de Gruyter Studies in Organization 20

Capitalism in Contrasting Cultures

de Gruyter Studies in Organization

An international series by internationally known authors presenting current fields of research in organization.

Organizing and organizations are substantial pre-requisites for the viability and future developments of society. Their study and comprehension are indispensable to the quality of human life. Therefore, the series aims to:

— offer to the specialist work material in form of the most important and current problems, methods and results;
— give interested readers access to different subject areas:
— provide aids for decisions on contemporary problems and stimulate ideas.

The series includes monographs, collections of contributed papers, and handbooks.

Capitalism
in Contrasting Cultures

Editors
Stewart R. Clegg · S. Gordon Redding
assisted by Monica Cartner

Walter de Gruyter · Berlin · New York   1990

Stewart R. Clegg
Professor of Sociology, Dept. of Management, University of St. Andrews, St. Andrews, Scotland, U.K.

S. Gordon Redding
Professor of Management Studies, Head of Department of Management Studies, University of Hong Kong, Hong Kong

Monica Cartner
The Graduate School of Business and Government Administration, The Victoria University of Wellington, PO Box 600, Wellington, New Zealand

Library of Congress Cataloging-in-Publication Data

Capitalism in contrasting cultures / editors, Stewart R. Clegg, S. Gordon Redding ; assisted by Monica Cartner.
  (De Gruyter studies in organization ; 20)
  "Selected papers from a conference held in Hong Kong in April 1988 ... organized within the Department of Management Studies of the University of Hong Kong under the auspices of APROS (Australian and Pacific Researchers in Organization Studies)" — Pref.
  Includes bibliographical references.
  ISBN 0-89925-525-6 (U.S.)
  1. Corporate culture — Cross-cultural studies — Congresses.
2. Capitalism — Cross-cultural studies — Congresses. I. Clegg, Stewart. II. Redding, S. G. III. Cartner, Monica, 1944 – .
IV. University of Hong Kong. Dept. of Management Studies
V. Australian and Pacific Researchers in Organization Studies (Organization) VI. Series.
HD58.7.C347 1990   89-23798
306.3′42 — dc20   CIP

Deutsche Bibliothek Cataloging in Publication Data

Capitalism in contrasting cultures / eds.: Stewart R. Clegg ; S. Gordon Redding. Ass. by Monica Cartner. — Berlin ; New York : de Gruyter, 1990
  (De Gruyter studies in organization ; 20)
  ISBN 3-11-011857-2
NE: Clegg, Stewart R. [Hrsg.]; GT

♾ Printed on acid free paper.

Typesetting: Arthur Collignon GmbH, Berlin — Printing: Gerike GmbH, Berlin — Binding: Lüderitz & Bauer GmbH, Berlin — Cover design: Johannes Rother, Berlin.

Preface

This volume contains selected papers from a conference held in Hong Kong in April 1988, titled 'Firms, Management, the State and Economic Cultures'. It was organized within the Department of Management Studies of the University of Hong Kong under the auspices of APROS (Australian and Pacific Researchers in Organization Studies) and co-convened by the senior editors, with administrative co-ordination from the assistant editor.

The conference was a follow-up to the 1985 APROS conference, also held at the same venue, the proceedings of which are available as *The Enterprise and Management in East Asia*. Hong Kong: Centre of Asian Studies, Occasional Papers and Monographs No. 69, University of Hong Kong, 1986.

It followed the unusual but, in our view, successful format pioneered in the earlier conference. It was designed to facilitate maximum substantive discussion by a small group of informed scholars. To this end, each discussion session was preceded by a reading session, long enough for three papers to be read quietly and without interruption. Discussion would then start *without* the formal 'giving' of papers by the authors. As well as dealing realistically with the facts that (a) people rarely read papers in advance and (b) presenters often waste time, this produced very rich, extended and penetrating debate.

A further unusual feature of the conference was that all thirty-seven participants were sole or joint authors of papers presented and thus had an equal stake in ensuring its success. This format is demanding not only of participants, who undoubtedly worked hard in absorbing other papers quickly and in substantiating their own, but also of the organizers, who need to determine final programming at short notice. We should like to thank all participants for making the conference a success and to recommend this format to other conference organizers.

Peter Standish was unable to attend the conference because of illness, but we should like to thank him for permission to include his paper, which was fully discussed in his absence and for his cooperation in revisions.

We were not disappointed in our hopes of attracting a wide range of papers with respect to discipline, subject matter and level of analysis. As always, selection of papers for publication proved a difficult task, but we trust this volume represents a real contribution to the field and reflects some of the diversity as well as the coherence of a very worthwhile conference.

We should like to thank Prof. Peter Berger of the Institute of Economic Culture, University of Boston, for his support. His seminal work in this field largely inspired the conference theme, and the conference was poorer for his unavoidable absence.

We should like to thank also the Department of Sociology's staff of the University of New England for their help in the early stages of planning and of the Mong Kwok Ping Data Bank and Department of Management Studies, University of Hong Kong, for their help and cooperation in the later stages and during the conference. Finally, but not least, we should like to thank Dr. Bianka Ralle of de Gruyter for her cooperation and support in this publication.

Stewart R. Clegg   *S. Gordon Redding*   *Monica Cartner*
University of   University of Hong Kong   University of Hong Kong
New England, Armidale

Table of Contents

Introduction:
Capitalism in Contrasting Cultures

Stewart R. Clegg and S. Gordon Redding

Each chapter in this volume is a testament to what Granovetter (1985: 481 – 482) has termed the 'embeddedness' of economic action: 'the argument that the behaviour and institutions to be analyzed are so constrained by ongoing social relations that to construe them as independent is a grievous misunderstanding'. Having contrasted 'over-socialized' and 'under-socialized' conceptions of economic action, Granovetter focuses on the central role of networks of social relations in producing trust in economic life. Granovetter's general approach is one that the editors would endorse. What is useful about this approach and implicitly present in many of the contributions to this volume, is the stimulus it provides for specifying the diverse descriptive particulars through which networks of social relations and stable features, such as trust, can be produced. The mechanisms may be diverse; for instance they may exist in the charismatic capitalist's commitment to a moral economy in which they trust because they are believed, valued and in turn trusted through its reproduction (see the chapter by Biggart); trust may be reproduced through the importance of the Chinese family business and its inheritance conventions for the complex networks of economic action which characterize overseas Chinese business people (see the chapters by Redding and Whitley, Tam); other mechanisms are manifest in the contrasting content but functionally similar role that is provided by comparing economic embeddedness in 'communitarian' Japan, 'patrimonial' South Korea, 'patrilineal' Taiwan and 'representational' Sweden (the chapters by Hamilton, Kim and Zeile; Clegg, Higgins and Spybey). Other examples abound in the volume.

This widespread re-discovery of what Berger (1987) has termed 'economic culture', embedded in the heartlands of contemporary capitalism, is quite at odds with the conventional conception not only of most of economics but also of the central traditions of the sociology of economic life and organizations which derive from the work of Max Weber. For Weber, the existence of culture and meaning in the economic code of modern capitalism would have been an agreeable paradox. Agreeable, because his basic conception of economics was not one which stressed it as a natural science, but instead regarded it as a cultural science. The paradox would arise because it was Weber's view that although modern industrial capitalism had been forged in the heat of religious values and culture it was set in a mould from which these sources of meaning were draining away. The pan-cultural value of 'rational action' would transform the contours of modern capitalism to a uniformity in which cultural value was absent.

Ideas such as these are at the crux of the Weber (1930) hypothesis concerning the 'Protestant Ethic'. In this work he implicates the specific cultural embeddedness of Protestantism as a major causal agency in the genesis of modern capitalism, an analysis which is elaborated and extended rather than undercut in his later work (Weber 1923, see Collins 1980). *The Protestant Ethic and the Spirit of Capitalism* posits a gloomy and unprepossessing view of his future and our present. Weber anticipated an horizon of meaninglessness, an 'iron cage' of bureaucracy entrapping us as 'little cogs' in a vast machinery of effort expended to no higher purpose, to no other cultural ideals than those of dull compulsion, necessity and relentless striving. Weber's was a characteristically modernist yet retrospective vision; the same sense of gloomy foreboding, the creative individual's despair at the advent of mass society and the domination of the machine, was one echoed across the human sciences, aesthetics, cinema and other visual arts in the texts of his near contemporaries such as Walter Benjamin, Charles Chaplin, Georg Simmel and T. S. Eliot. Modern times, dominated by art produced in and by the age of machinery, were articulated in what were taken to be some of their most representative experience, as a meaningless wasteland. By the 1950s and 1960s this aesthetic experience had become the normal science of modern sociology, encapsulated in works such as W. H. Whyte's (1956) *The Organization Man* or Herbert Marcuse's (1964) critique of *One-Dimensional Man*. Later, it was to join ranks with romantic currents in the modernist project, culminating in Braverman's (1974) wholesale critique of *The Degradation of Work in the Twentieth Century*, giving rise to a 'labour process debate' through which William Morris' ghost might just, sometimes, be visible.

Meanwhile, outside of the aesthetic mainstream and the representations of the world which expressed its concerns, there was an undercurrent of solid industrial anthropology in both Europe and America which was less inclined to accept the modernist prognosis of cultural denudation than were the 'normal science' heirs of Weberian rationalism. In Europe writers like Jaques (1951) in *The Changing Culture of a Factory* and Crozier (1964) in *The Bureaucratic Phenomenon* had plumbed the organizational depths of cultural despair and found them to be, in contrast to the received wisdom, rich and fertile grounds of human imagination, purpose and achievement, even if this occurred within the more general bureaucratic bondage. In the United States researchers like Roy (1960) were coming to similar conclusions: within the iron cage, whether its frame was cast from a capitalist or a bureaucratic shell, culture was alive and well, meaning existed. The radical twist to modernism saw this occurring in spite of the iron cage of capitalist relations even as it irrevocably reproduced them (Burawoy 1979, Willis 1977), while more conservative prognoses saw in this discovery of culture the 'salvation' of capitalism, its revitalization, its holy grail of 'excellence' (Peters and Waterman 1982).

Weber no longer needed repairing or correcting or rounding out, as an earlier generation of scholars had done (e. g. Blau and Scott 1963, Gouldner 1954). The empirical limits of Weber's (1978) ideal type of bureaucracy could now be delineated through types that were not so much accidental or designed deviations from the ideal (e. g. Burns and Stalker's [1961] 'organic' type or Emery and Trist's [1965] 'socio-technically' designed system) as exemplifications of a reality barely visible in the representations of modernism.

Two distinct 'alternative realities' were initially addressed: those of counter-cultural 'alternative organizations' (Rothschild and Whitt 1986) and those of the 'clannish', but, to a modernist, rationalist aesthetic, equally strange world of Japanese organizations (Ouchi 1980). Much of this volume is concerned to explore some of the major implications of the latter alternative and to address its distinctiveness in analytical and empirical terms. The former, it had been thought, was of little value to an understanding of other than ideologically motivated, 'radical', alternative and small organizations (Clegg and Higgins 1987). However, there does in fact appear to be a major organizational type which is different from bureaucracy, but whose difference is expressed, not in politically radical ideological terms, as in Rothschild and Whitt's (1986) collectivist organizations, but in terms of a radically conservative ethic of 'charismatic capitalism'. There are, indeed, more niches whereby the alleged meaninglessness of the modern world might be avoided than were dreamt of in any of the modernists' imaginations.

In her contribution 'Charismatic Capitalism: Direct Selling Organizations in the USA and Asia' Nicole Woolsey Biggart delves into a world many of us must know of from Tupperware parties or from 'Avon calling', but have, perhaps, never seriously considered as an organizational form. Direct selling organizations employ 5% of the U. S. labour force and are spreading rapidly in Asia where the cultural affinities and material circumstances of a vigorous capitalism, extended familism, subordinated labour force participation by women and a strongly moral ordering of status hierarchies resonate harmoniously with a mode of organization and marketing sprung from the suburban community of the United States.

While economic actors who are strongly motivated by politically ideological beliefs are an apparent embodiment of cultural embeddedness, it would be a mistake to think that religious beliefs can no longer fulfil the role that Weber originally drafted for them. As the delightful ethnography of the 'Duck Islanders' by Acton demonstrates, strongly held and communally reinforced religious beliefs can function as a means of ensuring that highly successful economic networks of social relations may be reproduced across both space and time.

Both Biggart and Acton's contributions point to the consequences of quite specific cultural configurations for economic action. They may be said to be concerned with a more micro, localized conception of culture as it is lodged in particular capitalist enterprises constituted within specific cultural configurations. Both chapters identify a particular cluster of values at the level of individual actors and point to the consequences of these for those organizations that 'contain' these individuals and which assemble distinctive economic action premised precisely on these particulars. Each contribution is generated from an intensive ethnography of a particular moral community.

Of far more general scope is the contribution which opens our consideration of 'Culture's Consequences' in the last part of the book, where the three more explicitly micro-level conceptions of culture as an individual phenomenon are located. Indeed, following on from the path-breaking work of Hofstede (1980) (to whom with due respect we owe the title of this section), Bond and Hofstede, the authors of 'The Cash Value of Confucian Values', propose that culture should best be understood at the individual level as 'the collective programming of the mind which distinguishes the members of one category of people from another'. While most of the other contributions to this volume focus on mechanisms of what Bond and Hofstede term 'collective programming', in this contribution they focus instead on measuring culture's effect in the minds of individuals, through a concept of 'dimensions of culture'. Standardized on a vast research effort, spanning 53 nations, the project identified four main dimensions of culture: power distance, individualism, masculinity versus femininity and uncertainty avoidance. In the research reported in this chapter the data on these dimensions for the 53 countries were correlated with measures of per capita GNP and economic growth to track the relationship between culture and economic performance. However, no consistent causal pathway from culture to economy could be established on these measures.

The absence of a finding in the original data is not the end of the story. Bond subsequently conducted a Chinese Value Survey, based not on the original Western project of *Culture's Consequences* (Hofstede 1980) but on values grounded in Chinese culture. Three of the same dimensions recurred in this data as were found in the Hofstede study: these were the dimensions of power distance, individualism and masculinity — femininity. However, no dimension that corresponded to that of uncertainty avoidance in the original study could be found. It appeared to be so foreign to the Chinese value-set that a concern with transcendental issues of truth and the search for it was absent. Instead, a fourth dimension of 'Confucian dynamism' was evident. The variable nature of this dimension ran from a dynamic future-oriented mentality to one which was more static and tradition oriented.

While none of the earlier dimensions of culture had any consistent relationship with economic growth, this was not the case with Confucian dynamism. It correlated consistently with economic growth in terms of higher scores on its positive pole, and lower scores on the negative pole. The conclusions that Bond and Hofstede draw from this finding are that there is a Confucian cultural ethic and that it is causally linked to economic success. In addition, they argue, there is also a Western transcendentalist ethic concerned with the search for Truth (uncertainty avoidance) whose focus on analysis, rather than the synthesis of the Confucian value, is in the present world an economic handicap. It is to the conjunction of these factors that they are inclined to attribute East Asian success.

The contributions in the final part of the book all reflect an individual-level concern with culture, from the grounded ethnographies of Biggart and Acton to the psychometrics of the Bond and Hofstede project. The latter touches on a far more global and macro issue, a concern for which will recur in other contributions to the volume: can specific conceptions of an economic culture be adduced, and if so, what is the nature of the institutional frameworks which serve to scaffold, support and sustain this culture?

Such issues may be raised at either a more meso-level or a more macro-level conception of an economic culture. For instance, the contribution to this volume by Wilks on 'The Embodiment of Industrial Culture in Bureaucracy and Management' addresses the concept of an 'industrial culture', a level of somewhat more focused applicability than the general concept of economic culture as Berger (1987) introduced it. While the general concept designates a macro arena of nationally or culturally bounded characteristics, industrial culture refers to more specifically meso-cultural phenomena: the attitudes to state intervention held by key institutional elites. Such attitudes are taken to be tacit but specific guides to action embodied in patterns of recruitment, financing, structure and process in organizational norms: what Clegg (1981) has referred to as 'sedimented selection rules' or Offe (1975) has referred to in state organizations as 'structural selectivity'. There are evident similarities of focus and conceptualization between Wilks' view of industrial culture and the institutional stress in the economic culture perspectives of Clegg, Higgins and Spybey. Both papers identify the importance of the way in which the normative and institutional frameworks influence rational action and calculation. Together with the other papers in Part One they also focus explicitly on the challenge posed for the Western economies by the forms of enterprise and organization which have sustained the competitive edge that East Asia is now widely regarded as having developed.

Wilks, following the critique of 'English peculiarities' launched by *New Left Review* in the 1960s, iterates how there developed a civil service culture in Britain which crucially handicapped the deepening and development of the first 'capitalist revolution'. By contrast, distinctive patterns of culture which were more facilitative of the state fostering industrial development came to characterize Germany, France and Japan.

The German case is marked both by more specifically interventionist ministries in the economic arena, as well as a much less 'liberal' tradition of politics and a far more 'organized' capitalism than occurred in Britain. France has been even more characterized by a close coordination at the elite level between governmental bureaucracy and industry, leading some observers (Karpik 1987) to speak of a 'French industrial system' spanning both the public service and industrial enterprises.

Not since Comodore Perry's ships opened up the cultural delights of Japan to Victorian appreciation and taste through the conduits of Gilbert and Sullivan, the Victoria and Albert Museum and other cultural centres of Europe, has Japan enjoyed a vogue so fashionable and appreciated as it does today. Once more, despite the prosaic stuff of economics and technology, it is overwhelmingly in cultural terms that Japan is appreciated. But how appropriate is such appreciation and the subsequent sequestration premised on it? Wilks and Clegg, Higgins and Spybey cast a sceptical eye over the culturalist interpretation of the Japanese 'economic miracle', with its celebration of 'groupism', 'consensus' and 'Confucianism'. While Clegg and his colleagues seek to demonstrate the realities of the industrial structure which they perceive beneath the surface of the consensualist gloss, Wilks presents a realist's guide to the nature of Japanese bureaucracy. One aspect immediately strikes those familiar with, for instance, the British or Australian situation. First, there is neither Treasury dominance over the arena in which promotion is determined as in Britain, nor is there the rapid circulation of public service personnel through different departments which characterizes Australia. In the latter, the preponderance of economics graduates (which, given the nature of the discipline in Australian universities, tend to an orthodox market and liberal stance) and the sheer centrality and weight of Treasury leads to a discursive dominance of categories of 'economic rationalism'. In Japan, in contrast to both countries, Treasury appears not to be wholly pre-dominant nor are individual careers made on the terms of a perceived loyalty, commitment and expertise to a generalized service ethic, however expressed: as, for instance, either the traditional conception of British gentlemanly amateurism or more recent notions of economic rationalism. By contrast, in Japan one joins a Ministry and remains in it, and loyal to it, for one's working life. Embeddedness as practical policy, one might argue.

As Clegg, Higgins and Spybey observe, this continuity of career in one organization also characterizes the Swedish social democratic economic culture. To have identified one variable constant across two such diverse types of economic culture but such consistently successful ones, suggests that its importance should not be overlooked. A free market in careers and loyalties may not be the most effective and efficient means of generating national economic success, precisely because of the extent to which it disembeds economic action. Also, in both countries, someone schooled in the more adversarial style of decision making favoured in the Anglo-Saxon nations would be totally confounded by the absence of what they took to be normal correlates of management. Given the greater cultural distance, this is, perhaps, even more striking with respect to Japan. In both Sweden and Japan the hand of the state is extremely visible. The rhetoric of the New Right in its advocacy of free markets, monetarism and deregulation would appear as exotically strange in both of these countries as their institutional fabrics — each strikingly dissimilar in most respects, especially the crucial one of representation — appear to Anglo-Saxon observers.

The question which Wilks addresses is how was it that this Anglo-Saxon exotica, which to Japanese or Swedish eyes would appear to be a bizarre liberalism, with its commitment to markets, individualism and voluntarism, how was it reproduced from its petty-bourgeois roots in early British industrial capitalism? (It is important to distinguish industrial capitalism from primary production, resource exploitation, agrarian capitalism and more speculative ventures in this respect: these were frequently aristocratically sponsored.) How did this first economic miracle happen? Wilks nominates as explanatory factors the following: the underdevelopment of a British managerial cadre; a correlating aversion to technological involvement in production, leaving such work to intermediaries (a factor also highlighted by Clegg, Higgins and Spybey) and the relatively weak peak organization and representation of the British industrial elite. This is in marked contrast to West Germany, France, Japan and (*pace* Clegg, Higgins and Spybey) Sweden. The difference can not be attributed to any underlying national cultural explanatory variable, but the outcome is a distinct culture, one embedded in and constructed out of a complex institutional frame, differently crafted in each situation. On this Wilks and Clegg as well as Higgins and Spybey are in agreement. What it boils down to is a question of institutionally constructing culture as more or less functional or dysfunctional.

The issue of functionality necessarily raises the issue of functional for whom? In an implicit way this issue is also raised by Wilkinson and Oliver's consideration of the impact of Japanese industrial culture in Britain, particularly as it re-shapes the frame of British industrial relations practice and its central actor: the British worker. In so many accounts such workers have been cast as the villains in a heroic struggle to achieve an economic breakthrough which crashes through the blockages to organizational adaptation, so often seen as endemic to Britain. Of course, there is a refraction of this which, through the same glass, but darkly, sees the militant worker as being in the vanguard of revolutionary struggle. Heroes and villains, although they make for good traditional stories, may not serve the task of social analysis so well as a focus on the structures which contain both types of excessive individualism.

Other papers in Part Three of the volume also take up this theme of blockages and breakthroughs in organizational adaptation. For instance, Boisot and Child focus on the limits to the 'capitalist revolution' which some authors have predicted for China (Cheung 1986), while Mannari and Marsh focus at the organization level on correlates of successful adaptation within the overall category of Japanese enterprise. This is particularly useful because it enables one to focus on the more specific organization-level correlates of what is often treated as an aggregate case. Marceau's paper performs a similar disaggregational function for another much vaunted aggregate category of economic success: that of the small firm. We shall return to the other papers in this part of the volume subsequently. For the present we will discuss Marceau.

'The Dwarves of Capitalism', as Marceau calls them, have been subject to almost eulogistic political prognoses for their contribution to OECD economic growth during the 1980s. Instead, Marceau argues, as do other contributors to this volume, small firms have to be seen within the broader context of the economic relations that locate them in the economics of larger firms. On this basis the economic cultures of these small firms will vary, depending on the nature of their embeddedness within the economy dominated by larger firms. One type of economic culture is exemplified by the craftsman-entrepreneur, drawn from the ranks of the working class, producing traditional products for stable markets. Such small firms tend to be risk averse, conservative, uninnovative and low in market orientation. By contrast, opportunistic entrepreneurs will be far more middle class, better educated, managerially skilled, innovative, risk taking and market oriented.

These distinctions characterize a scene which is rapidly changing throughout the OECD. The changes are being structured through the opportunities posed by the radical nature of new technologies. Two of these are of particular consequence for the argument of the chapter. First, their adoption may lead to major readjustments in the market between large and small enterprises. Second, these may in turn stimulate the generation of small enterprises through a reorganization of the division of earlier forms of manufacturing production. Consequent upon such reorganization and redivision, new forms of organizational control and coordination are developing which challenge the notion of the individual firm as the appropriate unit of analysis. The challenge is raised precisely because of the nature of these firms as an embedded network, particularly through forms of contracting relations rather than through the classic hierarchical modes which have preoccupied organization theory from its precursors in Max Weber to the present day. This is not to imagine some liberal utopia devoid of hierarchy and composed only of markets: on the contrary, it is to acknowledge a world in which there exists a complex hierarchy of market relations under the dominance of large enterprises, enterprises whose organizational boundedness is not enveloped within their legal form but which holds sway over those networks of relations that they create and join.

One of the major ways in which cultural isomorphism of organizational forms may develop is through the conscious importation and borrowing of ingredients from recipes which appear to have worked well elsewhere. At the vanguard of such importation one will frequently find foreign national firms who are directing investment into offshore production facilities. A significant part of the revival of Mrs. Thatcher's 'enterprise culture' in Britain has been the encouragement of such investment from Japan, which, as Wilkinson and Oliver's contribution to this volume demonstrates, has also been a source for conscious adoption and diffusion of practices isomorphic with what are taken to be the essence of Japanese management. However, their adoption, diffusion and encouragement has not been without resistance, as they elaborate.

'We're Brits not Nips' must be one of the most emphatically nationalist, not to say racist, slogans under which working class action and resistance has been organized since the demise of the Australian labour movement's commitment to 'White Australia' as a bastion of antipodean social democracy. At root the slogan has gained currency in the United Kingdom as a means for tapping a tacit conception of what being a British worker means in terms of a moral community. Against single enterprise or no unionism it means a traditionally craft fragmented labour unionism; against a communitarian ethic in the firm it pits an individualistic or adversarial ethic, with community reserved for the locales of club, home and class; against flexible working arrangements it opposes a dogged determination to abide by hard-won demarcations achieved through past struggles: in short, against current conceptions of a reasonable and responsible worker it upholds what is so often caricatured as the 'bloody-minded' anti-business ethic of British unionism.

For the last decade, both inspired by and taking issue with the work of Braverman (1974), a leading theme of much British industrial and organizational sociology has been to point up the 'rationality of resistance' implicit in this 'bloody-mindedness'. Given a conception of economic organization involving 'us' and 'them', 'two sides of industry', and the 'class struggle', then a zero-sum conception of power will pervade both the literature and organizational life. From this perspective workers' bloody-minded resistance and reluctance to change is simply a rational defence of gains laboriously achieved in past struggles, against those strategies of management and capital which are designed to intensify the terms of the effort bargain by which labour is employed.

The most effective way of short-circuiting the necessary struggle attendant on the givens of a zero-sum conception of the game is to change the rules in such a way that winning, losing and the nature of play are redefined. Management consultants refer to this as achieving a 'win-win' situation. It is a realization of and a resistance to this ploy which is so starkly expressed in the claim 'We're Brits not Nips'. The ploy — let us call it the Nipponization move — seeks to redraw the game by re-drafting the rules. In Britain the Nipponization of the industrial culture is well under way, as Wilkinson and Oliver address in their contribution 'Japanese Influences on British Industrial Culture', not only through direct investment but also through the conduits of cultural example and economic comparison (also see Wilkinson and Oliver's 1988 issue of the *Industrial Relations Journal*). In short, there is every reason to assume that 'Brits' may well become more like 'Nips' in their work practices in the foreseeable future.

What is involved in the Nipponization move is simple in principle, if more difficult to achieve in practice, as Wilkinson and Oliver outline. Essentially, it involves the construction of a flexible, efficient manufacturing system, involving tight discipline, the elimination of down time from the working day, tight quality control and scheduling, often on a just-in-time basis, the creation of a solidaristic ethic based on the corporation rather than on cross-cutting affiliations and an attempt to construct a harmony of interests between management and workers rather than a relationship based on antagonisms and contradictions. As they identify it, a central feature in facilitating this achievement is the 'Company Advisory Board', in which joint negotiations between workers and management take place, often outside the union structure, in order to produce binding arbitration. Contracts in which trust can be vested are the desired outcome of such negotiations.

If trust is to be secured intra-organizationally, it must also be the basis of inter-organizational relationships, particularly with subcontracting firms, if Nipponization is to be fully implemented. In part (as is also stressed in the contribution by Clegg, Higgins and Spybey), an important element in this is time: one must have a basis for reasonably stable expectations about the future if one is to trust one's plans. If a key component of the economic culture which Nipponization moves to achieve is a context of trust, then, as Clegg, Higgins and Spybey point out in their chapter on ' "Post-Confucianism", Social Democracy and Economic Culture', it is as well to realize that the evidential basis for ceding that Japanese economic culture is particularly harmonious and based on trust is somewhat more ideological than is often appreciated. As a number of revisionist writers on Japan have suggested, the trust, harmony and groupism striven for in Nipponization is a socially constructed myth about Japanese reality, carefully nurtured by the Japanese elite. Beneath the mythical surface is a contested terrain in both recent history and current practice. While current practice may be less violent than recent history, it belies the superficial picture of happy, loyal, company song-singing drones depicted by both the proponents and antagonists of the consensus view of Japan. Instead, as is stressed both by Wilkinson and Oliver with respect to Japanese practice in Britain, and by Clegg, Higgins and Spybey with respect to Japan, the crucial characteristics of Japanese economic culture are far more institutional than some of the proponents of a unique 'post-Confucian' cultural configuration might allow. Key features, in addition to those previously noted in Wilkinson and Oliver, include internal labour markets (which we also find in banking: see Lewis and MacGregor's paper in this volume); a divided labour movement in both the party and union sphere, company towns, extensive levels of subcontracting and out-working as the easily expended basis for flexible production; all of this institutional framework sustains a small core of workers rigorously selected from elite schools based on competitive examination from kindergarten level onwards who are consciously incorporated into a 'corporate culture'.

Institutional features, considered at the macro-level, are clearly important in considering Japanese economic performance. In addition, it is important to understand the internal organizational relationships which are conducive to successful performance, particularly as there is reason to believe that these arrangements are relatively stable across countries and thus across different cultural and institutional frameworks (Donaldson 1986). Japan is of the utmost interest to such analysis because it is in and with respect to this country that the culturalist explanations have had their fullest expression. Consequently, the chapter by Mannari and Marsh, based on solid empirical data collected at the organization level, is of particular importance.

Mannari and Marsh report on a longitudinal study which compares 48 manufacturing organizations in one prefecture. Unlike most other large-scale comparative analyses the research is not simply cross-sectional; they are able to study structural change in the organizations over time. The contribution, 'Organizational Change and Stability in Japanese Factories: 1976 – 1983', marks a substantial revision of not only received wisdom on the importance of cultural specificity but also on the nature of structural causality in organization analyses. Hitherto there have been two main axes to this debate constructed around two contrasting dichotomies: those of power vs. efficiency (one thinks of the debates between Perrow [1986] and Williamson [1985]) and of size vs. technology, the classical leitmotif of so much work in the Aston School (e. g. Pugh and Hickson 1976).

One implication of Mannari and Marsh's contribution is that the way in which these dichotomies force us into either/or consideration is something which can be short-circuited by causal, longitudinal analysis. Thus, in the explanation they present of the substantial changes that occurred over the period studied, both power, size, technology and efficiency enter into the explanation. More automated technology is important in explaining the increasing use of both mechanized quality control and greater R & D expenditure and sales per employee: the latter through the causal path of mechanized quality control. Each of these factors has been stressed in the literature in Japanese organizations as an aspect of Japanese uniqueness: the low rejection rate resulting from tight quality control: the greater productivity resulting from enhanced R & D expenditure and the achievement of more competitive products. In Mannari and Marsh's explanation each of these phenomena is seen to be an effect of increased automaticity of technology. However, the more advanced the technology used it appears that there is a weakening reliance on university-educated personnel. This would seem to support the views of those writers who stress the close relationship between power and technology, observing how routinization of professional determination is effectively eroding some spheres of professional discretion (Clegg and Dunkerley 1980, Clegg, Boreham and Dow

1986, Fox 1974, Perrow 1986). In addition, greater use of automated technology leads to weaker interdependency between sub-units.

If some aspects of the argument from technology (and power/technology) are supported, so too are aspects of the arguments from size. Greater size, measured best in terms of personnel, leads to the use of more electronic data processing technology, proliferating job titles and a greater span of control for first line foremen, as well as more interdependence among work flow segments and a greater probability that a labour union will be recognized.

Rate of change in size also proved important; as it was greater so the value of production rose and, against conventional wisdom, voluntary turnover declined. Moreover, larger firms were more likely to have differentiated management from ownership. Both size and an entrepreneurial foundation have a positive relationship with increased differentiation; the latter diminishes both vertically and horizontally with the centralization of authority. Size increases may generate increasing structural differentiation; alternatively it may be that developing new product lines leads to additional units not only of production but also of control. Of necessity, increasing control leads to greater administrative functional specialization as it becomes more and more difficult with increasing size for direct control to be sustained. Delegation to functional specialists is the means of extension of direct control and hence a cause of greater complexity.

While increasing size leads to a transition from more direct control to administrative control, it does so only where it is 'new-product' driven. It is product diversification, leading to increased scale of operations and decreased central direct control, which is of causal importance. Whether it leads to greater administrative formalization or not is contingent in large part on the degree of autonomy in itself and the accountability to external control that an organization has. Large autonomous organizations have less formalization than large dependent organizations. The size argument can not be dissociated from the power argument.

While it would seem to be the case that size and power can not be deemed entirely separate explanatory factors, it would also seem that power can not be cordoned off from efficiency explanations either. In declining organizations managers and supervisors are less likely to lose their jobs than workers. Why? Mannari and Marsh speculate that it will be because supervisors remain necessary while there is functional superordination and subordination in their section: in other words, as long as power prevails. Managers are shed more slowly because, they suggest, their task is to scan and manage the external environment and to counter the organizational decline, although one could readily adduce a power explanation here as well.

Some organization sociologists have followed Braverman (1974) in being attracted to a 'de-skilling' hypothesis: one which is now under considerable suspicion as a general explanation (Attewell 1987). The suspicion is not lessened by Mannari and Marsh's contribution. It was those organizations which did not develop more advanced technologies rather than those which did, which contributed disproportionately to unemployment.

At the core of the Japanese organization model, looked at through the standard concepts of the sociology of organizations rather than through the lens of cultural specificity, the explanatory focus shifts back to quite prosaic phenomena by contrast with the macro-cultural argument. The focus is on adopting new technologies, developing new products, generating R & D, in the context of a contingency framework. If these phenomena are the essence of Japanese economic success, they are readily diffusable, if, that is, other countries' organizations can learn from Japan's competitive edge before their own competitive capacity is crippled. As the research by Wilkinson and Oliver suggests, on a detailed unit cost comparison, Japanese firms in Britain are far more efficient and competitive than are comparable British firms. They too stress the role of successful quality control and enterprising innovation. Perhaps, with macro-institutional adjustments which continue to weaken labour and strengthen markets, and with organizational changes oriented to more and better products, means and methods of production, 'Brits' may be able to become more like 'Nips' after all. But, one might wonder, may not the localized cultures of resistance serve to undercut the achievement of a similar competitive edge?

The success of Japan has often led commentators to generalize cultural explanation from it to the economic achievements of the 'little dragons' of Hong Kong, Taiwan, South Korea and Singapore. Sometimes, the same underlying logic of explanation for all these countries, as in the argument from 'post-Confucian' economic culture, is employed. However, as the contributions of Redding and Whitley; Tam; and Hamilton, Kim and Zeile make clear, it would be mistaken to regard these countries as essentially similar in their patterns of economic success. They have quite distinct foundations which are sufficiently different as to counter any too easy reliance on a view of a single 'post-Confucian' way. Nor would it be appropriate, as Hamilton, Kim and Zeile make clear, to substitute one mono-causal explanation with another.

Mono-causal explanations abound. From the economics discipline and from the political right there has been no shortage of explanations couched in terms of 'market forces' as to why the East Asian NICs have achieved economic growth. Such explanations are not supported by this text.

Concentrating on Japan, South Korea and Taiwan, Hamilton, Kim and Zeile present an empirically based comparison of 'business group structures', the form of the characteristic organizational patterns in which this economic growth has been embedded. Business groups

are composed of a set of legally independent firms which may or may not have economic or fiscal relationship among themselves and which normally have no overarching accounting or management systems that coordinate the activity of member firms. In some cases, all the firms in the group are at least partially owned by a core firm, sometimes a holding company, a bank, or a key manufacturing firm. At other times, an individual or a small group of individuals, sometimes a family, owns or controls all the firms in the group. In a few cases, however, particularly in the Japanese case, which is the key example of an economy organized through business groups, no one firm or set of individuals owns or controls the business groups. Therefore, even consolidated ownership is not their defining characteristic. Instead, the defining characteristic of business groups is that they are organized networks of independent firms, with the nature, manner and consequence of their organization left open to investigation (Hamilton, Kim and Zeile, this volume).

The economists' explanation for the East Asian preponderance of these business groups attempts to bring them into the framework of the theory of the firm as a particular form of transaction which deals with market imperfections through the quasi-authoritative organization of the business group. A contrasting view is derived from political economy and from scholars usually of a more 'dirigiste' orientation. Rather than stressing micro-economic phenomena concerned with market-clearing, these accounts stress the role of the state in facilitating collusive elite linkages.

Both political economic and market economic explanation founder on the reef of sustained empirical investigation. For one thing, although each might seem to offer the best explanation of some aspects of some of the countries, neither scores across the board. Political economy is of some explanatory importance in South Korea, where the state created modern capitalist enterprise. This was not the case in Taiwan in the major sectors of economic growth. The particular small firm configuration in Taiwan has to do with inheritance laws which pass on assets on an 'equal shares' basis to the sons of a family. It is not market competitiveness which maintains small firm size in Taiwan. Japan, like South Korea, had business groups before it had economic growth.

Explanation of these differences must look elsewhere, to the central role of institutional variation in national legal, financial and accounting conventions, and the distinct types of authoritative structures which they produce.

The focus which is called for by many of the contributions to this volume has its roots in the organization analysis exemplified by Mannari and Marsh in their concern with classic organization level variables. However, in many cases the focus has been extended from categories of 'the organization' per se to the wider set of relations in which organizations are embedded. This is most explicitly so in Redding and Whitley's contribution.

'Beyond Bureaucracy: Towards a Comparative Analysis of Forms of Economic Resource Co-ordination and Control' contains a strong argument for analyzing organizations in their embedded networks of social relations, focusing in particular on what the authors see as three dominant East Asian forms; the Japanese *kaisha*, the Korean *chaebol* and the Chinese family business. Their argument is that the individual organization is hardly the appropriate unit of analysis as the economic actor in the business world of the region, and that the same stricture would apply in other regions such as Europe. Using an approach which owes some debt to Ragin's (1987) advice on the comparative method, they propose the bases for two taxonomies useful in unravelling the complexities of economic culture.

The first concentrates on the economic actors, and notes the way in which different 'recipes' emerge as dominant in different societies. The agenda is to differentiate the recipes by specifying their ingredients, and the ones proposed are: delegated discretion, centralization, inter-enterprise co-ordination, managerial integration, personalized authority, emotional loyalty of the workforce. In this regard, critical features of economic action, such as Japanese ties with subcontractors, Korean government-business relations and Chinese family business networks, are brought into account and help to enrich understanding.

Why such combinations of ingredients become dominant is a matter of tracing determinacy in the societal contexts where they achieve stability. For this, a parallel taxonomy is proposed using the following components; patrimonial authority patterns, trust relations, nature of the state elite, basis of societal elite formation, inheritance system.

The work of Redding and Whitley contributes to the task of dislodging organization theory from its traditional foundations in Western empirical reality, and its traditional difficulty of coming to terms with alternative frameworks for cooperation. By positing that there are economic structures out there in conceptual space 'beyond bureaucracy', a challenge is implied and the need for a new paradigm declared.

The paper by Tam follows this theme by concentrating on the process of growth in Hong Kong Chinese and Japanese organizations, attempting to come to terms with the question, put simply, of why Japanese organizations grow large and Chinese do not. He proposes two configurations of characteristics; the Japanese centripetal business system and the Chinese centrifugal system, explaining in the process much about the differences between the structuring of the Japanese and Hong Kong economies. Nor is it difficult to extrapolate from the Hong Kong case to the Overseas Chinese throughout East and Southeast Asia.

More significantly perhaps, Tam then goes on to tackle the deeper question underlying such conceptual work: how is it that they are both successful in world market terms? This discussion focuses on five anomalies which emerge from the comparison of Hong Kong against Japan: (1) How can industrial power be released from atomistic firms? (2) How can excellent performance be achieved without management development? (3) How can an economy made of conservative firms display constant renewal? (4) How can an effective workforce result from using disloyal, uncommitted employees? (5) Are there hidden economies of small scale? The resolving of these anomalies produces revealing insights into the workings of non-Western capitalist systems and, by facing the issue of performance, albeit in abstract terms, brings forward a number of highly intriguing agenda for future research.

The paper by Tricker, also set in the context of East-West comparison, with Overseas Chinese as the Asian focus, looks at corporate governance, a new but increasingly significant field for research. In this he argues that the main vehicle of capitalism, the company itself, is designed largely as an extension of Western ideals about cooperation. Although it can be, and is, adopted within other societies, it is not adopted without adjustment. Such adjustment, exemplified by Hong Kong experience, includes elaborate means for retaining family control after a company goes public, retention of power and prestige by the paterfamilias, and the use of extensive informal networks rather than managed hierarchies, to deal with co-ordination between firms.

With the field of corporate governance being so commonly one in which legislation is rife, it becomes important to understand the different premises on which governance has evolved in practice. Again, the question of an economic system's success is salient, and there is some inevitability in the question of whether the governance of entrepreneurial, venture-capital firms in the West might not be more effectively designed if it took account of oriental solutions to the issues.

A number of contributions to this volume indicate the central importance in explaining economic performance, of the stability or otherwise of the framework within which economic calculation takes place. It is a theme taken up not only by Hamilton, Kim and Zeile, but also by Clegg, Higgins and Spybey; Standish; Redding and Whitley; and Wilkinson and Oliver. It underlines the points made about economic embeddedness by Granovetter (1985).

An important outcome of the broad comparative focus reflected in the papers in this volume, drawing as it does on work from North America, Europe and the Asia-Pacific region, is to underscore the ways in which institutional variations can be subject to design and control. 'Culture', seen as an emergent effect of practices within institutional frames, becomes less an underlying catch-all explanation, but something which is itself to be explained. One fruitful way of doing this is via an understanding of the forms of calculation available for economic actors in particular settings. At this level, because these are usually nationally bounded, it is eminently reasonable to talk of a nation and a culture in the same terms. For instance, Wilkinson and Oliver note towards the end of their argument that a recent House of Lords Select Committee in the U. K. (whose report has been spurned by the government) proposes a set of institutional changes which would facilitate the Nipponization of British economic culture. Amongst the measures recommended is a shift from the 'tyranny' of quarterly financial reporting. It is precisely the national variations in financial reporting which are highlighted as central aspects of the institutional framework by Clegg, Higgins and Spybey in their comparative anaylsis. Manufacturing decline in the West, and the 'economic miracles' of East Asia, rather than being solely attributable to an idealist conception of culture, are instead, they propose, a result of institutional frameworks supporting distinct cultures. Economic calculations thus proceed on diverse assumptions, and not all assumptions are equally efficacious in sustaining manufacturing activity. Some are downright prejudicial, particularly those that pertain in Britain, the USA and Australia. In Japan, by contrast, the emphasis is on longer-term, stable financial sourcing and reporting than in the English-speaking countries. Consequently, manufacturing logic predominates over a more speculative financial logic (see also Abegglen and Stalk 1985).

It is not only in Japan that institutional mechanisms for more stable manufacturing can be found. Hamilton, Kim and Zeile also identify similar mechanisms operative in Taiwan and South Korea as well. What makes them similar in their underlying logic, despite apparent differences, is a stable set of inter-organizational relationships between key firms and sectors of economic activity. Consequently, the market principle is subordinated to mechanisms ensuring long-term manufacturing strategies and viability, rather than the more rapacious and speculative business behaviour displayed in the US, British and Australian penchant for takeovers, mergers, greenmail, and so on. Concurring with Weber's (1930) original emphasis on accounting in his classic analysis of economic culture in *The Protestant Ethic and the Spirit of Capitalism*, Clegg, Higgins and Spybey argue that the institutional mechanisms producing financial hyperactivity, in contrast to the more orderly Japanese scene, are diverse accounting schema and systems.

As is already evident from Tricker's paper, which surveys briefly the history of corporate regulation, there are clearly differences of approach, even within Europe, and they have understandably different origins. Taking a part of this larger question, Standish focuses on financial accounting and reporting, in the chapter: 'Accounting: The Private Language of Business or an Instrument of Social Communication?'. In this he identifies one of the tensions which produce different emphases in national accounting as both an instrument of state surveillance and an informational resource for ordering the market. Not only is it the case that these tensions can produce distinct national expression, they can also produce distinct theories of accounting as an activity, as Standish suggests. These interact with the special national emphases and political currents that prevail in particular times and places. For instance, as Clegg, Higgins and Spybey argue, the contrast between the affinities for and effects of the recent British, American and Australian Governments' (with Lewis and MacGregor's contribution, one can add New Zealand) monetarist leanings have legitimated an 'agency' view of accounting; by contrast the social democratic party which has enjoyed hegemony in Sweden for half a century, has produced a far more radical form of accounting theory and practice. Standish notes the contrasts between the English-speaking countries and French practice while Clegg, Higgins and Spybey contrast them with both Japan and Sweden.

The Swedish, French and Japanese institutional fabrics vary markedly. Accounting practice is central to long-term national planning in a way which is also quite differentiated between English-speaking countries. In large part, Standish explains, this difference is attributable to national variations between the 'community' and 'market'-oriented practices of accounting, in the English-speaking cases, compared to a more *dirigiste* or concerted governance in the other countries. The provision of standardized financial information becomes a major factor in such governance. Both *etatism* and corporatism require quite different forms of accounting practice to those characteristic of the communitarian-market tension of the English-speaking countries.

The English-speaking countries in the OECD which have been dealt with thus far include the United Kingdom, United States, Australia and New

Zealand. The United Kingdom and the United States have had politically conservative parties in office during the 1980s while, in the latter cases, for most of the 1980s labour parties have held office. Despite these political party differences, each of the four countries has had some similar policy experiences in the past decade.

During the 1980s there has been a trend towards more market-oriented and de-regulatory policies, often legitimated in part by the 'need' for a more flexible response to the Japanese and Asian challenge. It was in terms of this rhetoric of response that the financial markets of Australia and New Zealand were rapidly de-regulated in the mid-1980s, in order to facilitate the greater availability of capital for re-structuring of manufacturing industry. Despite taking place under labour Governments, the rhetoric has been aggressively 'New Right'.

The New Right monetarist-inspired phenomenon of de-regulation clearly has cultural just as much as economic auspices. Indeed, in the concepts of 'enterprise culture' (U. K.) or 'productive culture' (Australia), the debate has directly tapped this dimension. However, one aspect of the debate has gone largely unremarked: exhortation in the political arena by national government and even de-regulation of aspects of economic activity do not necessarily nor unproblematically translate into a culture of 'efficiency and effectiveness' at the organization level. One can change the rules of the game, one can change the motivational rhetoric of the national captains – but does this necessarily produce the desired changes in actual behaviour at the level of organizational action?

As Lewis and MacGregor argue in their discussion of 'De-regulation and Degradation in Managerial Work', issues of de-regulation understood at the organization level need to touch base with the issues that have been central to labour process theory: control and resistance. De-regulation in the finance industry has been driven by technological changes which have made possible significant changes to the nature of work and organization in banking. Indeed, in organization terms, de-regulation might more accurately be specified as re-regulation: a move from one form of regulation to another.

The first wave of technological change in banking had produced a stable administrative bureaucracy as the normal form of direct control at the level of branch operations. It was a control system that was explicitly gendered: men controlled women; men had access to career ladders while women did not. During the 1950s and 1960s a second wave of technological change occurred, carrying with it a re-regulation of organizational relations. The major components of this second wave were micro-electronic technology, one effect of the adoption of which was to vest increased centralization and control in automatic data processing operations rather than in direct control of subordinated clerical labour processes at the branch level. Control moved up and out of the branch managers discretion: to centralized bank offices; into programmes which were routinely accomplished by lower level branch staff working with automatic computer equipment. Branch managers who had been previously middle level managers in the national framework, while simultaneously top managers who exercised considerable local discretion at the branch level, found that important areas of their roles disappeared with this re-regulation. Decision making had been transformed into centralized head office functions organized on a divisional form which became implemented at the branch level through the provision and supply of standardized information via electronic data processing.

According to the arguments of contingency theory (Donaldson 1985), one would anticipate that the move towards the divisional form would enhance efficiency by effecting an improved fit between form, function and environment. One should note two important considerations, however. First, the environment has not had its effect through either the implicit competitive or evolutionary tendencies that figure in contingency accounts. Determination was political: the rhetoric of the New Right was strongly ensconced in the economics discipline in both Australia and New Zealand: key staff in Treasury in both countries were committed de-regulators, and the incoming labour Treasurers in both countries supported much of their general position, in part because New Right critiques of the lack of de-regulatory nerve of their conservative predecessors had gained considerable media exposure.

A second important consideration in respect of this move to a divisional form is that, by contrast to what one would expect from the contingency argument, the effects at the organizational level of the branch have been neither effective nor efficient in the terms anticipated by both New Right and contingency views. To understand this, one needs to harness an 'institutional' view of organizational culture to a grasp of the dialectics of control and resistance at the banch level, as Lewis and MacGregor propose.

In order to achieve efficiency in marketing services in a de-regulated environment, the discretion and control previously exercised by branch managers has been eroded. Despite this, they are now the front line marketers of the range of financial services that the banks are trying to market through the branch structure. The data clearly indicate that branch managers deeply regret the loss of control and career opportunities once open to them. However, they are ill-equipped to resist an increasing regime of control by re-regulation/de-regulation because of an extreme dependence by them on their employing organization. There are no countervailing loci of power in a solidaristic trade union; they are tied to the bank by the 'golden chains' of an internal labour market, low mortgage rates and firm-specific superannuation schemes. Yet they are able to find and exploit a point of resistance to an increasingly stressful and resented work organization. Resistance takes the form, precisely, of not being efficient and effective in the very area that strategically guided the re-structuring and re-regulation which has so transformed their work-selling: they resist through not selling; through this refusal to market they are, in terms of the micro-politics of the local organization, effectively and unwittingly resisting, however temporarily, the 'logic of capital' as it is expressed through a specific re-regulated/de-regulated regime of accumulation.

The implications of this analysis are far broader than they might initially appear to be. The de-regulatory thrust is not confined to the finance industry nor to Australia and New Zealand. It is a plank in political strategies in many of the OECD countries as they seek to retain the competitive edge lost to Japan and the NICs of East Asia. What Lewis and MacGregor's analysis suggests is that even in the most propitious circumstances of no union, an existing internal labour market and an ideologically conservative non-working class labour force, grand strategies derived from ideological world views, such as those of the New Right, may not achieve the efficiency and effectiveness claimed for them. Strategies at the macro level necessarily entail individual and organizational action whose intent can rarely be assured in the arena of micro-politics.

One thrust of the concluding section of Clegg, Higgins and Spybey's consideration of economic culture is to suggest that where a broad-based, popular and interstitially embedded social movement succeeds politically in the way that social democracy has done in Sweden, then the expanded representational basis for active citizenship at all levels, from local micro-politics to the macro considerations of state planning, does a great deal to facilitate the effective achievement of overall strategies. Consequently, they maintain, the arguments for a social democratic economic culture (in contrast to the authoritarian democratic culture of East Asia or the liberal democratic culture of the English-speaking OECD nations) are not simply ideological — a matter of elective affinity and political preference — but also functional: expanded representation is a more secure basis on which to build a modern, industrially efficient economic culture than is exclusion. As Standish implicitly argues, exclusion may not only occur in terms of formal political and organizational arrangements. The absence of a standardized framework for interpreting the information contained in accountancy practice can itself give rise to distorted communication and function as a barrier to entry into full representational citizenship, as it were.

It is not just in the explicitly capitalist world that grand strategies have been undercut by local politics and practice which are deeply embedded in organizational routines. The same has been true of the People's Republic of China (PRC). Indeed, at one level the China case offers a striking counter-factual to the importance of institutional frameworks and cultural embeddedness for economic success. If in the Japanese and NIC cases one looks for examples of facilitative institutions and cultures with respect to economic efficiency, in the PRC one would more usually tend to look to institutional and cultural blockages. Not surprisingly, some similar cultural features fulfil the diverse analytical roles of facilitator and foe of economic efficiency in the understanding of Chinese economic action in the PRC compared to that of the Overseas Chinese in South East Asia.

Max Weber (1978) stressed the necessity of rationalization obliterating the status desiderata of pre-modern feudal societies if a market-based economy and society were to be achieved. In the PRC this has yet to occur. It is an irony of recent scholarship that the very Confucian values of familism, tradition, face-to-face trust, which some observers see as quintessential contributions to the 'post-Confucian' economic successes of Japan and the NICs — the 'groupism' and familial centred provisioning of welfare — are regarded by observers like Boisot and Child as obstacles to the same goal, in their chapter on 'Efficiency, Ideology and Tradition in the Choice of Transactions Governance Structures: The Case of China as a Modernizing Society'. Their argument is that the feudal nature of traditional Chinese social relationships has in some important local respects survived intact into the present day: the 'war-lords' have changed, but practices of the fief have remained remarkably constant. Local patrimonialism and a negotiated absolutism characterize the relations between enterprises and their municipalities, trapped in a web of conflicting regulations and, on the enterprise's part, transactional dependencies. Just as for capitalism to flourish in Britain, the Tudor absolutist state had to be dismantled by the post-restoration state, particularly from the mid-eighteenth century on, so the state in the PRC is the only economic actor that has sufficient capacity to effect the rationalization through which greater elements of a market society might be constructed. In other words, concerted political action is required to found market institutions. The PRC's problem, contrary to the views of many outside observers, is not the omnipotence of state regulation but the weakness of its implementation in key areas. However, they suggest, it may not need to proceed as far down the path of bureaucratic regulation as nineteenth-century precursors such as Bentham designed for the Indian Civil Service, or as Weber found in the Prussian bureaucracy. Modern forms of electronic communication may enable rationalization and codification at a lower level of regulation: where the medium is the message, or at least part of it, the constraints of an excessively formalized regulation via the written word might be minimized. In the land of Confucius, the home of the mandarin, this hope may prove too optimistic to entertain, if the more cultural-oriented explanations are to be believed.

The chapters in this volume are diverse, but as this introduction has sought to establish, they do share common themes in their perspectives on *Capitalism in Contrasting Cultures*. First, the importance of analyzing what Granovetter (1985) refers to as the embeddedness of economic action. The majority of the contributions to the volume achieve this focus; most do it with a comparative focus although some are more particular case-studies (e. g. Acton, Biggart and Lewis and MacGregor). Consequently, the 'space' dimension of embeddedness is well covered here: the focus ranges across Europe, the United States, Asia and the Pacific. However, economic relations are not only differentially embedded in spatial terms; they also achieve differential embeddedness across temporal continua as well, although only the contribution by Mannari and Marsh achieves this rare level of analysis. In doing so, interestingly, it is the contribution which sticks closest to a disembedded view of the organization as the unit of analysis. For the future, it would be of evident value if the kind of longitudinal analysis offered by Mannari and Marsh could be integrated with the more institutional perspective of many of the other contributors to this volume.

Mention of an institutional perspective brings us to a second major common point among many of the papers. Within the ranks of organization analysis there is a new social movement gathering pace which is collecting disparate themes and authors under the banner of 'institutionalism', a movement over which Scott (1987) has recently cast a paternalist eye. He identifies five main variants of the institutionalist perspective. It will be useful to connect these to the chapters collected here.

The origins of the institutional school have been attributed by Scott to the work of Selznick (1957), in particular a focus on institutionalization as a means of instilling value, of supplying intrinsic worth to a structure or process which previously had only instrumental utility (Scott 1987). The contribution which comes closest to this perspective is that by Wilkinson and Oliver in their focus on attempts to 'Nipponize' British workers and industry. A clear attempt is being made to overturn instrumentalism and instil an expressive dimension to economic life.

A second perspective within the institutionalist movement is identified by Scott as a concern with institutionalization as a process of creating reality, a stream he regards as heavily indebted to the work of Berger (Berger and

Luckmann 1967) in the sociology of knowledge. The concern is with the paradox 'that man is capable of producing a world that he then experiences as something other than a human product' (Berger and Luckmann 1967: 61). In organization analysis this stream is seen particularly in the work of Meyer and Rowan (1977). In this volume the focus on the processes whereby phenomena come to take on a rule-like nature in thought and action is probably best seen in the focus on forms of calculation in Clegg, Higgins and Spybey's chapter. However, 'Nipponization', the focus of Wilkinson and Oliver's piece, or the concern with 'Corporate Governance' in Tricker, as well as the focus on the language of accounting in Standish, may all be seen to explicate the 'rational myths' that are the focus of Meyer and Rowan's influential work.

A further strand of institutional theory is apparent in Meyer and Rowan's (1977) work, according to Scott's (1987) analysis. Its identifying feature is a concern with those relational networks whose 'rules define new organizing situations, redefine existing ones, and specify the means for coping rationally with each'. As they add, not only do they 'enable', but 'often require, participants to organize along prescribed lines' (Meyer and Rowan 1977: 344). Relational networks as the focus of analysis, looking not to the organization per se but to its embeddedness within systemic and enduring features of the constitutive environment, are at the heart of the conceptualization advanced by Redding and Whitley; Hamilton, Kim and Zeile; Wilks; Tam; and Marceau. Each one of these contributions focuses on the institutional environment conceived in network and cultural terms.

A major thrust of post-functionalist social theory has been to specify the nature of social life as institutionally loosely coupled, rather than being tightly coupled under any single, overarching normative order. Alford and Friedland (1987) have developed this point by noting how different institutional spheres sustain distinct belief systems, and how these may aid in reproducing the spheres. Most contributions to this volume take this approach to institutions as distinct societal spheres. Acton, for instance, focuses on the inter-relationship of the religious sphere of belief systems with the sphere of economic organization. The former is causally efficacious for the latter, he argues, in respect to the Duck Islanders. Biggart similarly focuses on the relationships between belief systems, concentrating on more general aspects of ideology rather than on religious belief. In her contribution, as well as in Acton's, the significance of the value sphere for economic action is underlined. The contribution by Bond and Hofstede focuses on the values acquired through primary socialization in the family and the ways in which these provide sustaining motivational resources for economic action. Each of these chapters regards the sphere of culture,

broadly and differently defined in substantive terms, as having consequences in the institutional sphere of economic action.

Finally, in this synoptic review of institutional affinities, we may note that
the contribution by Boisot and Child comes closest to a concern with what
Scott (1987) terms the 'new institutionalism'. In this perspective, developed
in Boisot and Child's case from elements of Dore (1973), Kroeber and
Kluckhohn (1952) and Williamson (1975), the emphasis on symbolic aspects of economic action is captured in the notion of transactional structures and modes, applied at a macro level, focusing on the semi-autonomy
of commune and firm and their inter-relation, within the context of the
PRC's policy environment.

It would be spurious to pretend that all the papers collected in this volume
share an essential unity or perspective. However, by focusing their attention
on issues surrounding conceptions of economic culture related to the sphere
of economic action and organization, a number of general issues which
are locatable in current concerns with 'embeddedness' and 'institutionalism', have emerged. This introduction has sought to not only display these
themes but also to serve as a synoptic review of the individual chapters.
It does not substitute for them. They should be read in their own right
and not necessarily through the editorial interpretation. Consequently, we
conclude.

References

Abegglen, J. and G. W. Stalk (1985): *Kaisha,* New York: Basic Books.
Alford, R. R. and R. Friedland (1987): *Powers of theory: capitalism, the state and
democracy,* Cambridge: Cambridge University Press.
Attewell, P. (1987): The deskilling controversy, *Work and occupations* 14, 3: 323–
346.
Berger, P. L. (1987): *The capitalist revolution,* London: Wildwood House.
Berger, P. L. and T. Luckmann (1967): *The social construction of reality,* Har-
mondsworth: Penguin Press.
Blau, P. M. and R. W. Scott (1963): *Formal organizations: a comparative approach,*
London: Routledge and Kegan Paul.
Braverman, H. (1974): *Labour and monopoly capital: the degradation of work in the
Twentieth Century,* New York: Monthly Review Press.
Burawoy, M. (1979): *Manufacturing consent: change in the labour process under
monopoly capitalism,* Chicago: University of Chicago Press.
Burns, T. and G. M. Stalker (1961): *The management of innovation,* London:
Tavistock.
Cheung, S. S. (1986): *Will China go capitalist?* London: Institute of Economic
Affairs, Hobart Paper 94 (2nd ed.).

Clegg, S. R. (1981): Organization and control, *Administrative Science Quarterly* 26: 545 – 562.

Clegg S. R. and D. Dunkerley (1980): *Organization, class and control,* London: Routledge and Kegan Paul.

Clegg, S. R. and W. Higgins (1987): Against the current: sociology, socialism and organizations, *Organization Studies* 8, 3: 201 – 221.

Clegg, S. R., P. Boreham and G. Dow (1986): *Class, politics and the economy,* London: Routledge and Kegan Paul.

Collins, R. (1980): Weber's lost theory of capitalism, *American Journal of Sociology* 45: 925 – 942.

Crozier, M. (1964): *The bureaucratic phenomenon,* London: Tavistock.

Donaldson, L. (1985): *In defence of organization theory: a response to the critics,* Cambridge: University of Cambridge Press.

Donaldson, L. (1986): Size and bureaucracy in East and West, in: S. R. Clegg, D. C. Dunphy and S. G. Redding *The enterprise and management in East Asia,* 67 – 92, Hong Kong: The Centre of Asian Studies, University of Hong Kong.

Dore, R. P. (1973): *British factory, Japanese factory,* Berkeley: University of California Press.

Emery, F. E. and E. L. Trist (1965): The causal texture of organizational environments, *Human Relations* 18: 21 – 31.

Fox, A. (1974): *Beyond contract: work, power and trust relations,* London: Faber and Faber.

Gouldner, A. (1954): *Patterns of industrial bureaucracy,* New York: Free Press.

Granovetter, M. (1985): 'Economic action and social structure: the problem of embeddedness,' *American Journal of Sociology* 19, 3: 481 – 510.

Hofstede, G. (1980): *Culture's consequences,* London: Sage.

Jaques, E. (1951): *The changing culture of a factory,* London: Tavistock.

Karpik, L. (1987): Success and limits of French corporations: industrial elite, structure and society, Paper presented to ISA RC-17 Conference: 'Critical perspectives on organization theories' Wassenaar, The Netherlands, July 1987.

Kroeber, A. L. and C. Kluckhohn (1952): *Culture: a critical review of concepts and definitions,* Cambridge, Mass.: Peabody Museum of American Archaeology and Ethnology, Harvard University.

Marcuse, H. (1964): *One-dimensional man,* London: Routledge and Kegan Paul.

Meyer, J. and B. Rowan (1977): Institutionalized organizations: formal structure as myth and ceremony, *American Journal of Sociology* 83: 340 – 363.

Offe, C. (1975): The theory of the capitalist state and the problem of policy transformation, in: L. Lindberg, R. R. Alford, C. Crouch and C. Offe (eds.), *Stress and contradiction in modern capitalism,* 125 – 144, Lexington, Mass.: Lexington Books.

Ouchi, W. G. (1980): Markets, bureaucracies and class, *Administrative Science Quarterly* 25: 129 – 140.

Perrow, C. (1986): *Complex organizations: a critical essay,* Glenview, Ill.: Scott, Foreman and Co.

Peters, T. J. and R. H. Waterman (1982): *In search of excellence: lessons from America's best-run companies,* New York: Harper and Row.

Pugh, D. S. and D. J. Hickson (1976): *Organizational structure in its context: the Aston programme 1*, Farnborough, Hants.: Saxon House.

Ragin, Charles C. (1987): *The comparative method*, Berkeley, Cal.: University of California Press.

Rothschild, J. and J. A. Whitt (1986): *The co-operative workplace: potentials and dilemmas of organizational democracy and participation*, Cambridge, Mass.: Cambridge University Press.

Roy, D. F. (1960): Banana time: job satisfaction and informal interaction, *Human Organization* 18: 156−168.

Scott, W. R. (1987): The adolescence of institutional theory, *Administrative Science Quarterly* 32, 4: 493−511.

Selznick, P. (1957): *Leadership in administration*, New York: Harper and Row.

Weber, M. (1923): *General economic history*, London: Allen and Unwin.

Weber, M. (1930): *The Protestant ethic and the spirit of capitalism*, London: Allen and Unwin.

Weber, M. (1978): *Economy and society*, Berkeley, Cal.: University of California Press.

Whyte, W. H. (1956): *The organization man*, New York: Simon and Schuster.

Williamson, O. (1975): *Markets and hierarchies: analysis and anti-trust implications*, New York: Free Press.

Williamson, O. E. (1985): *The economic institutions of capitalism*, New York: Free Press.

Wilkinson, B. and Oliver, N. (1988): Guest editorial, *Industrial Relations Journal* 19, 1 Spring: 7−10.

Willis, P. (1977): *Learning to labour: how working class kids get working class jobs*, Farnborough, Hants.: Saxon House.

Part I
Capitalism's Cultures — Lessons from Asia?

'Post-Confucianism', Social Democracy and Economic Culture

Stewart R. Clegg, Winton Higgins and Tony Spybey

Introduction

The concept of culture, according to one of its foremost students, 'is one of the two or three most complicated words in the English language' (Williams 1976: 77). In all its early uses it was employed as a noun of process: the tending of something, a meaning which, from the early sixteenth century onwards, was extended in application from nature to human development as an object of intervention (see Bauman 1973, 1976). An extension of this noun of process to economic husbandry has a long if frequently implicit history in the social sciences. Its still implicit character is revealingly apparent from its absence in Swedberg's (1987) definitive review of 'economic sociology'.

Despite this absence, notable contributions to the career of the implicit concept are many. One thinks, for instance, of Weber's (1930) reflections on the 'Protestant Ethic'; Schumpeter's (1944) concern for the decline of 'heroic capitalism'; Wiener's (1981) charting of the decline of the English 'entrepreneurial spirit' or Anderson's (1964, 1986) critiques of the 'peculiarities of the English'. Moving further afield from the European heartland, one can point to the contemporary American literature on 'corporate culture' (Peters and Waterman 1982) together with the closely allied fascination for Japan, understood in terms of its 'economic culture' (Ouchi 1981) or the more general fixation on 'post-Confucian culture' (Clegg, Dunphy and Redding 1986 a): all of these serve as indices of the salience of this particular concept for contemporary social science, a concern currently capped by Berger's (1987) important work on *The Capitalist Revolution*.

The reasons for this continuing fascination are not difficult to fathom. In each of the major conceptualizations referred to the impetus has been to understand the salience of specifically 'cultural' factors for the dynamics of economic 'success' or 'decline' in either specific capitalist economies (Dunphy and Redding 1986 a; Schumpeter 1944; Weber 1930; Wiener 1981) or specific capitalist firms (Ouchi 1981; Peters and Waterman 1982). We may, for the sake of simplicity, refer to these as a concern with macro-economic culture and meso-economic culture respectively.

Any conception of 'economic culture' will, in Berger's (1987: 7) terms, 'explore the social, political, and cultural matrix or context within which particular economic processes operate'. For any culture of economic processes to be recognizably reproduced, certain practices would have to be routinized in such a way as to develop both structural properties, in the form of rules and resources, and systematic properties, in the form of regular social practices or reproduced relations (Giddens 1984). At the heart of the matter is the manner in which culture, as a process, tends, cultivates and regulates particular types of economic outcomes. It is through analysis of these structural and systemic regulatory properties that the features of an 'economic culture' can be addressed.

Conceptions of an 'economic culture' are often, in the popular press at least, identified with an 'enterprise culture'. However, it is not clear that the concept of 'economic culture' does carry an ideological load; certainly its primary contemporary proponent, Berger (1987: 9 – 10) suggests it does not. Nonetheless, in the Western capitalist nations, particularly in the last decade of emphasis on de-regulation, it has often seemed as if the notion of a 'successful economic culture' has carried with it a strongly liberal, laissez-faire bias espousing free enterprise, an anti-bureaucratic, anti-state orientation and a strong endorsement of markets over politics as sources of effective resource allocation and decision making. In part, surely, this is because the concept has been applied particularly to notions such as Mrs Thatchers' endorsement of an 'enterprise culture', an endorsement often refracted through a broader cultural commitment to the renewal of some older, almost mythical, 'Victorian values'.

Elsewhere, however, it is less to history than to contemporary East Asia that many advocates of the importance of economic culture would refer, including Berger (1987). Like many other observers he has been impressed by the economic success of Japan, Hong Kong, Singapore, South Korea and Taiwan, countries whose post-war economic growth has consistently outstripped OECD annual average growth rates during the same period, in terms of GDP (Gross Domestic Product) per capita. Despite the undeniably impressive gains made by these countries, some caution may be required in interpreting their economic record. One should not be too sanguine about the meaning of these economic growth rates. For one thing, GDP growth is somewhat limited as an indicant of performance. It makes no reference to the quality of work, leisure or life more generally. Moreover, the fact that these Newly Industrializing Countries (NICs) have a high growth rate is hardly surprising (although this does not alter the fact that their growth, comparatively, is significant). For those nations which are initially worse off, then economic growth, where it is achieved, will tend to be generally higher than the average for more mature economies. This was the case in the initial post-war era of Japan's economic miracle, for instance. However, by the 1970s the growth rate had fallen to the 3% − 4% range, which, while still at the leading edge of OECD nations, was clearly within their standard range (Quiggin 1987). Despite this caution one must still acknowledge that the Newly Industrialized Countries of East Asia did achieve, in their economic growth, something which most other post-war 'underdeveloped' countries did not achieve. The interesting question is thus why it was that it was these countries, rather than other Asian, African or Latin American nations, which became the NIC powerhouses. Economic explanations alone seem inadequate to this explanatory task (Clegg, Dunphy and Redding 1986 a). Having explored and run up against the limits of economic factors, many explanations of this success have sought instead to understand it in terms of the cultural factors we have alluded to. The focus has been on the cultural context in which such successful economic husbandry has occurred; the specificity of this context has been defined in terms of a 'post-Confucian' economic culture.

While the Pacific Region may be the context of this latest application of an 'economically cultural' explanation, it is noticeable that not all states in the region are able to forge a post-Confucian way. Amongst these is Australia, a state not characterized by a largely ethnic Chinese business sector, but one which, as a matter of government policy, is seeking to emulate the export-led growth of these other Pacific region states. Interestingly, in this country the prescription for an 'economic culture' has been sought not in nearby East Asia but in faraway Scandinavia. It is not just chauvinism on the part of two of the authors of this paper which leads us to pose the question of economic growth and economic culture from within the antipodean context. There are two other important reasons. First a matter of local detail; if Britons have been hectored to acquire the advantages of an 'enterprise culture' by their government, then in Australia key ministers have been no less avid in promoting a similar idea. Locally it goes by the name of developing a 'productive culture', and the political resonances are evident. The issue of 'economic culture' is clearly on the Australian political and economic agenda.

The second reason for posing issues of economic culture from an Australian perspective is a matter of analytic strategy. Berger's (1987) book poses a choice between 'capitalism' and 'socialism', and comes down firmly on the side of capitalism in terms of arguments of both equity and efficiency. We doubt if these terms of debate are contentious. However, what would be of greater salience and of incomparably more policy relevance would be a comparison of capitalisms. In the modern world capitalism must be considered in the highly plural and diverse forms in which one encounters it in various nation states and regions. To regard its form of articulation in South Africa, for example, as the same as its present development in Denmark would not get one very far. Certainly, property may be basically privately owned and controlled and labour formally free — but the nature of that formal freedom varies considerably with the nature of the state and civil society which constitutes it. In turn, the possibilities for capital formation are contingent not only on resources and infrastructure but also the modes of labour organization and discipline which have been constructed. A singular category of capitalism is not very useful.

Some states are faced with more strategic choices than others in the construction of contemporary capitalisms. Recent research by Calmfors and Diffil (1988), reported in *The Economist* (13 – 19 February, 1988: 86), suggests that a key contingency in comparing capitalisms is the type of wage-bargaining system which is institutionalized in different national settings. Studies have consistently shown a relationship beween this variable and selected macro-economic outcomes such as the levels of unemployment and inflation (Clegg, Boreham and Dow 1986). Three types of arrangement are identified by Calmfors and Diffil (1988). Focusing on inter-employer and inter-union cooperation in wage-bargaining, they split seventeen OECD countries into those characterized by centralized, decentralized and intermediate bargaining patterns. These types were then related to a range of macro-economic outcomes such as levels of inflation and unemployment. Those countries which were either highly centralized or highly decentralized in their wage-bargaining system consistently outperformed those in the intermediate category. Included in this intermediate category were both Australia and New Zealand, as well as West Germany, Holland and Belgium; Britain, they suggest, probably belongs here as well. These countries clearly have considerable incentive to re-think their strategies in terms of either a more or a less centralized wage-bargaining system if they are concerned with achieving more effective macro-economic outcomes. Those countries at either end of the spectrum are necessarily more 'locked in' to their design by virtue not only of institutional isomorphism but also the performance advantages that this goodness of fit produces. It is those countries which are least isomorphic in their institutional arrangements which have the greatest freedom of movement and choice either way.

It is a consequence of the choices facing countries such as Australia that the 'economic culture' debate takes on an important policy dimension. To the extent that there is an elision in the terms of the debate, and the concept of an 'economic culture' *per se* is aligned with that of an enterprise culture, then the terms of debate and choice are unnecessarily restricted. Moreover, the Scandinavian prescriptions would seem ill-advised. Consequently, the discussion of the 'economic cultures' of Pacific examples, such as Japan and the East Asian NICs, needs to be balanced with discussion of less 'economically liberal' and more 'social democratic' cultures, such as that which prevails in Sweden, for example. When posed in these terms, as we shall see, the issue of choice becomes more acute.

If we concentrate only on Japan and the East Asian NICs, the choices, although somewhat inchoate between national strategies, do appear to have some common elements oriented towards recasting the industrial relations into terms consonant with those which have marked the 1980s revival of neo-conservative liberal analysis applied to 'political culture'. Recipes for success will be sought in de-regulation, in de-unionization or enterprise unionism, in state intervention oriented to curbing the excesses of democracy, administrative overload, ungovernability and so on. (For an account of the general arguments, consult Clegg, Dow and Boreham 1983: 34 – 38.) When the political and economic imagination is confronted by the economic success of an economic culture which is in many respects an alternative to those Pacific examples, such as that of social democracy typified here by reference to Sweden, the implicit choices really do become quite evident. They will be seen to hinge on the central notions of citizenship and representation: on the one hand, the deepening and extension of these on a universalistic basis in not only the political but also the economic sphere; on the other hand, their restriction not only within the economic but also the political sphere. Consequently, it is through consideration of these issues that one might be attracted to what, in any economically liberal conception of an economic culture, would hardly be a promising example. The rationale for our chapter is now clear.

The framework for the remainder of the chapter is as follows. First we will establish that with respect to the cases of the East Asian economic success stories there are evident limits to an understanding couched solely in conventional economic terms. It is for this reason that in the past decade increasing recourse has been made to conceptions of 'economic culture' in explaining this success, attributing it to some underlying set of 'post-Confucian' value-clusters. Our second task is to cast a sceptical eye over these explanations and to suggest that they have recourse to what we consider to be an underlying 'essentialism' as a strategy of argument: the cultural essence becomes capable of explaining whatever economic phenomena are to be explained. Our third task is to attempt to sketch the institutional framework within which the 'social, political and cultural matrix' of economic process has been lodged in the pre-eminent case of Asian economic culture; that of Japan. One consequence of this will be to cast a further sceptical eye over culturalist explanations as they have been developed for the Japanese case. By contrast, we would want to concentrate explanation rather more on the institutional frame and rather less on the allegedly causal role of a unique culture. Our fourth task is to try and develop some conceptual order within which such discussion may in future be framed. In order to do this we focus on the limits to univariate explanation which we assemble by reference to cultural, market, state and organizational contingencies. This discussion focuses more widely than on Japan alone: it also includes the 'four dragons' of Taiwan, Hong Kong, Singapore and South Korea.

The framework of cultural, market, state and organizational contingencies impinges on the forms of economic calculation which are available to dominant economic actors. Two aspects of this are focused on: the technical considerations surrounding production (which we will identify as having been of particular importance in the Japanese case) and the forms of financial calculation which are systematically available to economic actors within diverse national frames. Again, the focus is comparative, broadened to include not only East Asian economic successes but also some less successful cases in recent times: Britain, the United States and Australia. Stability in economic calculation appears as a key factor, thus underscoring the argument from Calmfors and Diffil (1988). However, at this stage in the argument our elective affinities become evident. We consider it important to understand that not only are stability and consistency in institutional frameworks important, but that it is also necessary to consider the basis upon which this order is constructed. Is it one which extends or restricts the distribution of those desiderata we value, all things being equal? The direction of our argument thus becomes apparent. It is our concern not only with macro-economic efficiency but also the basis on which this is achieved, in terms of the public sphere of citizenship, which guides the argument. Consequently, our penultimate two sections open up consideration of a social democratic example of an economic culture, which in our final section we contrast with the two types which have been implicit in our earlier discussion: a liberal democratic and an authoritarian democratic type. On this comparative basis of alternative frameworks better informed policy choices may be constructed.

Having outlined the logic of our subsequent argument it is appropriate to commence it. We begin with a consideration of the East Asian conjuncture in which the economic culture concept first explicitly developed.

The Limits of Economic Explanation for East Asia

The limits to economic explanation are readily appreciated. Intuitively economic explanations which stress cheap labour or government subsidies or the inexpensiveness of transport costs to major markets do have a certain plausibility in explaining economic performance: but it is one which is limited; on these criteria the debt-ridden nations of Latin America would have seemed a better proposition for economic growth than did those of East Asia in the post-war period. Casting the net a little wider, other explanations have stressed the importance for the East Asian NICs of factors such as their being extremely market-oriented economies tightly organized around the price mechanism, having liberal doses of entrepreneurialism, high domestic savings and 'free' labour markets. Although these factors are not applicable across the board, such elements would seem to conform precisely to the liberal conception of an economic culture to which we have already alluded in the introduction.

Market conditions have invariably been paid most attention, stressing phenomena such as labour intensive export-oriented policies and free trade conditions existing for exporters, policies underlined by specific frameworks of interest rate, agricultural, educational and anti-labour support. While consideration of these issues would offer some explanatory purchase on how these East Asian economies were able to rapidly industrialize, they do not specifically focus on their successful export-orientation.

Some considerable ingenuity has been exercised in explaining this successful export-orientation: it was due to factors in scarce supply, such as a lack of natural resources, of land and of a large domestic market, at least where the city-states are concerned. The 'advantage' of a total lack of natural resources has often been regarded as a factor in Japan's success. The ingenuity is only exceeded by the implausibility of these explanations. Although the idea of countries not having the luxury of options and being forced to export or perish is intuitively attractive, there are still many countries where the same might apply and apparently does not.

Spurred by the lack of explanatory content of these factors, some recent contributors to the debate have, as we have indicated, sought to introduce an 'economic cultural' explanation. What characterizes these arguments is the use of long-standing and pervasive cultural attitudes and institutions which are identified as the source of East Asian success. It is here that the social conditions of 'entrepreneurialism' are sought. In the East Asian case this explanation has come increasingly to be made in terms of what has been called the 'post-Confucian hypothesis'.

Post-Confucian Economic Culture

The post-Confucian hypothesis was first explicated by Herman Kahn (1979), who proposed that the success of organizations in Japan, Korea, Taiwan, Hong Kong and Singapore was due in large part to certain key traits shared by the majority of organization members which were attributable to an upbringing in the Confucian tradition. Classically, the key notion of Confucianism was that of *Chün-tzu*, a concern for the courteous and correct conduct of one's duties, particularly towards the family, based on a profound respect for social conventions. In this respect Confucianism, in its concern with ritual, order, imperial patrimonialism, service and the meritocratic achievement of these virtues, was profoundly anti-individualist: it legitimated a corporate, bureaucratic elite unified around the highly developed monopoly of complex literacy enjoyed by the mandarinate. One might, in view of this characterization, be tempted to think that the only commonality between Confucianism and post-Confucianism is a shared stress on familism, collectivism defined in terms of the family, and a meritocratic stress on education as the means to collectively consolidate family wealth. The elite, ascetic, other-worldy characteristics are lacking.

Some aspects of the post-Confucian argument are appealing in precisely the same terms as are similar ideas about the role of Protestantism in forming a 'capitalist ethic' in nineteenth-century Europe and America. This is, that in the initial stages of capitalist development, either ethic could provide at least some of those conditions of capital formation which are necessary for initiating sustained production and accumulation. To reinvest capital to the glory of God or to that of the family will, if diligence, application and market conditions allow, achieve the same end of deferred consumption and increased investment leading to greater productivity. There is a sting in the tail, however. Precisely to the extent that such ethics are capitalistically successful, their success will begin to undermine the conditions that first produced them, as Weber was well aware in his prognosis for the future of the Protestant ethic:

Where the fulfillment of the calling cannot directly be related to the highest spiritual and cultural values, or when, on the other hand, it need not be felt simply as economic compulsion, the individual generally abandons the attempt to justify it at all. In the field of its highest development, in the United States, the pursuit of wealth, stripped of its religious and ethical meaning, tends to become associated with purely mundane passions, which often actually give it the character of sport (Weber 1930: 182).

It is not simply the character of the meaning structure which regulates economic activity in its drive, its production, which can serve to undercut an economically cultural ethic. As Marcuse (1964) observed, the very conditions for successful mass production are those least likely to reproduce the ascetic conditions of the initial economic success. Mass production, at least in its early twentieth-century form, was premised on mass markets and mass consumption. Against this orchestrated conformity of consumption Marcuse imagined that the hedonism which it unleashed would lead to an eventual revolt, not of mass producers, but of those excluded from a mass society whose life style was consequently no longer shaped by an ethic of asceticism. However, although the most recent era has witnessed a 'revolt into style', it has done so not as a spectacle of rebellion but as one of highly differentiated consumption premised on ever more fine-grained flexible production and niche marketing, within the mass form. Japan, in particular, has been in the vanguard of these new forms of flexible production. The implications of this are important for the general cultural explanation of post-Confucianism.

While it can be seen that a norm of *ascetic* individualism would seem destined to wither with the full flowering of an era of mass consumption, a collectivist, familist ethic would appear to be much hardier. For one thing, mass consumption, centred on the familial household, would serve to reproduce these households as the appropriate social unit of consumption. The very social forces that undermined a Protestant, ascetic ethic while leaving its individualism with relatively unbridled opportunities for hedonistic development could serve to reproduce an ethic based on the collective, familial household. However, the sting is not entirely absent.

East Asian economic success, particularly that of Japan, has been in large part premised on a keynote of flexibility in producing highly specialized variants of basically mass produced goods. These have depended upon pin-point accuracy in differentiating and positioning commodities in the market. Any visitor to the highly fashion conscious centres of Hong Kong, Singapore or Tokyo cannot fail to be impressed by the success with which advertisers have created an individualist ethic of consumption in these 'post-Confucian' heartlands. One does not have to be a latter-day Marcuse to ask whether or not mass marketing, demographic analysis and urban density will produce conditions which may not reproduce the initial conditions posited for the economic success: familism, deferred consumption and disciplined order can be and are undercut by marketing strategies oriented to individual differentiation. Evidence in support of this proposition may be drawn from a cross-national survey of youth from 18 to 24 years of age which the office of the Prime Minister of Japan conducted in 11 countries. Japanese youth came out as more 'highly egoistic, self-centred and oriented to personal interests' and with the highest 'levels of frustration against family and school' among the nations surveyed, as Sugimoto (1986:

66) reports from the *Mainichi Shinbun* of February 12 and 13, 1984. The sting is evident: if the post-Confucian hypothesis is to be accepted, then the highly differentiated consumption characteristic of its success would appear to undermine the productive basis of this post-Confucian economic culture's core-values of familism, deferred consumption and disciplined order. That is, if one accepts that these values play the role that has been suggested for them by the culturalists.

What conclusions can be drawn from this 'cultural' and 'economic' explanation? Well, if one were a 'non-Confucian' who was persuaded by the post-Confucian hypothesis, one might take comfort in imagining that in the longer term East Asian managers will confront precisely the same social fabric and workforce characteristics that European and American managers presently face. But this would be false comfort, we will argue, because, contrary to popular consensus, the success of Asian business can not be attributed so simply to cultural factors, despite the stress on these in the literature. Consequently, the concept of 'economic culture', inasmuch as it is hinged on this literature, requires reconsideration. We can begin to re-specify it by focusing on the Japanese literature.

The 'Culture' of Japanese Management

The literature on Japanese management has expanded exponentially since the 1960s. There is widespread agreement that Japanese distinctiveness relates primarily to personnel practices, decision-making processes and manufacturing philosophies and practices, but there are also distinctive differences in relationships with stakeholders, in enterprise goals and in structures. Dunphy's (1986) research suggests that while distinctive production methods and workforce skilling are clearly linked to productivity, it is harder to conclude that such a causal link exists between productivity and those practices that are supposed to lead to loyalty and commitment. It is not only that these Japanese management practices do not seem to generate higher worker satisfaction in Japan. It is also the case that these practices of loyalty and commitment cannot be regarded as unproblematically as they have been portrayed in so much of the Western literature on Japan. A representative example of this literature can be culled from one of the most recent of its exponents: in his treatment of the 'Shadow of Confucius' Ketcham (1987), in illustrating the nature of 'groups' in the workplace in Japan, depicts the following world of work:

the crux is a pervasive, emotional commitment to the group as a group. Everything depends on the closeness and assurance of the bonds within the group, and the willingness of everyone in it to share its tasks and accept the moral and emotional responsibilities that go with prolonged intimate association. The group develops a keen sense of camaraderie and commonly spends long hours together, day after day, at work and in relaxation. Individuals are valued and trusted, all speak up and make important contributions, each member knows the abilities and weaknesses of the others, personal idiosyncracies are acknowledged, and the needs of all are attended to thoughtfully — yet the essential verticalness is never relinquished. All are deeply aware of, utterly imbued with the clear hierarchies of every relationship within the group (Ketcham 1987: 106).

We are not inclined to treat this representation lightly. It has echoes of a distant drum. In the nineteenth century the fading conservative dreams of a cosy, warm, intimate *Gemeinschaft* could only be constructed as a moral retrospect, functioning discursively in much the same way as the Marxian utopia of a dawn prior to the division of labour (Clegg and Higgins: 1987). Which is to say: mythically. In the 1980s the mythology rises like a phoenix in the east, clothed in Chinese characters, kindled from the ashes of Confucianism. Although such views are widespread in much of the literature dealing with Japan, we are inclined to regard such depictions as more ideological than literally empirical in function. The search for moral community has rarely been absent from the more explicitly conservative social analysis, even in areas as pragmatic as organization theory (Clegg and Dunkerley 1980). Japan has become the contemporary vehicle of its expression, we suggest. The stress on 'groupism' functions in part as a means of ideological wish-fulfilment. (However, we would not want to dismiss the cultural explanation entirely: some aspects of primary socialization in the family do seem to be of importance in producing competitive workers who are also compliant.)

Amongst some Japanese scholars, such as Murikami (1986), the cultural explanation is adopted but given a different specificity than in the general 'post-Confucian' case. Japan, he suggests, should be differentiated from other 'Confucian' societies. The cultural specificity of Japanese industrialization was premised not on a religious ethic but on distinctively pre-industrial patterns of social organization:

Its unique characteristic was the preindustrial basic unit of social group formation called *ie*, which had exceptional compatability as a production unit in industrial society (Murakami 1984) — The *ie* had exhibited strong capabilities for expansion, efficiency, and achievement, as well as for creating and thriving within a system of functional hierarchy. However, a basic group unit similar to the *ie* is rarely found in other agricultural societies. Therefore, I argue that the *ie* has been one of the main reasons Japan could adapt its indigenous culture to industrialization with extraordinary rapidity. This also is the reason Japan should be distinguished from other societies of the China periphery type and why in all likelihood it will remain a unique case among societies achieving industrialization (Murakami, 1986: 229).

Stressing the *ie* social group formation locates Japanese 'groupism' not in Confucianism but in forms of samurai-led agro-military organization, the key aspects of which were stable authority structures capable of guaranteeing the land rights of local peasantry. Murakami (1984, 1986: 230) argues that central features of this social organization survived sucessive transformations into the present day, including: functional rather than kin membership, membership homogeneity rather than stratification, and a consequently functional hierarchy rather than one of class or status discrimination. What is crucial for accounts such as Murakami's (1984, 1986), Ketcham's (1987), and Nakane's (1973) is a focus on the 'group' qualities of Japanese employment and social relations, whether the origin is attributed to a Confucian or to a samurai ethic.

Other writers, whose views we endorse here, have had a more sceptical regard for this 'group-centred' 'Japan-model' as Sugimoto (1986) and Sugimoto and Mouer (1985) have termed it. From their perspective much of Japanese 'groupism' and 'consensus' is not so much an effect of culture as of control from above, an element of control missed by those Western scholars whose research only samples the elite and their institutions in the Japanese context. (The myth of consensus, they suggest, should be regarded as an elite construct: as Berger [Berger and Luckmann 1967] has counselled elsewhere, the social construction of reality should never be regarded as a disinterested affair.) One way of testing this hypothesis, that the 'culture of consent' and 'groupism' is an effect of elite control of the mechanisms of ideological transmission rather than being more deep-rooted within Japanese life, is to consider the historical record. If Japan's economic success since the Meiji Restoration of 1868 is due to a unique economic culture rooted in post-Confucian consensus and groupism, then the historical record of Japanese labour relations should display this fact.

It is worth considering just how unique the putative achievement of a mature industrialization without conflict would be. Probably a majority of sociologists, outside of either extreme functionalists or extreme Marxists, would not accept the 'dominant ideology thesis' (Abercrombie et al. 1980). Instead, judged on the empirical record, industrial societies have come to be regarded as having fragmented and diversified cultures, as displaying a plurality of world-views and experiential frameworks rather than an all-embracing unitary culture or dominant ideology or hegemony. The sociology of deviance (Taylor et al. 1974) would also seem to confirm this hypothesis: modern societies are composed of subcultures rather than a singular, all-embracing coherent normative order.

The study of Japanese industrial relations (Gordon 1985) appears to offer a striking disconfirmation of any historically rooted Japanese national consensual culture. Instead, the standard struggle attendant on the 'making' of a working class from a traditionally recalcitrant peasantry was as typical of Japan as it has been elsewhere (Vlastos 1986).

If the myth of consensus has any historical root, it is to the 1930s and 1940s that we must look. In the 1930s, as Japan prepared for war, a combination of government legislation, a strong police force, factory owners and their hired gangs of factory-employed thugs succeeded in creating an apparently calm industrial relations atmosphere. Trouble, defined in employers terms, was largely eliminated by the simple expedients of efficient coercion and repression. The post-war era differed somewhat. As part of the United States programme of post-war democratization of Japan, trade unions, which had been repressed entirely during the war, were once more allowed. During 1946 the membership of the trade unions grew rapidly from nil to five million, and the unions quickly developed a political role, with their political allegiances being split between the socialist and communist parties. However, they also engaged in more direct forms of democracy. Workers took over factories, expelled bosses and managers and during the first six months of 1946 practised workers control. This occurred in 255 factories involving 157,000 workers (Gordon 1985). It did not last for long: the occupying American forces together with the Japanese Government drastically weakened the labour movement; tough anti-labour legislation was introduced and in 1950 12,000 workers were expelled from the Japanese industrial system's core enterprises because they were considered to be communists. Meanwhile, the 'human relations' precursor of today's 'groupism' was introduced under American tutelage. It was on these bases that the post-war 'economic miracle' was constructed in Japanese enterprises.

What are some of the characteristics of post-war Japanese enterprises? First, there is a pronounced split between those workers integrated into the 'company world' of the internal labour market, with its 'seniority wage' system and 'lifetime employment', and other workers. Those within the 'company world' of Japan amount to less than one third of the industrial labour force: these are the members of the enterprise unions whose main function is as 'an auxiliary to management in the personnel sector' (Kawashini 1986: 156). They are to be found in the *enterprise groups* (Orru, Biggart and Hamilton 1988) which dominate the peaks of Japanese enterprise. Within these groups, core workers within the individual enterprises will belong to enterprise-specific unions: each company has its own local wage scales premised on managerial evaluation of the skill requirements of a labour capacity which is itself constituted within the 'company world'. These are the elite of Japanese industrial workers, held securely in place by the 'golden chains' that the company proffers (Muto 1986).

Enterprise unions may be the prevalent pattern, but there are also some corporations which are characterized by a 'plural type' union situation, in which not only is there a majority union, but a breakaway minority union born after some decisive event in the previously enterprise union. About 12 per cent of unions which belonged to Sohyo (the 'left wing' union peak organization, with particular strengths in the iron and steel, chemical, machine-manufacturing industries and the public sector [Deutschmann 1987 b: 468]) are plural-type unions, amounting in 1982 to 768 unions. Such unions generated a disproportionate percentage of labour disputes handled by the Central Labour Relations Committee (*Churoi*) in the private sector, some 41 per cent in all (Kawashini 1986: 141). Such plural-type unions are particularly evident in the public sector. Outside the core workers in the enterprise groups, organized into enterprise, or more rarely plural-type unions, there are a great many medium and small companies which do not form part of the 'company world'.

The contemporary union picture in Japan is rapidly changing. Institutional arrangements such as those depicted in the sphere of union peak organization by Deutschmann (1987 b) no longer exist. In November 1987 the private sector trade unions became unified under a single umbrella organization known as Rengo — the National Federation of Private Sector Unions. Domei, the other main union peak organization, and Sohyo are now incorporated under this new umbrella structure, having been formally dissolved in November 1987. Speculation has been widely entertained that with the establishment of Rengo as a peak organization, leaving out only Toitsu Rosokon with its links to the Japanese Communist Party, the hitherto fragmented socialist and social democratic opposition parties may be closer to achieving unity in the future (see *Far Eastern Economic Review*, 14 January, 1988, pp. 16−18). Presently this is not the case, nor is it immediately likely to be. Consequently, in both the industrial and political arenas labour is relatively weak. This weakness is exacerbated by both spatial and contractual considerations.

In spatial terms, big name companies and their 'company world' will sometimes dominate whole towns, like Toyota, Hitachi, Kawasaki Steel or Chisso corporation do. The big name companies also cast a contractual shadow over the employment scene. Whether or not towns are literally company towns, the enterprise groups dominate whole areas of employment through a vast number of subcontract firms. Although formally independent, these are highly structured, semi-formalized and enjoy on-going relations with the enterprise group core companies. Effectively, in Muto's (1986: 135) phrase, they are 'vassals' of the big companies. In turn, many of the subcontracting firms themselves rely on work subcontracted out to smaller subcontractors who in turn sub-contract to female domestic outworkers who work on piece-wage rates far removed from those of the enterprise union members. In the Japanese automobile industry, for instance, 75 per cent of work (as compared to 50 per cent in the United States) is sourced outside the big name firms to primary subcontracting firms, which in turn may subcontract to secondary firms, which in turn may subcontract to tertiary outworkers, who will be paid at a fifth of the rate of workers in the larger subcontract firms (Muto 1986: 135).

Some of these subcontracting workers may well work within the big name firms factories, on a modern day version of 'internal contracting' (see Clegg, Boreham and Dow 1986 b: 93–97; Littler 1982): the *Oyakata* system, where subcontracted labour is provided for a lump sum. Alongside them may be temporary, seasonal workers, frequently drawn from the agrarian sector (disproportionately large in Japan due to deliberate government policy of tariff and quota exclusion of imports and of subsidies to primary producers) or from the ranks of part-time workers, usually housewives. Their ease of recruitment and dismissal is a major basis of Japanese flexibility, together with the 'enterprise' base of the unions themselves. Data from 1970 shows that 12 per cent of the workforce employed in large companies of more than 500 workers, in major industries such as steel, shipbuilding, automobiles and construction, were such temporary workers, compared to only 2–3 per cent in companies employing 30–99 employees (Muto 1986: 136).

For those workers fortunate enough to have gone to the elite schools and universities favoured in recruitment by the big name firms and whose personal background passes scrutiny (see Rohlen 1974), the firm will proceed to train these core workers. At this level a particular 'corporate culture' does seem to come into play. Training is firm specific; it is oriented not only to 'functional qualifications' but is also 'a process of moral socialization into the community of the firm' (Deutschmann 1987 b: 45). Indeed, Deutschmann suggests that the corporate culture in this respect does build on more general cultural phenomena in terms of the primary socialization role of the family, a family conceived as a cooperative community (Deutschmann 1987 b: 44). To Western observers it seems to be an extremely patriarchal (in an older sense of the term) system. The scope of the system can best be seen in the extent to which work time and work relations are routinely organized into the time and space outside of work. Lifetime employment is the cost and the benefit of this system. Cost, because it precludes any external labour market options for most workers. They are simply not trained for other enterprises and would not consider or be considered for such employment. Insofar as it does deliver employment security (which it does not always achieve and is less likely to in the future with the rapidly changing role of Japan in the world economy), then this is indeed a benefit. However, this security is of employment, not employment status: marginalization and downgrading to occur.

The point of entering into this institutional fabric in some detail is to stress that consent, where it is achieved, may well have rather more of a material than a cultural basis alone. This is not to deny that Japan has built an effective basis for an industrial economy. Undoubtedly it has, as Japanese success attests.

The Japanese succeed not only on the backs of highly segmented workers but also in part because they pay a great deal of attention to factors directly related to particular performance measures. Work practices are subordinated to these, especially with respect to quality controls. The percentage of final output inspected correlates most highly with productivity level, followed by attention to various aspects of machine technology (like computer usage), utilization of plant capacity and budget accountability. Characteristically, major enterprises in Japan have married successful quality control with enterprising innovation (Dunphy 1986).

These performance measures and the segmentary work practices seem to be at the root of Japanese economic success, rather than an economic culture which stresses 'post-Confucian' values of consensus and group harmony. 'Groupism' variables in Japanese organizations are not associated positively with performance (or, as in the case of morning ceremonies, they may even be negatively associated with performance). This suggests that such practices have been systematically overrated by those Western observers who have advocated cultural sequestration in order to increase performance. Such practices may well be culturally compatible and decorative additions to the Japanese economic machine, rather than its essential mechanism, much as Dunphy (1986) suggests.

Further evidence of the non-essential nature of 'culture' in producing Japanese productivity is what happens to it in subsidiary overseas operations. While there is evidence that some important and distinctive features of Japanese personnel policy (such as participative decision making) are transferable to other cultures, Japanese firms tend to drop many of these practices in their overseas operations. This can be demonstrated by considering the example of Japanese firms in Singapore, for instance. Milton-Smith (1986) has documented the difference between Japanese business ideology and practice in Singapore. Difficulties are experienced by the Japanese in operating in a different business culture to that of Japanese ethnocentrism. Personnel and labour management, often cited as the cultural locus of the organizational expression of 'post-Confucianism', are, in fact, the weak points of Japanese management overseas. In particular, the increasing integration of subsidiaries into the global marketing strategies of the Japanese parent mean that these strategies predominate over concern for the welfare of local employees. In addition, the exclusion from decision making of non-Japanese, locally hired, subsidiary managers would suggest that Japanese companies will experience increasing difficulty in hiring and retaining bright, ambitious local managers. Thus many of the much-debated Japanese personnel policies may prove to have no real impact on organizational performance in Japan and to be a handicap in adapting cross-culturally, even in East Asia. This would be a significant problem in view of Japanese industries increasing direct investment abroad as a result of the strong Yen.

Managerial skill in relating organization variables, such as technology or semi-autonomous work groups to productivity increases, product quality and innovation, seems crucial. The organization of the labour market into both an internal labour market in the big companies, with a highly unprotected and secondary sphere outside it, is a vital adjunct of this. The contribution made by various aspects of personnel policy to performance at the enterprise level remains controversial. It is not clear the extent to which various aspects of personnel policy contribute to performance, detract from it, or are merely cultural accretios of ethnographic interest but of no relevance to performance. What does appear to be clear is that particular aspects of personnel policy may contribute to performance at home but be non-exportable without some 'functional equivalent' for the material, institutional underpinnings. If exportable, they may, nevertheless, become a liability in another cultural setting.

Cultural, Market, State and Organizational Limits to Univariate Explanation

It is clear that Japan and the other East Asian NICs have developed within their own economies rational policies which take advantage, in various ways, of global economic developments, while organizing and taking into account the relative power of diverse institutional actors and organization stake-holders in each national setting. One of the critical factors behind East Asian economic success has sometimes been considered to be their political stability. Cultural grounds have been sought to explain this stability. These nations have been high on both power distance and collectivism, values which reinforce respect for authority and the sacrifice of individual interest to collective welfare (Hofstede 1980). The leaders of the nations of East Asia have attempted to develop effective means of managing this potential 'consent'. Various forms of either a paternalist-welfare capitalism or a repressive state have developed which restrict what in the West would usually be regarded as 'labour rights'. Typically, they reinforce a unitary rather than pluralist view of political interests in which states and markets are strong.

Opposition to 'strong states' is variable in the countries in question. South Korea is clearly the least stable, and has had the greatest levels of labour and political mobilization. The factors which contribute to this seem to be tied up with aspects both of its route to modern industrialization and its state development. The former has been founded on the creation of very large, centralized urban enterprises, in which an independent unionism has flourished, despite official sanction against it. This labour organization has become a major actor in the struggles for democracy which characterize South Korea and which make it distinct from the East Asian countries under review. As Koo (1987: 11) notes 'Frequent state interventions in labour conflicts led to the politicization of labour relations and to the development of alliance between labor movement and other political movements'. Consequently, South Korea has the industrial structure which, of the East Asian economies, is closest to that which Marx in the Communist Manifesto thought most conducive to proletarian class formation. This has taken place in a nation which has long had a vociferous and highly political student body: together these social movements confront a state regime which differs significantly from those of the other East Asian countries under consideration. It was founded in the immediate post-war era in close concert with the leading industrial enterprises and in alliance with a landlord class whose legitimacy was tarnished by war-time collaboration with the Japanese colonialists. Consequently, the South Korean state, suggests Koo (1987), has never enjoyed civil hegemony. It continues to use 'systematic torture' in order 'to intimidate and suppress political opposition [...] carried out with the tacit approval of senior officials' (International Commission of Jurists Report on South Korea; *Sydney Morning Herald*, January 14, 1988: 10). Nor are the other countries immune to charges of considerable official neglect of what are the norms and procedures of their own constitutions with respect to the use of forced confessions, torture and due process, as McCormack (1986) and Igarashi (1986) discuss with respect to Japan.

While the South Korean state has not enjoyed civil hegemony, this is true of neither the post-war Taiwanese, Japanese nor Singaporean state: Hong Kong's legitimacy was premised less on its state form and more on its being an industrially and capitalistically dynamic haven for refugees fleeing from Chinese Communism. Civil hegemony does not just happen. State and organizational relations are not necessarily imbued with legitimate authority. It has to be produced and re-produced where it exists. Where it does not have a strong root, then indeed a strong state may be a necessity. The East Asian NICs have expended considerable effort on 'manufacturing consent' (Burawoy [1979]; see Sugimoto [1986] for Japan and Wilkinson [1986] for Singapore, in particular). With the partial exception of South Korea, with its strong civil movements for democratization, they have achieved considerable success in quelling opposition. Not only that, one should acknowledge with Berger (1987) that they have done so on the basis of profound economic growth and prosperity, which is itself legitimating. The role of the state must enter into specific explanations for the economic success of the East Asian NICs.

The argument purely from culture is questionable. The proposed singularity and coherence of 'post-Confucian' culture can not be sustained upon detailed investigation, nor, unambiguously, is it a historically derived residue of Confucianism. While culture can explain some common patterns across the East Asian societies, such as familism, what it cannot do is explain the variations within and between these societies. These are of considerable importance at the enterprise level (Hamilton and Biggart 1985). Moreover, if the cultural factors are deep rooted in the historical 'collective consciousness', why do they only become effective in the post-war era and under certain, diverse institutional conditions? It is an irony of contemporary sociology that factors which an earlier generation of scholars, such as Weber, saw as inimical to rational, efficient capitalism, should now be seen as central to its very essence!

Suspicion of purely cultural explanation does not mean that we should reconsider the explanatory role of more purely market factors. Market explanations, in the East Asian context at least, are certainly correct in emphasizing phenomena such as de-regulated labour markets, a highly educated population, an export-orientation and a high level of domestic savings for investment. However, why this particular mix of phenomena should have occurred is less clear: these factors are invariably seen as the unproblematic effect of underlying 'good policies'. The nature of these policies is left under-determined, other than to make reference to either the more market-oriented aspects (e. g. de-regulated labour markets) or the more politically oriented aspects (e. g. the role of Japan's MITI), depending on the ideological elective affinities of the authors concerned.

If, notwithstanding the role of the state, neither purely cultural nor market explanations are sufficient, then what role does organization play? At the organizational level, the extreme variation in enterprise form from the primarily market co-ordinated multiplicity of small, family controlled, subcontracting Taiwanese firms, to the large hierarchically, impersonally controlled Japanese enterprise groups, South Korean state-financed enterprises or Singaporean foreign-owned multinationals, seems sufficient to suggest that performance cannot be adduced solely to the level of organization variables (Hamilton, Zeile and Kim, this volume). Organizationally, to the extent that these variables are important, they seem to hinge on control of the core technologies and performance measures, as well as of the organization of labour, rather than the cultural trappings whereby these are assembled and contained. The average size of enterprises in the national economy does not seem to be a major factor. (This is not to deny that it has a role in limiting types of structure: see Donaldson [1986].) The size of organizations typical to an economy does not strongly or easily correlate with the overall effectiveness of the economy, in terms of its growth rates. In fact, the typical enterprise size will depend very much on the state's role in developing the economy, the capital market, regulating inter-organizational relations, and so on.

In these East Asian economies certain institutional arrangements appear to be decisive. It would be quite inappropriate to read a general principle into these institutional arrangements. What is important is the stable integration and development of these within the wider political and normative context, the institutional framework for economic culture, rather than the imposition of any one model derived from a quite different national context. In effect, what we require is a 'contingency-framework' at the national, institutional level. As comparisons of Malaysia and Thailand with Hong Kong and Taiwan demonstrate (Levin, Nihei and Ohtsu 1986), a culture of consent may be more or less premised on either intra-organizational discipline and control or on the discipline of the labour market. The latter will hardly be an effective contingency in a 'full employment' social democracy such as Sweden or Norway. The effectivity of institutions is nationally contingent.

For the future, understanding will be enhanced not by focusing on any univariate or single factor model which can be assumed to be appropriate for all countries. Social reality is too complex for any single factor model or single discipline to adequately represent its processes. While the market may be important in explanation of Taiwan and Hong Kong, it is of less importance in Japan than an appreciation of the role of the Japanese Industrial System (McMillan 1984) or, for instance, that of the state corporations in the financing of enterprises in South Korea. Not only are there specificities: there are also commonalities. Authoritarian repression of labour is important in each of these countries. Singapore is also a singular case. The multi-national penetration of Singapore, much of it Japanese as well as British and American, is not mirrored as extensively elsewhere. It would seem that the major variables of culture, market, state and organization bear differential explanatory weight in each case, as a different balance of factors comes into play in each country.

Consequently, undue stress on either simple market-based explanation such as the need to 'break' unions and screw down wages in the context of that odd couple, the 'strong state' and 'small government', or a search for post-Confucian cultural equivalents for excellence, will be as vain as the search for the Holy Grail. Empirical findings from another arena of comparison demonstrate this clearly. Detailed comparative study of differential OECD inflation, unemployment and economic growth rates in the post-war era has failed to identify any single factor, such as a market commitment or small public sector, as a causal mechanism of success for these indicants of economic performance (Clegg, Boreham and Dow 1986: 352). Instead, the complex, interactive interdependency of a number of factors becomes apparent (see Dow, Clegg and Boreham 1984; Schmidt 1982).

Economic Culture and Economic Calculation

Economic culture has been considered more or less explicitly in terms of economic success stories. The focus has been very much on East Asia, reflecting Berger's (1987) emphasis. In particular, we have focused on Japan's economic culture. In consequence, some re-specification of the terms of the concept have been proposed. Its expression as a culture of 'groupism' and compliance was argued to have been overdrawn in the literature. Behind the explanation from culture, it was argued, there stood important aspects of an institutional framework, expressed in Japan in terms of patterns of market structure (both labour and capital), union structure and contractual relations which helped to support both elite workers, and elite enterprises with a discernible patterning of corporate culture. However, economic success in Japan, it was suggested, was less easily adduced to this cultural configuration than to certain technical considerations in production. In Japan these are managed in such a way that the complex and often large-scale physical conversion processes of manufacturing, with their attendant immutable time frames and physical and technical givens, have achieved adaptation of processes and products to customers' needs and purposes (Higgins and Clegg 1988).

We can abstract from this Japanese success some general lessons concerning the management of technology and applied technique in manufacturing enterprise. One of the most important and least understood aspects of manufacturing enterprise is its relationship to technology and applied technique. As some organization sociologists, economic historians and management theorists have long recognized, contrary to a widespread view (not least among economists), technique is not a commodity to be bought, but a vital aspect of manufacturing organization. This is clear in the sense that applied technique includes the human organization or system that sets equipment to work; but equally importantly, the concept includes the physical integration of a new piece of equipment into a production process and its subsequent refinement and modification at the hands of the technically skilled workforce.

Many manufacturers have come to grief on the belief that technical solutions can be bought pre-packaged. This is to ignore, precisely, that in operation these are always socio-technical solutions. What is at issue is precisely the 'cultural' context in which these solutions have to work. What issues do socio-technical solutions have to address? Studies have shown that equipment users rather than makers develop major process innovations (thus stealing a march on their competitors) and that small, imperceptible 'everyday rationalizations' account for the lion's share of productivity gains in an ongoing manufacturing business. For this reason, 'learning by doing' and making the best organizational and technical use of 'what you've got' is far more important than acquiring the latest 'state of the art' process technology (Ewer, Higgins and Stephens 1987, ch. 4). This is not an argument for technological obsolescense, for hanging on proudly to the engineering achievements of the Victorians, such as might be embodied in the steam turbine or coal burning engine. On the contrary, it is to foster sufficient incrementalism as to be able to know when to scrap past achievements. Whether an enterprise is capable of these two vital learning processes is very much an institutional question. The crucial benefits to productivity, quality and ultimate market position, are not quantifiable, least of all in advance.

In establishing and maintaining its productive base, a manufacturing firm continually faces highly technical life-and-death issues; starting with the amount of capacity it needs and can justify in terms of scale economies and present and foreseeable markets. Where it operates related facilities, it has to develop the right configuration to match up the various plant capacities in order to avoid bottlenecks, uneven throughput and product inflexibility. To maximize market position and competitive advantage, it has to judge the degree of flexibility and scope for product diversification that it can demand of its processes without jeopardizing the specialization and 'focus' necessary to maximize efficiency and meet quality requirements. These issues are enormously complicated by time frame. To make the most of equipment and plant once it is put in place, a firm has to adapt it, update it and operate it as close as possible to full capacity over a long life-cycle covering several product generations, during which time markets and competitors behave unpredictably. For technical reasons decisions about acquiring items of physical capital often have a long lead time, and capacity thus has to be added in 'chunks', not in small increments to match sales recorded from time to time. Yet too much or too little capacity at any one time can spell commercial disaster, not least in a capital-intensive industry.

The combination of technical constraints and complexities, on the one hand, and the constant need to adapt to and anticipate changes in processes and products, on the other, calls for peculiar organizational features, above all flexibility in work practices and a skilled and constantly reskillable workforce. Economic culture is not unimportant here, as we have seen in the case of Japan. We have also seen how conceptualization of this economic culture requires embedding within its institutional frame. Technical and organizational aspects of production have to be integrated into a wider (even national) institutional setting that accounts for financial provision, marketing and research and development. Finally, the complexities of these issues and their time dimensions call for deliberate strategic thinking and consistent decision making and implementation in which technical competence is always at a premium, but optimal strategies are never guaranteed.

No matter how well an organization's actors perceive these issues and pursue solutions, they must still secure organizational dominance and consensus, or at least obedience, for their goals, and they will still have to depend on a national institutional environment if their strategy for the organization is to succeed. Its most urgent need will invariably be sources of long-term credit to finance major new investments, to maintain debt-to-equity ratios consistent with minimal capital costs, and to cushion the inevitable destruction of capital that flows from basic innovations. Given current trends towards 'neo-mercantilism' and 'administered' markets and prices, it will need public financial assistance to meet the 'front end' costs of marketing and establishing distribution and service networks, and public policies to protect it on the domestic market from other governments' predatory trade strategies, such as dumping and providing credit packages on tenders for major development projects. It will need an industrial relations system that does not put arbitrary limits on technological innovation and the upgrading of work practices (Williams, Williams and Thomas 1983: see the introduction). Finally, usually it will depend for its technical inputs of equipment and components, and for its markets on its insertion into a diversified manufacturing sector, in which public policy plays a coherent role in establishing and maintaining linkages. To gloss all of this complex totality as an 'economic culture' may be a useful shorthand, but it may also be analytically restricting.

It would also be analytically restricting to consider only successful economic cultures. Most mature capitalist industrialized countries, in contrast to the East Asian examples considered earlier, exhibit symptoms of manufacturing decline, but significantly enough, it is in the historically leading industrial powers, Britain and USA, that the symptoms are most striking. Britain's balance of trade in manufactures has deteriorated steadily over 35 years, and she now has a large and growing trade deficit in this sector (Williams and Haslam 1985: 53). The USA became in 1971, and remains, a nett importer of manufactures. That country's sharp decline in research and development expenditure, productivity growth and technological leadership is particularly spectacular. An American firm held the original patent for home video recorders, but imports now account for 100 per cent of U.S. sales; in 1977 the export and import of machine tools balanced, but the USA has now ceased exporting them and imports 36 per cent of its own requirements; in 1982 U.S. industry operated 4 robots per 10,000 employees compared to Sweden's 30 and Japan's 13; and the list of eclipsed major U.S. industries goes on, including computers, semi-conductors, cars, steel and consumer electronics (Thurow 1984). Each case tells a familiar story of ageing plant and shoddy products.

Our review of organizational issues underpinning differential manufacturing performance stresses the institutional roots of such industrial disorders in Britain and the USA. In particular, it would home in on the strategic failure in enterprise of the new 'professional managers in terms of both a failure to conceive strategies and to implement them, as well as a systematic choice of self-defeating strategies' (Hayes and Abernathy 1980). Unlike his/her predecessor who typically worked up through the various functional departments and divisions of the enterprise gaining 'hands on' experience, the new manager cultivates a 'fast track' career by job-hopping and scoring up quick symbolic 'wins'. He/she replaces 'non progressive' knowledge of the specific business grounded in its local culture with an analytic detachment borne of de-contextualized and portable skills gained at business, accountancy or law school. Apart from the formal accomplishments of law, accountancy and financial management, these skills restrict themselves to formalized consumer analysis, market survey technique, matrixes and learning curves. He/she supplements ignorance of technical contingency with 'technology aversion' and an elitism that prevents either being remedied (Pascale 1984). Institutionally cultivated individual career strategies for organizational dominance contribute to organizational decline.

Two prominent analysts of the Harvard Business School, Hayes and Abernathy (1980: 74), have branded the new managers as 'pseudo-professionals' who systematically mismanage a manufacturing business. They regard plant as an embarrassing constraint on financial manoeuvrability and try to buy pre-packaged solutions, commonly on an inappropriate and grandiose scale. But what they do well is more damaging than what they do badly. 'Managing by the numbers' collapses time frames: individual businesses have to show quick returns on minimal outlays or be deliberately run down and liquidated; in conglomerates, individual businesses are reduced to bargaining chips, quickly acquired and shed. 'A "successful" American manager doesn't plant or harvest', Thurow (1984: 23) comments, 'he is simply a Viking raider'. Clearly, such individuals are strategically ill-equipped to address the substantive issues of manufacturing management, and obsolescence, lack of fit, quality and labour problems result.

For many writers, the investigation of manufacturing decline stops here, and they propose solutions accordingly. At the most extreme, Pascale (1984: 65) suggests that rationality as such is an ethnocentric cul-de-sac, and the standard business journal exercise of learning-from-the-Japanese for him boils down to a flight from rationality and emulating the inspired but erratic hit-or-miss business behaviour of Soichiro Honda. 'The givens of organisation', he reminds us, 'are ambiguity, uncertainty, imperfection and paradox': he thus follows the organization theory of March and his associates (Cohen, March and Olsen 1972) towards the conviction that strategic and structural responses carry their own falsehood. The more common remedies are no less fanciful and voluntaristic, from exhumation of the Schumpeterian entrepreneur to proposals for corporate cultural revivalism (see Ray 1986) and an evangelical faith in the explanatory purchase of 'economic culture' in its post-Confucian mode, an explanation to which can be attributed both the 'decline of the West' and the rise of East Asia.

It would, however, be a vulgar sociologism which rested content with an explanation of manufacturing decline that simply posited a sudden, collective conversion to false gods on the part of managers and their academic mentors. The striking mismatch between managerial and manufacturing processes must surely reflect an overdetermining congruity between managerial forms of calculation − Giddens' (1984) rules, resources and regular social practices − and the institutional environment. The economists' most rational forms of calculation may themselves give rise to the substantive irrationality productive of manufacturing decline. At the heart of this, we suggest, is the relationship between financial institutions and manufacturing industry.

The Framework of Financial Calculation and Managerial Economic Culture: National Variations

Giddens' (1984) 'systematic properties' aspect of culture, when considered economically, must make reference to the available 'vocabularies of motive' which managers can routinely draw on in constructing their managerial practices. A key component of these will be the forms of financial calculation which frame the managerial action they are able to take. Elements of both financial and managerial accounting will enter into this. The institutional relationship between financial institutions and manufacturing firms varies enormously from country to country, but in each case it is crucial to an understanding of manufacturing performance: manufacturers need access to long-term credits and new equity to finance strategic investment and to maintain a favourable debt-to-equity ratio. There is, however, an endemic problem in the relation between the sectors: as dealers in money or liquifiable assets, financial institutions seek to lend short term at high rates of interest, against securities that can be liquidated at any time; whereas manufacturers need inexpensive long-term credits or stable venture capital. From the manufacturers' point of view, this problem calls for institutional measures that subordinate financial logic to manufacturing. In Japan, for instance, the appropriate relation has in the past been achieved through straightforward regulation of banks, channelling semipublic funds directly into manufacturing, and through the strong institutional links which include a system of 'stable shareholders' who take up new share issues in manufacturing firms and undertake not to trade in them. In recent years, however, the relationship with banks has become somewhat weaker. Many firms have begun to rely more on the stock market and on internally generated funds (Kosai and Ogino 1984). Both bank and internal sourcing ensure that, economically, cultural continuity can thus be constituted at the enterprise level. Relative success in this was clearly evident in the recent behaviour of the Tokyo market subsequent to the October 19, 1987 stock market crash.

What is evident in considering not only Japanese, but also Taiwanese and South Korean firms, is that each of these successful East Asian countries has developed stable institutional frameworks in which manufacturing logic is predominant. What is evident is that they have done so neither through cultural happenstance nor through any one economically rational 'best way'. These conclusions are drawn from the research of Orrù, Biggart and Hamilton (1988). They conclude that one common feature of each of the three East Asian economies which they studied was the existence of an industrial manufacturing system centred on an organization of business groups. These are distinct patterns of firm relations that express themselves as inter-firm networks. Different forms of these are found in each of the three countries.

Some of the characteristic features of the Japanese system are already evident from our earlier discussion, including the vertical organization of subcontracting firms, known as *keiretsu*. However, there are important additional features such as the 'inter-market' groups of firms cross-linked across the different economic sectors each one occupies. It is within the 'inter-market' groups that the stable sources of finance and shareholding have been organized, as well as more general matters of strategic policy. Those firms which are members of 'independent groups', groups that are vertically rather than horizontally organized, typically cluster around a big name firm. Such firms organize satellite subcontractors and are interlinked through stable mutual shareholdings with other enterprise groups. At least part of the Japanese answer to the need for integrated financing, manufacturing and market structures thus emerges.

A similar integration is achieved in South Korea with different mechanisms. Here the enterprise groups (*chaebol*) are usually owned and controlled by a single person or family, and generally operate in a single industrial sector. They do not rely on stable subcontract relations but vertically incorporate most component producers. While control is associationally negotiated in Japanese firms, in the South Korean enterprise it is familially unified. Consequently, while financial stability is achieved in Japan by highly organized joint stockholding, in Korea it is achieved by family control and financing, together with board links to government-controlled financial institutions, the major source of externally generated capital. Family control ensures continuity of purpose and ownership.

Family control also characterizes Taiwan, but here, however, family sources of finance are of most importance: Orrù, Biggart and Hamilton (1988: 22) report that over 60 per cent of capital is derived from family and friends. Consequently, business groups here are familially interlinked through individual family members holding positions in multiple firms. Those firms are on average much smaller than the larger Japanese or still larger South Korean enterprises, a factor primarily explained through inheritance laws which fragment assets generationally.

In each of these countries distinct features of the institutional environment sustain a stable set of expectations about manufacturing activity, in which a manufacturing logic is not subordinated to a logic of profit per se. Which is, of course, not to say that they are not profit oriented: it is only to note that the profit orientation is predicated on industrial success rather than paper entrepreneurialism. Orrù, Biggart and Hamilton (1988: 25) see the commitment to manufacturing taking different institutional form in each country: in Japan in a communitarian ideal; in South Korea in a patrimonial principle; in Taiwan in a patrilineal principle. The economic culture appears to have less to do with post-Confucianism and more to do with a stable institutional framework, capable of variable expression cross-nationally, in which the market principle is subordinated to mechanisms ensuring long-term manufacturing strategies and viability.

Britain, Australia and USA represent the other extreme. The banking sectors in Britain and Australia are unique among almost all major manufacturing countries in assessing a manufacturer's creditworthiness on a liquidation basis – which is highly unfavourable given the nature of its assets rather than on a going concern basis. This favours old, established firms with large assets but possibly little future as against newer, more dynamic ones. Bank lending policies thus place an enormous constraint on strategic investment and capital budgeting (Ewer, Higgins and Stephens 1987: ch. 4).

Stock exchanges in these countries, relatively speaking, play an exaggerated role in the capital market, but their hyperactivity is hardly productive of new equity capital in the manufacturing sector, and counterproductive in terms of the forms of calculation they impose on manufacturers. The two major stimulants of this hyperactivity are both antithetical to the logic of financing manufacturing enterprise. The first is the rise of institutional investors pursuing the highest possible rate of short-term monetary return with no responsibility for national manufacturing performance. Their preponderance in the capital market and preference for non-industrial placements starve manufacturers of external finance. The second is the attempt by manufacturing enterprises themselves, having been unable to find finance for internal expansion, to expand externally through mergers or takeovers, to 'diversify', or simply to pursue financial placements as an alternative to the vagaries of manufacturing. At best, mergers and takeovers are a dubious avenue to rationalization, and few in any event have this motivation (Newbould 1970). At worst, this activity distracts managerial attention and dissipates resources from the needs of manufacturing. The constant fear of stock exchange 'raiders', in its turn, imposes an obsession on management – now formalized as business-school orthodoxy — to maintain share values at all costs (Thompson 1978: 420).

There are two related mechanisms whereby short-term financial calculations induce manufacturing miscalculation in the mature industrialized countries under discussion. The first is the imposition of financial criteria from the outside by banks, financial institutions and stock exchanges. But the second is the internalization of short-term financial criteria by manufacturing enterprises, an internalization which the institutional power of finance imposes. 'Corporate portfolios' provide a clear example of this second tendency. Corporate portfolio management was a technique first developed for individual and institutional investors with no more than rentier pretensions, as a way of spreading risk and maximizing annual returns. But *industrial* corporate managements now consciously practise it as a mode of diversification, and it has led in turn to decision making one manager describes as 'excessively cautious, even passive; certainly over analytical and, in general, characterized by a studied unwillingness to assume responsibility and even reasonable risk' (Hayes and Abernathy 1980: 71).

At its worst the 'over analytical' component can produce quite unanticipated consequences: this can be seen in the strategy of 'portfolio insurance' which some analysts, including the U. S. Presidential Task Force on Market Mechanisms (*Sydney Morning Herald*, January 11, 1988: 25, 26), have suggested was a root cause of the Wall Street crash of October 19, 1987. 'Portfolio insurance' is not insurance in the usual sense but is a computerized-trading strategy based on analytical buying and selling rules incorporated into a computer programme. It has been widely used by large institutional investors in the 1980s to protect paper gains or to offset losses on their corporate portfolios. One consequence of the strategy is that computers can generate trade that results in orders to sell huge amounts of stock. It is automatic, reactive selling which, on the instructions programmed into the insurance strategy, will liquidate large fractions of the portfolio of stockholdings, regardless of price. The Presidential Task Force report suggests that this is what happened: 'The formulas used by portfolio insurers dictated the sale of $ 20 billion to $ 30 billion of equities' between October 14 and October 20, 1986 (*Sydney Morning Herald*, January 11, 1988: 25). Automatically unloading so much stock in such a few days, not surprisingly, sent the market plummeting. Another automatic computer trading strategy, 'stock index arbitrage', probably exacerbated the selling at sensitive points in the market's downward spiral, the Report suggests. (Stock index arbitrage works through computers taking advantage of tiny discrepancies between stock index futures and present underlying stock values.)

In the manufacturing sectors of Britain, USA and Australia, the major institutional loci of internalized financial calculation antithetical to industrial activity are conglomerates, themselves largely the product of the capital-market disorders already mentioned. A manufacturing firm's facilities, workforce and distribution network impose their own constraints on its technologies and markets, and thus their own limits on rational diversification. Recognizing those limits is a matter of fine judgement; expensive mistakes, resulting from uncoordinated manufacturing strategies and managerial distraction, can occur even in the cases of integration and diversification motivated solely by manufacturing considerations. But they occur much more frequently in the case of mergers and takeovers that represent a second-best to internal expansion, and the situation is much worse in the usual case where businesses are acquired with no manufacturing rationale at all. Thus arises the typical conglomerate of, say, 20 or 30 unrelated businesses presided over by a single head office which, however, bears ultimate responsibility for their strategic decision making. Mergers and acquisitions do not necessarily produce rational reconstruction on divisional lines but can produce conflicting authority structures based on disparate organization cultures and systems resistant to the new loci of control.

In such a situation the head office's necessary lack of insight into the dynamics of the individual businesses is compounded by its overreliance on the major formally rational means of control over local management and assessment of business prospects; that is dependence upon financial calculations and accounting techniques premised on the divisional form. The degradation of subsidiary businesses to 'profit centres' in contemporary managerial jargon tells the tale plainly enough. Centralized cost-accounting and capital-budgeting systems are the new organs of control to whose simplistic quantifications all complex technical and organizational questions, as well as future production and marketing imponderables, have to be reduced. 'Profit-centre' managers in their turn submit to the iron law of quarterly or annual return-on-investment (ROI) calculation, which hardly encourages them to become farsighted captains of industry. Thurow's (1984) investigation of a conglomerate with 30 subsidiaries revealed an average time-horizon of 2.8 years, hardly adequate for planning investments in processes with life-spans covering several product-generations! Analysts of manufacturing decline almost unanimously pinpoint the rise to prominence of ROI calculations as the immediate cause of the sharp decline in expenditure on new process technologies, facilities and research and development.

This brings us to the interesting question of the dynamics and distortions accounting practices as such impose on manufacturing enterprise, a question taken up below. It is vital to note, however, a point that has only been touched on so far: forms of enterprise calculation are to a large extent moulded by national 'rules of the game'. These comprise the institutional fabric of the national economy shaping an 'economic culture', including not only the variable factors already mentioned, such as corporate and inter-corporate structure and institutional links between manufacturing and finance, but also market structure, the government's role and policies, and the industrial relations system (cf. Williams, Williams and Thomas 1983, and Redding and Whitley in this volume).

The concept of 'economic culture', as Weber's (1930) analysis of 'the Protestant ethic' suggests, has at its institutional core the conventions of particular accounting practice. A couple of general contemporary observations are in order. Especially in Britain, the accountancy profession exercises an extraordinary autonomy in defining accounting best practice and thus in regulating corporate behaviour. Yet the adoption of one or other accounting convention has real material consequences. The most important general example is the use of modified historic-cost accounting in Britain and Australia which systematically overstates profits by understating the value of real capital, and this in turn may lead to inadequate retention of operating surpluses and the winding down of the assets of the business.

Another arbitrary — if formally rational — aspect of accounting practice is the choice and weighting of time-frames. Profit is struck on an annual basis, and the time-frame and weighting of anticipated returns can vary greatly. The financial institutions' separation from, and domination of, manufacturers gives yearly accounts a much greater salience than in countries where financial institutions are made more receptive to manufacturers' requirements, and this in turn highlights the artificial distinction between operating costs and capital outlays.

Some recent American writers strongly argue that current ROI calculations and capital budgeting techniques bear a heavy inherent bias to conservative investment behaviour and short-term management of manufacturing enterprise. The quarterly or annual ROI calculation presents an unambiguous case and a very strong influence on local managerial behaviour because it is the main — and often only — form of control over, and measure of, its success. Quite simply, it is much easier to improve 'performance' on this measure by decreasing the denominator, than by increasing the numerator, which can take a long time, involves risk and has to be discounted for taxation. A profit centre manager can achieve quicker, surer and easier results by delaying replacement of old or worn-out equipment, replacing equipment eventually with technologically dated or inferior substitutes, skimping on maintenance, research and development and personnel development, in other words, by disinvestment and technological stagnation (Hayes and Garvin 1982: 74; Hayes and Wheelwright 1984: 11–13). In the seventies, for instance, in the car industry robots did not meet ROI criteria in either Japan or USA. The Japanese introduced them anyway, and thereupon gained market dominance through the much higher quality achieved. As a result, robots were paying for themselves within two and a half years (Thurow 1984).

Even more insidious, perhaps, is the rapid acceptance of capital-budgeting techniques which involves discounting calculations for assessing strategic investments. The amount and timing of future cash flows resulting from a proposed investment, are estimated and then they are discounted by the estimated return on an alternative, external investment of the same size, and aggregated to produce a 'net present value'. This procedure provides plenty of room for fudging the figures and building in arbitrary assumptions. In particular, it relies on estimating the final cost of the investment, the amount and timing of returns, the rate of return on the alternative investment (the 'hurdle rate') and the rate of real deterioration of items of productive capital. Some of the antipodean heroes of the entrepreneurial culture have already found this game too difficult to play successfully on the more 'sticky wicket' that has prevailed in the post-October 19, 1987 market milieu.

Even if used sensibly, capital-budgeting procedures will tend to discourage major initiatives and indicate strategies aimed at short-term returns. In practice, hopelessly unrealistic assumptions and expectations are often built into these 'analyses', like payback periods of three years or less, and very high, rule-of-thumb hurdle rates that bear no relation to the real cost of capital to the business or actual rates achievable from external placements. (Net present value calculations can, however, be bent the other way, to justify massive strategic overkill with catastrophic socio-economic – and political – consequences. Perhaps the best examples of this mistake were The British National Coal Board, British Steel Corporation and British Leyland, all of which had strikingly similar histories: see Higgins and Clegg 1988.)

What appears to be important from our discussion thus far is the existence of an economic culture which steers economic activity in a stable manner and which achieves a goodness of fit within particular national frameworks. We have expended most time thus far on discussion of the Japanese case: it is, after all, invariably regarded as the most significant success. A contrasting counter-factual logic guided discussion of Britain and the United States. With respect to the Japanese case (which should be extended further than we have done to each of the other East Asian NICs) we have noted the effectiveness of forms of both capital, labour and manufacturing organization. However, our view is that the costs of the forms of labour organization which can characterize economic success are considerably less in some other institutional frameworks for economic culture. For us, that makes such options preferable: we accept that our view of costs may well be some other person's view of benefits.

At the crux of our concern, as we indicated at the outset, is the issue of representation, its fullest expression politically and its extension on a model of citizenship rights from civil to economic rights (Abrahamson and Brostrom 1980; Turner 1987). The analysis of 'economic culture' can only be facilitated by such broader comparisons, particularly ones which are drawn from a different framework than those of the most frequently cited enterprise cultures of East Asia. It is to Sweden that we now turn in order to develop a more strategic and policy-oriented approach to 'economic culture' and institutional constructions and intervention.

The Practice of Swedish Social Democracy

The Swedish system involves a combination of organized labour's high profile in economic decision making, with free enterprise (90 per cent of Swedish industry is privately owned) and state surveillance and co-ordination (mechanisms exist for capital to be channelled in particular directions, especially into product development and new technology). This is a particularly successful example from the economic point of view and one which in 1987, according to both *Business Week* and *The Economist*, could fairly be claimed to have shown real signs of re-emerging from the international recession.

Even the US-based Brookings Institute was moved to report recently that despite − or because of − (the) defiance of orthodoxy, Swedish industry had adjusted to changed economic circumstances at least as well as the allegedly more flexible free market American or Japanese economies (*The Guardian*, August 4, 1987).

Sweden thus offers a remarkable comparison to the usual liberal market connotations for the use of the term economic culture. In that country a new economic culture emerged with an ascendant social democratic labour movement.

The Swedish Social Democratic Party (SAP) was founded in 1889 as an affiliate of the Second International. Like the German parent party, the Swedish social democrats began with an uncomfortable mixture of Marxist and Lassallean strategic perspectives which was gradually subordinated to a distinctively Swedish strategy, albeit under the guise of German 'orthodox' and then 'revisionist' Marxism until the twenties. On the conventional interpretation of social democracy's history (Tingsten 1967), the movement's political trajectory was a long 'maturation' process, oscillating in the 1930s from revolutionary Marxism to welfare liberalism. Undoubtedly, the latter years of the party's first generation leadership up to the mid-twenties were marked by hesitation, but far from the latter stemming from forsaken socialist goals, it signalled confusion over how to pursue those goals under the newly won universal suffrage (Higgins 1988). Neither the political problem nor its novel solution figure in the conventional historiography, but the solution underpinned the party's subsequent unique political success, and so constitutes a major clue in our pursuit of a distinctively social democratic economic culture.

The definitive formulation of social democracy's problem in the twenties, and the strategic re-orientation to overcome it, was above all the work of Ernst Wigforss, the party's main theoretican (and the country's treasurer 1925 — 26 and 1932 — 49). Briefly stated, he saw the party as unable to attain an electoral majority while it failed to challenge orthodox public economic management and thus colluded in the typically free-market outcomes of macro- and micro-economic inefficiency and social inequity. Mass unemployment was the most topical such outcome. The party could only aspire to majoritarian rule if it contested free-market economic rationality by proposing the comprehensive reform of macro- and micro-economic institutions in the overt pursuit of efficiency, equity and democracy as mutually reinforcing goals (Higgins 1985b, 1988). On this basis the party launched its spectacularly successful electoral offensive in 1932, in the aftermath of which it has been in government ever since, with the exception of the non-socialist interregnum of 1976 — 82. The Wigforssian politics of contesting free-market economic rationality have not only made the Swedish social democrats the West's most successful electoral party, but have also moulded what have become distinctively Swedish institutional innovations and proposals: indicative planning, the public orchestration of economic development, a direct role for organized labour in macro-economic management, and industrial and economic democracy.

The Swedish blue-collar union movement (LO) has from the twenties been an important bearer of the politics of economic rationality, and indeed the main bearer since the late forties. It is also uniquely successful among its Western counterparts, both in terms of union density (around 85 per cent), institutional development, its direct part in public and 'private' economic management, and in overtaking its affiliated party as the labour movement's major policy initiator. It took up this latter role in the late forties. It did so by developing its own distinctive policy regime (the Rehn-Meidner model adopted in 1951), in order to perpetuate full employment while at the same time counteracting inflationary pressures at their source, in substantively irrational investment behaviour — rather than in what is presumed conventionally to be their source in wage movements (Higgins 1985a, Higgins and Apple 1983). Whether one comes down on the side of 'corporatism' or 'political unionism' in analysing organized labour's salience in public and private economic management (Fulcher 1987; see also Pontusson 1987), one can hardly gainsay the stark contrast between Swedish arrangements on the one hand, and the exclusion of organized labour's influence in both the East Asian cases and our British and American examples of industrial decline.

Sweden's comparative economic performance under these peculiar institutional conditions is also unambiguous. Since the non-socialist interregnum between 1976 and 1982 the SAP has steered the Swedish economy away from the verge of decline and into a new resurgence, with economic growth currently at 2 per cent, unemployment at 2 per cent, inflation a little over 3.5 per cent, the budget deficit down from 13 to 2 per cent and the balance of payments in surplus. For most observers, these would be successful economic outcomes.

Perhaps the most important features of the Swedish economic culture are twofold. First, the electoral success of the SAP is based mainly on the fact that the majority of Swedes associate the party not only with the beginnings of their economic success but also with its continuation (see Himmelstrand 1981). Second, even many Swedish business people have faith in the economic culture that has been created, and tend to be suspicious of change. Industrial leaders — for example Curt Nicolin, a former chairman of the Swedish employers' federation (SAF) — have gone on record as saying that they prefer to deal with a social democratic government because 'they have a better understanding of the rules of the game' on the labour market. Moreover, the 'fast tracking' we have identified in the USA, for instance, with its characteristic 'job-hopping', 'short tenure' and consequent non-responsibility in the future for one's past decisions in the same firm, do not characterize Swedish managers (Lawrence and Spybey 1986). There are clear hints here of important aspects of an economic culture and of its broad appeal in terms of stable expectations.

Of course, there is also opposition to social democratic policies as well. One can see this particularly in the face of the SAP's support, albeit lukewarm, for wage-earner funds which LO proposed in 1976 in order to boost industrial investment and to introduce a democratic element into resource allocation. The watered-down version of the funds scheme which was introduced in 1983 provided that proportions of both wage rises and company profits should be put into five funds for investment under tripartite control in Swedish industry. This is not, however, the first example of the socialization of the investment function, to use Keynes' term. In the late thirties the social democrats pioneered an investment reserve fund mechanism to re-phase and promote investment during recessions. The scheme became operative in the fifties, and allows Swedish firms to retain pre-tax profits in frozen Central Bank accounts. The government 'releases' the funds in downturns, and, provided the firms then invest them appropriately, they do not attract tax. The National Labour Market Board (AMS — *Arbetsmarknadsstyrelsen*), which has a majority of union delegates, exercises a degree of influence over these releases. The main activities of this important state organ consist in retraining, relocation of labour and job creation, all of which also constitute indirect levers into investment decisions.

The three funds generated by the supplementary pension scheme (ATP funds) represented a higher level of ambition in both income redistribution and public influence over the level and direction of investment. This system began in 1960 and represents a landmark in the development of Sweden's social democratic economic culture. The funds met the requirement in the Rehu-Meidner model for a shift from private to public saving and investment. Within a few years they represented 40 per cent of the credit market and their placements reflected the labour movement's developmental priorities. In the seventies a fourth fund was created and was empowered to take up equity shares. As we shall see below when we return to the wage earner fund proposal, the latter represented a still higher level of ambition in socializing the investment function.

All these institutional arrangements contribute to a system of sticks and carrots intended to draw capital into the renewal and expansion of the manufacturing sector, where they have stimulated investment levels and shored up substantively rational forms of calculation. The latest experiment in this series comes in the form of 'developmental funds' which harness excess liquidity in firms to training and research and development programmes. The evident common inspiration behind all this institutional creativity points to a coherent social democratic economic culture.

Against this, the non-socialist opponents to the SAP presided over a blow-out of the budget and balance of payments deficits and an industrial contraction between 1976 and 1982. The non-socialist governments were unable to exploit the strength of the Swedish institutional frameworks that embody the economic culture, while those strengths effectively prevented them from developing 'free-market' alternatives. For instance, these governments did not tamper with the welfare state in an era when public sector spending was under attack everywhere else in the West.

A Social Democratic Economic Culture

The Swedish system has often been cited as the best example of social democratic 'corporatism' (see Clegg, Boreham and Dow 1986: 378 — 388). As we have seen, the political party of the labour movement has been in government almost uninterruptedly since 1932. Not only has social democracy worked in close cooperation with the unions but it has also developed a preference for conflictual compromise rather than for industrial conflict as theatrical or gestural politics in its relations with the employers. The remarkable success of Swedish industry, of worldwide proportions and yet operating from a nation of only 8.5 million people, further serves to enhance its reputation. But it is also interesting to see the ramifications of economic culture in public administration.

The key to the Swedish economic culture, in constitutional terms, is representation (in stark contrast to the East Asian examples). To a considerable extent, it is organized from the grassroots upwards. Sweden has local government written into its constitution, so that its basic structure cannot be tampered with by the government in power, and it operates at county (*landsting*) level and at municipal (*kommun*) level. In particular, the former has been responsible for health care and the latter for education (the provision of schools – since 1969 of the comprehensive type). An additional, lower tier of district councils is being tentatively introduced by some municipal councils although, as a local politician has pointed out, the cost is very high. This is being done in an explicit attempt to counter charges of 'bureaucratic remoteness' from local communities. This is a reminder that democracy does not come cheap but that the explicit democratic principle is held as important in Sweden. Nevertheless, Swedish pragmatism is reflected at the same time, in a need to demonstrate the compatibility of democracy with efficiency (Czarniawska-Joerges 1986).

Some observers (see, for instance, Gidlund 1987) feel that future developments will see the disappearance of county government, the encroachment of the municipal tier and the universal adoption of the lower tier of sub-municipal government. This would be an extension of representation at 'grass-roots' level but, not surprisingly, the county government administrators see it differently, with their role preserved at the very least as a kind of central planning agency. Civil servants tend to resist plans to devolve administration, whilst all the political parties except the conservatives support it.

It is worth noting, however, that the SAP in government, with its practical responsibility for budgets and tax collection, currently urge the county and municipal administrations to avoid increases in expenditure. Normally the latter two take it in turns to increase taxation. Overall, a majority of the highly taxed Swedish people see themselves as consumers of state services by choice and so do not mind paying taxes so much if they can see that they are getting value for money. Contrary to economic liberal hypotheses, there is no widespread Swedish 'tax revolt'. To a significant extent, controversy tends to be over the 'value for money' in public spending rather than over taxation itself. This is important for the concept of an economic culture because it reflects the high acceptance in Sweden of public sector spending, as for instance in the cases of virtually universal state education and state health care. Here the point has to be made that, given middle-class support for the provision of state services, these become quality services.

We have been reviewing 'bottom-up' arrangements for representation: but there are also two kinds of 'top-down' arrangements. The first is in the form of the *lanstyrelser*, which are outpost representative boards of the civil service, responsible for regional planning, tax collecting, vehicle licensing, etc. The second, more interesting for the present concern, are the tripartite boards of which the National Labour Market Board, mentioned above, is a good example. The Board is an offshoot of the Department of Employment, but there are also regional labour market councils and the local labour exchanges, the latter operating with what Rothstein (1985) refers to as 'street level bureaucracies'. The term is appropriate in this context. The SAP, in pursuit of an 'active' labour market policy, has from the early post-war period broken the tradition of meritocratic recruitment of bureaucrats in order to put individuals who are more in sympathy with their policies into contact with concrete labour market problems at the grass-roots level. Rothstein describes this as 'cadre activity' on the part of the Social Democrats. Certainly it has to be seen as determination on the part of the Social Democrats to make inroads into the 'conservative' civil service in order the better to accommodate their reform programme, especially in the areas of the labour market, education and agriculture. Despite the enabling policies of the Social Democrat government in this area, implementation is time-consuming in terms of voluntary work. This fact is a tribute to the Swedish dedication to democratic participation, a tradition that goes back at least to the emergence of popular rural and then working-class movements in the nineteenth century (Therborn 1983–4), especially when one considers the competing commitment to 'private life' in the national culture. Swedes can put the family before all other activities, and yet it is common for voluntary, democratic work to take up to four evenings a week. Too strong a sense of familism would not sustain this.

The labour movement invests the Labour Market Board with great importance, particularly for its support of the broader policy ambition of keeping wages high, even if this forces weak firms to the wall. Indeed, precisely because it does force weaker firms to the wall: as the Rehn-Meidner model problematized wage differentials, why should it be the case that low wage workers subsidize inefficient firms? The labour market policies board deal with any problems of re-deployment (rather than unemployment). The national board handles macro-level planning and industrial relocation, the regional boards concentrate on job-creation, re-training and re-deployment in the regions, and the labour exchanges are equipped (and financed) to deal effectively and sympathetically (from the labour point of view) with individual cases.

At this point it should be made clear that, despite Rothstein's (1985) argument, this is not just a case of the Social Democrats filling the various levels of public administration with their party nominees, but rather of a highly specific institutional model being implemented, with these boards made up, at both national and county levels, of nominess from government, employers and unions plus other interest groups, where appropriate. In recent years policy has returned to 'economic realism' in the denial of public money to declining industries after the non-socialist governments' lavish support of doomed industries like shipbuilding. Instead, a network of local investment corporations has been set up to solicit private invest-ment and these, incidentally, have tended to be over-subscribed.

Meanwhile, in the case of larger problems, such as those encountered in the formerly highly successful shipbuilding industry, Sweden's large com-panies have been mobilized into the breach, with some financial encour-agement. In the case of the closing down of the large Uddevalla shipyard, a new Volvo plant was built, and in the more recent case of the Kockums yard at Malmo, a new Saab plant is planned. The future may be more difficult because, as a Ministry of Industry official pointed out, there is not an endless supply of possibilities on this scale. As a counter example, it is interesting to note that in 1987 when the Dannemora and Grangesberg iron ore mines were threatened with closure the government compromised its policy and underwrote a five year extension. To some extent this highlights the status of miners as a special case almost everywhere but also reflects the relatively small scale of the problem with only about a thousand jobs to be protected. From a different perspective, in the case of Uddevalla and Malmo it should be noted that the result is 'state of the art' technology for Volvo and Saab, already known for their innovation in manufacturing technology and organization (Sandkull 1986).

The institutional innovations characterized here as constituting a new, efficient, social democratic economic culture in Sweden amount to a permanent advance on laissez-faire public economic management. As we have seen, the original Rehn-Meidner model and its institutional ramifi-cations (above all the ATP funds and the labour-market planning appa-ratus) successfully sought to perpetuate full employment and economic dynamism under socially equitable and increasingly democratic conditions.

It tackled the main enemy of the full-employment economy — inflation — at its source in the irrationality of unregulated private investment behaviour. High wages and wage equalization featured as centrepieces, and the model prescribed a direct and gowing role for the union movement in policy making and implementation. But from the beginning of the early seventies many LO strategists and union activists perceived a need to take the model a great step further. The original model had served well in the stable, expansionary conditions of the long boom and while Swedish industry was in the hands of competent industrialists. But, as this model stood, it was less well equipped to deal, from the seventies, with the international economic contraction and destabilization on the one hand, and the internationalization of financial markets on the other — a change that made Swedish industry, too, prey to predatory financial interests and their anti-manufacturing forms of calculation. The Swedish union movement responded to these new conditions by extending the model, and thus evolving the social democratic economic culture still further. Concretely, it did so by mounting two simultaneous campaigns, for industrial democracy and for economic democracy in the form of wage earners' funds (Higgins and Apple 1983). Both arose out of the movements' penchant for collectivist and democratic solutions rather than a relapse into economic liberal atavism.

Both industrial democracy and wage-earners funds proved non-negotiable with the employers' federation (SAE) and thus necessitated resort to both legislation and intense mobilization of the rank and file. A series of statutes, known as the Aman laws, redefined the rights of shop stewards and safety committees and employees in general, as well as imposing obligations on employers to accept worker directors and to disclose and negotiate over all corporate plans affecting their workforces. Despite employer resistance, the industrial-democracy campaign has left its mark in the qualitatively heightened ability of local union organizations (backed by central union resources) to enter into corporate planning and decision making. They do so as the bearers of a substantive industrial rationality which is often at loggerheads with the paper entrepreneuralism of the new major players on the capital market.

The second union campaign from this period, the wage-earner fund proposal, shared the same rationale. Although its original pretext was to cream off and thus sterilize a proportion of excess profits that otherwise stimulated wage drift, a major motive of the funds was to secure the re-investment of those profits in industry at a time when the country's capital resources were being diverted into speculative and purely financial placements. More broadly, the proposed reform aimed to partially fulfil the traditional social democratic goal of democratizing economic life, in this instance by bringing the all-important function of resource allocation under gradually increasing social control. In the event, a failure of political will on the part of the social democratic party resulted in the enactment of a wage-earner fund scheme that was too watered down to achieve any of these ambitions. However, the present scheme may prove the precursor of democratic reforms in capital formation that come closer to fulfiling the original ambitions of the wage-earner fund concept.

In concluding this section, we come back to the point that the basis for the East Asian nation's economic success was the effectiveness of their capital, labour and manufacturing organization. On each of these points Swedish social democratic economic culture offers an alternative solution, one whose contingencies appear to have achieved a goodness of fit within the isomorphism of the Swedish economy. Collective capital formation, empowered and democratized labour and a high-wages-forced national manufacturing rationality (rather than a rationality premised on either internationally comparatively lower wages and/or much longer hours of work by segmented and divided workers) are the hallmark. The key to this close contingency or elective affinity is the extension of institutions of representation throughout society, rather than their restriction.

Conclusions

Three types of institutional framework for the cultural organization of economic action have been identified. First we considered the East Asian type, which we will term *an authoritarian democratic* type. This was characterized by stable associational linkages between firms with relatively low levels of inter-capital predatory behaviour. We noted that important variations existed within the type constructed. In Japan the organizing principle was a communitarian ideal, in South Korea a patrimonial principle and in Taiwan a patrilineal principle. Accounting conventions favour a logic of manufacturing production rather than a more short-term and speculative policy of trading in assets. In each case the labour market is relatively highly segmented, with comparatively fewer rights for labour and a more arduous regime of work: one with longer hours and shorter recreation. (Annual average working hours of a Japanese worker amount to more than 2,100 hours: by contrast, in Britain and the USA the average is 1,800 – 1,900, with about 1,650 the norm in the Federal Republic of Germany: see Deutschmann 1987 a.) However, it is worth noting that not all of these are particularly 'low-wage' economies: certainly not Singapore and Japan. The state, comparatively, tends to the 'strong state' type in its dealings with its subjects. Within the general type some states, such as Hong Kong, are less democratic while others, such as South Korea, are more authoritarian. Second, we considered the *liberal democratic type*, which we may typify by Britain, the United States and Australia. Here the emphasis was on the role of accounting conventions in producing less than stable capital organization, indeed capital disorganization (Lash and Urry 1987). Less attention was paid to labour market and state organization: had it been, then variations from a more highly organized labour market in the Australian case, with relatively lower rates of ethnic segmentation and higher rates of gender segmentation, compared to a moderately organized British and less organized and more segmented American cases would have been noted. On a continuum, Australia is closer to the third type, a social democratic type, than are either Britain or America. Sweden was our exemplar of the *social democratic type*, whose keynote we consider to be expanded forms of democratic representation compared with the other types. The organization of capital we regarded as stable rather than competitively predatory, largely because of the existence of collective, democratically conceived financial, accounting and capital formation conventions which perform as 'functional equivalents' to the sources of institutional stability in the East Asian authoritarian democratic type. Just as there is more than one way to skin a cat there is more than one to achieve a successful economic culture.

It may be conceded that we have sketched a working model of social democratic 'economic culture' and its institutional formation in one country. However, critics may well be sceptical about the generalizability of this model to other nations (Hicks 1987). The central objection must surely be that the class formation, the political hegemony enjoyed by the Swedish social democrats, and the resultant political economy are such that they would be impossible to replicate elsewhere. This is correct. However, the institutional framework can be a source of concrete examples for political actors elsewhere, as indeed can any national pattern of institutional arrangements.

What is important in our argument is the following. First, the social democratic construction of an 'economic culture', as we have sketched it, is not culturally specific but institutionally produced. Second, some of these institutional conditions are, in principle, capable of replication elsewhere. The central thrust of the recent landmark publication in Australian economic policy formation, *Australia Reconstructed* (ACTU/TDCS 1987), explicitly recognizes this fact (see also Higgins 1987). A party of labour in government; a strong and centralizing union structure; and peak tripartite institutions in which priorities and policy commitments can be hammered out concerning wages, investment and industry policy, all point to the possibility of developing a social democratic economic culture. This development is institutionally feasible at the national level, despite the increasing interdependence of national economies and their susceptibility to economic factors outside their control (Bruno and Sachs 1985, Hicks 1987). In fact, these international interdependencies make national institutional factors of more, not less, importance. None of this is to say that institutional and policy development is unproblematic: of course not. What is important is that the social democratic path to an 'economic culture' does at least provide a counterweight to the substantive implications which are evident in other claimants to the title, such as 'post-Confucianism'. While the latter has had scant respect for developing the panoply of citizenship rights for its national subjects, this is not the case in the social democracies. Indeed, what is important, as has been argued elsewhere (Clegg, Boreham and Dow 1986), is that the relationship between citizenship rights, institutional frameworks and economic indicators is reciprocally productive in the social democratic case. It is not the case, as many market-oriented advocates of an economic culture would propound, that large public sectors and democratic entitlements necessarily mean economically inefficient cultures (Clegg, Boreham and Dow 1986). No causal empirical relationship between these factors has been adequately established.

Consider the alternative 'economic culture' arguments from the perspective of national economic managers in a country such as Australia. 'Post-Confucianism', if identified in wholly cultural terms, is simply not a possible strategy, for obvious reasons. If re-defined in institutional terms, it would hardly be desirable nor even feasible. Moreover, it would be incoherent: which of the various post-Confucian pathways would one follow? Strong authoritarian states (South Korea, Singapore)? State-financed enterprises (South Korea)? Market and familial linkages (Hong Kong, Taiwan) or complex corporate interdependencies (Japan)? Enterprise unions (Japan) or a largely non-unionized workforce (Taiwan)? Perhaps all that one could cull from the cases in common would be a general cultailment of citizenship rights as we associate these with advanced economic social democracies: a substitution of market for civil entitlement with respect to health, welfare, education and some other areas citizens of the social democracies have achieved as a component of their universal citizenship rather than as something to be bought through their particular market power.

Of course, at the end of the day, thinking of certain characteristics of both British and Australian politics, with which we are especially familiar, the reason for the seeming 'elective affinity' between the advocacy of an 'economic culture' and an 'enterprise culture', where the notion of enterprise takes on a rugged caste opposed to state and governmental intervention, may well be on grounds also of political principle. Thus, all the more reason, on grounds of political principle, to display such elective affinities alongside others which at least have the merit of being less abstracted culturally and more attuned to relatively expanded conditions of citizenship as they exist in nations such as Sweden, rather than those which prevail in South Korea, Taiwan, Singapore, Hong Kong or Japan.

At the root of any notion of 'culture' is the tending, the cultivating of something in order to achieve some desired state. We conclude by counselling attention to the political implications of this root meaning when considering 'economic culture'. The choice within established capitalist nations is not just between policies derived from the evident success of the capitalism of East Asia and those drawn from the illiberal socialism of the Eastern European and other members of the communist bloc. The crucial choices are between forms of liberal capitalism which extend and deepen democratic representation and economic efficiency compared to those whose economic efficiency is premised on the restriction of democratic representation. On these grounds, which are both empirical and comparative, our cultural affinities are clear while at the same time our argument remains open to disconfirmation.

References

Abercrombie, N., S. Hill and B. S. Turner (1980): *The dominant ideology thesis,* London: Allen and Unwin.

Abrahamson, B. and A. Broström (1980): *The rights of labour,* London: Sage.

ACTU/TDCS, Australian Council of Trade Unions/Trade Development Council Secretariat (1987): *Australia reconstructed,* Canberra: Australian Government Publishing Service.

Anderson, P. (1964): Origins of the present crisis, *New Left Review* 24: 26 – 53.

Anderson, P. (1986): The figures of descent, *New Left Review* 161: 20 – 77.

Bauman, Z. (1973): *Culture as praxis,* London: Routledge and Kegan Paul.

Bauman, Z. (1976): *Towards a critical sociology,* London: Routledge and Kegan Paul.

Berger, P. (1987): *The capitalist revolution: fifty propositions about prosperity, equity, and liberty,* London: Wildwood.

Berger, P. and T. Luckmann (1967): *The social construction of reality,* Harmondsworth: Allen Lane.

Bruno, M. and J. D. Sachs (1985): *Economics of worldwide stagnation,* Cambridge: Harvard University Press.

Burawoy, M. (1979): *Manufacturing consent,* University of Chicago Press.

Calmfors, L. and J. Diffil (1988): Bargaining structure, corporatism and macroeconomic performance, *Economic Policy* 6, I: 13 – 62.

Clegg, S. R. and D. Dunkerly (1980): *Organization, class and control,* London: Routledge and Kegan Paul.

Clegg, S. R. and W. Higgins (1987): Against the current: organizations, sociology and socialism, *Organization Studies* 8, 3: 201—222.

Clegg, S. R., P. Boreham and G. Dow (1986) *Class, politics and the economy*, London: Routledge and Kegan Paul.

Clegg, S. R., G. Dow and P. Boreham (1983): Politics and crisis: the state of the recession, in: S. R. Clegg, G. Dow and P. Boreham (eds.), *The state, class and the recession*, 1—50, London: Croom Helm.

Clegg, S. R., D. Dunphy and S. G. Redding (eds.) (1986): *The enterprise and management in East Asia*, Centre of Asia Studies: University of Hong Kong.

Cohen, M. D., J. G. March and J. P. Olsen (1972): A garbage can model of organizational choice, *Administrative Science Quarterly* 17, 1: 1—25.

Czarniawska-Joerges, B. (1986): De-centralization in Swedish local governments: a change by ideological control, Paper presented to the Conference on the Bureaucratization and De-bureaucratization of Social Welfare, Gottlieb Duttweiler Institute, Rushlikon, Zurich.

Deutschmann, C. (1987 a): The Japanese type of organization as a challenge to the sociological theory of modernization, *Thesis Eleven* 17: 40—58.

Deutschmann, C. (1987 b): Economic restructuring and company unionism — the Japanese model, *Economic and Industrial Democracy* 8, 4: 436—488.

Donaldson, L. (1986): Size and bureaucracy in East and West: A preliminary meta-analysis, in: S. R. Clegg, D. Dunphy and S. G. Redding (eds.), *The enterprise and management in East Asia*, 67—92, Hong Kong: Centre of Asian Studies University of Hong Kong.

Dow, G., S. R. Clegg and P. Boreham (1984): From the politics of production to the production of politics, *Thesis Eleven* 9: 16—32.

Dunphy, D. (1986): An historical review of the literature on the Japanese enterprise and its management, in: S. R. Clegg, D. Dunphy and S. G. Redding (eds.), *The enterprise and management in East Asia*, 343—368, Hong Kong: Centre of Asian Studies, University of Hong Kong.

Ewer, P., W. Higgins and A. Stephens (1987): *Trade unions and manufacturing strategy*, Sydney: Allen and Unwin.

Fulcher, J. (1987): Labour movement theory versus corporatism: social democracy in Sweden, *Sociology* 21, 2: 231—252.

Giddens, A. (1984): *The constitution of society*, Cambridge: Polity Press.

Gidlund, J. E. (1987): The future of local government in Sweden, Mimeo, University of Umea.

Gordon, A. (1985): *The evolution of labour relations in Japan*, Cambridge: Massachussetts.

Hamilton, G. and N. W. Biggart (1985): Market, culture and authority: a comparative analysis of management and organization in the Far East, Paper presented to the Pan Pacific Conference II, Seoul, Korea, May 11—13.

Hayes, R. H. and W. Abernathy (1980): Managing our way to economic decline, *Harvard Business Review* 58, 4: 67—77.

Hayes, R. H. and D. A. Garvin (1982): Managing as if tomorrow mattered, *Harvard Business Review* 60, 3: 70—80.

Hayes, R. H. and S. C. Wheelwright (1984): *Restoring our competitive edge: competing through manufacturing*, New York: John Wiley and Sons.

Hicks, A. (1987): Socialism: scientific and utopian, *Contemporary Sociology* 16, 5: 661 – 664.

Higgins, W. (1985 a): Political unionism and the corporatist thesis, *Economic and Industrial Democracy* 6, 3: 349 – 381.

Higgins, W. (1985 b): Ernst Wigforss: the renewal of social democratic theory and practice, *Political Power and Social Theory* V. 5: 207 – 250.

Higgins, W. (1987): Unions as bearers of industrial regeneration: reflections on the Australian case, *Economic and Industrial Democracy* 8, 2: 213 – 236.

Higgins, (1988): Swedish Social Democracy and the New Democratic Socialism, in: D. Sainsbury (ed.) *Democracy, state and justice: critical perspectives and new interpretations,* Stockholm: Almavist an Wiksell International.

Higgins, W. and N. Apple (1983): How limited is reformism? *Theory and Society* 12, 3: 603 – 630.

Higgins, W. and S. R. Clegg (1988): Enterprise calculation and manufacturing decline, *Organization Studies* 9, 1: 69 – 89.

Himmelstrand, U., G. Ahrne, L. Lundberg and L. Lundberg (1981): *Beyond welfare capitalism,* London: Heinemann.

Hofstede, G. (1980): *Culture's consequences: international differences in work related values,* London: Sage.

Igarashi, F. (1986): Forced to confess, in: G. McCormack and Y. Sugimoto (eds.), *Democracy in contemporary Japan,* 195 – 214, Sydney: Hale and Iremonger.

Kahn, H. (1979). *World economic development: 1979 and beyond,* London: Croom Helm.

Kawashini, H. (1986): The reality of enterprise unionism, in: G. McCormack and Y. Sugimoto (eds.), *Democracy in contemporary Japan,* 138 – 156, Sydney: Hale & Iremonger.

Ketcham, R. (1987): *Individualism and public life,* Oxford: Blackwell.

Koo, H. (1987): Industrialization and labor politics in the East Asian NICs: A comparison of South Korea and Taiwan, Paper presented to the American Sociological Association Annual Meetings, Chicago, August 17 – 22.

Kosai, Y. and Y. Ogino (1984): *The contemporary Japanese economy,* London: Macmillan.

Lash, S. and J. Urry (1987): *Disorganized capitalism,* Cambridge: Polity Press.

Lawrence, P. and T. Spybey (1986): *Management and society in Sweden,* London: Routledge and Kegan Paul.

Levin, D. A., Y. Nihei and M. Ohtsu (1986): Industrialization, ownership and employment practices: a comparative study of allocation and wage structure of seven garment plants in four Asian countries, in: S. R. Clegg, D. Dunphy and S. G. Redding (eds.), *The enterprise and management in East Asia,* 187 – 228, Hong Kong: Centre of Asian Studies, University of Hong Kong.

Littler, C. R. (1982): Deskilling and changing structures of control, in: S. Wood (ed.), *The degradation of work? Skill, deskilling and the labour process,* 122 – 145, London: Hutchinson.

Marcuse, H. (1964): *One-dimensional man,* London, Routledge and Kegan Paul.

McCormack, G. (1986): Crime, confession and control, in: G. McCormack and Y. Sugimoto (eds.), *Democracy in contemporary Japan,* 186 – 194, Sydney: Hale and Iremonger.

McMillan, C. J. (1984): *The Japanese industrial system,* Berlin: De Gruyter.

Meidner, R. (1978): *Employee investment funds: an approach to collective capital formation,* London: Allen & Unwin.

Milton-Smith, J. (1986): Japanese management overseas: international business strategy and the case of Singapore, in: S. R. Clegg, D. Dunphy and S. G. Redding (eds.), *Enterprise and management in East Asia,* 395–412, Hong Kong: Centre of Asian Studies, University of Hong Kong.

Murakami, Y. (1984): Ie society as a pattern of civilization, *Journal of Japanese Studies* 10, 2: 281–363.

Murakami, Y. (1986): Technology in transition: two perspectives on industrial policy, in: H. Patrick (ed.) with the assistance of L. Meissner, *Japan's high technology industries: lessons and limitations of industrial policy,* 211–241, Seattle and London: University of Washington Press.

Muto, I. (1986): Class struggle in post-war Japan, in: G. McCormack and Y. Sugimoto (eds.), *Democracy in contemporary Japan,* 114–137, Sydney: Hale and Iremonger.

Nakane, C. (1973): *Japanese society,* Harmondsworth: Penguin.

Newbould, G. D. (1970): *Management and merger activity,* Liverpool: Buthstead.

Orrù, M., N. W. Biggart and G. Hamilton (1988): Organizational isomorphism in East Asia: broadening the new institutionalism, in: W. W. Powell and P. DiMaggio (eds.), *The new institutionalism in organizational analysis,* Chicago: University of Chicago Press.

Ouchi, W. (1981): *Theory Z: Now American business can meet the Japanese challenge,* Boston, Mass.: Addison-Wesley.

Pascale, T. (1984): Perspectives on strategy: the real story behind Honda's success, *Californian Management Review* 26, 3: 47–72.

Peters, T. and R. Waterman (1982): *In search of excellence,* New York: Harper and Row.

Pontusson, J. (1987): Radicalization and retreat in Swedish Social Democracy, *New Left Review* 165: 5–33.

Quiggin, J. (1987): White trash of Asia, *Current Affairs Bulletin* 64, 2: 18–25.

Ray, C. (1986): Social innovation at work: the humanization of workers in twentieth century America, Ph.D., University of California, Santa Cruz.

Rohlen, T. (1974): *For harmony and strength: Japanese white collar organization,* Berkeley: University of California Press.

Rothstein, B. (1985): The success of the Swedish labour market policy: the organizational connection to policy, *The European Journal of Political Research* 13: 153–165.

Sandkull, B. (1986): Industry, government and the public — the public role of big corporations, in: R. H. Wolff (ed.) *Organising industrial development,* 59–75, Berlin: Walter de Gruyter.

Schmidt, M. G. (1982): The role of parties in shaping macroeconomic policy, in: F. Castles (ed.), *The impact of parties, politics and policies in democrat capitalist states,* 97–176, London: Sage.

Schumpeter, J. H. (1944): *Capitalism, socialism and Democracy,* London: Allen and Unwin.

Sugimoto, Y. (1986): The manipulative basis of 'consensus' in Japan, in: G. McCormack and Y. Sugimoto (eds.), *Democracy in contemporary Japan*, 65 – 75, Sydney: Hale and Iremonger.

Sugimoto, Y. and R. Mouer (1985): *Images of Japanese society*, London: Routledge and Kegan Paul.

Swedberg, R. (1987): Economic sociology: past and present, *Current Sociology* 35: 1.

Taylor, I., P. Walton and J. Young (1974): *The new criminology*, London, Routledge and Kegan Paul.

Therborn, G. (1983 – 4): The coming of Swedish social democracy, *Annali della Fondazione Giangiacomo Feltrinelli* 527 – 593.

Thompson, G. (1978): Capitalist profit calculations and inflation accounting, *Economy and Society* 7, 4: 395 – 429.

Thurow, L. (1984): Revitalising American industry: managing in a competitive world economy, *Californian Management Review* 27, 1: 9 – 40.

Tingsten, Herbert (1967): *Den svenska socialdemokratins id. utveckling* Vols I – II, Stockholm: Aldus/Bonniers.

Turner, B. S. (1987): *Citizenship and capitalism: the debate over reformism*, London: Allen and Unwin.

Vlastos, S. (1986): *Peasant protests and uprising in Tokugawa Japan*, Berkeley: University of California Press.

Weber, M. (1930): *The protestant ethic and the spirit of capitalism*, London: Allen and Unwin.

Wiener, M. J. (1981): *English culture and the decline of the industrial spirit 1850 – 1950*, Cambridge: Cambridge University Press.

Wilkinson, B. (1986): Emergence of an industrial community? The human relations movement in Singapore, in: S. R. Clegg, D. Dunphy and G. S. Redding (eds.), *Enterprise and management in East Asia*, 111 – 128, Hong Kong: Centre of Asia Studies, University of Hong Kong.

Williams, R. (1976): *Keywords*, Harmondsworth: Penguin.

Williams, K. and C. Haslam, (1985): Accounting for failure in the nationalised enterprises, Mimeo, University College of Wales, Aberystwyth.

Williams, K., J. Williams and D. Thomas (1983): *Why are the British bad at manufacturing?* London: Routledge and Kegan Paul.

Beyond Bureaucracy:
Towards a Comparative Analysis of Forms
of Economic Resource Co-ordination
and Control

S. Gordon Redding and Richard D. Whitley

Introduction

Over the course of the 20th century new forms of business organization have developed in East Asia which have become increasingly significant in terms of world business competition but which do not yield easily to analysis within traditional Western frameworks. They are, as the title of this paper implies, outside the normal conceptual boundaries of the classical bureaucratic model of formal organizations and yet appear to be economically successful. Their success suggests the need for broader frameworks for comparing business structures across societies than the standard measures of bureaucratization and for more attention to be paid to societal contexts in which different sorts of enterprise forms become dominant and successful.

In particular, the increasing acknowledgement of the 'embeddedness' of economic action (Granovetter 1985) has led to a more pointed and more urgent renewal of interest in how different ways of organizing economic activities are related to their broader contexts. Although this is especially obvious in the case of Asian systems, there has also been a growing awareness of variations in European business structures, and of the relatively idiosyncratic nature of the United States' experience (Chandler and Daems 1980, Granick 1972, Locke 1984). As a consequence of such comparisons, the generalization of rational-legal authority principles and formal bureaucratic control systems as the only efficient way of co-ordinating and directing economic resources in competitive markets seems less valid than it did to Max Weber; and their efficacy much more dependent on extra-economic institutions than most management textbook authors have recognized. Anglo-Saxon conceptions of the legally bounded form as the basic unit of economic action are inadequate to explain the economic actions and structures of *chaebol* and Chinese family businesses, both of which have complex extra-firm linkages influencing decision making (Jones and Sakong 1980, Redding 1990, Redding and Tam 1985).

Furthermore, such linkages are often not only contractual or bureaucratic, as Williamson (1975) proposed in his opposition of markets and hierarchies, but can also be highly personal and family dependent. Just as cartelization and interlocking shareholdings amongst members of European industrial groups (cf. Bauer and Cohen 1981, Kocka 1980) can, as means of co-ordinating economic actors' activities, be considered viable alternatives to the diversified multi-divisional enterprise, so too can kinship-based trust relations be effective ways of integrating diverse activities in Chinese family businesses.

These points suggest that the traditional focus on firms as independent legal entities which are well bounded and distinct from their environments needs to be modified, and the institutionalization of such atomistic firms as the dominant form of economic actor seen as a contingent historical phenomenon which is by no means essential to economic development. It is now clear that different forms of economic resource co-ordination and control can be equally successful in world markets, and such success can only be understood in terms of the broader social context in which they develop and become institutionalized. Theories of economic activity and change which treat dominant economic actors as discrete, homogenous entities pursuing identical 'rationalities' need, then, to be replaced by approaches that consider their form and operation as contingent, socially contextual phenomena varying across cultures and historical periods (Whitley 1987).

In proposing a comparative analysis of forms of economic co-ordination and control in this paper we wish to emphasize the need to go beyond previous discussions of organizations and their 'environments' that presume the unproblematic nature of the boundaries and identity of economic actors and examine how particular co-ordination and control systems develop and are institutionalized in particular societies. Rather than just 'breaking down' the organization, as Callon and Vignolle (1977) have suggested, we propose to consider the different processes by which different sorts of economic actors are 'built up' in distinct socio-cultural contexts and are able to compete internationally in world markets. Essentially, the questions to be addressed are: how do different forms of economic organization become established in different societies, how do they co-ordinate and control different sorts of human and material resources and how do they manage extra-enterprise connections and develop distinctive strategies in different social contexts? As a preliminary step in dealing with these general questions we will outline the sorts of considerations which we think are critical to a comparative analysis of economic activities and briefly describe how these are manifested in the cases of the overseas Chinese family business, the Korean *chaebol* and the Japanese *keiretsu* and *kaisha.* Initially, we consider the problem of identifying the appropriate unit of analysis for comparing economic actors and then propose a set of dimensions for describing and contrasting dominant organizational configurations in different societies. These dimensions will be illustrated with national examples, and then we briefly suggest some of the major characteristics of societies which help to explain why different sorts of business structures become dominant in different contexts.

The Unit of Economic Action

In comparing dominant types of actor and explaining why they vary across human societies, it is clearly critical to be able to identify the same unit of analysis in different contexts. Equally clearly, the way in which this is done will substantially affect any subsequent analysis since what is 'inside' or 'outside' organizational boundaries in different societies, and so an important feature of forms of economic organization, will have already been determined. In dealing with this difficulty, and others, it is important to bear in mind the theoretical purpose of the analysis here which is the comparison of forms of economic resource co-ordination and control. The unit of analysis, then, is the entity which acquires, allocates, directs and sells economic resources in a relatively cohesive and reproducible manner in order to generate products or services that are traded in some market system. As Penrose (1959) suggests, 'firms' in this sense are administrative structures which select and combine human and material resources and manage their transformation into productive services in a coherent and co-ordinated way. Economic actors are, then, the relatively autonomous entities which organize resources in particular ways and reproduce themselves as distinct social systems making economic decisions. Their key features can be summarized as:

a. relative autonomy as resource acquirer, disposer and controller,
b. some reproduced administrative system which is minimally stable and
c. a relatively integrated and co-ordinated information and strategic decision-making system.

This system is responsible for business entry and exit decisions, product and market changes, major technical investments, senior management appointments and rewards and overall financial policies. In considering, for example, whether Japanese *keiretsu* and French industrial groups or their constituent 'firms' should be considered the dominant economic actors, the critical questions are: which entity controls senior personnel selection decisions, decides retention ratios and allocation of profits, major investment decisions and market changes and becomes the dominant unit of loyalty and identity for senior managerial personnel. In practice, of course, it is rarely possible to identify unequivocally the locus of these sorts of decisions but it is usually feasible to make considered judgements about the dominant economic entity on the basis of case studies and general economic histories. It seems clear, for instance, that the once dominant position of the traditional general trading company based industrial groups in the Japanese economy has declined in the past 20 or so years and newer, independent *kaisha* which group subcontractors around a dominant manufacturing concern have become significant economic actors (Abegglen and Stalk 1985, Aoki 1987, Kiyonari and Nakamura 1985). In analyzing contemporary Japanese enterprises, then, both types of economic actor have to be considered and the processes by which the once dominant from changed spelled out.

Having identified, however tentatively, the dominant forms of economic co-ordination and control in different societies, the next task is to identify the major dimensions on which they vary and develop so that the significant differences between them can be understood in terms of their contexts. In addition to the traditional means of distinguishing formal organization structures, such as those developed for comparing 'Western' managerial bureaucracies, these need to include broader characteristics such as the relations between economic institutions and other major social institutions, especially kinship groupings and state agencies (Hamilton and Biggart 1988), and general principles of authority and loyalty. They also have to incorporate processes of inter-enterprise co-ordination and co-operation as well as variations in the scope of economic activities undertaken and in the institutionalization of enterprise boundaries. These dimensions summarize differences in particular 'recipes' for organizing economic actors which have been established in different ways and are derived from particular features of their societal contexts. We now consider how these recipes can be differentiated, illustrating this with examples of three Asian types.

Dimensions for Distinguishing Major Types of Economic Actors

Given that economic actors are relatively autonomous collective entities manifesting some discretion over resource acquisition, combination and use, then critical aspects of their organization and functioning reflect the sort of agents who are able to establish and control administrative systems, how they co-ordinate and control them, how they deal with extra-enterprise uncertainties and dependencies and how they develop and change. These broad aspects can be reduced to six basic dimensions for comparing dominant forms of economic co-ordination and control across societies which summarize the major respects in which the three Asian types vary and also can be applied to Western forms of business organization.

The first dimension, the degree of delegated discretion, refers to the extent to which control over economic resources is delegated by dominant groups to separate 'management teams' (Penrose 1959: 21−2, Whitley 1987). Typically discussed under the heading of the separation of ownership and control, this deals with general questions of discretion and trust and the processes by which particular groups are able to establish and maintain enterprises in particular systems of power relations. Where institutional mechanisms for establishing trust and reciprocal obligations between economic agents are weakly developed, such delegation is unlikely to be high and enterprises are unlikely to be directed by managerial teams selected on purely universalistic criteria. Instead, strategic decisions will be dominated by owners and their personal contacts.

Related to this dimension, but varying partly independently of it, is the second aspect − the centralization of authority within enterprises. Societies in which trust is difficult to establish on an impersonal basis, and thus where discretion over economic resources is rarely delegated substantially, are unlikely to encourage much decentralization of decision making within firms, but the relationship does not appear to be direct. Managerially dominated enterprises vary considerably in their degree of centralization as numerous organizational studies have shown and so do dominant economic forms, as the comparison of British and French large companies shows (Bauer and Cohen 1981, Granick 1972).

Thirdly, enterprises differ in the degree to which their activities are regularly and systematically integrated with those of others within and between industrial sectors. Where they are members of industrial groups as in France and Japan (Clark 1979: 73−87, Encaoua and Jacquemin 1982, Hamilton et al., this volume, Levy-Leboyer 1980) their strategies and senior personnel are more closely linked with those of allied firms and banks than where they largely operate as separate entities with purely contractual connections to other enterprises. This sort of 'horizontal', co-ordination can be differentiated from 'vertical' co-ordination in which central agencies such as large banks or state ministries channel funds and other resources to particular sectors and enterprises and attempt to organize leading firms around general industrial and societal goals. This sort of co-ordination typically occurs in what Johnson (1982: 17−23) termed 'developmental' states such as Korea and Japan (Cumings 1987), although the French planning system in the 1950's and 60's also attempted central state co-ordination of firms' investment strategies (Suleiman 1978: 252−65). Bank- or general trading company-centred groups in which strong central direction dominated enterprise strategies also exemplify vertical co-ordination as the pre-war Japanese *zaibatsu* illustrate (Yasuoka 1976).

This sort of inter-enterprise co-ordination is connected to the degree of vertical and horizontal specialization of enterprises in particular activities and their tendency to remain in a single industry segment. According to Clark (1979: 50−64, cf. Tsuchiya 1976), Japanese companies tend to concentrate on one industry and often rely on trading companies and other firms to negotiate links with suppliers and customers. Like many British textiles firms (Lazonick 1986), they focus on a limited range of economic activities − typically production − and maintain a clear identity within particular industries. Clearly, where such specialization is high, firms have to develop connections with purchasing and selling agents but these can be purely contractual or based on personal trust or more elaborate co-ordinating mechanisms involving joint ownership and intra-group managerial mobility. Conversely, where the dominant economic actor is the large, diversified corporation integrating varied activities through a Chandlerian managerial hierarchy, high levels of inter-firm co-ordination are not to be expected, although interlocking directorships with financial institutions and similar efforts to reduce uncertainty and manage the 'environment' are a common feature of such economic systems (Scott and Griff 1984).

As well as varying in the extent to which strategies and activities are integrated across firms and sectors, dominant types of enterprises differ in their systematic co-ordination of activities within their boundaries to realize economies of scale and 'synergy' in the use of human and material resources. Granick (1972) has suggested that large British companies in the 1960's preferred to rely on market contracting models for integrating their different activities rather than developing formal procedures and rules in comparison with French and Unites States' firms and linked this to a general cultural preference for market contracting. Generally, we can distinguish between dominant types of firms which seek the maximum benefit from systematically integrating different sets of resources around related activities from those which diversify opportunistically to reduce risk and realise *ad hoc* gains in relatively unrelated activities. The latter tend to rely on financial means of control, while the former co-ordinate investment plans and flows of inputs and outputs as well as the competitive strategies of operating units through hierarchically controlled procedures.

Fifthly, the extent to which managerial authority is primarily based on the personal qualities of top management as opposed to their formal status and expertise clearly varies considerably between enterprise types, as does the tendency to identify with individual leaders rather than the organization as a whole. 'Legal-rational' forms of managerial authority emphasize loyalty to positions and competence rather than individual incumbents and are, in principle, unlimited in application, whereas personal authority is dyadic and restricted in range.

Finally, loyalty and personal identification vary across enterprise types in terms of the dominant unit of attachment and the extent of commitment to entire corporations. In some societies workers and managers identify primarily with relatively narrow professional and technical specializations rather than with particular employing organizations. Similarly, within large enterprises they may demonstrate more loyalty to particular departments or operating units than to the whole entity and, in general, we can differentiate between firms where strong vertical bonding all the way up the hierarchy is evident from those in which it is weak and/or subsidiary to horizontal identification with particular occupational specialisms and strata.

We now turn to a brief discussion of the three major types of economic actor in East Asian societies before considering how they each manifest these dimensions to different degrees. They can be summarized as the Chinese family business, the (South) Korean *chaebol* and the Japanese *keiretsu/kaisha*.

The Chinese Family Business

The Chinese family business is the dominant form of economic structure used by the Overseas Chinese, of whom there are approximately 40 million in Hong Kong, Singapore, Taiwan where they dominate, and in Thailand, Indonesia, Malaysia and the Philippines where they form an ethnic minority but are still very significant economically. Their collective GNP, were it separable, would amount to somewhere between 150 and 200 billion US dollars.

The form of organization which they adopt is remarkably consistent across a diverse region, and it could be argued to contribute to their success in dominating economies in which their demographic minority is tiny (e. g. Indonesia 4%, Philippines 1%), and also in achieving the competitive efficiency in the international market place visible in exports to the developed world.

Their consistently found characteristics are as follows (cf. Redding 1990, Silin 1976):

1. small scale, and relatively simple organizational structuring;
2. normally focused on one product or market with growth by opportunistic diversification;
3. centralized decision making with heavy reliance in one dominant executive;
4. a close overlap of ownership, control and family;
5. a paternalistic organizational climate;
6. linked to the environment through personalistic networks;
7. normally very sensitive to matters of cost and financial efficiency;
8. commonly linked strongly but informally with related but legally independent organizations handling key functions such as parts supply or marketing;
9. relatively weak in terms of creating large-scale market recognition for brands;
10. a high degree of strategic adaptability.

The characterization of Chinese family business as preponderantly small scale does not rule out the possibility of large-scale enterprises emerging, but it does call into question their likely effectiveness given the constraints on scale implied by some of the key features such as centralization of decisions, or nepotism. In practice, the few very large companies have tended to stay within boundaries where they have political protection and are not subject to the full onslaught of international competition (Limlingan 1986, Yoshihara 1988). Either that or they have kept to one specialism such as property or shipping where the strategic judgement of the dominant executive can be relatively easily exploited.

The Korean *Chaebol*

Although it is by no means the only economic form in South Korea, the large conglomerate form known as the *chaebol* has come to be dominant. The ten largest now account for over half the country's exports and the top thirty for three quarters of the country's total output of goods and services (Koo 1987, Woronoff 1983, Yoo and Lee 1987). The ten largest were sponsored in the 1960s by the Korean government in answer to the perceived threat from Japanese corporations, and in line with a reluctantly acknowledged emulation of the Japanese formula for post-war economic growth. There are, however, two key differences between the *chaebol* as they have developed so far, and the *zaibatsu* which can trace a much longer, if interrupted, lineage. The *zaibatsu* tended to conglomerate around a 'city' bank and trading company which operated in relatively open capital markets and served as the main source of credit; the *chaebol* on the other hand have been, and remain, heavily dependent on the government as the main source of finance. Their dependence on the state is thus much higher. Secondly, each *chaebol* remains very closely associated with a dominant family, that of the entrepreneur chosen for government support; this tradition, visible in pre-war Japanese industry, has now been replaced there by a much wider spread of ownership between firms within business groups and financial institutions together with the emergence of a distinct managerial elite which does not own many shares (Clark 1979, Futatsugi 1986, Yasuoka 1976).

The key characteristics of the *chaebol* may be summarized as follows (Koo 1987, Woronoff 1983, Johnson 1987, Jacobs 1985, Jones and Sakong 1980, Yoo and Lee 1987):

1. large conglomerates, e. g. Samsung 27 companies, Daewoo 17;
2. tendency to focus on one or a small number of industrial sectors, such as heavy industry, construction, electronics;
3. grouped around 'general trading companies' spearheading the government push to export;
4. monopolistic and oligopolistic access to raw materials, production facilities, markets and government-backed research;
5. funded by very high debt and low equity, with government as creditor;
6. strategy making dominated by 'government as chairman of the board';
7. founding families still in dominant decision-making positions;
8. atmosphere of paternalism but with a strongly disciplined flavour;
9. Extensive welfare provisions but no permanent employment, long working hours and low wages.

Thus the dominant form of economic structure in Korea presents a dramatic contrast with that found among the Overseas Chinese, and the understanding of this difference requires some acknowledgement of factors found operating only in the Korean milieu.

The Japanese *Keiretsu/Kaisha*

The classification of forms of economic co-ordination and control in the Japanese economy is made difficult by the semantic confusion involved in the transfer of Japanese phrases into the Western literature. Common reference is now found to *zaibatsu*, *sogo shosha*[1], *kaisha* and *keiretsu*, all

---

[1] The phrase 'Shosha' is a shortened form of 'Shoji Kaisha', meaning trading company. 'Sogo' means 'all round' or general.

of which are significant types, and partially overlapping. It is necessary to clarify what these mean.

A *zaibatsu* is a type of organization, inevitably very large, which typically comprises a bank, an insurance company, a trading company and many industrial companies (Yoshihara 1982: 301). It is particularly associated with pre-war Japan when the four largest (Mitsui, Mitsubishi, Sumitomo and Yasuda) controlled 544 companies accounting for 25% of all industrial capital in Japan. Such organizations were at that time centrally co-ordinated and directed through family-controlled holding companies which were dissolved in 1946 (Yasuoka 1976).

A *sogo shosha* or general trading company is a post-war phenomenon in its current form, the Japanese phrase having been coined in 1954. Yoshihara (1982: 10) suggests that for a trading company to be a *sogo shosha* it should deal with many products, both export and import, have international offices, and wield considerable power in marketing and finance. In particular, it should derive most of its revenues from trading, so that, for instance when Mitsubishi changed its English name in 1971 from Mitsubishi Trading Company to Mitsubishi Corporation, three quarters of its profits were then coming from trading. There are now nine companies which meet these criteria, but that number may shrink as manufacturing interests begin to displace trading as the main source of revenue[2] (McMillan 1985: 230–242).

The word *keiretsu*, which means business group, is used for the modern version of the *zaibatsu*. It stands for the groups which contain a core 'city' bank, but such groups are less centrally co-ordinated than were the *zaibatsu* (Hamilton et al. in this volume). Their strength lies in co-operation via lending and intra-group trading as well as exchanges of directorships and shares (Futatsugi 1986). The concept overlaps with that of *sogo shosha* but allows for the inclusion of many other bank-centred groups whose main role is other than trading.

The recent move away from such large groups towards individual manufacturing companies and their associated subcontractors, or *kaisha*, in Japan is proclaimed by Abegglen and Stalk (1985: 189) in the following terms:

When a list is made of the companies that have led the growth and success of the postwar Japanese economy, few are group members. Toyota, Honda, Hino, and Suzuki in vehicles; Kubota in farm machinery; Shiseido, Kao and Lion in personal

---

[2] In order of size these are Mitsubishi Shoji, Mitsui Bussan, C. Itoh, Marubeni, Sumitomo Shoji, Nissho, Toyo Menka, Kanematsu, Nichimen.

products; Hitachi, Sharp, Sanyo, Matsushita and Sony in electronics; Shionogi and Fujisawa in pharmaceuticals; and Fuji Film, Canon, Ricoh, and Seiko are neither group members, nor bank dependent [...]. They are highly independent companies, with recent entrepreneurial origins. They are the *kaisha* that have succeeded in the sectors of fast-changing consumer markets and high technology. Companies in the traditional groups are large, ponderous and slow-moving. Their businesses are mostly in declining industries (cf. Aoki 1987).

The key characteristics of *kaisha*, as identified by Abegglen and Stalk, are in many ways text book examples of universally relevant efficiency principles. And yet they have a subtle Japanese flavour. Their embeddedness is hinted at by Abegglen and Stalk (1985) when considering the problems of stretching such organizations multinationally.[3]

Many of their strengths arise out of special aspects of Japanese society and culture [...]. These very strengths turn to disadvantage as the *kaisha* must try to deal with personnel, legal structures, and social customs as participants in other societies (1985: 283).

A summary of their main features is as follows:

1. an intensive strategic sensitivity to competitiveness;
2. integrated internally via a powerful corporate culture and a unified workforce (e. g. company union, management not a separate group);
3. high levels of worker commitment via long working hours, low absentee and dispute rates;
4. shareholder as investor rather than controller, with dividends related to par value of shares rather than profit, and an 'inside' board appointed from management ranks. Thus relatively autonomous from short-term financial pressures;
5. linked with an extensive network of subcontractors who are highly dependent but at the same time are supported with technological help;
6. employees, subdivided into a favoured group of permanent skilled employees, and less favoured groups of temporary and part-time employees. Different wage rates;
7. high workforce flexibility based on extensive training in a variety of skills (cf. Koike 1987);
8. salience of seniority as criterion for promotion and status;
9. dedicated to technological innovation as a strategic weapon;
10. open to influence and 'guidance' from government but fundamentally self-governing.

---

[3] On this same point, see also a series of articles on Americans working for Japanese companies in the *Los Angeles Times*, July 10–13, 1988; also Clark 1979, Fukuda 1988, Yoshino 1979.

Enterprise Types in East Asia: Six Dimensions of Variation

These three — or four if we separate *keiretsu* from *kaisha* — types of enterprise structure can now be more systematically compared and contrasted in terms of the six dimensions sketched previously. We begin with the degree of delegated discretion.

In the case of Japan, the move to extensive delegation of resource acquisition and control, although it had been growing throughout the pre-war years, was greatly boosted by the McArthur period of reform and democratization in which the *zaibatsu* were re-organized as public corporations with a wider spread of ownership and with full-time, non-family executives. It could be argued that this trend has gone further than in the U.S., as shareholder influence on the company has declined. As Abegglen and Stalk (1985) note:

The board of directors of the Japanese company consists almost entirely of inside board members, that is, of the senior management of the company. They achieve board member status as they move up in the executive ranks; they are career employees. To the extent that they might be seen as representatives of a constituency, their constituency is the career employees of the company (1985: 185).

This contrasts dramatically with the Chinese family business, where discretion is hardly delegated at all outside the owning group. The family grip on strategy, as on shareholding, is very firm, and the separation of ownership and control is evident in only the rarest of cases.

In Korea the *chaebol* grew at a time when the devastations of war had left a shortage of experienced entrepreneurial talent. Given what Jacobs (1985: 168) has termed 'the time-honoured Korean patrimonial notion of how to organize and exploit an economy', the government's solution was to find trusted entrepreneurs whom it could back with support and to encourage them to build enterprises owned by them but strongly influenced by government. Control of capital by government gave it the ascendancy. This case is thus different again, and suggests that strategic control of the enterprise goes no further down than the dominant coalition of government and family. Inevitably this will be changing as the sheer volume of managerial needs brings non-family managers into the boardroom, but the dependence on state-controlled financial support remains high, and critical for determining the allocation of influence.

The centralization or decentralization of power within the enterprise, although obviously related to the previous dimension, is analysable at a different level of analysis from it. The former takes account of delegation societally; this takes account of delegation organizationally. The former does not necessarily determine the latter, as the contrast between a divisionalized U.S. corporation and a centralized French industrial group indicates.

The Japanese *kaisha* displays extensive decentralization of discretion in decision making down to middle-management levels (Noda 1979). This common characteristic of the Japanese organization is absent in the Chinese family business where power is centralized and where organizational size, in consequence, remains restricted (Pugh and Redding 1986). In the Korean case research data are not currently available to describe the degree of centralization in the *chaebol*, but Korea's patrimonial tradition would suggest strongly that delegation of discretion has not proceeded to anywhere near the same extent as in Japan (cf. Yoo and Lee 1987). Even though organizational size and complexity would inevitably require some downward spread of power, this may be more a matter of what Jacobs terms 'deconcentration' which (albeit in the field of Korean politics) means 'the periphery was mandated to carry out centrally determined initiatives, with local decision-making limited to whatever the centre offered patrimonially on grace or deemed residual to its interests' (1985: 32). Liebenberg's (1982) metaphor for the Korean decision-making style is militaristic, and the disciplined organization, sensitive to hierarchy and patronage, leads us to conclude that centralization is more likely to be natural.

While delegation is clearly a necessary condition of managerial discretion and autonomy, it does not always lead to economic autarky since enterprises may be interlinked, as industrial groups are in France (Levy-Leboyer 1980) and Japan (Hamilton et al., this volume) or may be heavily dependent upon bank credit or state support. An organization such as a 'general trading company' can develop informal ties which are longlasting and stable, and which must be brought into account to explain the organization's behaviour. In the Japanese case the strength of ties with subcontractors is such as to make them, in many senses, *de facto* components of the larger body (Clark 1979) with long-term contracts, extensive training assistance, help with technology, imposition of standards, all flowing downwards to cement the connection. The advantage for the core organization is that it is absolved from legal ties of obligation in matters of employment and finance, and thus the larger enterprise structure is built with great flexibility around the edges, and a consequent ability to resist the shocks of market volatility.

In Japan also, the horizontal ties between organizations have traditionally been significant, especially in the *keiretsu* which are extensively networked by mutually convenient bonds of trading, finance and boardroom information, although they are not managerially co-ordinated from a centre (Clark 1979). The increasing significance of the independent *kaisha* does however suggest an adjustment to this tradition, as it appears to display more manoeuvrability in establishing relationships (Aoki 1987).

Vertical co-ordination in Japan raises the question of government influence on business policy, and here the impression gained is of subtle but indirect strategic guidance and only limited use of open suggestion (Johnson 1982: 265 – 274, Vogel 1978, Hamilton and Biggart 1988). Nevertheless, the influence of government on industry in Japan cannot be denied and must be included in any account of large-enterprise behaviour.

The position in Korea is different. The *chaebol* is much more tightly integrated into being a large and centrally directed conglomerate than would be the case in Japan. Also its links with government are more subservient, depending on government as it does for finance and often for market access. Korea is much more a 'hard' state, where government intentions are carried deep into the base layers of the economy (Jones and Sakong 1980).

In the Overseas Chinese case, co-ordination between enterprises is at the same time informal and stable. The typical Chinese family business tends to stay in one field of specialism, and not to develop a conglomerate form. There are exceptions but they tend to become increasingly unstable, as the central co-ordinating impetus of patrimonialism is diluted. In the typical small-to-medium sized firm extensive networks develop to secure reliable bonds in the interests of assuring inputs and markets. A factory may well use one distribution system in the form of another independent company for decades, rather than develop its own marketing function. Vertical integration is not normally handled within the enterprise but rather by the building of trust bonds between enterprises. The result is that the understanding of how economic action takes place needs to acknowledge the workings of the 'molecular' structures (Redding and Tam 1985).

The role of government for the Overseas Chinese varies substantially within their diaspora. In Hong Kong and Taiwan it is minimal; in most of ASEAN it is a potentially, and often actually, malign force to be co-opted where possible. In these latter cases co-ordination may be at least partly explained by the influence of government but such influence is indirect, and more a matter of a firm adjusting to the realities of government power rather than following a government policy. If anything, ASEAN government policies have hindered the formal co-ordination of large enterprises by the Overseas Chinese (Yoshihara 1988).

In general, the delegation of discretionary control over resource allocation and use can vary independently of enterprise interdependence and co-ordination. The Chinese family business seems to combine a high degree of integration of ownership with managerial direction and control, although 'sleeping partners' are quite often found as well (Silin 1976: 24 – 29) – with considerable reliance on trading houses and domestic and overseas agents (Tam, in this volume). The Korean *chaebol* manifests rather more separation of operational control from family ownership and a correspondingly greater reliance on non-kin managerial hierarchies all in the broad context of considerable inter-enterprise co-ordination by the state Economic Planning Board (Johnson 1987, Jones and Sakong 1980). In contrast, Japanese *keiretsu* and *kaisha* exemplify high degrees of delegation of strategic and operational control from property rights holders and considerable interdependence between members of business groups and between core enterprises and major subcontractors (Hamilton et al., in this volume) all in the broad context of state 'guidance' and 'targeting' by MITI (Johnson 1982: 256 – 303, 1987). In many respects the combination of high delegation and discretion and considerable interdependence and state steering is similar to the large French industrial groups, including their strong ties to jointly owned banks, although family ownership remains important in many French groups (Bauer and Cohen 1981, Levy-Leboyer 1980). Finally, the Chandlerian integrated and diversified U.S. corporation represents relatively high degrees of discretion and low degrees of corporation interdependence and strategy co-ordination.

The question of managerial integration is in essence a question of how much 'management' there is in the enterprise, the implication being that where managerial integration reaches high levels there are:

a. large numbers of professional managers spread throughout the system;
b. management control is exercized systematically, and in pursuit of negotiated and rational objectives;
c. strategy is formulated by managerial teams pursuing their own goals rather than those of major shareholders;
d. an organization structure and a set of operating systems are designed to foster co-ordination both vertically and horizontally.

On these criteria, management in the *kaisha* is highly sophisticated, and corporate loyalty and identity also reinforce formal processes of co-ordination (Noda 1979). Similarly, in the *chaebol*, extensive systematization has taken place, but here the top-down decision-style, and the retention of family dominance in strategy making, make for a different balance of forces, and a relative weakening in the impact of 'professional' management. In the Chinese family business the overt paternalism and the smallness of scale militate against managerial integration and produce an enterprise type at the other end of the spectrum from the Japanese.

It is also worth noting that the Overseas Chinese family business exhibits high degrees of vertical specialization reminiscent of the early British textile industry in Manchester (Lazonick 1986) and diversification into unrelated businesses as the dominant growth strategy. Co-ordination of the different activities is primarily through financial means and kin-based obligations (Redding 1980). In contrast, most other sorts of business enterprise manifest greater degrees of vertical integration and more related diversification strategies together with systematic planning of investments and product flows.

Such integration is at the centre of the concerns in this paper, in that we are advocating a unit of analysis for understanding economic activity which in many cases extends beyond the boundaries of the firm as legal entity. In the Overseas Chinese case, products and services reach the market as a result of coalitions of separate family businesses acting together but basing that action not on legal contractual ties but on ties of informally co-ordinated mutual benefit. This is the means whereby the size limitations are surmounted. An owner-dominated organization, unable to delegate power, will be unable to control many functions within itself if they become very complex. It can, however, be part of a larger network. A factory, for instance, can function as a production department. A shipping and forwarding agent can function as a transport department. A sourcing company can function as a buying department. The informal networking of a series of family businesses can function as the equivalent to the large, integrated bureaucracy in terms of economic resource co-ordination and control.

The question thus arises: what is the unit and what is the sub-unit? If we apply the principle that the end-result of economic resource co-ordination and control is the creation of a product or service, then the unit of analysis for the Overseas Chinese case is a network of small organizations, something termed by Redding and Tam (1985) the 'molecular organisation' in order to capture the idea of a set of connected particles.

Under this definition the integration of such units is at a low degree of formality. Firms move in and out of the arrangement according to market forces. At the same time, because of the high value attached to mutual obligation, the system has more inherent stability in this society than might be the case elsewhere. Integration is thus capable of working effectively without contractual ties or hierarchy.

The integrating process, based as it is on personalistic bonding, reflects Chinese behavioural norms about specific friendship ties, in turn deriving from Confucian teaching. These act as the basis for the reduction of uncertainty in economic transactions and allow the general problem of mistrust to be handled adequately (cf. Zucker 1986).

There are clearly connections between the dimensions under consideration. An organization which is low on formalization and differentiation, and thus tending to be high on more personalistic means of control, is likely at the same time to be highly centralized. Without the formalization of organizational processes it is difficult to maintain predictability of action if decentralization takes place. At the same time, if personalism is the principle means of achieving co-ordination between the sub-units of the economic resource co-ordination system (i. e. separate family businesses closely focused on specific functions), then that system may be taken to have a medium to high score on co-ordination. The force of centralization will play a part here because of the power attached to the head of the organization. Co-ordination becomes a matter of connections between 'all-powerful' individuals and, as long as those connections are mutually beneficial, Chinese social norms will ensure their stability and reliability.

Personalized authority is at first glance connected negatively to the previous dimension of managerial integration but the case of the *chaebol* indicates that they are not mutually exclusive dimensions. The workings of person-alized authority go further than the spread of power from a charismatic chief executive/owner, and the dimension reflects a societal difference in authority patterns. In organizations where authority is personalized, ver-tical ties of obligation which have an emotional content are an important component of the organization's design. The upward flow of loyalty and conformity is exchanged for the downward flow of protection, and this serves to stabilize the structure and to damp down the resentment of subordination which otherwise is institutionalized in industrial relations structures. This characteristic is a standard feature of both the Chinese family business and the *chaebol*. It has also been commonly described for Japan (Clark 1979, Doi 1973, Rohlen 1974, Yoshino 1968) but, in Japan, the ultimate source of an individual manager's authority is an enterprise system designed for the common good of all its members, and he does not thus represent a particular person at the top of the organization. In the Korean case he does.

Silin's (1976) account of Taiwanese enterprises exemplifies highly personal authority principles which result in essentially dyadic relationships between managers and the boss, and little scope at intermediate levels to develop discretion and foster the emergence of distinct units with some autonomy. This focus on personal loyalty and the moral superiority of the leader leads to high degrees of centralization of strategic and operational control, broad and rather diffuse specifications of roles and responsibilities and a low degree of collegiality and co-operation among peer groups. This lack of co-operation and a general lack of trust between non-kin managers stems from such commitment and loyalty being conditional and 'rational' according to Silin (1976: 54 − 67) rather than being emotional as well and linked to a strong sense of identity with the collective enterprise. The moral superiority of enterprise leaders arises from their expertise in understanding the natural and social order and it is manifested by their economic success. As such, they are able to command respect and obedience because of the established norms of piety. Thus, although loyalty is personal, it is not emotionally based and can be withdrawn − as it often is by managers leaving to start their own businesses (Redding 1990). This contingent commitment and the lack of institutionalized trust relations beyond kinship groups in Chinese society encourage insecurity and a fear of non-cooperation in enterprise leaders which in turn encourage classic divide and rule tactics, a lack of delegation and a lack of respect for formal boundaries and roles.

A similar degree of personal loyalty and domination by the enterprise founder and his family seem characteristic of the Korean *chaebol* but they also manifest greater trust in managerial subordinates and a willingness to delegate more operational control and discretion (Cumings 1987, Jones and Sakong 1980). Post-war Japanese companies, in contrast, are more decentralized and rely on elaborate formal hierarchies and boundaries to delimit activities and co-ordinate them. Loyalties are primarily to the work group and the larger enterprise and leaders are not regarded as superior in all areas of expertise but rather in their co-ordination skills. Thus they do not need to resent subordinates' initiative and ability but are rewarded for harnessing it for the success of the work group (Rohlen 1974, Silin 1976: 131 − 138). This emphasis on the work group and collective achievement in Japanese enterprises means that job descriptions and responsibilities are not highly specialized and formally specified, and that co-operation within such groups and departments is relatively easy. This example shows that a lack of strong reliance on personal loyalty need not imply a lack of personal identification with collective enterprises for an entirely formal co-ordination and control system. Instead, large Japanese enterprises seem to combine a high degree of vertical and horizontal solidarity on the basis of extensive training and indoctrination programmes and mutual trust between corporate employers and employees (Abegglen and Stalk 1985: 191 − 213). On the other hand, a high degree of reliance on formal relationships and rule governed compliance can be accompanied by a lack of trust between *cadres* and a highly centralized decision-making system as in the case of many French enterprises (Callon and Vignolle 1977, Crozier 1964, Granick 1972). Here the promotion and stratification system prevents strong identification with the enterprise, and the legitimacy of the top management group stems from their success in the educational system rather than their collective achievements in the firm.

This discussion demonstrates that highly personal authority principles and bases of compliance need not necessarily be associated with strong loyalty to, and identity with, enterprises, although it can do, as Biggart's account of Direct Selling Organizations shows elsewhere in this volume. It also suggests that decentralization does not always accompany formal, legal-rational bases of legitimacy and control, although highly personal loyalty systems do seem to imply a high degree of centralization and relatively diffuse and unstable role specifications, together with rather informal and personal co-ordination and control systems, including appraisal and reward standards.

Societal Contexts

It is clear from the discussion so far that many of these characteristics of dominant forms of economic co-ordination and control are closely associated with those of the societal contexts in which they have become established.

We suggest these societal contexts can be analysed in terms of five main interconnected characteristics, namely:

1. patrimonial authority patterns;
2. trust relations;
3. nature of the state elite,
4. basis of societal elite;
5. inheritance system;

which we will now briefly discuss.

Patrimonial Authority Patterns and Trust Relations

Authority principles within enterprises, of course, are dependent upon general principles of legitimacy and domination in broader social entities such as the different forms of patrimonialism (Hamilton 1984) and legal rational authority. Where the dominant authority system in a society is based on legal-rational norms, highly personal forms of authority in large enterprises are unlikely to prove stable on their own. Equally, managerial control presuming common adherence to 'rational' means of legitimation is unlikely to be effective in patrimonial societies.

A second, related, characteristic concerns trust relations beyond kinship groups. Where these are not strongly institutionalized, large, semi-autonomous managerial bureaucracies are unlikely to become established as Silin (1976) points out. This relative lack of trust and commitment to non-kinship based collectivities has been linked to the particular form of patrimonial authority characteristic of Chinese society for a considerable period (Redding 1990, Silin 1976) in which the right to authority is determined primarily by moral and intellectual considerations and acquired through education and civilized behaviour. The key contrast between this form and Japanese feudalism is the Chinese lack of any reciprocal system of rights and duties between different strata of society and thus of a means of vertically integrating loyalties.

Because the Chinese state bureaucratic elite derives its ascendancy traditionally by exhibiting morally superior qualities, it has no need to demonstrate its efficacy in achieving broader social goals or to justify its authority in terms of fulfilling particular functions. Obligations are thus based on moral status rather than collectively focused achievements and are owed by the morally inferior to the state elite as a matter of role' performance (cf. Hamilton 1984). A further point about Chinese patrimonialism in comparison with Japanese feudalism is its apparent lack of mediating strata and institutions linking the state elite with the mass of the population which could serve as the focus of loyalty and identity (Redding 1990). In Jacobs' (1985) account of Asian patrimonialism this lack of intermediary institutions is the result of deliberate policies of the state bureaucratic elite adopted to prevent any challenge to its power and privileges (cf. Hall 1988). Whatever the reason, it clearly hinders the development of collective social structures, such as large economic enterprises, which could attract loyalty and commitment on an impersonal basis, as it inhibits the necessary de-personalizing of relationships and the growth of alternative norms governing social co-ordination.

In the case of Korea, Jacobs argues that it shares the patrimonial social order of the Asian mainland in contrast with the feudal social order of Japan and that Korea currently exhibits what he terms patrimonial modernization (Jacobs 1985: 8). The related question of trust in the societal context of economic organisations can be characterised in terms of norms of reciprocal obligations between strangers. Essentially, Japanese and Western industrial societies seem to have institutionalized trust relations between relative strangers so that general rules and conventions are followed by large numbers of, for example, employees who do not have strong personal ties to their initiators. Similarly, outside the organizations, transactions can be concluded efficiently between strangers without the commitment of time in establishing a personal trust bond. In many of such aspects the

Western position is more strongly developed than the Japanese, where interpersonal trust would still appear to be quite salient.

There remains, however, a strong contrast in the Chinese case, where obligations and dependence are much more tied to personal bonds. Here it would be irrational to expect strangers to follow general norms of reciprocity in the same way (cf. Gouldner 1956). Thus we could say that obligations are much broader and more intense among Chinese people than in the West, but are restricted to fewer social relationships and ones in which personal knowledge is critical.

Nature of the State Elite and the Basis of Elite Formation

A further aspect of societal authority systems concerns the nature of state elites. Where these do not seek legitimacy from sustained economic growth, are relatively cohesive, and are intolerant of alternative resource-controlling institutions, the development of large, relatively stable economic enterprises controlling substantial resources is unlikely and economic activities will be left to non-elite groups who are not linked to powerful networks. Thus, state legitimacy, autonomy from traditional elites and tolerance of institutional pluralism are critical features of societal contexts in addition to the existence of reciprocal relations of rights and responsibilities between superiors and subordinates.

The main feature which affects the sorts of people who establish and control economic entities and their connections to dominant social institutions is the general pattern of elite formation and activity in a society. Where dominant groups control resources through rentier type activities, either based on land ownership or privileged access to state controlled resources such as licenses and foreign exchange, their involvement in building up large, administratively co-ordinated, economic enterprises is unlikely to be high and, indeed, most entrepreneurial, or putatively entrepreneurial, groups will be more concerned with gaining access to such privileges than establishing independent managerial hierarchies. In these circumstances integrated industrial groups in capital-intensive industries are unlikely to develop and remain significant economic actors, and owners of economic enterprises are unlikely to be accorded high social prestige. Equally, they are unlikely to develop a high degree of cultural self-confidence and security, or invest large resources for long-term growth strategies. This characteristic of elite formation and activity is obviously linked to patterns of land ownership and tenure, and this in turn is connected to the autonomy of the state elite and its willingness and ability to dispossess the traditional land-owning class and push them into economically productive activities. It is clearly not coincidental that Japan, Korea and Taiwan have all undergone major land reforms in the course of their industrialization and that, for different reasons, state elites in these societies have been able to exercise considerable independence of traditional landowners (Cumings 1987, Koo 1987).

Inheritance System

A further important factor in considering the differences between East Asian industrializing societies is the nature of the inheritance system. In Chinese society this is egalitarian while in Japan inheritance is governed by primogeniture. In Korea the system is traditionally egalitarian but with some small advantage provided to the eldest son. Even if in practice unequal inheritance is practised in many expatriate Chinese communities, the strong cultural preferences for equal division of family property acts as a constraint on the reproduction of large, stable economic enterprises controlling substantial resources. As long as they are viewed as part of the family assets and governed by family obligations, such enterprises, by being continually broken up, are unlikely to continue as major economic actors in societies dominated by egalitarian inheritance patterns and thus, in patrimonial societies, be able to function independently of the state bureaucracy (cf. Jacobs 1985: 204–207).

The great longevity of many Japanese economic institutions, with many current firms dating back to the eighteenth century or earlier, is in stark contrast to the Chinese case, where firms normally break up in the third generation. Korea, in this respect, again takes a middle position, and, as Jacobs observes:

Although the Korean patriarch never was as strong as his Japanese counterpart, perhaps because he never absolutely controlled his lineage's common property and was not chosen for his pragmatic ability, nevertheless he was stronger than his Chinese counterpart (Jacobs 1985: 209).

Conclusion

The growth of East Asian economies and business has highlighted the variety of forms of business organization that are economically viable in post-war world markets. In particular, it emphasizes the limitations of the

Chandlerian model of enterprise development and the contingent nature of bureaucratization of economic actors. Chinese family businesses are small, family dominated, centralized, informally but effectively coupled, eschew professional management, rely on personal authority, and do not assume workforce loyalty. They have sprung from an environment of patrimonial authority, general but not specific mistrust, aloof government, a free entrepreneurial environment, and traditions of equal inheritance.

Chaebol are also family dominated, but less centralized, grow extremely large, are elaborately and formally co-ordinated, extensively reliant on professional management, and attract some loyalty from workers. Their environment is also patrimonial, less fraught with mistrust, has a similarly Confucian moral-based government, but highly interventionist, a somewhat free entrepreneurial environment, and a modified version of equal inheritance.

The *kaisha* is 'professionally' managed and decentralized, can become very large, is elaborately co-ordinated, has significant vertical linkages, relies on less personal authority, and attracts high workforce commitment. Its historical context is a state which traditionally fostered local autonomy feudally rather than patrimonially, where trust across society is high, where government retains an aloof but influential position, where entrepreneurship is fostered, and inheritance based on primogeniture.

Forms of economic co-ordination and control thus vary and are closely related to particular features of the context in which they have become institutionalized and develop. In this paper we have sketched briefly some of the ways in which such variations occur and the sorts of contextual factors which affect them.

We have also drawn attention to the critical theoretical issue of the unit of analysis in studying business structures across societies. It is quite clear that the Anglo-Saxon legal-financial entity is only one sort of economic actor, and there are many other ways of structuring business units and co-ordinating their activities. How organizations and firms are constituted and inter-connected are key questions for any comparative analysis of enterprise structure and development and clearly depend on particular features of their societal contexts. We suggest that concentrating on the dominant units of economic action helps to overcome some of the problems of comparative organizational analysis and forces us to consider how these particular kinds of units develop and become established in different kinds of ways in different sorts of society.

References

Abegglen, J. and G. W. Stalk (1985): *Kaisha*, New York: Basic Books.

Aoki, M. (1987): The Japanese firm in transition, in: K. Yamamura and Y. Yazuba (eds.), *The political economy of Japan I: The domestic transformation*, 159 – 206, Stanford, Cal.: Standford University Press.

Bauer, M. and E. Cohen (1981): *Qui gouverne les groupes industriels?* Paris, Seuil.

Callon, M. and J. P. Vignolle (1977): Breaking down the organization: local conflicts and systems of action, *Social Science Information* 16: 147 – 167.

Chandler, A. D. and H. Daems (eds.) (1980): *Managerial hierarchies*, Cambridge, Mass.: Harvard University Press.

Clark, R. (1979): *The Japanese company*, New Haven: Yale University Press.

Crozier, M. (1964): *The bureaucratic phenomenon*, London: Tavistock.

Cumings, B. (1987): The origins and development of the Northeast Asian political economy, in: F. C. Deyo (ed.), *The political economy of the new Asian industrialism*, 62 – 95, Ithaca, N. Y.: Cornell University Press.

Deyo, F. C. (ed.) (1987): *The political economy of the new Asian industrialism*, Ithaca, N. Y.: Cornell University Press.

Doi, T. (1973): *The anatomy of dependence*, Tokyo: Kodansha International.

Encaoua, D. and A. Jacquemin (1982): Organizational efficiency and monopoly power: the case of French industrial groups, *European Economic Review* 19: 25 – 51.

Fukuda, K. J. (1988): *Japanese-style management transferred: the experience of East Asia*, London: Routledge.

Futatsugi, Y. (1986): *Japanese enterprise groups*, Kobe: University School of Business Administration.

Gouldner, A. W. (1973): The norm of reciprocity, in: Gouldner, A. W., *For sociology: renewal and critique in sociology today*, New York: Basic Books.

Granick, D. (1972): *Managerial comparisons in four developed countries*, Boston, Mass.: MIT Press.

Granovetter, M. (1985): Economic action and social structure: the problem of embeddedness, *American Journal of Sociology* 91, 3: 481 – 510.

Hall, J. A. (1988): States and societies: the miracle in comparative perspective, in: J. Baechler et al. (eds.), *Europe and the rise of capitalism*, 121 – 159, Oxford: Blackwells.

Hamilton, G. (1984): Patriarchalism in imperial China and Western Europe, *Theory and Society* 13: 393 – 426.

Hamilton, G. and N. W. Biggart (1988): Market, culture and authority: a comparative analysis of management and organization in the Far East, *American Journal of Sociology*, Special Supplement on The Sociology of the Economy.

Jacobs, N. (1985): *The Korean road to modernization and development*, Urbana, Ill.: University of Illinois Press.

Johnson, C. (1982): *MITI and the Japanese miracle*, Stanford, Cal.: Stanford University Press.

Johnson, C. (1987): Political institutions and economic performance: the govt-business relationship in Japan, South Korea and Taiwan, in: F. C. Deyo (ed.),

The Political Economy of the New Asian Industrialism, 139–162, Ithaca, N.Y.: Cornell University Press.

Jones, L. P. and Il Sakong (1980): *Government, business and entrepreneurship in economic development: the Korean case,* Cambridge, MA: Harvard University Press.

Kiyonari, T. and H. Nakamura (1980): The establishment of the Big Business system in: K. Sato (ed.), *Industry and business in Japan,* 150–192, New York, M. E. Sharpe.

Kocka, J. (1980): The rise of the modern industrial enterprise in Germany, in: A. D. Chandler and H. Daems (eds.), *Managerial hierarchies,* 77–98, Cambridge, Mass.: Harvard University Press.

Koike, K. (1987): Human resource development and labour-management relations in: K. Yamamura and Y. Yasuba (eds.), *The political economy of Japan I,* 206–224, Stanford, Cal.: Stanford University Press.

Koo, H. (1987): The interplay of state, social class, and world system in East Asian development: the cases of South Korea and Taiwan, in: F. C. Deyo (ed.), *The political economy of the new Asian industrialism,* 41–61, Ithaca, N.Y.: Cornell University Press.

Lazonick, W. (1986): The cotton industry, in: B. Elbaum and W. Lazonick (eds.), *The decline of the British economy,* Oxford: Clarendon Press.

Levy-Leboyer, M. (1980): The large corporation in modern France, in: A. D. Chandler and H. Daems (eds.), *Managerial hierarchies,* 32–56, Cambridge, Mass.: Harvard University Press.

Liebenberg, R. D. (1982): Japan Incorporated and 'The Korean Troops': a comparative analysis of Korean business organizations, unpublished MA dissertation, University of Hawaii.

Limlingan, V. S. (1986): *The overseas Chinese in ASEAN: business strategies and management practices,* Manila: Vita Development Corporation.

Locke, R. (1984): *The end of the practical man,* Greenwich, Conn.: JAI Press.

McMillan, C. (1985): *The Japanese industrial system,* Berlin: de Gruyter.

Noda, K. (1979): Big Business organization, in: E. Vogel (ed.), *Modern Japanese organization and decision making,* 31–59, Tokyo: Tuttle.

Penrose, E. T. (1959): *The theory of the growth of the firm,* Oxford: Blackwell.

Pugh, D. S. and S. G. Redding (1986): Variations in formalization: a study of Chinese and Japanese contrasts, International Association of Psychologists Conference, Tel Aviv, 1986.

Redding, S. G. (1980): Cognition as an aspect of culture and its relation to management processes: an exploratory view of the Chinese case, *Journal of Management Studies* 17, 2: 127–148.

Redding, S. G. (1990): *The spirit of Chinese capitalism,* Berlin: de Gruyter.

Redding, S. G. and D. S. Pugh (1986): The formal and the informal: Japanese and Chinese organization structures, in: S. R. Clegg, D. C. Dunphy and S. G. Redding (eds.), *The enterprise and management in East Asia,* 108–132, Hong Kong: Centre of Asian Studies.

Redding, S. G. and S. Tam (1985): Networks and molecular organizations: an exploratory view of Chinese firms in Hong Kong, in: K. C. Mun and T. S. Chan (eds.), *Perspectives in international business,* 129 – 142, Hong Kong: Chinese University Press.

Rohlen, T. P. (1974): *For harmony and strength: Japanese white-collar organization in anthropological perspective,* Berkeley, Cal.: University of California Press.

Scott, J. and C. Griff (1984): *Directors of industry,* Oxford: Polity Press.

Silin, R. H. (1976): *Leadership and values: the organization of large-scale Taiwanese enterprises,* Cambridge, MA: Harvard University Press.

Suleiman, E. N. (1978): *Elites in French society,* Princeton, N. J.: Princeton University Press.

Tsuchiya, M. (1976): Management organization of vertically integrated non-zaibatsu business, in: K. Nakagawa (ed.), *Strategy and structure of Big Business,* 109 – 145, Tokyo: University of Tokyo Press.

Vogel, E. (1978): Guided free enterprise in Japan, *Harvard Business Review* 56. 3: 161 – 170.

Whitley, R. D. (1987): Taking firms seriously as economic actors: towards a sociology of firm behaviour, *Organization Studies* 8: 125 – 147.

Williamson, O. (1975): *Markets and hierarchies,* New York: Free Press.

Woronoff, J. (1983): *Korea's economy: Man-made miracle,* Seoul: Si-sa-yong-o-sa Publishers Inc.

Yasuoka, S. (1976): The tradition of family business in the strategic decision process and management structure of *zaibatsu* business, in: K. Nakagawa (ed.), *Strategy and structure of Big Business,* 45 – 70, Tokyo: Univ. of Tokyo Press.

Yoo, S. and S. M. Lee (1987): Management style and practice of Korean *chaebols,* *California Management Review* 29: 95 – 110.

Yoshihara, K. (1982): *Sogo Shosha: the vanguard of the Japanese economy,* Tokyo, Oxford University Press.

Yoshihara, K. (1988): *The rise of ersatz capitalism in South-East Asia,* Singapore, Oxford University Press.

Yoshino, M. Y. (1968): *Japan's managerial system,* Cambridge, MA: MIT Press.

Yoshino, M. Y. (1979): Emerging Japanese multinational enterprise, in: E. F. Vogel (ed.), *Modern Japanese organizational decision-making,* 60 – 87, Tokyo: C. E. Tuttle.

Zucker, L. G. (1986): Production of trust: institutional sources of economic structure 1840 – 1920, *Research in Organizational Behaviour* 8: 53 – 111.

The Network Structures of East Asian Economies

Gary G. Hamilton, William Zeile and Wan-Jin Kim

Introduction

East and Southeast Asia continues to develop economically at a rapid rate. During the 15-year period between 1965 and 1980, Japan and the East Asian NICs[1] grew at an average annual rate of 8.8%. The four major ASEAN-member economies[2] followed closely behind with an average annual growth rate of 7.1%. These growth rates compare with a 2.9% average annual growth rate for the United States economy and a 3.7% average rate for all industrial market economies during the same period. More recently, in the period 1980−85, despite a downturn in the world economy, the East Asian NICs slowed only slightly to an annual growth rate of 6.6%. In the same interval Japan's average annual growth rate dipped to 3.8%, and that of the industrial market economies to 2.5%[3]. Japan, of course, remains by far the largest and most developed capitalist economy in the area, but the other NICs are nearing, if they have not already entered, the period of mature capitalism.

Underlying this rapid economic growth has been the parallel development of powerful business groups. There is a large literature in Western languages on modern Asian economies, most of which attempts to explain the fact and rapidity of growth. But Western scholars have written relatively little on the organizational patterns of Asian economic growth[4]. Therefore,

---

[1] The countries being considered in these figures are Japan, South Korea, Taiwan, Hong Kong and Singapore.

[2] These four are Malaysia, Thailand, Indonesia and the Philippines.

[3] The above figures are all unweighted averages calculated from the *World Development Report* 1987, except for the Taiwan figures, which were calculated from *Taiwan Statistical Data Book* 1987.

[4] Much of the development literature on East Asia focuses on the export-oriented policy regimes of the region's most successful economies. Recent examples include the contributions in Balassa et al. (1982), Galenson (1985) and Bradford and Branson (1987). There does exist a fairly extensive literature on Japanese industrial organization, some of which deals with Japan's business groups. Examples include Rotwein (1964), Caves and Uekusa (1976), Sato (1980) and Aoki (1984).

although Asian business groups are a common topic for Asian journalists, they are rarely the subject of scholarly attention.

Despite the lack of detailed analyses on Asian industrial organization, scattered writings reveal the presence of large, economically powerful groups throughout the entire region. Phipatseritham and Yoshihara (1983) discuss the basic set of groups that control important segments of Thailand's rapidly developing economy. In an important and provocative study of capital formation in Indonesia Robison (1986) shows that a handful of politically blessed business groups control much of the private sector of the economy. Lim Mah Hui (1981), Gale (1986) and Sieh (1982) have discussed a similar set of groups that undergird the Malaysian economy, and Lim Mah Hui and Fong (1986) make a similar argument for Singapore, as does Yoshihara (1985) for the Philippines. Very little has been written about business groups in Hong Kong, but even a cursory look at the stock exchange statistics (Stock Exchange of Hong Kong 1986) shows that one business group alone, the Hong Kong and Shanghai Bank group, consisting of over 34 subsidiary (over 50% ownership) and associated (under 50% ownership) firms (Hong Kong and Shanghai Banking Corporation 1987), controls over 12% of the total market capitalization for the colony[5].

In all these locations throughout Southeast Asia business groups dominate the economic landscape, where they comprise a significant percentage of the modern industrial and financial sectors of these economies. Business groups, however, are also significant and economically powerful in the most developed industrial economies of the region: in Japan, South Korea and Taiwan. In this paper we offer an empirically based, comparative analysis of business group structure in these three countries. In the following sections we show that what is defined as business groups in the economic literature is, in fact, not a unitary phenomenon, but rather differs in important ways in each location. At a minimum, business groups should be conceptualized as networks of firms, but it should be recognized from the outset that these networks are configured differently, and perform different economic operations, in different locations. The respective business groups grew at approximately the same rate or faster than that of the

---

[5] The Hong Kong and Shanghai Banking group of firms is an international network of largely financial firms. This 12% figure, however, only includes Hong Kong located assets. In addition to the bank itself, several other subsidiary companies are listed on the Hong Kong Stock Exchange, including the Hang Seng Bank, of which Hong Kong Bank owns over 60% of the shares. According to the *Asian Wall Street Journal* (April 11, 1985, p. 1), the Hong Kong Bank itself holds 'more than ⅔ of the net worth of all Hong Kong incorporated banks. It holds an estimated 60% of local deposits and issues the bulk of Hong Kong's currency'.

general economy, but in each location they grew in distinctive ways. These findings suggest that an adequate theory of business groups needs to go beyond narrowly defined economic and political dimensions to include institutional and organizational features of the host societies.

Business Groups

What is a business group? Perhaps one of the reasons that business groups have only rarely been the subject of systematic investigations is that they are usually equated with what is, in the United States, a corporate form of business organization. Business groups, however, are not corporations in the conventional meaning of that term[6]. As a rule, business groups are composed of a set of legally independent firms which may or may not have economic or fiscal relationships among themselves and which normally have no overarching accounting or management systems that coordinate the activity of member firms. In some cases, all the firms in the group are at least partially owned by a core firm, sometimes a holding company, a bank or a key manufacturing firm. At other times, an individual or a small group of individuals, sometimes a family, owns or controls all the firms in the group. In a few cases, however, particularly in the Japanese case, which is the key example of an economy organized through business groups, no one firm or set of individuals owns or controls the business groups. Therefore, even consolidated ownership is not their defining characteristic. Instead, the defining characteristic of business groups is that they are organized networks of independent firms, with the nature, manner and consequence of their organization left open to investigation.

Using this sort of minimalist definition, a small group of analysts have begun to examine business groups in a number of developed and developing market economies[7]. A large portion of the existing studies deal with mature capitalist societies (Caves 1987), particularly with Japanese business

---

[6] In the United States, corporations have a precise legal meaning. In much of the business history and economic literature (e. g., Chandler 1977) the corporation refers, in a more restricted sense, to multi-divisional business organizations.

[7] For a survey of some of this literature, see Caves, forthcoming. A much larger literature about these business groups exists outside of economics, most of which deals broadly and often impressionistically with the political economies of capitalist societies. Hamilton and Biggart (1988) give some indication of this literature in regard to Asian business groups, and Stokman, Ziegler and Scott (1985) in regard to European business groups.

groups[8], but also with French (Encaoua and Jacquemin 1982), Belgian (Daems 1978, Stokman et al. 1985) and West German (Cable 1985, Stokman et al. 1985) examples. There is also a smaller and, generally speaking, less economically sophisticated literature on business groups in developing societies. In addition to those examples in Southeast Asia cited above, scholars have examined business groups in Central and South America and in South Asia[9]. Although the literature is scattered and written from diverse points of view, one can, nonetheless, conclude that business groups are neither products of particular stages in economic development nor products of particular cultural groups. What they do stem from, however, is less clear.

Generally speaking, analysts offer two types of explanations for business groups. The first and most developed type of explanation draws, more or less exclusively, upon economic factors and generally rests upon theories of market imperfections. These 'market imperfection' explanations treat business groups as outward extensions of firms, as organizational layers that exist between firms and markets, which allows firms to operate with greater efficiencies in market economies (Caves 1987, Goto 1982). With this explanation, the phenomenon of business groups is brought under the general theory of the firm (see Putterman 1986) and explained by it.

From this point of view, analysts argue that firms develop more complex organizational structures in response to market constraints. In the hypothetical situation in which markets operate with perfect efficiency, and in which market transactions allocate all resources, firms will remain small and business groups will not develop at all. What causes firms to expand and business groups to form are imperfections in the market's ability to allocate resources efficiently. Given imperfect markets, firms and groups of firms administer the allocation process through authoritative organizations, in the case of firms, and through quasi-authoritative organizations, in the case of business groups. In this sense, business groups should be viewed as a type of organizational network located between firms and markets. As Goto (1982: 69) notes, 'the (business) group is an institutional device designed to cope with market failure as well as internal organization failure. Under certain circumstances, transactions within a group of firms are more efficient than transactions through the market or transactions through the internal organization of the firm'.

---

[8] For a survey of the relevant Japanese literature on Japanese business groups, see Orru, Hamilton and Suzuki (1987). Also see Gerlach (1987).

[9] For a bibliography and summary of these studies, see Leff 1978.

A variant of this explanation is that, in those countries having underdeveloped markets, business groups develop to counter the absence of markets in certain products and services. According to Leff (1978: 667), 'the institution of the group is thus an intrafirm mechanism for dealing with deficiencies in the markets for primary factors, risk, and intermediate products in the developing countries'. Leff (1978: 667) views the formation of business groups as constituting an entrepreneurial breakthrough that opens channels of inputs and outputs 'where routinized market mechanism does not exist'.

Market imperfection theories offer a 'bottom-up' explanation for business groups that gives causal priority to a narrow range of economic variables. Businessmen seize the opportunity to reduce transaction costs between firms and thereby achieve greater allocative efficiencies and competitive advantages vis-à-vis other firms in the same market, by establishing networks of firms. Firms are the basic unit of the process, and business groups represent outward extensions that allow firms to co-ordinate their activities in ways that neither markets nor firms are able to accomplish.

From this point of view, a reasonable test of the efficacy of business groups is whether or not such networks offer greater allocative efficiencies than would occur without them. On the one hand, a finding that they, in fact, offer greater efficiencies would imply, in theory, that the economy in which they are found contains systematic market constraints that undermine fully efficient markets. Business groups would then represent a 'natural' organizational response designed to overcome existing market imperfections to attain, through networking, what can neither be attained through markets alone nor through expanding the size of firms (i. e. vertical integration). On the other hand, a finding that business groups offer fewer allocative efficiencies would imply that they are 'artificial' or 'unnatural' groups, which in themselves, by forming a cartel, undermine efficient markets. This is the substance of the second type of explanation.

The bottom up economic theories are in direct contrast with the 'top down' political theories for business groups offered by political economists. From a political economy perspective, business groups form as a result of collusions between political officials and business elites. In this sense they are 'unnatural' monopolies that represent 'corruptions' of both political and economic processes. Robison (1986), for instance, argues that Indonesian business groups represent long-term, mutually enriching alliances between the local military forces and Chinese businessmen. Similarly, Evans (1979) shows that the prominence of Brazilian capitalists, as well as the firm networks they have created, can be explained by showing their linkages to the state and to international capital. A number of similar explanations exist for East Asian business groups. Koo (1984) argues that Korean business groups (called *chaebol*) were a creation of an authoritarian state. Hadley (1970) and Johnson (1982) show the linkages between the Japanese state and the Japanese business groups. Numazaki (1986) and Gold (1986) show the same relationship between the Taiwan state and business networks. Finally, Cumings (1984) and Haggard and Cheng (1986) give a political economy explanation for the economic success, as well as for the formation of business groups, throughout the region.

The political economy explanation of business groups has not been set down in a formal manner. Bruce Cumings (1984), however, gives one of the best summaries of the principal elements in reference to Northeast Asia. Cumings argues that bureaucratic, authoritarian states characterize many of the countries outside the capitalist core, including those in East Asia. States in this area, however, have been particularly successful in their attempts to industrialize, because the capitalist core gave them favored treatment resulting in what Wallerstein (cited by Cumings 1984) calls 'development by invitation'. In East Asian countries, as well as in other newly industrializing countries, the state apparatus itself directs the economic development of the society through preferential linkages between indigenous business elites and international capital. Such linkages allow business elites to develop oligopolistic control over key industrial sectors, thus creating business groups — the skewed formations of large firms and the politically supported networks linking them.

Although there is, conceivably, some overlap between the two types of explanations[10], in theoretical terms, they are opposed. The economic theories explain business groups from the bottom up, as a result of essential economic processes in flawed markets, and the political theories, from the top down, as a result of collusive, authoritarian and sometimes straightforwardly corrupt political practices.

In the following analysis we argue that both the market imperfection and the political economy explanations of business groups focus too narrowly on single sets of causal variables. They both miss the crucial organizational features of business groups that explain their structural form as well as their operational characteristics within economies. By means of our comparative analysis, we suggest that market and political factors are both

---

[10] An implicit overlap is found in Gerschenkron's theory (1965) that successful late developing societies require strong states to direct resources and create markets where there were none previously or where so many impediments existed that no market developments could occur.

important, but that both are mediated through an institutional framework that shapes their influence.

The first step in our analysis is simply to describe the role of business groups in the three economies. Afterward, we analyze some of the network characteristics of each country's business groups. In the conclusion, we contrast the economic and political explanations with the institutional explanation that we develop.

East Asian Business Groups and Economic Concentration

In this section, we describe East Asian business groups in terms of economic concentration. Conventional measures of concentration rest upon the firm as the basic unit of analysis (Curry and George 1983). The most common measure represents a ratio of the cumulative share of the Kth firm. For the aggregate concentration in the total economy, the 'top 100' is the most frequently used figure for K. For industrial sectors, the values assigned to K are more varied (normally between 3 and 8), but regardless of the value of K, firms remain the basic unit of measurement[11].

Measuring the economic concentration of business groups raises some conceptual as well as some measurement problems. This is not the location to discuss these problems in detail[12]. It is sufficient to note that firm-based and business group-based concentration measures are incommensurable.

Table 1 outlines the general characteristics of the business groups in each of the three countries. Tables 2 and 3 show the differences between the two ways to calculate aggregate concentration for the three societies. As

[11] There are a number of alternative ways to measure firm concentration at the individual market level, including the widely-used Herfindahl – Hirschman Index. In this paper we are concerned with measuring aggregated concentration, rather than monopoly power in narrowly-defined markets.

[12] If economic concentration is to be a useful concept that reflects or at least describes actual features of an economy, then the basic units of measurement should reflect these features. The United States has an economy in which business groups, though present, are not a dominant organizational feature. Therefore, using the firm as the basic unit to measure aggregate concentration is appropriate. However, to assess concentration in Asian economies where business groups do matter, with only conventional firm-based measures, misses some of the basic features of concentration. Using both firm- and group-based measures, and determining the relation between the two sets of measures, allows much greater precision in actually assessing economic concentration in East Asia, as well as understanding the impact of industrial organization upon these economies.

Table 1   General Characteristics of Business Groups

	Japan 1982 Keir + IGs	Korea 1983 50 *chaebol*	Taiwan 1983 96 BGs
Total Sales	217,033 Bill. Y	54,663 Bill. Won	633.7 Bill. NT$
Equivalent Billion US$	871.26	68.32	16.48
No. of Workers	2,841,000	795,000	330,000
No. of Firms	1,001	552	745
Firms/Business groups	62.60	11.04	7.76
Workers/Firm	2,838	1,440	444
Percentage of Total Workforce	9.5	5.5	4.7

Sources: Dodwell 1984, Hankook Ilbo 1985, Zhonghua Zhenxinso 1985.

the tables reveal, the set representing the top 100 firms neither is contained within nor is conterminous with the set of firms that are members of business groups. In all three locations business groups contain firms of many different sizes, the majority of which are quite modest[13]. This mixture of firm size within business groups, as well as the variation in this characteristic among the three countries, is an important feature of their operation within the respective economies. Moreover, especially for Taiwan, some of the largest firms in these economies are not members of business groups[14].

Table 3 also shows that business group concentration differs markedly in the three societies. Korean business groups make up a very large proportion of the total economy, as measured in various ways. Japan and Taiwan business group concentrations fall somewhat behind that of Korea, but they still reveal that business groups form sizeable proportions of the totals.

What is most significant, however, is not the aggregate figure, but rather the lack of an even distribution of business groups through these economies. As shown in Table 4, business group concentration varies considerably between sectors within economies, as well as between countries. In all three

---

[13] For example, even in the case of Korea, the country with the largest firms on average, the top 20 business groups average some 17 member firms. However, for most groups the top four firms account for over 70% of aggregate group sales turnover (Lee 1985).

[14] Some of the largest firms in both Taiwan and Korea are government or quasi government firms. This is especially the case in Taiwan, where 19 of the largest 50 companies are government-run enterprises. In 1981 public enterprises accounted for 17.9% of Taiwan's total industrial production, including 14.5% of manufacturing and 44.7% of mining production (*Taiwan Statistical Data Book* 1987). Public enterprises in Korea accounted for an average 8.6% share of GDP during the period 1975–80 (Song 1985).

Table 2 Aggregate Concentration Ratios for Top 100 Non-financial and Manufacturing Enterprises (Percentages)

	Share of assets (non-financial enterprises)	Share of assets (manufacturing)	Share of sales (manufacturing)	Share of employment (manufacturing)	Number of group member firms among top 100 enterprises[7]
Japan (1980)[1]	24.1	33.8	27.3	—	65
South Korea (1980)[2]	—	—	46.3	19.4	53[8]
Taiwan (1981)[3]	—	21.2	19.7	8.9	40
Unites States (1976)[4]	30.6[5]	45.5	(34)[6]	24.0	—

[1] Nakamura 1984: 50−90 and Dodwell 1984−85.

[2] Chu 1985.

[3] Figures for Taiwan are for the top 100 private manufacturing firms (State-run enterprises are not included). China Credit Information Service, *Top 500: The Largest Industrial Corporations in the Republic of China, 1982; Report on 1981 Industrial and Commercial Census, Taiwan-Fukien Area, Republic of China,* v. III; and China Credit Information Service, *Business Groups in Taiwan,* 1985.

[4] White 1981, 223−230.

[5] Figure for 1975.

[6] Share of value added.

[7] Group membership defined as financial association with 16 major industrial groups in Japan (using the broadest definition given by Dodwell), ownership by top 30 *chaebol* in Korea, and ownership by top 96 business groups in Taiwan. 'Top 100 enterprises' refers to top non-financial enterprises in Japan and South Korea and to top private manufacturing enterprises in the case of Taiwan.

[8] Figure for 1977.

countries business groups' sales represent a large proportion of the total sales in manufacturing, but a much smaller share of sales in mining. Business groups dominate the financial sector in Japan and account for a sizeable share of construction in Korea. Business group activity in trade and commerce is quite large in both Japan and Korea, but quite small in Taiwan[15].

[15] This is explained by the presence in Japan and Korea (and the absence in Taiwan) of large general trading companies affiliated with the major business groups. Japan's general trading companies *Sogo Shosha* have a long history of association with business groups. Today the top nine companies presently handle 45% of Japan's exports and 77% of its imports. Korea's general trading companies were created in 1975 as part of the government's effort to promote exports. Today the seven major general trading companies (all *chaebol*-member firms) handle 48% of Korea's exports and 17% of its imports (Lee 1987).

Table 3   Business Group Concentration Ratios (Percentages)

	Proportion of total paid-up capital (non-financial enterprises)	Ratio: total non-financial sales to GDP	Value-added contribution to GDP	Manufacturing sales ratio	Manufacturing employment ratio
Japan (F. Y. 1982)[1]					
6 intermarket groups	18.4	61.7[4]	–	20.3	12.6
16 major groups	25.9	81.2[4]	–	33.2	20.4
Taiwan (1983)[2]					
Top 20 groups	–	17.6	–	14.1	8.3
Top 96 groups	–	27.3	–	19.0	13.0
Korea (1983)[3]					
Top 20 groups	–	– (73.6)[4]	–	36.0	15.3
Top 50 groups	–	84.3 (89.6)[4]	19.1	45.4	22.9

[1] Dodwell 1984–85 and *Japan Statistical Yearbook, 1984*.
[2] *Business Groups in Taiwan 1983–84* (China Credit Information Service, 1983); *Report on Industrial and Commercial Surveys, Taiwan Area, Republic of China, 1983*; *Taiwan Statistical Data Book, 1987* (CEPD, 1987); and *Yearbook of Labor Statistics, Republic of China, 1986*.
[3] *Firm Directory of Korea for 1985* (Daily Economic News, 1986); *Korea's Fifty Major Groups for 1983 and 1984* (MERI, 1985); *Economic Statistics Yearbook, 1986* (Bank of Korea, 1986); Lee, Kyu-Uck 1986.
[4] Ratio of Total Sales (including Finance and Insurance) to GDP.

Within manufacturing, we see a large variation in business group sales shares across industrial sectors (Table 5). At this point, we can begin clearly to see systematic differences among business group concentrations in the three countries. In Taiwan business groups dominate (i. e. account for more than 50% of total sales) only one industrial sector (i. e. textiles) and make sizeable contributions (i. e. between 25 and 50% of total sales) in three more sectors; in Japan business groups dominate three industrial sectors (basic metals production, electrical and electronic products and transportation equipment) and make sizeable contributions in five others; but in Korea business groups dominate five industrial sectors (basic chemicals, petroleum, rubber products, electrical and electronics and transportation equipment) and make sizeable contributions to eight other sectors. Among the sectors dominated by business groups, there are only two overlapping cases among the three economies: the electrical and electronics products and transportation equipment sectors for Japan and Korea. For all three countries in common, business groups dominate or make sizeable contri-

Table 4   Business Group Shares by Broad Economic Sector

Sector	Japan (Sales share of 16 major groups, fiscal year 1982)[1]	Korea (1986 value added share of top 50 chaebol)[2]	Taiwan (1983 sales share of 96 largest groups)[3]
Mining	17.6	4.1	0.0
Manufacturing	33.2	28.3	19.0
Construction	14.7	31.9	5.6
Transport & Storage	22.1	19.7	1.8
Banking & Financial Services	84.6	−	5.8
Trading & Commerce	24.2	17.0	4.1

[1] Calculations based on sales data for all sectors except Banking, for which the share of total bank loans was calculated. The ratio reported for Transport & Storage is for Land and Marine Transport only Dodwell 1984−85 and *Japan Statistical Yearbook, 1984*, Tables 11-1 and 12-8.

[2] *Financial Analysis Note of Top 50 Chaebol of Korea* (1986) and *Economic Statistics Yearbook, 1987* (Bank of Korea 1987).

[3] For Construction, the 1983 total sales figure used to calculate the ratio was estimated using reported index numberes for building construction and the transactions figures in the 1984 Input−Output Tables for Taiwan. Total sales figures for the other sectors come from the 1983 industrial census. For the Transport & Storage and Banking & Financial Services sectors, revenue figures are used. [*Business Groups in Taiwan 1983−84* (China Credit Information Service 1983); *Report on Industrial and Commercial Survey, Taiwan Area, Republic of China, 1983*; *1984 Input−Output Tables, Taiwan Area, Republic of China*; and *Taiwan Statistical Data Book, 1987* (CEPD 1987).]

butions to sector sales in just four cases: textiles, chemicals, non-metallic mineral products and electrical and electronic products.

If we only consider such aggregate measures of concentration, one might conclude that Korean business groups are substantially more significant to the Korean economy than they are in the other two cases. Although Korean business groups certainly dominate that economy, the comparative assertion of their significance needs some qualification. The reason is that these measures of concentration do not also control for differences in the placement and organization of business groups within the economy. If we examine each of these industrial sectors in terms of product characteristics (i. e. proportion of intermediate and final products, relative factor intensity in production and proportion of products exported), then further differences emerge among the three locations.

Table 6 reports the correlations for each country between business group concentration in manufacturing sectors and product characteristics of those sectors. The results indicate that Taiwan business groups predominate in

Table 5 Business Group Shares by Manufacturing Sector (Percentages)

	Japan (16 major enterprise groups)[1]	Korea (top 50 *chaebol*)[2]	Taiwan (96 largest enterprise groups)[3]
Food Products	18.2[4]	33.7	26.3
Beverage & Tobacco	–	27.6	3.8
Textiles	28.2	38.4	50.7
Garments & Apparel	–	12.6	12.0
Leather Products	–	15.2	9.1
Lumber & Wood Products	–	31.5	4.0
Pulp & Paper Products; Printing & Publishing	17.7	6.5	20.1
Chemical Materials	40.0[5]	54.3	42.4
Chemical Products	–	24.0	8.4
Petroleum & Coal Products	40.2	91.9	0.0
Rubber Products	37.5	76.8	13.0
Plastic Products	N. A.	0.1	5.4
Non-Metallic Mineral Products	29.0	44.6	47.6
Basic Metal	58.1	28.0	7.8
Metal Products	4.0	26.7	6.0
Machinery	19.5	34.9	3.6
Electrical & Electronic Products	55.4	50.9	22.7
Transportation Equipment	80.7	79.0	23.6
Precision Machinery	12.3	14.0	0.0
Miscellaneous Industrial Products	3.0	5.2	10.7

[1] Calculated from sales data for fiscal year 1982. Dodwell 1984–85 and *Japan Statistical Yearbook, 1984,* Tables 6-6 and 11-1.

[2] Calculated from 1983 sales data for each *chaebol*-member firm and 1983 industrial census data. [*Firm Directory of Korea for 1985* (Daily Economic News, 1986), *Korea's Fifty Major Groups for 1983 and 1984* (MERI 1985), and *Report on Industrial Census for 1983* (EPB 1985).]

[3] Calculated from 1983 sales data for each group-member firm and 1983 industrial census data. [*Business Groups in Taiwan 1983–84* (China Credit Information Service 1983) and *Report on Industrial and Commercial Survey, Taiwan Area, Republic of China, 1983.*

[4] Includes Beverage and Tobacco.

[5] Chemical Products aggregated together with Chemical Materials.

intermediate goods sectors, and thus have important forward linkages with other sectors in the economy. In contrast, business group concentration in Japan and Korea is only loosely associated with production for intermediate use[16]. For all three economies, business group concentration by sector

[16] Note the difference between the manufacturing sales share for Korea's top 50 *chaebol* and their value-added share in GNP (Tables 3 and 4). This can be explained by the presence of large *chaebol* enterprises in downstream positions in the flow of production, since the value of sales of final goods embodies the value added in all previous stages of production.

Table 6   Correlations Between Business Group Sales Shares and Sector Characteristics (20 Manufacturing Sectors for Korea and Taiwan, 13 Manufacturing Sectors for Japan)[1]

Sector Characteristics[2]	Japan (16 major groups, fiscal year 1982)	Korea (top 50 *chaebol*, 1983)	Taiwan (96 largest groups (1983)
Intermediate Demand Ratio[3]	0.152	0.197	0.419 (0.496)
Labour Share of Value Added[4]	−0.303	−0.487	−0.065 (−0.406)
Export Share[5]	0.234	−0.005	−0.273 (−0.354)

[1] Manufacturing sectors and corresponding business group sales ratios for Korea and Taiwan are those reported in Table 5. For Taiwan, the correlation coefficients reported in parentheses are for 19 observations, excluding Petroleum & Coal Products (which is dominated by government enterprises). The 13 manufacturing sectors for Japan are those for which business group sales data is reported in Dodwell 1984−85. They correspond to the sectors listed in Table 5 for which the Japanese business group sales ratio is greater than zero, with the exception of Rubber Products and Miscellaneous Industrial Products. Basic Metal is disaggregated into two sectors (Iron & Steel and Non-ferrous Metal Products) and the Pulp & Paper Products sector excludes Printing and Publishing.

[2] Calculated from transactions data in the Input−Output Tables for each country, aggregated to match the sectors reported in Table 5. [*1980 Input−Output Tables: English Summary* (Administrative Management Agency, Japan 1984); *1983 Input−Output Tables* (Bank of Korea 1985); and *1984 Input−Output Tables, Taiwan Area, Republic of China* (1986).]

[3] Ratio of total intermediate demand to total (intermediate plus final) demand for the output of the sector.

[4] Total payments to labour input divided by total value added (net of indirect taxes) for the sector.

[5] Ratio of exports to total domestic product for the sector.

is negatively correlated with the degree of labor intensity in production[17]. This is especially the case for Korea, indicating that the *chaebol* are largely concentrated in highly capital-intensive manufacturing activities. Finally, for the correlations between group concentration and export share of production, we note that the sign of the correlation coefficient varies between countries. Japanese business group strength in manufacturing is weakly associated with export activity, while business groups in Taiwan appear to be more concentrated in import-substitution sectors. In Korea business group concentration is fairly evenly divided between export and non-export sectors, and thus not correlated with either.

These differences in correlations suggest that business groups play important, though differing roles in each economy. These differences further

---

[17] Note that, when the outlying observation for 'petroleum products' is excluded, the correlation coefficient for Taiwan increases dramatically. This sector, the most capital-intensive sector of all, is effectively monopolized by state-run enterprises.

suggest that, without knowing the configurations of business groups within the total economy, one cannot assess the degree of importance of business groups solely on the basis of aggregate concentration.

Network Configurations

One of the ways to examine these differences in configuration is to look at the network structures of business groups in each location. By network structure, we mean the stable (but not necessarily long-term) linkages between firms. Analytically, one can distinguish four distinct types of such inter-firm networks:

1. ownership networks (i. e. firms linked through common ownership),
2. investment networks (i. e. firms linked by capital and investment),
3. production networks (firms linked by production sequences),
4. distribution networks (firms linked by the distribution of commodities).

A full analysis of these networks would contain an examination of how these four types of firm networks work out empirically in each location and then to contrast these network configurations across societies. We address this task more fully elsewhere (Orrù, Biggart and Hamilton, forthcoming), but for the sake of showing the different configurations of East Asian business groups, it is sufficient here to outline only two of the four types of networks: ownership and production networks.

Who owns these East Asian business groups and how do ownership networks relate to production networks? The answers sharply vary across the three societies, but are strongly uniform within each location[18].

Japan

In Japan business group firms mutually own each other[19]. Typically, individual ownership, whether through stock or through private holdings, counts for very little of the total ownership of Japanese business groups.

---

[18] In an earlier paper (Orru, Biggart and Hamilton, forthcoming) we have shown that business group networks in each society are, generally speaking, isomorphic. All four types of business groups networks are very similar within countries, but differ systematically across countries.

[19] This section is drawn from a much more complete analysis of Japanese business groups found in Orru, Hamilton and Suzuki (forthcoming).

Most firms are publicly listed on one of Japan's several very large stock exchanges, where only a small percentage of the total shares are actually available for purchase. Most equity in business group firms is held by other firms in the same business group. Partly to prevent hostile takeovers and unwanted mergers and partly to demonstrate their mutuality, the managers of the member firms of business groups have worked out complicated joint shareholding arrangements.

There are two major types of shareholding ownership networks, one that is, and another that is not, conterminous with production networks. At the top of the Japanese economy are six major business groups, called intermarket groups or *kigyo shudan*[20]. The major firms in these groups are roughly equal and are sometimes called 'president's club' firms, signifying that the top managers meet regularly to discuss the situation of the group as a whole. Although there are significant transactions and loan relationships between these firms, the ownership (and investment) network represented by president's club firms is not conterminous with production sequences; they are normally non-competitive and occupy different industrial, commercial and financial sectors. Presidents' club firms individually hold something less than 5% of each other's shares, but collectively they own between 14 and 28% of all the shares of group firms and between 38 and 72% of the shares ownes by top 10 shareholders. Controlling interest, therefore, is held by the group as a whole, and not by any one firm within the group, and the group as a whole strives, in competition with other intermarket groups, for larger shares of the total Japanese economy.

All of the major presidents' club firms specializing in manufacturing, as well as another set of very large independent firms (e. g., Toyota), have developed a second type of ownership network, called *keiretsu*, that overlaps directly with production sequences. These major manufacturing firms have created or merged with a set of auxiliary and subsidiary firms to carry through the entire process of production[21]. The major firm will normally control 20 to 50% of the equity of subsidiary firms. Investigators have shown that the major firms handle securing and distributing the upstream supplies, the initial input; subsidiary firms then manufacture the basic parts; labor-intensive aspects of the production sequence are often further subcontracted to small- and medium-sized independent firms, with

---

[20] The six intermarket groups are as follows: Mitsubishi, Mitsui, Sumitomo, Fuyo, DKB and Sanwa. The ten independent groups are Tokai Bank, IBJ, Nippon Steel, Hitachi, Nissan, Toyota, Matsushita, Toshiba-IHI, Tokyu and Seibu.

[21] The Japanese literature refers to this tendency as 'one setist behavior'. One setist behavior 'for an enterprise group [...] implies that all the raw materials needed for production can be procured within the groups' (Futatsugi 1986: 57).

whom they have long-term stable manufacturing relationships, but no actual ownership. The major firm then undertakes the final assembly of the commodities; in the case of Toyota this is an aspect of the *kanban* system, which is the 'just-in-time' (*kanban*) inventory and assembly process made famous by this business group. *Keiretsu* group firms, therefore, occupy intermediate and final positions in overall production sequences, even though these firms sometimes subcontract to small independent firms a large portion of their actual production.

South Korea

Unlike their Japanese counterparts, South Korean business groups, called *chaebol*, are owned by individuals and not firms[22]. By and large, the ownership networks of *chaebol* are clearly delineated. At the head of each *chaebol* is the individual who, together with his immediate family, owns or controls all the firms in the business group.

These business groups developed rapidly in the 1960's and 1970's when state officials earmarked specific industries for rapid economic growth and loaned large amounts of money to selected individuals in an effort to build state-of-the-art factories that could compete in world markets. Using such generous, low cost loans, these individuals created networks of vertically integrated firms that centered on large core firms. Ownership and managerial control of subsidiary firms was and still remains centralized in the hands of the *chaebol* owners. In recent years, in order to reduce the debt ratio, the government has encouraged *chaebol* owners to list a few key *chaebol* firms on Korea's very small stock exchange, thereby allowing *chaebol* to raise their capital through equity markets. Although most large *chaebol* have listed a few firms, the owner and his family still maintain controlling shares in those firms. On average, only about 20 to 25% of business group firms are listed on the stock exchange, however; the unlisted firms remain solely in the private control of the *chaebol* head.

Production networks are largely conterminous with ownership networks. Because state officials selected and financed specific *chaebol* to accomplish state economic goals, the Korean economy is structured so that *chaebol* often enjoy monopolistic and oligopolistic advantages in the sectors in which they predominate[23]. Therefore, in some sectors, such as in chemicals,

---

[22] For a fuller discussion of South Korea *chaebol* and relevant sources, see Hamilton and Biggart (1988), Orru, Biggart and Hamilton (forthcoming) and Zeile and Kim (1988).

[23] In fact, considerable competition exists among a few *chaebol* in such specific sectors as transportation equipment and electronics.

construction, and petroleum, *chaebol* are intermediate producers that sell most of what they produce to other domestic firms. *Chaebol* in other sectors, such as in electronics and transportation equipment, produce final products especially designed and built for export markets.

Within their own production areas, *chaebol* owners have normally created or have otherwise taken over firms that were necessary to complete their own production. *Chaebol* rely very little on stable domestic subcontracting relations with non-*chaebol* firms. This pattern of self-sufficiency in production seems to have accelerated the vertical integration within business groups by encouraging the *chaebol*'s forced acquisition of small- and medium-sized firms in the same production areas, a practice that earned them the name 'octopus legs'. As a consequence of this self-sufficiency, *chaebol* factories are on average larger than those in Japanese business groups and much larger than those in Taiwan. Instead of subcontracting locally, *chaebol* have more commonly developed joint manufacturing projects with foreign firms, thus allowing major components to be supplied from elsewhere. For instance, Mitsubishi makes the engines for Hyundai's main export automobile, the Excel.

The network structure of Korean *chaebol* tends to be economically self-sufficient within their own areas of economic activity or to develop joint ventures with foreign firms to supplement their own production. Because they have been heavily capitalized, *chaebol* owners have developed the largest, if not always the most efficient, factories in each of the sectors they dominate. Because they do not rely heavily on non-*chaebol* domestic firms as a source of subcontracting, they have come to dominate, in terms of ratio of total production, most manufacturing sectors. Although *chaebol* are certainly the most prominent economic organization in modern South Korea, they tend to segment rather than to integrate the total economy in the way that Japanese business groups do. Therefore, the high concentration figures for Korean business groups are somewhat misleading, or at least are not directly comparable with those of Japanese business groups.

Taiwan

In both Japan and South Korea production and ownership networks of business group firms directly overlap, although in very different ways[24]. In Taiwan these networks tend to be much more distinct. The ownership

---

[24] For amore complete discussion of Taiwan business groups, including relevant sources, see Hamilton and Kao (1987).

of Taiwan's business groups, generally known as *qiyejituan*, is overwhelmingly in the hands of private individuals. Family ownership is most frequent, but limited partnerships between unrelated individuals are also common. Unlike in South Korea, the Taiwan government does not select or make long-term, low interest loans to private individuals in order to stimulate the economy. And unlike in Japan, stock equity is relatively unimportant, although that is changing somewhat in recent years. Instead, entrepreneurs generate most of their investment capital through nongovernmental sources, usually through personal networks of family, friends and fellow regionals. As a consequence, firms within a business group may have a number of active owners and silent partners, and the specific group of owners may differ for each firm. Ultimate control of resources, as opposed to fiscal ownership, however, tends to be concentrated in the hands of just a few, or perhaps even one, readily identifiable individual. Often observers associate this person or persons with a family *(jia)* and consider the business group to be a family business. Other times these individuals are unrelated, but are known to be active business partners. Ownership networks, therefore, are not as concentrated as they are in South Korean *chaebol*, but are no less private.

Production networks, however, differ greatly from those found in South Korea. Whereas, by comparison, *chaebol* consist of vertically integrated firms, Taiwan's business groups normally represent sets of modest-sized firms engaging in unrelated businesses. In the top 96 Taiwan business groups there is an average of seven firms per business group, and these firms are spread across an average of four industrial sectors[25]. Based on self-reported information, over 40% of Taiwan's business groups reported that none of their member firms were linked by ongoing business transactions. An additional 33% reported five or fewer routine transaction linkages among member firms[26]. Production sequences primarily link business group firms with non-business group firms in a system known locally as *weixing gongchang*, or a satellite production system. With this system a group of independent firms, each producing some component part, jointly manufacture a specific finished product. For instance, key business groups, such as Tatung, have a large share of the total market in making electronic products, but many other independent firms also make component parts for Tatung products, as well as for other manufacturers. Therefore, although business group firms have only a modest portion of total sales,

---

[25] This is calculated at a four-digit level of industrial sector aggregation.
[26] The reliability of this information, which has been tabulated from the Zhonghua Zhengxinso survey (1985), is doubtful, but indicative nonetheless.

their upstream locations suggest greater importance than aggregate concentration figures would indicate.

This is particularly the case when one investigates production sequences in a temporal fashion. As indicated earlier, many of the largest and most profitable Taiwan business group firms maintain forward linkages with the main commodity production networks. For instance, 25 business groups produce over 50% (by total sales) of all cloth woven on the island, and these groups sell most of their cloth to small and middle non-business group firms, which produce 88% of the total sales of all finished garments and other apparel made in Taiwan, about 75% of which is exported. Similarly, the production of raw plastics is dominated by a handful of very large business group firms, which in turn sell their products to scores of small- and medium-sized firms, which, in turn, make finished products.

Combining both the aggregate statistical and the network descriptions, then, we can summarize the three countries as follows:

In Taiwan major firms in many business groups seem to dominate intermediate production locations and a few key 'downstream' production sites; in both locations they cooperate closely with an array of non-affiliated firms, hence the most successful Taiwan business groups appear to produce for and to participate in production networks composed of firms that are not owned by the top business groups themselves. When compared with the concentration statistics for Japan and South Korea, therefore, Taiwan's smaller figure should not necessarily mean that business groups play an insignificant role within that economy, but rather simply a different role.

In South Korea business groups control capital intensive sectors; some of these sectors produce intermediate products (steel) and others finished products (automobiles). The sharp divisions between those sectors in which business groups predominate and those sectors in which they participate very little suggest that business group firms do not develop sub-contracting relationships with smaller firms in the same sector as much as is commonly the case in Taiwan and Japan. The larger aggregate concentration figure of business groups in Korea is misleading without also knowing that Korean business groups do not serve to integrate the total economy in the same way that business groups do in Japan, and to some extent in Taiwan as well.

Finally, in Japan the major business groups sit atop and integrate that economy in a way not found in the other two societies. Japanese business groups systematically both span across industrial sectors and develop strong vertical linkages between firms within industrial sectors. In addition, business groups firms develop long-term subcontracting relationships with a vast array of small independent firms. Aggregate concentration figures only hint at the vast, largely unquestioned influence that business groups exert within the Japanese economy.

As the above discussion shows, the configurations of ownership and production networks vary considerably among the three societies. In the final section we want to discuss briefly some of the implications of these differences.

Conclusion:
Institutional Influences on Network Configurations

What factors best explain these network configurations? Can one explain each country's network patterns, as well as the differences in patterns among countries, by using the bottom – up economic explanations for business groups? Or should one use the top – down political explanation? In each case it would not be difficult to construct a post hoc explanation around either set of explanations. Clearly, both economics and politics are important in all three societies. But what is significant in this context is that politics and economics are not important in the same ways.

In any explanation of Korean business groups the political dimension is an essential feature. In Korea the government decreed the success of business groups through its comprehensive planning and strongly enforced implementation policies. To seal the matter, the government created fiscal institutions that used indebtedness as the means to finance, but also to control, the large vertically integrated *chaebol*. This government strategy allowed *chaebol* to expand and to prosper and the *chaebol* now to become contenders for power in their own right. Bottom – up market explanations do not work as well, in large part because one can clearly show, temporally, that Korea's industrial structure precedes market involvement, and thus was not a consequence of it.

This same top – down political explanation, however, recedes in importance when applied to Taiwan. To be sure, in Taiwan the government built an infrastructure and dominates import-substitution industries, such as petroleum and steel making. But the largest portion of Taiwan's economic growth has occurred in the private manufacturing sectors in which the government has had very little direct involvement. The government does not finance big business and leaves the private sector largely to its own devices. The business group configurations that have emerged in Taiwan are primarily the result of non-state factors.

This conclusion, of course, begs the question as to whether they are, therefore, by default, the result of market factors. The answer to this question, however, must also be no. The reason is that market explanations would predict that business groups expand from firms in order to reduce transaction costs and, thereby, achieve greater allocative efficiencies. Market explanations, therefore, would predict a direct overlap between ownership and production networks, but that outcome seems not to have occurred in Taiwan. A better explanation for the relative absence of vertical integration centers on non-economic factors, the most important of which may well be inheritance patterns. At the death of the father, all sons may equally split the assets of the family. This practice, along with other factors, has the effect of promoting diversified investment patterns, so that non-entangled independent firms can be divided among sons.

For Japan, neither political nor economic dimensions seem to offer satisfying explanations for the extensive, as well as intensive, firm networks found there. As with South Korean *chaebol*, Japanese business groups precede market growth. Founded in the early years of the Meiji period, the first three *zaibatsu*[27] arose from differing sources, one growing out of a successful merchant house and the other two representing coalitions of former elites. Political collusion is, of course, a factor here, but the continued success, particularly in the post-World War II era, does not result from politics alone. Indeed, in the absence of strong political centers, politics are less important now than before the war. But, even in the postwar era, market factors do not seem sufficient to explain the success of networks that have no parallel elsewhere. How can such a unique configuration be explained by processes assumed to be universal?

If neither political nor economic theories explain individual cases, then it is certainly true that they cannot be used to explain all three cases in the same terms. What one is left with, however, need not be an ad hoc, eclectic theory. A large part of the problem is the lack of clarity in what political and economic theories are best at explaining. These theories best explain the reasons for instead of the actual patterns of growth. Rather than growth, what most need to be explained in these cases are the patterned interlinkages between firms, the networks themselves. This is not simply a question of economics or of politics. Rather, it is a question of organization and of the factors that are known to influence the process of organizing.

---

[27] 'Zaibatsu' is a type of organization, inevitably very large, which typically comprises a bank, an insurance company, a trading company, and many industrial companies. (Yoshihara, K. 1982: *Sogo Shosha: the vanguard of the Japanese economy* Tokyo: Oxford University Press. pp. 301).

What is needed, then, are macro-organizational theories of economies. Certainly efficiency in the allocation of resources and the state's control of businesses are both important parts of such theories, but these factors are not singular in nature, universal in character and unambiguous in practice. These factors reflect their social location. State structure greatly differs among the three societies, and such economic institutions as banking structures and stock markets are distinctive in each case. Moreover, these highly complex factors themselves do not exert their influence in a vacuum, apart from other, equally complex factors; thus, state control and economic institutions do not interact in the same way in different locations. Therefore, to analyze adequately the firm networks in any one society is essentially to have organizational theories, in each location, of how that society is put together. Such organizational theories should not create, in a Parsonian fashion, an abstract world of pattern variables, but rather should concentrate on real worlds of human activity and of distinctive cultural meanings. Although many diverse analytic traditions provide beginnings for such theories, these macro-organizational theories remain promising tasks for the future.

References

Aoki, Masahiko (1984): *The economic analysis of the Japanese firm,* Amsterdam: Elsevier.

Balassa, Bela et al. (1982): *Development strategies in semi-industrial economies,* Baltimore, Md.: Johns Hopkins University Press.

Bradford, Colin I., Jr. and William H. Branson (eds.) (1987): *Trade and structural change in Pacific Asia,* Chicago: University of Chicago Press.

Caves, Richard E. (1987): International differences in industrial organization, Discussion Paper Number 1321, Harvard Institute of Economic Research, Cambridge, Mass.: Harvard University.

Caves, Richard E. and Masu Uekusa (1976): *Industrial organization in Japan,* Washington, D. C.: Brookings Institution.

Chandler, Alfred, Jr. (1977): *The visible hand: the managerial revolution in American business,* Cambridge, Mass.: Harvard University Press.

Chu, Jong Hwon (1985): *Chaebol Kyungjeron* (Economics of *chaebol*), Seoul: Cheonghum Munhwasa.

Cumings, Bruce (1984): The origins and development of the Northeast Asian political economy: industrial sectors, product cycles, and political consequences, *International Organization* 381: 1–40.

Curry, B. and K. D. George (1983): Industrial concentration: a survey, *The Journal of Industrial Economics* 31, 3 (March): 203–255.

Daems, H. (1978): *The holding company and corporate control.* Leiden: Martinus Nijhoff.

Dodwell Marketing Consultants (1984): *Industrial groupings in Japan, 1984—85,* Tokyo: Dodwell Marketing Consultants.

Encaoua, David and Alexis Jacquemin (1982): Organizational efficiency and monopoly power: the case of French industrial groups, *European Economic Review* 19: 25—51.

Evans, Peter B. (1979): *Dependent development: the alliance of multinational, state and local capital in Brazil,* Princeton, N. J.: Princeton University Press.

Futatsugi, Yusaku (1986): Japanese enterprise groups, Monograph No. 4, Kobe: The School of Business Administration.

Gale, Bruce (1986): *Politics and business: a study of multi-purpose holdings Berhad,* Singapore: Eastern University Press.

Galenson, Walter (ed.) (1985): *Foreign trade and investment: economic development in the newly industrializing Asian Countries,* Madison, Wisc.: Unversity of Wisconsin Press.

Gerlach, Michael Lloyd (1987): Alliances and the social organization of Japanese business, Unpublished Dissertation, Yale University.

Gerschenkron, A. (1965): *Economic backwardness in historical perspective,* New York: Praeger.

Gold, Thomas B. (1987): *State and society in the Taiwan miracle,* New York: M. E. Sharpe.

Goto, Akira (1982): Business groups in a market economy, *European Economic Review* 19: 53—70.

Hadley, Eleanor M. (1970): *Antitrust in Japan,* Princeton, N. J.: Princeton University Press.

Haggard, Stephen and Tun-jen Cheng (1986): State and foreign capital in the 'Gang of Four', in: Federick Deyo (ed.), *The new East Asian industrialization,* 84—135, Ithaca, N. Y.: Cornell University Press.

Hamilton, Gary G. and Nicole Woolsey Biggart (1988): Market, culture, and authority: a comparative analysis of management and organization in the Far East, *American Journal of Sociology* Special Supplement on the Sociology of the Economy.

Hamilton, Gary G. and Cheng-shu Kao (1987): The institutional foundations of Chinese business: the family firm in Taiwan, Program in East Asian Culture and Development, Working Paper Series, No. 8. University of California: Institute of Governmental Affairs.

Hamilton, Gary G., Marco Orru and Nicole Woolsey Biggart (1987): Enterprise groups in East Asia: an organizational analysis, *Shoken Keizai* (Financial Economic Review) 161: 78—106.

Hankook, Ilbo (1985): *Pal ship O nyndo hankook ui 50 dae jae bul* (The 50 top 'chaebol' in Korea), Seoul, Korea.

Hong Kong and Shanghai Banking Corporation (1987): *Annual Report 1986,* Hong Kong: Hong Kong and Shanghai Banking Corporation.

Johnson, Chalmers (1982): *MITI and the Japanese miracle: the growth of industrial policy, 1925—1975,* Stanford, Cal.: Stanford University Press.

Koo, Hagen (1984): The political economy of income distribution in South Korea: the impact of the State's industrialization policies, *World Development* 12; 1029—1037.

Lee, Kyu-Uck (1986): The concentration of economic power in Korea: causes, consequences and policy, in: Korea Development Institute (ed.), *Industrial development policies and issues,* 235 – 251, Seoul: Korea Development Institute.

Lee, Sung-Soo (1987): Korea's general trading companies, *Monthly Review* (Korea Exchange Bank) 21: 3 – 19.

Lee, Young-Ki (1985): Conglomeration and business concentration – The Korean case, in: Korea Development Institute *Industrial policies of the Republic of Korea and the Republic of China,* 235 – 251, Seoul: Korean Development Institute.

Leff, Nathaniel H. (1978): Industrial organization and entrepreneurship in the developing countries: the economic group, *Economic Development and Cultural Change* 26 (4): 661 – 675.

Lim, Mah Hui (1981): *Ownership and control of the one hundred largest corporations in Malaysia,* Kuala Lumpur: Oxford University Press.

Lim, Mah Hui and Teoh Kit Fong (1986): Singapore corporations go transnational, *Journal of Southeast Asian Studies* 17, 2 (September): 336 – 365.

Nakamura, Takatoshi (1984): Japan's giant enterprises – their power and influence, *Japanese Economic Studies* 12: 80 – 90.

Numazaki, Ichiro (1986): Networks of Taiwanese big business, *Modern China* 12 (4): 487 – 534.

Orrù, Marco, Nicole Woolsey Biggart and Gary G. Hamilton (forthcoming): Organizational isomorphism in East Asia: broadening the new institutionalism, in: W. W. Powell and P. DiMaggio (eds.), *The new institutionalism in organizational analysis,* Chicago: University of Chicago Press.

Orrù, Marco, Gary G. Hamilton and Mariko Suzuki (forthcoming): Patterns of domination in Japanese business, *Organization Studies.*

Phipatseritham, Krirkkiat and Kunio Yoshihara (1983): Business groups in Thailand, Research Notes and Discussions Papers No. 41, Singapore: Institute of Southeast Asian Studies.

Putterman, Louis (1986): The economic nature of the firm: overview, in: Putterman, Louis (ed.), *The economic nature of the firm,* Cambridge: Cambridge University Press.

Robison, Richard (1986): *Indonesia, the rise of capital,* Sydney: Allen and Unwin.

Rotwein, Eugene (1964): Economic concentration and monopoly in Japan, *Journal of Political Economy* 72: 262 – 277.

Sato, Kazuo (ed.) (1980): *Industry and business in Japan,* New York: M. E. Sharpe.

Sieh, Lee Mei Ling (1982): *Ownership and control of Malaysian manufacturing corporations,* Kuala Lumpur: UMCB Publications.

Song, Dae-Hee (1985): The role of public enterprise in the Korean economy, in: Korea Development Institute (ed.), *Industrial policies of the Republic of Korea and the Republic of China,* Seoul: Korean Development Institute.

Stock Exchange of Hong Kong (1987): *Fact book 1986,* Hong Kong: The Stock Exchange of Hong Kong Limited.

Stokman, Frans N., Rolf Ziegler and John Scott (eds.) (1985): *Networks of corporate power: a comparative analysis of ten countries,* London: Polity Press.

Taiwan Statistical Data Book 1987 (1987): Council for Economic Planning and Development, Republic of China.

White, Lawrence (1981): What has been happening to aggregate concentration in the United States? *Journal of Industrial Economics* 29: 223–230.

World Bank (1987): *World development report 1987,* New York: Oxford University Press.

Yoshihara, Kunio (1985): *Philippine industrialization: foreign and domestic capital,* Kuala Lumpur: Oxford University Press.

Zeile, William and Wan-jin Kim (1988): Industrial policy and organizational efficiency: the Korean chaebol examined, Program in East Asian Culture and Development, Working Paper Series, No. 29, University of California: Institute of Governmental Affairs.

The Embodiment of Industrial Culture in Bureaucracy and Management

Stephen Wilks

The general concern of this chapter is with the broad span of social science analysis dealing with state intervention in the economy. Comparative analysis in this area is largely, and quite understandably, refracted through a lens of cultural preconceptions which condition us to expect certain national characteristics in how governments relate to industry. We expect American companies to be independent and to 'capture' government agencies rather than vice versa; similarly in Britain a liberal, arms-length relationship is expected; West Germany is marked by capitalist self-regulation through the banks with government interest, but minimal involvement; while France and Japan are characterized by such close, intimate relations between government and industry that it can be difficult to distinguish where government ends and industry begins; here industrial development is government led. These substantive national variations in the proclivity to intervene, have been labelled by Dyson 'industrial culture' (1983: 42). He argues that countries have evolved their own distinctive industrial cultures which reflect traditions of public authority but are also moulded by the historical conditions of industrialization. Such industrial cultures are expressed in attitudes and behaviour but are also embodied in institutions and form a mediating factor in the policy process. The term 'industrial culture' is an earlier and more specific formulation of the same contextual pressures which Berger has labelled 'economic culture' (1987: 25). Dyson's use of the term must be seen as an articulation of an analytic school of historically based political and economic writers which expresses interventionary variations in terms of the power of 'the state' contrasting 'weak' and 'strong' states (for an outline of these themes see Wilks and Wright 1987).

It is on this concept of 'industrial culture' that I propose to focus. The term 'culture' is a provocative one. It easily lends itself to caricature with throw-away references to French 'dirigisme' or 'Japan Inc' and this has led some analysts to reach for their guns when they hear the term culture and to eliminate it as a garbage can, residual category of no serious utility. This is an over-reaction, but if culture is to be retained as a valid concept, it needs to be saved from promiscuous, universalistic usage. Industrial culture can be treated as an aspect of political culture. The common usage

and development of political culture has been to analyse the pre-requisites
and socialization suitable for democratic citizenship, and the circumstances
in which voters and groups within society attach legitimacy to the constitutional or political system. In contrast, this chapter considers attitudes to
state intervention held within significant institutional groupings within
society and, in particular, attitudes held in the bureaucracy, in industrial
management, by organized labour and within the political parties. It
concentrates on the first two of these four categories while bearing in mind
that a full analysis, which space does not allow here, should incorporate
party and labour.

The idea of 'attitudes' to state intervention needs elaboration. We are
concerned with the 'norms' pertaining to state intervention (defined as
tacit but specific guides to action; as opposed to values, explicit but non-
operational beliefs), how those norms originated but also how they have
been expressed in organizational form. To what extent, in other words,
have organizations incorporated such norms in their recruitment, financing,
structure, processes and in their patterns of linkages with other organizations. One can thus talk of norms being 'embodied' in bureaucracy and in
management. They became an inseparable and defining aspect of national
organizations and, in turn, these abstract presumptions are given substance
in the patterns of behaviour and approaches to problem-solving which can
be observed in the typical practices of the organization. Norms become as
much a part of the organization as recruitment practices or hierarchical
gradings. It is therefore necessary, in a cross-national comparison, to study
these 'embodied' norms as well as more overt organizational procedures
and structures.

As an aside, the contemporary relevance of this debate in the U. K. should
be stressed. Cultural interpretations of British economic decline have become dominant. In his influential study Martin Wiener encapsulated twenty
years of debate when he wrote of Britain's 'anti-industrial culture' and of
the 'cultural domestication of the industrial revolution' which spread across
all the social groupings (including industrialists) of the 'Establishment'.
Wiener clearly felt his analysis to be exportable, hence

we have come to see that Japan's startlingly rapid development owes at least as
much to peculiar features of Japanese society and culture — the 'tribal' character
of work relationships and the inner discipline [...]. No one can fully understand
the Japanese economic miracle without grasping the working principles of Japanese
culture (Wiener 1981: 5).

In an equally erudite study Barnett (1986: 209, 215) rails at the 19th-
century development of the Christian gentleman ideal with its romantic

idealism and the 'liberal knowledge' which became the basis for the British state bureaucracy.

In the most direct way this theme of cultural inadequacy has been taken up by Conservative ministers. First Sir Keith Joseph and now Lord Young have vigorously maintained the argument that Britain needs an 'enterprise culture'. A recent White Paper incautiously subtitled the Department of Trade and Industry as 'the Department of Enterprise' and argued that, since 1979, Britain has recovered on the basis of policies calculated to release 'the enterprise of our people'. It argued that a cultural change has taken place in the 1980s but that 'individuals need positive encouragement to participate actively in the challenge of creating prosperity, if only to combat the past anti-enterprise bias of British culture' (CM 278 1988: 3).

The chapter continues in four sections. The first two review culturally based interpretations of bureaucratic norms and of managerial norms looking first at Britain, then comparatively treating West Germany, France and Japan. The third section presents an argument about the origin and retention of cultural positions within institutions, and the fourth section presents some conclusions.

The 'Culture' of the British Civil Service

In Britain it is widely accepted that there is a well-developed antagonism to the principle of state intervention in the economy, the institutions of both state and industry are not closely related and, while intervention does take place, it is neither systematic nor usually successful. This is the British 'liberal' or *'laissez-faire'* inheritance which is well attested in a series of studies of industrial policy (see Dell 1972, Wilks 1988). We can examine the manifestation of that inheritance first in the bureaucracy.

For thirty years now, since the publication of Lord Balogh's scathing polemic (Balogh 1959), the British civil service has suffered a torrent of criticism, little of which had significant impact until civil service reform became a preoccupation of the Thatcher governments. There is a rich seam of cultural criticism here which centres on the education, selection, values and competence of the senior civil service, formerly known as the administrative class, now more prosaically termed 'grades 1 to 7'. The British model of the 'talented all-rounder' was once regarded as the quintessence of civilized values but is now lampooned as an archaic, self-indulgent reservoir of incompetence. The following quote from Barnett is simply the most recent of a long line of similar attacks.

'Thus in the 1850s was born the Whitehall mandarin, able at a touch to transmute life into paper and turn action to stone. Henceforward the British governing elite was to be composed of essay-writers rather than problem solvers — minds judicious, balanced and cautious rather than operational and engaged [...]. Moreover, this was to be an elite aloof from the ferocious struggle for survival going on in the world's market place; more at home in a club or senior common room than a factory. And where would such mandarins be recruited other than from Oxford and Cambridge? [...]' (Barnett 1986: 215).

This is all very well but such statements are far too sweeping, they appear almost to attack the civil service with its own weapons, a literary attack on a literary problem. Let us rather try to disentangle some of the characteristics of the civil service in the shape of six norms of behaviour.

In descending order of reliability the first norm is that decisions are taken on an intelligent but dispassionate balancing of the arguments. This is the famous 'generalist' ethos of the service known as amateurism by its enemies, judgement by its friends and summarized in the cricketing metaphor of the 'all-rounder'. The concept of the generalist administrator is defensible but the British generalist is a very peculiar phenomenon. The model stresses abstract, individual intelligence measured according to Oxbridge criteria in areas such as classics or literature and it is associated, of course, with a disparagement of technical education and vocational training. The practical effect is of non-programmatic policy making with a tendency towards ad-hocery and improvisation. The second norm is one of self-confidence, verging on the arrogant. An important criterion in selection and promotion is assurance, an urbane capacity to make the best of even a poor case. This sense of 'effortless superiority', of imperturbability, has taken some blows since 1960 but it could still be said of the senior British civil servant, as it was said of Lyndon B. Johnson's adviser, Walt Rostow, that he was 'often wrong, but never in doubt'.

A third, well-remarked norm of the British civil service is its concern with policy at the expense of management. The orientation of the higher civil servant is upwards, to his minister, and outwards, towards society, rather than towards the internal organization and operation of his own department. The self-definition of the British civil servant has traditionally been as a 'statesman in disguise', a position bolstered, argues Thomas (1978) by a set of humanistic, ethical principles which are not openly articulated but bear comparison with the scientific management popularized within the American federal service in the 1920s and 1930s. It is this norm which has borne the brunt of the reforming onslaught of the Conservatives since 1979. The Conservative reforms have had more impact on the service than any other post-war initiatives. Nevertheless, they are still widely regarded as transient. They have not been concerned with structure and formal process but rather with the system of expectations, incentives and attitudes within the service. The Government has tried to change what they describe as the 'culture' of the service from an impartial weighing of policy options towards committed managerialism (see Richards 1986, Metcalfe and Richards 1987).

The fourth, fifth and sixth norms are inter-related and are more concerned with policy priorities rather than with attitudes to the job itself. Briefly there is a norm of conformity with liberal values; a norm of undervaluing industrial success; and a norm of operating according to *laissez-faire*, free market assumptions. There are many theoretical currents and counter currents packed into these simple assertions and, at this point, the argument becomes controversial, polemical and deserves far more elaborate treatment. In essence, however, one can observe a mix of attitudes within the civil service which have been repeatedly diagnosed as antagonistic to constructive engagement of government with the industrial economy. Liberal values translate into a traditional concern with liberty, with individualism and hence into reactive, non-interventionist government. The disparagement of industry is seen in the pre-industrial, aristocratic value system of the British establishment which regarded 'trade' as vulgar and demeaning and which, in Pollard's terms, finds expression in the Treasury's perennial 'contempt for production' (Pollard 1982). The devotion to the market reflects the rise and dominance of *laissetz-faire* doctrine in the early 19th century which became part of the outlook of the service and has persisted with remarkable vitality ever since.

The norms outlined above have been analysed and re-analysed sufficiently frequently for the arguments to sound almost ritualistic. Defenders of the service are thin on the ground with criticism coming from the libertarian right of the Conservative party, from centrist analysts and from the left. The following discussion draws on writers of the left, stressing that much of their analysis is widely accepted.

The mix of norms which characterize the British civil service has been identified as part of a wider syndrome in the development of the British state. Britain is said still to be 'pre-industrial' in its political institutions, to be dominated still by aristocratic values and, despite historical orthodoxy, is said never to have experienced a full bourgeois revolution. Hence

The pioneer modern liberal-constitutional state never itself became modern [...] the industrialisation which it produced, equally pioneering and equally world-wide in impact, never made England into a genuinely industrialised society.

And:

The cost (of peaceful change) was the containment of capitalism within a patrician hegemony which never, either then or since, actively favoured the aggressive development of industrialism or the general conversion of society to the latter's values or interests. Permanent social limits were thus imposed upon the 'industrial revolution' and the British entrepreneurial system (Nairn 1981: 22, 32).

This argument has been advanced directly, indirectly, and with varying degress of clarity by a series of political and economic historians including Perry Anderson, John Eatwell, Andrew Gamble and Colin Leys. The most elegant and impressive recent deployment is by Geoffrey Ingham who argues that

Britain has retained important characteristics beyond a time when [...] they should have ceased to function effectively [namely ...] the persistance of traditional cultural forms and ideological legitimations; a powerful traditionally or aristocratically based element within the elite or ruling class; an unusually dominant 'financial' sector in the City; and, conversely, a relatively weak industrial bourgeoisie (Ingham 1984: 2−3).

This so-called 'exceptionalism' thesis is not only described by Ingham but he traces its institutionalization in the City − Bank of England − Treasury nexus which has sustained City interests and reproduced both policy patterns and cultural forms.

The culmination of this argument can be found in a recent article by Peter Gowan. Like most observers he agrees that the British civil service was moulded between 1850 and 1880 and its contemporary practices and traditions are still to be seen as the product of that creative process. He goes on, however, to argue that the creation of the service was an elaborate and autonomous conspiracy conceived by a Gladstonian group of 'radical conservatives'. Specifically, the Northcote-Trevelyan reforms of 1854 were designed to 'weaken the capacity of [...] [the urban middle classes] to penetrate the upper reaches of the service, thereby strengthening the hold of the landed classes on administrative power' (Gowan 1987: 18). But Gladstone, Jowett and the Oxford reformers were, he argues, replacing the rising bourgeoisie with a positive alternative, they were undertaking a secret 'cultural revolution within the ruling class'. The form of that revo-lution was to create in the administrative class of the civil service a body of 'highly cultured and devout individuals rooted in the landed interest, the aristocracy and the ancient institutions'. The inspiration, asserts Gowan, can be found in the devotion of Gladstone and his associates to the ideas of Coleridge and to his ideal of the 'clerisy'.

Hence,

Gladstone's great achievement, when the aristocratic-gentry and their educational institutions feared their demise within the parliamentary apparatus, was to find a way of consolidating the landed interest within the state while presenting this political organisation in the colours of the urban middle classes, as a purely administrative-efficiency reform based on objective tests and meritocratic criteria.

To round off the argument, Gowan suggests that this pattern has persisted throughout the 20th century but reached its Waterloo with the failure of the civil service under Heath in 1973 — 74. Now, he believes, Mrs Thatcher is in the process of breaking up the mandarinate. Credibility might be lent to this belief by the fact that in 1986, for the first time in over 100 years, the civil service fast stream recruited under 50 per cent of its entrants from Oxbridge.

There is no doubt that the British civil service is a distinctive institution with a distinct culture, although characteristics do vary from department to department (see Wilks 1987). Equally, it is beyond serious doubt that the service is both unwilling and unsuited to pursue extensive intervention in the industrial economy. Whether one accepts Ingham's stress on City privileges, or Gowan's identification of a century-old class conspiracy is more questionable. Certainly the idea that the author of *Kubla Khan* and the *Rime of the Ancient Mariner* is directly responsible for our current administrative failings may be hard to swallow suggesting, as it does that:

We have been too long
Dupes of a deep delusion! Some, belike,
Groaning with restless enmity, expect
All change from change of constitutional power;
As if a Government had been a robe ... .
(Samuel Taylor Coleridge from 'Fears in Solitude', April 1798).

Continental Comparisons of Bureaucracy

Although the British civil service has a distinctively distant and uneasy relationship with industry, all bureaucracies experience a tension over issues of industrial development. Armstrong's comparative analysis of the elite adminstrator's role in relation to economic development highlighted the archaic and irrelevant values and style of the British elite but identified parallel problems in the German bureaucracy. He found the traditional values of Prussian administration to be non-interventionist (Armstrong 1973: 30) and the German legal training to be as limiting as the British dependence on the Oxbridge degree. Thus

in both cases a relatively unchanging field of study, deriving its inspiration from pre-industrial periods, has prevailed. Like most stable bureaucracies of the past (the Chinese mandarins or the Byzantine literati come to mind), the German and the British have prepared their aspirants by mastery of intricate, often graceful patterns of words and categories which bear little direct relation to social patterns (Armstrong 1973: 173).

Indeed, Armstrong depicts both the British and West German bureaucracies becoming steadily weaker and 'retreatist' as their training and attitudes have increasingly less to offer in controlling and guiding economic development.

Although the modern German civil service may share elements of the first three of the norms identified in the British case, it does not share the latter three, the 'anti-industrial' attitudes. This makes relations between government and industry far more amicable and constructive. Over the post-war period the relative fragmentation of the German civil service, federally and departmentally, has enabled individual units to evolve a degree of understanding of industry. This particularly applies to the Federal Technology Ministry which controls research funding and has earned an interventionist reputation. But, in any case, the necessity for intervention is less acute because, while industrial self-organization is weak in Britain, it is strong in West Germany. This rather anticipates the later discussion of management but Germany has never been a 'market economy' in the sense of accepting *laissez-faire* principles. The civil service has been able to play a passive, facilitative role in permitting neo-corporatist industrial adaptation through devices such as cartelization and relying on the leadership of the big universal banks. The whole 'social market' philosophy is at best a half-truth. While the British were pursuing *laissez-faire* under the influence of Adam Smith and the free traders, the Germans were reading Friedrich List's strictures on the necessity of a 'national' approach to economic development. Published appropriately in the same year as the Northcote-Trevelyan Report, 1854, List's *National System of Political Economy* saw English liberal political economy as an 'insane doctrine which sacrifices the interests of agriculture and manufacturing industry to the pretentions of commerce — to the claims of absolute free trade' (quoted in Ingham 1984: 156). List's influential doctrine had a limited effect on administrators but it did strengthen the strong-state philosophy which Dyson sees in the German industrial culture. German industry, he feels, shares a concept of good citizenship in which public obligations take precedence over the private concerns of 'selfish' individuals (Dyson 1983: 32). As Armstrong (1973: 62) confirms, 'List's doctrines appealed mainly to entrepreneurs and managers. His doctrine served to strengthen the St. Simonian legitimisation of private entrepreneurs who saw themselves as serving societal interests rather than purely private achievement.'

Extending the comparison to France runs the risk of being engulfed in a huge cliché. The French civil service has been celebrated since the early

1960s as a self-confident, assertive technocracy which has pulled French industry struggling into the 20th century. Clearly French government has been far more closely involved with industry than that of Britain or Germany, and French administrators have been accordingly more closely and naturally concerned with industrial affairs. In conformity with the Gerschenkronian schema of late developers utilizing the machinery of the state, public officials in France have been used to involvement with infrastructure investment, with running nationalized industries, with moving through *pantouflage* into the private sector, with the allocation of industrial finance and have enjoyed a more technical training. This has produced a close integration of the bureaucracy with industry and, while the elite corps of finance inspectors, auditors and lawyers might share some of the generalist concerns of the British or German officials, the elite technical corps of the Mines and Ponts et Chaussees are technocratic, orientated towards management and industry. Perhaps the only norm which the French bureaucracy fully shares with the British is that of self-confidence verging on arrogance. Unlike the British, however, there appears to have been a discontinuity in administrative attitudes since 1945. A pre-war stalemate society in France marked by bureaucratic fragmentation and political stagnation gave way to a more self-confident mobilizing and modernizing post-war posture. The movement associated with Monnet and the planners gave a more entrepreneurial tone to the administration, permitted greater freedom to firms and replaced state direction with the idea of the 'concerted economy'. The industrial culture of the French administrative elite stresses nationalism, a presumption in favour of action, a willingness to define industrial goals, a sense of responsibility and a realistic ability to act founded on the availability of a range of policy instruments.

Japanese Bureaucracy and Industry

Japanese industrial culture is the stuff of which myths are made. Even among economists only the most dessicated could write about Japan's unnerving post-war economic success without making some reference to distinctive institutions and attitudes. Central to virtually all interpretations of Japan's growth has been a view of the role played by the bureaucracy. At first sight there are some similarities between the Japanese and the British higher civil services. They share characteristics of elite recruitment (from Tokyo and Oxbridge); of generalist dominance; of well-developed 'old-boy' networks; and of collective decision-making — seen as collegiality (and omnipresent committees) in Britain and consensus in Japan. But when it comes to dealing with industry, all similarity ceases. If the British civil service has been portrayed as a conspiracy against industrial growth, then the Japanese has been seen as a conspiracy in favour of industrial growth; and a poorly guarded conspiracy at that. Books such as Wolf's *The Japanese Conspiracy* present MITI's modest Tokyo headquarters as the central command of the unified public and private troops of 'Japan Inc' (Wolf 1983).

Analysis of Japanese industrial culture since the late 1960s has laid emphasis on patriotic capitalism and state leadership. The former can be dated from the 'opening up' of Japan in 1854 by Commodore Perry's superior naval forces and the subsequent 1868 Meiji Restoration, although it was obviously powerfully reinforced by defeat in the Pacific War. The latter provides the text-book example of rapid industrialization under state-leadership. The exploitation of state authority mobilized through a technocratic bureaucracy is increasingly popularized in the expression 'the developmental state' and has affinities with German thinking and French practice. For Johnson, "Japan's political economc can be located precisely in the line of descent from the German Historical School − sometimes labelled 'economic nationalism'" (1982: 17). Emphasis has also been laid on less universal, more esoteric, aspects of Japanese culture.

The apparent lack of conflict in Japanese government, industry and, especially, in labour relations has led to an emphasis on 'groupism' and 'consensus'. The techniques for acquiring group harmony have become well known and management consultants have restocked their shelves with concepts such as 'quality circles', *'ringi'* decision making and, in government, *'nemawashi'* consultation and advisory councils. The roots of this apparently culturally specific harmony have been traced back to feudal times, to the cooperative necessities of rice cultivation, to the concentric loyalties to family, clan and province and even to the social pressure for courteous behaviour in cramped, overcrowded housing conditions. More recently anthropology has given way to theology with analysis of the distinctive variant of Confucianism which envolved in Japan and which stresses harmony, balance, virtue, modesty and respect for paternal authority. Hence Dore's recent work employs the Confucion metaphor for a mix of socially responsible attitudes while an ambitious recent book by Pye interprets Japanese authority as deriving from socialization within the Confucian family. This, he argues, induces

a Japanese craving for a dependency [...] this craving goes far beyond merely seeking to recapture the security of childhood [...] in that the dependant expects the suprior to express indulgences, sympathy, and a distinctively Japanese quality of 'sweetness'.

With the result that

Paternalistic authority works in Japan because the desire for dependency on the part of subordinates is so great that it often drives them to superhuman efforts. The fear of letting down the side, of breaking with consensus, of not meeting the expected standards provides the main psychological drive for generating what must be the most impressive political and social power in Asia (Pye and Pye 1985: 170, 176).

This is mystification of a high order. It overrates the significance of a psychological interpretation which is, in any case, contentious. Moreover it is clearly patronizing, it seems to illustrate what a cultural analysis should not be doing, and it demonstrates also why the 'anti-cultural' analysts of Japanese politics became quite so fervent.

Japanese bureaucracy has been extensively analysed but, even so, Johnson's remarkable study is a landmark. Drawing on his work, we can pick out some of the major norms of the Japanese civil service. First of all, the bureaucracy is the most prestigious career in Japan and the official enjoys extraordinary prominence and status. Senior civil servants form a frank meritocratic elite but without the arrogance that could be expected. The early bureaucracy was recruited largely from the Samurai class and is held to have adopted comparable ethical principles. Hence the theme of 'sacrifice for the public service' is drilled into new recruits as part of a code that has been likened to a 'way of the bureaucrat' (*kanryodo* as opposed to *bushido* — the way of the warrior) (Johnson 1982: 39). The ethic of public service is matched by substantial competence.

In a meritocratic society the public service, and particularly the elite Ministries of Finance and of Trade & Industry, stand at the pinnacle. To an uncanny degree the elite administrators are recruited from Tokyo (and Kyoto) Universitites, and then from the Law Faculty. They study public and administrative law, although in a fashion closer to Anglo-Saxon political science, and also economics. The senior civil service entry examinations cover vocational subjects from administration to civil engineering so that the new recruit may have had a 'general' education but will have covered practical and relevant subjects in some depth. The managerial utility of this preparation can be inferred from the fact that the major companies similarly seek the best Tokyo Law graduates, often those who have failed the civil service exam (about 39 out of every 40) (see Komiya and Yamamoto 1981: 606−7, Johnson 1982: 62, Clark 1979: 37). The features of Japanese bureacracy in operation are relatively familiar. They include an intense loyalty to the class of graduation and entry; early retirement by 55 which facilitates movement through *amakudari* to senior positions elsewhere; a strict seniority system and absolute loyalty to the one Ministry in which the whole of an official's career will be spent. Joining a Ministry is like joining a family and, as Johnson notes, the security provided "cause(s) a Minsitry to become a 'welfare community', which becomes in turn an object of affection for its members and not merely an impersonal office" (Johnson 1982: 79).

This formidable bureaucratic apparatus has been mobilized towards the overwhelming goal of economic independence. 'From about 1941 to 1961 the Japanese economy remained on a war footing. The goal changed from military to economic victory' (Johnson 1982: 241). Since the mid-1960s a concern with 'social development', the environment and the cost of growth have come to the fore (Dore 1986: chapter 1), nevertheless, economic growth has retained the top priority. There is no doubt that this priority is sustained with great commitment. Johnson notes that a leading MITI official "liked to use the derogatory term *keto* ['hairy Chinese', by extension 'unpleasant foreigner'] to refer to Japan's competitors" and that with its nationalism and loyalism 'MITI's spirit has become legendary' (Johnson 1982: 81), perhaps the best example of an industrial culture 'embodied' in a bureaucratic institution.

Despite this reservoir of ability and evidence of action, it remains difficult to see how leadership is exercised in Japanese government-industry relations. Indeed, Ketcham notes that

despite the pervasiveness of hierarchy and thus the multitude of leader-subordinate relationships, there is no word in Japanese that conveys the assertive connotations of the English word 'leadership'. The common Japanese word *shido* is literally 'finger-guide', and thus connotes more guidance than actual leadership (Ketcham 1987: 106).

There is an overwhelming bureaucratic preference for harmony and consensus, ostensible decisions are invariably decided well-beforehand and the Japanese bureaucracy has taken accomodation, consultation and conflict avoidance to an extreme. Western exponents of accountable management would indeed confront a gulf of total incomprehension in Japan. Nonetheless, exponents of the Japanese strong state are confident that the bureaucracy is the decisive force. To quote Johnson once again, 'the elite bureaucracy of Japan makes most major decisions, drafts virtually all legislation, controls the national budget, and is the source of all major policy innovations in the system' (Johnson 1982: 20). Yet this might understate the power of business within the system.

In a study of administrative guidance — the fabled power of Japanese bureaucrats to give non-legally binding (illegal?) instructions — Young concluded, boldly, that 'the regulated parties designed their own regulatory regimes' (Young 1986: 16). Regulation thus reflected government-structured bargaining so that the bureaucracy was simply facilitating a private ordering of priorities. Hence 'this view of the public-private relationship suggests that business actually has considerable, indeed almost overwhelming, power in the system' (Young 1986: 30). Certainly any adequate analysis must take note of political parties. The Japanese LDP, which has been in power since 1955, may be dominated by ex-bureaucrats, but is also extensively financed by business in a fashion which is only partially visible and is spectacularly corrupt.

Johnson's analysis is balanced and he is conscious of the strength of private interests. These interests have recently been re-emphasized by Samuels who declares that 'most available descriptions of the Japanese political economy exaggerate state power at the expense of private power' (Samuels 1987: 21). Instead, he says, 'although the Japanese state pervades the market, it does not lead, guide or supervise private interests. There is little evidence that state actors have ever been able to resist political pressures [...]. The Japanese bureaucracy does not dominate, it negotiates' (Samuels 1987: 260). He terms this a relationship of 'reciprocal consent' which "is quite different from 'consensus', that model of Japanese political life which stresses harmony and cultural adhesives" (Samuels 1987: 261). Here, then, we have an interpretation of government-industry relations which stresses conflict and which regards stability as dependent on satisfactory negotiations. A politically constructed cooperation rather than one natural or organic. The common ground is a deep distrust of the free market shared by bureaucrats and businessmen and hence agreement that 'capitalism needs the visible hand of the state' (Okimoto cited in Samuels 1987: 262).

Management and Industrial Culture

Among the most provocative and influential studies of business attitudes to state intervention is David Vogel's study of the American business philosophy. He suggests that 'the most characteristic, distinctive and persistent belief of American corporate executives is an underlying suspicion and mistrust of government' (Vogel 1978: 45). At the heart of his analysis are two values and two norms. The dominant value is an emphatically and sincerely articulated support for the 'free enterprise system' and associated with that is the practical norm of rejecting any action that inhibits management autonomy. More specific to government is a parallel value that wholeheartedly rejects the legitimacy of state intervention in the economy and a norm that is suspicious of the competence and the motives of public officials. Vogel has subsequently adapted the clarity of this position to argue that governments in the United States have pursued aggressive and important policies of industrial promotion, these have been made compatible with an adversary political culture by elaborate rationalization and concealment (Vogel 1986: 94).

In a recent study Vogel uses these concepts to help explain variations in the form and success of regulative policy in the U. K. and the USA, hence illustrating the utility of the approach. His findings are complimentary to British policy makers. He concludes that environmental regulation in Britain is cooperative and relatively successful, partly because the civil service is respected and business regards regulatory intervention as legitimate (Vogel 1986: 242). This perhaps demonstrates that where you get to depends on where you start and that Anglo-American comparisons produce different perspectives from Anglo-Japanese ones. However, Vogel is arguing that regulative policy is regarded as legitimate in Britain whereas promotional 'industrial policy' is not.

The effectiveness of British regulatory policy and the failures of British industrial policies are related. The very style of policy making that improves the effectiveness of the former diminishes the effectiveness of the latter. The government is unable to implement policies in either area without securing the consent and co-operation of the companies affected [...] both sets of policies have been, in practice, jointly administered by civil servants and industrialists. In neither case has the government been able to impose its priorities on industry; rather it has continually adjusted its policies to industry's own definitions of its needs and capacities (Vogel 1986: 284).

The idea that regulative policy rests within a different cultural tradition is important as is the idea of responsiveness to industry's needs. This recalls Samuel's conclusions on the Japanese state although we might be wary of seeing the problems through American eyes.

Industrial cultures which sanction or disapprove of a close relation between government and industry will be embodied in the bureaucracy but also in business. A business culture will be far more heterogeneous than that of the civil service. The classic 'fractions' of capital, finance and industrial; large and small; domestic and multinational; might be expected to vary in their attitudes to government intervention. Similarly the vexatious question of the control of business, whether by owners or by managers, adds a further layer of complexity. In Britain, however, it appears fairly clear that business has a strong antagonism to comprehensive or detailed governmental intervention into the structure, financing and control of industry. There is a marked opposition to 'industrial policy'. This is a cultural pattern less deeply founded than the equivalent mix of civil service attitudes. At times, as in the late 1930s and early 1960s, industry appeared more open and welcoming to ideas of industrial planning and a public-private sponsorship of industrial modernization. Here the obstructionism of the Treasury and the dogmatism of the Labour Party arguably strangled the development of a government-industry partnership although Ingham would also suggest that the City's power proved a decisive obstacle (Ingham 1984: chapter 9).

British industry, then, has retained a culture of individualism (or autonomy), voluntarism and commitment to the market. These features are recognizably similar to those identified by Vogel in the United States and are conventionally explained by the history of industrialization which in Britain was undertaken by small entrepreneurs, self-financed with minimal help, or even interest, from the state. Explaining the origin of this culture is relatively simple, it is less easy to explain how it has been perpetuated. There are, it seems, three important factors at work.

First, a professionalized managerial cadre has been slow to emerge in Britain. Despite the high level of concentration of British industry, the family firm and the conglomerate holding company forms persisted well into the 1960s. Channon's classic study found the multidivisional form of organization becoming widespread in the late 1960s, but, even then, 'the general officers of many corporations had not yet divorced themselves from the operations of the divisions in order to concentrate on their entrepreneurial role of strategic decision-making' (Channon 1973: 240). Hannah suggests that one reason for this was simply the pervasiveness and efficiency of the British market system which made it unnecessary for British firms to develop the elaborate hierarchical co-ordination through large enterprises, the state, or the banks as in the other, later, industrializers. He also, however, reminds us of the lower prestige of business and of underinvestment in managerial talent. Hence relatives went into family firms because no-one else would, the Oxbridge product (unlike the Tokyo product) was not available (Hannah 1980: 64−69). Thus the virtual absence of a managerial class inhibited the formulation and articulation of class interests. In Marxian terms the industrial bourgeoisie had not established an hegemony.

A second factor can be seen in the way that British management borrowed its attitudes and philosophies from elsewhere rather than developing a self-confident mission. Production techniques were borrowed from the United States but Lewchuck's recent excellent study of the motor industry shows how management backed away from taking direct responsibility for the shop floor (Lewchuck 1987). This theme is echoed by Anthony's defence of paternalism in which he argues that management has pursued a policy of insulation from labour. Insulation originated in traditional 'labour contracting' practices in the 18th century and early 19th century but was continued through the intermediation of the foreman and the role of the unions and company personnel departments. His argument is that management is insecure, unsure of the legitimacy of its real power (Anthony 1986). Some would go further. In a much quoted article Nettl argued that 'business in England lacks a social identity of its own', instead it has emulated 'a model of attitudes, procedures, institutions — an elite [...]. In Britain this is the higher Civil Service' (Nettl 1965: 25, 29). Nettl's argument has become rapidly outdated, it is also a fairly horrifying thought, given what we know of the managerial capacity of the civil service, but it does serve to emphasize a tendency towards complacency and deference in much of British management.

A third factor in explaining cultural continuity is the relative weakness of British industrial leadership. The institutions of collective industrial representation are under-developed in Britain when compared with Europe or Japan while the peak organizations themselves are weak. In a recent study Grant and Sargent (1987) bring together the results of many years study of peak organizations in Britain. They conclude that business finds it hard to formulate and express collective views and further, that it addresses its views to a very unresponsive state machinery. English individualism and corporate autonomy continue to be pursued with vigour and determination. At the risk of cultural obfuscation one is reminded of Macfarlane's assertion that English individualistic capitalism actually dates back to the 13th century, that 'English property relations were at the heart of much that is special about England, particularly in relation to industrialisation' (Macfarlane 1978: 200). As Berger (1987: 95) points out, Macfarlane's argument presents 'a total reversal of the conventional notion of causality: it is not modernity that has caused individualism, but, on the contrary, the individualistic patterns of medieval England made it possible for modernity to arise there'. Thus attempts to substitute collective for individualistic industrial leadership require a truly radical discontinuity. The autonomous English company is operating within a peculiar English tradition of at least six centuries in the making.

Continental and Japanese Comparisons

Space precludes an elaborate analysis of managerial attitudes to state intervention in West Germany and France. The generally accepted view would be that, while tension exists, the two values and two norms identified in the Anglo-Saxon cases would not hold true. In other words, management would be sceptical about the unfettered free market and would accept some limitation on managerial autonomy; similarly they would concede the legitimacy of state intervention and would concede a high degree of trust in the competence of state officials.

The Japanese position is even further away from the Anglo-Saxon model. As Clark notes, 'modern industries were created, largely by the state' (Clark 1979: 20) in the twenty years after 1868, they were then privatized. The industries were sold cheaply 'and many of the buyers were friends of senior officials'. He goes on to note that the early industrialists "tended to owe their success to two factors, determination [...] and good contacts in government. It is possible, perhaps to divide them roughly into two categories, 'merchants of fortune' and 'government proteges'" (Clark 1979: 212). Of the two most influential *zaibatsu* the founders of Mitsubishi he puts in the former category and Mitsui in the latter. There are plenty of subsequent examples of industry objecting to, resisting and failing to comply with government intervention but, as noted above, the right and the duty of the state to take responsibility for industrial development has never been in serious doubt.

Historical Origins of Cultural Attitudes

The discussion undertaken above draws on historical accounts of the evolution of attitudes to the role of government in the economy. These attitudes can be said to be culturally derived in that they are integrated into the socialization and education process, they are widespread, inarticulate, unquestioned and conform to societal expectations about the role of government. They are, in other words, a sub-set of a wider political culture. They appear 'natural' but are, in fact, constructed by social forces. This process of the 'manufacture' of culture and the institutionalization of it in organizations and processes is the central concern of this chapter. Culture used as in independent variable to explain all behaviour otherwise inexplicable becomes a generalized stereotype which is positively harmful. Culture used as a dependent variable to explain how a mix of historical, social and political forces have been fused to shape attitudes and expectations is an indispensable tool of cross-national comparison.

Using 'industrial culture' in this fashion requires that the origins, form and effect of culture be identified as part of a process of innovation. It also requires an explanation of how an industrial culture is sustained and reproduced.

Although he rejects the idea of a 'fixed notion of national character or national culture', Armstrong has expressed the above problematic admirably. He argues that Prussian and British administrative roles are expressed in socialization patterns,

these patterns originated during relatively brief periods of time scarcely exceeding a generation. At that time the socialization patterns served the interests of determinable groups. Although one may admit a certain inertia for patterns once formed, they persisted over long periods essentially because they continued to accord with the interests of these or other social collectivities (Armstrong 1973: 300).

What I have called 'culture' Armstrong terms 'ideology', hence "In employing 'ideology' we shall retain the basic sense in which Marx used the term i. e. an argument (more frequently an elaborate set of arguments) advanced to explain why an institution or value was introduced or maintained". Thus, in the British case, Armstrong uses this 'genetic approach' to argue that elite socialization was in the interests of the educational elite, although such groups may misperceive their interests which 'might have been better served by a more interventionist, hence more influential Administrative class'. Nevertheless,

once an administrative elite socialized in accordance with the Oxbridge prescription was firmly established, the administrators themselves acquired an interest in perpetuating the non interventionist role definition. An interventionist position would have revealed the specific inadequacies of their training, disrupted their corporate solidarity, and reduced their status in the general elite (Armstrong 1973: 301).

We might note Gowans argument that behind the interests of the administrative class itself stood the broader interests of the 'landed classes' which actually rejected interventionism while accepting the validity of Armstrong's methodology.

The British case may be fairly clear cut. There is wide agreement on the importance, if not the significance, of the period 1850−80 when the civil service was reformed. We can also, however, point to key cultural turning points in each of the countries discussed at which time industrial cultures were formulated and embedded in institutions, processes and attitudes. In Germany, for instance, the period 1870 (when the Deutsche Bank and Commerzbank were formed) to 1910 was the high tide of bank hegemony, the period which Hilferding immortalized in his model of finance capital and whose legacy continues to be influential. More recently we can look to the post-war reconstruction of the German union system which has played such a part in German industrial success. The well-known industrial unions were in fact based on divisions designed by the National Socialist union organization, but the concrete legislative reconstruction was consciously designed to facilitate industrial rationality. Thus the important works councils impose a set of obligations on works councillors. Their most basic duty is to 'cooperate with the employer [...] as well as the union and the employer's associations present in the plant for the good of the plant and its workers' (Article 2 of the 1952 Works Constitution Act, revised 1972, cited in Markovits 1986: 49). As Streeck (1984) has also argued, this system of industrial relations was constructed, it did not just 'happen', but once it had been constructed the pattern became routinized.

So also for France. Zysman, like Armstrong, rejects the blanket concept of culture as 'national character'. He puts the emphasis on the post-war movement towards the concerted economy symbolized by the role of the planners, Bloch-Laine and Monnet. Hence, he argues,

the interventionist state was not the product of some ingrained national character, of an ideology of etatism, or of a historical tradition of close involvement in the economy. [...] Embedded in old institutions [...] it represented an explicit political victory that shifted the relative positions of business leadership and state bureaucrats (Zysman 1983: 105).

The Japanese case is even more clear cut. In a fascinating example of real cultural manipulation Clark outlines the problem posed for Japanese industrialization by the fact that Confucion moral values regarded the businessman (merchant) as an inferior, 'clearly, views of business would have to change if the country were to become rich and powerful'. Business was legitimated by associating it with nationalism and public spirit. Shibusawa, a hugely successful entrepreneur of the 1870s and 80s is quoted as explaining 'My object does not lie in the increase of wealth, but from the nature of the business it so happens. That is all. Never for a moment did I aim at my own profit'. These notions, says Clark, endured. Especially 'the ideal of the businessman as the benefactor of the community and servant (though at a slight remove) of the state; and the precept that the businessman should be inspired more by altruism and high principle than profit' (Clark 1979: 26−9). This argument is echoed by Boyd who notes that classical free enterprise utilitarianism 'was regarded as unacceptably selfish in Japan' (Boyd 1987: 67). Similarly, while Berger notes that it is difficult to decide whether the Meiji oligarchs were pursuing insight, or were just lucky, it does appear that 'these individuals did accomplish a feat of ideological permutation that ingeniously combined traditional symbols with modern needs' (Berger 1987: 164 and 145). Thus, while the British were constructing a dysfunctional culture of a liberal bureaucratic elite, the Japanese were establishing the principled, altruistic businessman as the prestigious partner of government. 'This form of the government-business relationship' says Johnson (1982: 311) 'is not peculiarly or uniquely Japanese; the Japanese have merely worked harder at perfecting it'.

Conclusion

The chapter has defined industrial culture in terms of the values and norms held within society which express beliefs and expectations about the legitimacy of state intervention in the economy. It has rejected the idea that such cultures can be expressed and compared by reference to traditionally formed variants of 'national character' which are created in a deterministic process of historical inevitability. Instead, it has been argued, the characteristics and origins of industrial culture can be identified, as can distinct sub-cultures. The major economic groupings within society, bureaucracy, management, labour and political parties each have their variants on a national industrial culture; these may be synchronous, as in the Japanese case, or they may be conflictual, as in the United States or in Britain. What is more, although the argument has not been elaborated at this level, individual organizations, such as MITI or the German universal banks, will have a distinct industrial culture.

The tenor of the argument has thus been to downplay anthropological interpretations of culture in favour of a theory of political choice. Industrial cultures are created in a more or less comprehensible process, and enough has been said above to demonstrate the historical evidence for this assertion. Much attention is paid by political scientists and social theorists to the creation and implication of welfare states; equal attention is arguably merited in the case of what is increasingly known as 'developmental states'. Once created, industrial cultures are perpetuated by deliberate processes of socialization (the educational system) and rationalized by habit and tradition. Clearly industrial cultures must be, or be made, compatible with existing economic endowments, political realities and social mores but they constitute radical breaks with past patterns, breaks that have sometimes been allowed by military defeat. Perpetuation of culture is also dictated by organizational self-interest (public choice theory has something to offer here), and by continuous, conscious adjustment and maintenance. Political elites have to work at maintaining the system.

It follows that, having been manufactured, such industrial cultures can be changed. We are experiencing a period of such change in the U.K. The direction of change is towards an American rather than a Japanese model. It is individualistic, market orientated and clearly more compatible with historic British beliefs than would be the capitalist developmental cultures of France or Japan. It is far from clear that the direction of change is wholly appropriate. To allow the anthropologists back in, one is reminded of Ernest Gellner's magisterial remark on the *laissez-faire* project, 'the trouble with the programme is not simply that it will not work, but that, constituting as it does a logical absurdity, it does not correspond to any possible state of affairs' (1987: 121). More provocatively, like Ron Dore, it is possible to admire the potential for social responsibility in the Japanese industrial system which moved the early 1970s priorities away from polluting activities towards a greater concern with the (Japanese!) environment and towards 'knowledge-based' industries. Knowing one has choices is the first step on the road to using them intelligently.

References

Anthony, P. D. (1986): *The foundation of management,* London: Tavistock.

Armstrong, J. A. (1973): *The European administrative elite,* Princeton, N. J.: Princeton University Press.

Balogh, T. (1959): The apotheosis of the dilettante, in: Hugh Thomas (ed.), *The establishment,* London: Anthony Blond.

Barnett, C. (1986): *The audit of war: the illusion and reality of Britain as a great nation,* London: Macmillan.

Berger, P. (1987): *The capitalist revolution,* Aldershot: Gower.

Boyd, R. (1987): Government — industry relations in Japan: access, communication and competitive collaboration, in: Wilks, S. and M. Wright (eds.), *Comparative government — industry relations,* Oxford: Clarendon.

Channon, D. (1973): *The strategy and structure of British enterprise,* London: Macmillan.

Clark, R. (1979): *The Japanese company,* New Haven, Conn.: Yale University Press.

CM 278 (1988): Department of Trade and Industry White Paper, *DTI the department of enterprise,* London: HMSO.

Dell, E. (1972): *Political responsibility and industry,* London: Allan and Unwin.

Dore, R. (1986): *Flexible rigidities: industrial policy and structural adjustment in the Japanese economy 1970 — 80.* London: Athlone.

Dyson, K. (1983): The cultural, ideological and structural context, in: K. Dyson and S. Wilks (eds.), *Industrial crisis: a comparative study of the state and industry,* 26 — 66, Oxford: Martin Robertson.

Gellner, E. (1987): *Culture, identity and politics,* Cambridge: Cambridge University Press.

Gowan, P. (1987): The origins of the administrative elite, *New Left Review,* 162: 1 — 29.

Grant, W. with J. Sargent (1987): *Business and politics in Britain,* London: Macmillan.

Hannah, L. (1980): Visible and invisible hands in Great Britain, in: A. Chandler and H. Daems (eds.), *Managerial hierarchies,* 41 — 76, Cambridge, Mass.: Harvard University Press.

Ingham, G. (1984): *Capitalism divided? the city and industry in British social development,* London: Macmillan.

Johnson, C. (1982): *MITI and the Japanese miracle: the growth of industrial policy 1925 — 1975,* Stanford, Cal.: Stanford University Press.

Ketcham, R. (1987): *Individualism and public life,* Oxford: Basil Blackwell.

Komiya, R. and K. Yamamoto (1981): Japan: the officer in charge of economic affairs, *History of Political Economy* 13: 600−628.

Lewchuck, W. (1987): *American technology and the British vehicle industry,* Cambridge University Press.

Macfarlane, A. (1978): *The origins of English individualism,* Oxford: Basil Blackwell.

Markovits, A. (1986): *The politics of the West German trade unions: strategies of class and interest representation in growth and crisis,* Cambridge: Cambridge University Press.

Metcalfe, L. and S. Richards (1987): *Improving public management,* London: Sage.

Nairn, T. (1981): *The break-up of Britain,* London: Verso, second edition.

Nettl, J. P. (1965): Consensus or elite domination: the case of business, *Political Studies* 13: 22−44.

Pollard, S. (1982): *The wasting of the British economy,* London: Croom Helm.

Pye, L. W. with M. W. Pye (1985): *Asian power and politics: the cultural dimension of authority,* Belknap: Harvard University Press.

Richards, S. (1986): *The changing managerial culture of the civil service,* London: Business School.

Samuels, R. J. (1987): *The business of the Japanese state: energy markets in comparative and historical perspective,* Ithaca, N. Y.: Cornell University Press.

Streeck, W. (1984): *Industrial relations in West Germany: a case study of the car industry,* London: Policy Studies Institute/Heinemann.

Thomas, R. (1978): *The British philosophy of administration: a comparison of British and American ideas 1900−1939,* London: Longman.

Vogel, D. (1978): Why businessmen distrust their state: the political consciousness of American corporate executives, *British Journal of Political Science* 8: 157− 172.

Vogel, D. (1986): *National styles of regulation: environmental policy in Britain and the United States,* Ithaca, N. Y.: Cornell University Press.

Wiener, M. (1981): *English culture and the decline of the industrial spirit 1850− 1980,* Cambridge: Cambridge University Press.

Wilks, S. R. M. (1986): Government-industry relations: a review article, *Policy and Politics* 14: 491−505.

Wilks, S. R. M. (1987): Administrative culture and policy making in the Department of the Environment, *Public Policy and Administration* 2: 25−41.

Wilks, S. R. M. (1988) *Industrial policy and the motor industry,* Manchester: Manchester University Press, second edition.

Wilks, S. and M. Wright (eds.) (1987): *Comparative government-industry relations: Western Europe the United States and Japan,* Oxford: Clarendon.

Wolf, M. J. (1983): *The Japanese conspiracy: the plot to dominate industry worldwide − and how to deal with it,* New York: Empire Books.

Young, M. K. (1986): Administrative guidance and industrial policy: participatory policy formulation and execution in Japan, unpublished paper.

Zysman, J. (1983): *Governments, markets and growth: financial systems and the politics of industrial change,* Oxford: Martin Robertson.

Centrifugal Versus Centripetal Growth Processes: Contrasting Ideal Types for Conceptualizing the Developmental Patterns of Chinese and Japanese Firms

Simon Tam

Introduction

Economic growth in Japan and Hong Kong has been widely acknowledged, but the underlying organizational processes which contribute to their macro-economic growth have not been systematically compared. This chapter attempts to take the first step in filling this gap. It will try to contrast the patterns of organizational growth in these two economies. Given the nature of the task, substantial intra-country variations in organizational processes will be glossed over. What will be presented are two ideal typical images which, it will be argued, capture the basic patterns of organizational growth in Japan and Hong Kong. Given the magnitude of the task, the results presented here should be regarded as preliminary and tentative.

Events leading to this research have been the discovery of several anomalies in Hong Kong which are, in the light of the literature, highly antithetical to its economic achievement. These anomalies include, amongst others, widespread disloyalty and lack of commitment of employees to companies, pervasive neglect of human resource development within companies, extremely limited trust and openness between employers and employees, constant disintegration of firms into units of atomistic size, thereby sacrificing the economies of scale. And yet despite these anomalies Hong Kong has a highly effective workforce, an abundant supply of first-class entrepreneurs and businessmen, constant renewal of firms and gigantic industrial power. In fact, Hong Kong prospers along with these anomalies. Contrasting this with the principles found in the management literature, particularly in the light of the Japanese experience, the economic miracle of Hong Kong demands an explanation — an explanation which could not be furnished by our existing pool of knowledge. Perhaps a new conceptualization is required in order to understand the Hong Kong case.

It is against this background that an ideal-typical image of the Chinese Business System has been conceived.

Method

The basic method is longitudinal research and can be conceived of as comprising two major stages[1].

Stage One: Data Collection
Within this there are three sub-phases.

1. field visits to companies in Japan for a total of three months to obtain basic personal experience for detailed reading of the Japanese management literature.

2. longitudinal field studies of thirteen firms in Hong Kong. The firms are from the following industries:
   a) Textile: 1 dyeing and finishing factory.
   b) Garment: 1 knitwear factory,
                    1 woven-wear factory,
                    1 import/export firm
   c) Electronic: 1 computer company,
                    1 electronic product distributor
   d) Plastics: 1 plastic factory
   e) Printing: 1 printing company
   f) Jewellery: 1 jewellery company
   g) Food: 1 food product company

[1] I am extremely grateful to Professor Tom Rhoel of the University of Washington who oriented me so well to Japan and introduced me to Professor Kenichi Imai and his faculty in Hitotsubashi University. His faculty has been very generous in sharing their research results on Japanese organizations with me.

The Chinese Executive Club of Hong Kong organized a study tour to Japanese ministries, institutions and companies in 1985. I am grateful for its provision of this opportunity and for those participating businessmen who freely shared their experiences and observations of Japanese business with me. On that tour, MITI, the Japan Management Association, Nomura Securities, the HK Trade Development Council Japan Branch, Dai Nippon Printing, Sapporo Brewery, Toyo Glass, Nifco Fasteners, Isetan Department Store and Jukuba Expo plus a few subcontracting operations were visited.

I am also indebted to the Asian Productivity Organization for sponsoring me on the Senior Management Consultants Course which enabled me to investigate many companies in various parts of Japan, some in considerable detail. Acting through the Japan Productivity Centre, the course has channelled me to companies including Oki Electronic, Mitsubishi Heavy Industry, Tohuko Metal Industries in Sendai, Daiichi Yoshi in Osaka and Munakata of the Matsushita group, amongst others. I benefited greatly from the in-depth knowledge of Japanese enterprises of Mr. Akira Takanaka and Professor Tamaki and his team. I was carefully guided by Mr. Ueda and Mr. Adachi of JPC to the various facets of Japanese culture via personal experience. Without them this paper would not have been written.

h) Retail: 1 retail food chain,
                  1 photographic processing chain
h) Publishing: 1 magazine publishing company.

Because of the tendency of Chinese businesses in Hong Kong to be very secretive about their affairs, research in such companies is not generally favoured. To get around this problem, the basic strategy employed is through action research, that is, in-depth research opportunities are obtained through offering consultancy advice for firms facing problems. This proves to be effective but it has the problem of whether those cases studied constitute a representative sample. To balance this source of bias, an additional strategy of accumulating cases from key industries in Hong Kong over time is employed to build up the necessary coverage. In the course of accumulating research findings, major themes began to emerge. Such themes have enabled more focused and efficient exploration to take place in subsequent phases.

These basic strategies underwent modification and refinement as the research project unfolded. It was becoming clear that Chinese firms on the whole have not been successful in integrating their employees to the extent that their organizations are plagued pervasively by subterranean movements. As a result, a research method has to be redesigned to tap the intentions and activities of the underground layers. Arising from this need, informants from diverse sources and companies who could provide such information were extensively cultivated.

3. Extensive interviews with entrepreneurs and managers in Hong Kong (over 300 by now), collection of entrepreneurial career histories from diverse industries (over 335 by now), compilation of company histories (over 60 by now), analysing histories of industries in Hong Kong.

Stage Two: Conceptualization
Various anomalies proved to be avenues leading to discovery after uncovering of various fragments of the reality. A sequence of 'inspirations' from time to time — which unlocked the riddles one after another — finally culminated in one sudden moment when a configurational image of the Chinese Business System emerged. This process of gradual realization was concurrent with the re-constitution of an image of the Japanese Business System, thereby developing two contrasting ideal types. The usefulness of this contrast between Hong Kong and Japan was that during the conceptualization stage they proved mutually illuminating. But given the widely disseminated knowledge about the Japanese enterprise and the scarcity of information on its counterpart, the benefit of this contrast has been heavily in favour of the Hong Kong Chinese enterprise.

The construction of the ideal types has been given a sense of unity by the basic tendencies operating in the two systems, which can be viewed as polar opposites. The logic of construction is to see what are the major elements bearing on these basic tendencies and how these elements inter-relate and reinforce each other to give stability and coherence to the configuration. In actual practice, the process was rather more complex than reported here. This is because the process of reconceptualization has not been a linear one, it involved several blind alleys entered and a huge amount of mental experimentation before the mosaic took shape.

Contrasting Developmental Patterns

Perhaps the best way of presenting the operation of the two basic tendencies in the Japanese and Chinese Business Systems is by reference to the following diagrams:

Figure 1 refers to a particular phase of development in Mitsubishi Shoji, a gigantic trading arm of an enterprise group called Mitsubishi in Japan. Figures 2 and 3 refer to the histories of two companies in Hong Kong, one in trading and the other in manufacturing. Both of them point to the phenomenon of firms splitting up. This process is conducted at two levels: amongst the owners themselves and between the employer and the em-ployees.

Enterprise Development Pattern in Japan

Figure 1 is both typical and untypical. It is untypical because of the speed of consolidation. Immediately after the war and the allied dissolution, once the regulations were lifted, the collectivist tendency quickly became ap-parent. But this speed was because their former loyalties and ties remained unbroken. However, the basic tendency is unmistakable, it goes well beyond those with pre-war loyalties. There are new types of groupings as well. Yoshino has identified two distinctive types:

Type one refers to the corporate groups of large independent firms. Within this type there are several categories of which two are most important:

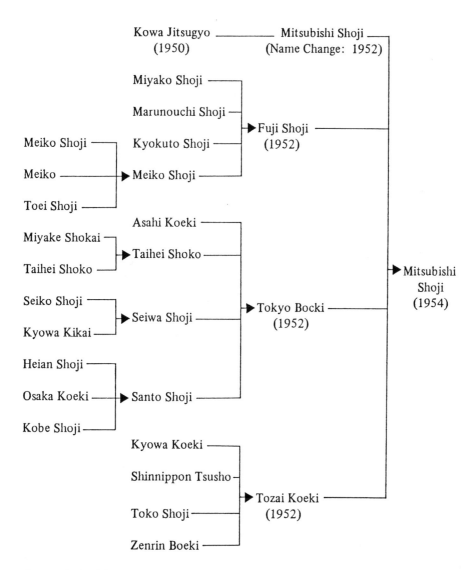

Source: Mitsubishi Shoji, *Mitsubishi Shoji, Sono Ayumi: 20-shunen Kinen-go,* 1974: 22.

Figure 1   The Rebirth of Mitsubishi Shoji

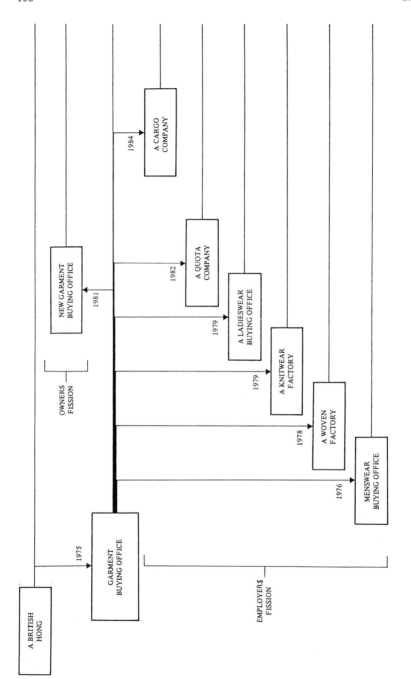

Figure 2 Developmental History of a Garment Buying Office in Hong Kong (1975—1984)

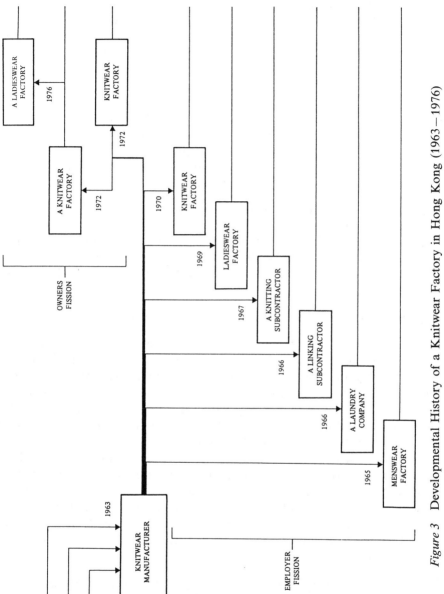

Figure 3 Developmental History of a Knitwear Factory in Hong Kong (1963–1976)

a. corporate groupings based on former Zaibatsu ties
   These include Mitsubishi, Mitsui and Sumitomo, the most important
   'Zaibatsu' before the war. The lesser pre-war 'Zaibatsu' had regrouped
   themselves as well. Prominent among these are Furukawa, Kawasaki
   and the Nissan groups. These latter three are also forging intergroup
   cooperation among themselves.
b. corporate groupings formed around major city banks
   These include Fuji, Mitsubishi, Sumitomo, Mitsui, Sanwa and Daiichi.
   These banks made a persistent effort in forging close links with prominent industrial firms by pursuing a preferential loan policy, whose
   objective was to establish a diversified industrial group as the nucleus.
   Such groupings began to take shape in the late 1950s.

Type Two is a loose, vertical hierarchy of small- to medium-size enterprises
organized around a single giant firm. The large firm has a network of
intricately related subsidaries, affiliated firms and subcontractors, which it
fosters and directs. Included in this type are names like Hitachi, Matsushita,
Toyota, Toyo Rayon, Yawata Iron and Steel, Tokyo Shibaura Electric etc.
(Yoshino 1968).

Economic re-concentration after the war has been very marked.

A study by the Fair Trade Commission in 1966 revealed that the aggregate
capital of the 100 largest corporations (exclusive of banking and insurance
firms) listed in the first section of the Tokyo Stock Exchange represented
39.4% of the total corporate capital in Japan. The total capital of the
firms linked to the six major city banks has reached nearly 63% of the
combined capital of all the firms listed in the first section of the Tokyo
Stock Exchange. It is also now a common phenomenon for large Japanese
firms each to be in effective control of a network of subsidiaries, satellites
of affiliated enterprises and a pyramid of subcontractors. The number of
small firms in each industrial group could easily be as high as several
hundred. They are dependent on the major concern not only for business,
but for financial, technical and managerial assistance, and their operations
are integrated to a considerable degree with those of the major concern
(Yoshino 1968).

This overall tendency for firms to congregate has been so pervasive that
the term 'enterprise group capitalism' has been coined to describe the
phenomenon (Yonekura 1985).

Table 1 Number of establishments and average employment in manufacturing, 1947 – 1983

Year	Est.	Emp.	Mean	Year	Est.	Emp.	Mean
1947	961	47,356	49.3	1966	8,941	346,990	38.8
1948	1,120	56,815	50.7	1967	10,234	399,918	39.1
1949	1,251	60,205	48.1	1968	11,667	472,412	40.4
1950	1,478	81,718	55.2	1969	14,078	524,371	37.2
1951	1,720	86,136	50.0	1970	16,507	459,178	27.8
1952	1,902	85,322	44.8	1971	18,612	564,370	30.0
1953	2,038	92,178	45.2	1972	20,474	578,855	28.2
1954	2,201	98,196	44.6	1973	21,470	581,701	27.1
1955	2,437	110,574	45.3	1974	31,318	600,128	19.1
1956	2,944	128,818	43.7	1975	31,034	678,857	21.2
1957	3,080	137,783	44.7	1976	36,303	773,746	21.3
1958	3,524	156,556	44.4	1977	37,568	755,108	19.4
1959	4,541	177,271	39.0	1978	41,240	816,683	19.8
1960	4,784	215,854	45.1	1979	42,282	870,898	20.1
1961	5,624	215,914	38.4	1980	45,409	892,140	19.6
1962	6,178	255,198	41.3	1981	46,729	904,646	19.3
1963	7,108	276,699	38.9	1982	46,448	847,194	18.2
1964	8,132	325,286	40.0	1983	47,081	848,703	18.0
1965	8,137	329,214	40.4	1984	48,992	904,709	18.4

Source: Redding and Hicks (1985)

Enterprise development pattern in Hong Kong

Figures 2 and 3, which were chosen as representative cases to describe Chinese-owned Hong Kong firms, display the reverse tendency. This tendency, which becomes obvious if we look at the firms' development over time, could be characterized as perennial fissioning. Data on development of firms in Hong Kong in general has so far been supportive of this observation, for instance:

1. The average size of manufacturing firms, which fuelled the engine of economic growth in Hong Kong, has been declining since 1950, when Hong Kong started to experience industrial expansion (Redding and Hicks 1983). This decline is shown in Table 1.

2. Two comprehensive surveys, one held in 1978, the other in 1987, in five manufacturing industries (garment, textiles, plastics, electronic and precision equipment), revealed that 80% of the entrepreneurs in those industries have undergone the typical pattern of firstly working in one job, accumulating capital and know-how, and then become employers. Only 5% of the entrepreneurs had never worked before they established their own factories (Sit and Wong 1988).

3. An interview study of textiles entrepreneurs in Hong Kong has identified a strong centrifugal force amongst the employees in that industry (Wong 1978).
4. Case studies by the author and colleagues over the years provide evidence supportive of these results (see, for example, Redding and Tam 1985, Tam 1987).

The Japanese Configuration

Here the underlying tendency discovered is centripetal. This concept is operationalized to mean that:

a. there is an inherent tendency for individuals to seek identity and to maintain existence and development by submergence in a collectivity. In this case the collectivity is an enterprise. And in the passage of time these individuals increasingly tend to deepen their bondage to each other and to the collectivity.
b. there is an inherent tendency for firms to affiliate themselves into groups of enterprises. And in the passage of time, these firms increasingly deepen their interdependence and solidify their relations.
c. that enterprise or groups of enterprises tend to seek improvement of their situation by aggrandizement: by securing more market bases, by including more members and by drawing more individual firms into their orbits.
d. A corollary of the above is a tendency for each member or each member firm which joins a collectivity increasingly to estrange himself or itself from other collectivities.

The above image has been gathered from diverse literature sources:

Theoretical discussion on (a) above has been refered to as the 'paternalism-lifetime commitment model' (Marsh and Mannari 1976). The most important statement in this regard is perhaps made by Dore (1973).

Description of interfirm bondage and affiliation can be found in Yoshino (1968) and Hirschmeier and Yui (1981). As has been noted, Yonekura (1985) labelled the Japanese phenomenon described in (2) as 'enterprise group capitalism'.

The imperative of growth as a strategic goal for Japanese firms is almost legendary (see, for example, Kagono et al. 1983). The competitiveness and mutual distancing amongst enterprises in similar markets and amongst enterprise groups is detailed in Hsu (1979).

The mutual exclusiveness of corporate groups referred to in (4) is portrayed in Cole (1971).

While these observations are now common knowledge (though their validity is not without debate), the task at hand is to compose a configurational image of Japanese enterprises in development terms so that comparison with the Hong Kong Chinese case can be made. For this reason it might be appropriate to address the issue of *why* this tendency should exist at all in the Japanese scene[2].

Again drawing together various pieces of the jigsaw puzzle from the literature, the underlying logic of the phenomenon could be reconstituted in the following way.

Basic Orientations

There seems to be a widely shared belief in the strength of a collectivity, such that individual identity is to be seen in the light of membership of a collectivity,

1. that it is through staying within a collectivity that one can seek dependence and security, and that the fate of both should be moulded into one. The prime responsibility of members in a collectivity is to ensure its permanent existence and prosperity (Doi 1973, Rohlen 1974).
2. that the membership for inclusion into the collectivity could transcend blood ties (Hsu 1963). This takes away an upper limit for size, at least theoretically.
3. that the existence of vertical orientation amongst the Japanese positively facilitates the enlargement of a collectivity by providing a orderly structural blueprint (Nakane 1970). The same orientation is expressed in the form of intense competition on ranking between corporate entities.

Centripetal Tendency in Enterprise Groups

These three principles have contributed to the centripetal tendency in enterprise groups via the following mechanisms:

A. When enterprises begin affiliating into groups, the collective strength arising from synergy tends to push corresponding competitors to join

---

[2] I am grateful to Prof. Koya Azumi for raising this issue during the APROS '88 Conference.

another group in oder to stay in the game. The rule of the game has been played historically in very similar pattern:

1. when the old Zaibatsu re-emerged after the war in a new form, their financial strength enabled those enterprises which they backed up to develop very fast. This worsened the position of the unassociated competitors, and their natural response was to try to associate with a powerful bank so as to enhance their financial backing.
2. expansion in the scale of business after the war had put the smaller banks in a vulnerable position because if they could not live up to their appetite for huge borrowing, their clients would be lost to the major banks. This triggered a series of mergers and amalgamations of smaller banks.
3. the re-unification of trading companies amongst Mitsui and Mitsubishi also triggered a series of *sogo shosha* realignments in other enterprise groupings to counteract their erosion of scale advantage (Hsu 1979).

It can thus be seen that once the race for affiliation and aggrandizement is on, enterprises and corporate groups seem to get caught in cycles of mutually aggravating escalation.

In fiscal 1963 one hundred largest non-financial corporations controlled 53.2% of all paid-in corporate capital in Japan − 39.4% directly, another 13.8% through affiliates (Caves and Uekusa 1976).
It is also significant that the rate of concentration steadily climbed from 32.1% in 1953 to 35.4% in 1958, and then to nearly 40% in 1964 (Yoshino 1968).

B. The synergistic effect of collectivity was actively exploited to attract further affiliations, strengthen internal cohesion and deepen the interdepence amongst the participating enterprises. Massive growth projects requiring interfirm pooling of technical, financial and managerial capacities began to be launched (Yoshino 1976).
C. Vertical and horizontal linkages amongst the participating enterprises were increasingly cultivated. Strategic composition of business lines whithin enterprise groups began to be developed (see, for example, the development and internal structuring of the Sanwa Group in Sato 1984).

Different enterprise groups compete in every respect with each other, from all the core businesses to new growth fields, at times carried to excess (Hirschmeier and Yui 1981). This tendency also allows each corporate group to achieve a certain degree of self-sufficiency, thereby having the power to undertake crucial exchanges with in-group firms and seal off contact points with out-group firms as much as possible.

Centripetal Tendency within Individual Enterprise

It can be seen from the above that there are forces in the situation which put the unaffiliated companies at a disadvantage in survival and growth terms and as a result one discovers a general inclination for firms to be associated with an enterprise group (Clark 1979). According to the survey by the Small Business Administration, about 60% of small manufacturing businesses belong to groups attached to large corporations. (A small business is defined as employing less than 300 employees [Kono 1984].)

What this general pattern implies is that a substantial proportion of firms in Japan enjoy a greater degree of economic stability and financial security than firms in Hong Kong. The oligopolistic control over the market, the support of in-group banking and financial institutions, the extensive use of cross-corporate shareholding, the in-group diffusion of information and technology, the generosity of extending managerial assistance and the ultimate back-up by the Ministries, together provide layer after layer of safety nets to enhance their chance of continual existence and prosperity.

Such security and stability enhance the possibility of a longer-term orientation. They also provide a favourable basis on which a firm can attempt to construct a context of mutual prosperity. The logic of the situation can be described in the following manner:

1. Enhanced security as a result of staying within a larger collectivity permits a firm to extend a long-term commitment to its employees. Integrative and paternalistic measures can be introduced in exchange for loyalty.
2. Deep-seated vertical orientation makes a long-term career passage with hierarchical gradation meaningful to members, thus providing the company with a highly effective tool to increase the anchorage of employees in the company over time.
3. The collective frame of action facilitates the development of mutual bondage for members over time.
4. Increasing unity within a collection of individuals also leads to estrangement from other groups and there are ample measures for a company to discourage interfirm mobility. Holistic provisions for employees add further to their embeddedness (Cole 1973, Rohlen 1974).

A holistic image of the configuration is presented in Figure 4, with the emphasis on the underlying centripetal tendency:

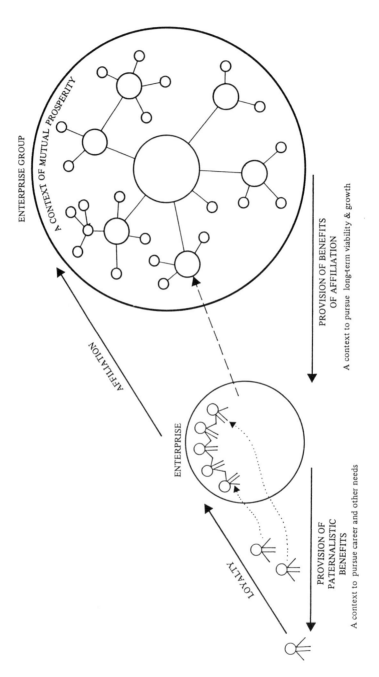

Figure 4   Centripetal Tendency: The Japanese Pattern

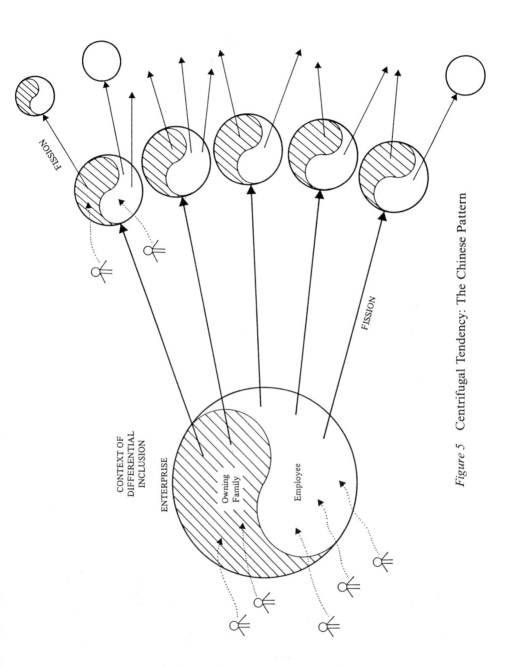

Figure 5 Centrifugal Tendency: The Chinese Pattern

The Chinese Configuration

Here the basic tendency is centrifugal (Figure 5). This concept is operationalized to mean that:

1. as far as possible, individuals are not prepared to subject themselves permanently to an enterprise, so that for the individuals concerned, the area of primary loyalty is not directed towards the enterprise;
2. there is an inherent tendency for individual firms to break-up into separate entities over time;
3. inter-firm associations and linkages tend to be shifting and temporal. As far as possible, a firm will avoid moving into a situation of over-dependence, and as far as possible a firm tries to move in the direction of independence.

These observations were formulated in the course of field research, but some evidence is already present in the existing literature, albeit in a scattered form. This presentation is structured according to the following sequence: anomalies which led to the discovery of major fragments of the configuration; initial evidence unearthed during field research; supporting evidence drawn from other researchers.

Anomalies

These features of the Chinese configuration appear anomalous when compared with the Japanese and the Western experience:

1. It is generally the case that firms increase in scale of operation to capitalize on a favourable macro-economic climate. Macro-economic growth in Hong Kong, however, has been accompanied by a consistent trend of dwindling in the average size of the firm, measured in terms of headcount. The average headcount per firm in 1950 was 55.2, this figure had shrunk to 18.4 by 1984.
2. It is widely believed that effective management of enterprises is a key factor in promoting macro-economic growth, and that management development effort is a key factor for enhancing managerial effectiveness (Handy 1987). The export sector has been the engine for the economic development of Hong Kong. But it is seldom realized that the leaders of the enterprises in this sector who are making this possible have so far received the most rudimentary form of management development provision. In a 1983 survey (Vocational Training Council Report 1983)

less than 6% of the entrepreneurial companies had managers and supervisors who had received any management training. 44.2% of the owner-managers had received primary education, 42.2% secondary education and only 13.6% post-secondary education. Most of the enterprises had no management development policies, nor internal training resources.

3. Egalitarian employment measures, consensus decision making, high wage homogeneity, employee empowerment and delegation are thought to be positively associated with performance. However, the reverse of all these normally cherished principles is enshrined within a typical Hong Kong enterprise. It is considered precarious to delegate; the more critical the function the less likely it would be delegated. Discriminatory employment practices are the norm. Decision making is centralized. Substantial differentials exist in the reward structure. It is amid this context that the economic miracle has occurred.

4. The employee loyalty and solidarity discovered in the Japanese milieu has been highly regarded and has been found to have positive links to company performance (Dore 1973, Vogel 1979). It is intriguing to note that most companies in Hong Kong have achieved their spectacular performance amid a context of rampant mobility, chronic factionalism, and covert and overt disloyalty.

5. Ongoing renewal of the firm has been considered a major managerial imperative. In the U.S. major enterprise renewal is typically achieved via the mechanism of leadership replacement (Hage 1980). The non-performing CEO is dethroned and a new leader is put in place to work out his new vision. He implements his new vision by adjusting the personnel, structure and systems to reflect the new emphasis. Should this work out, the company is revitalized. In the Japanese context the same effect is achieved by the mechanism of crisis excitement, with the leadership articulating the crisis, thereby appealing to and mobilizing the collectivity to respond to the new situation, capitalizing on the existence of a community sharing the same fate (Imai, Nonaka and Takeuchi 1984).

Given its chosen structure and systems, both routes are denied to the Chinese firm. There is no separation of ownership and management to make the leadership replacement option possible. (Research by Wong gives supportive evidence of the extent to which Chinese families maintain ownership control over enterprises in Hong Kong, which confirms the case findings of this author, further supported by evidence from extensive interviews of entrepreneurs by Redding; see Wong 1988, Redding 1990.) Also there is scarcely any integrative community in a Chinese firm to enable it to pursue the crisis excitement route either. Articulation of the possibility of crisis would most likely undermine the limited confidence of employees to the owning family and hasten their departure. And yet Hong Kong enterprises are constantly being revitalized.

Components of the Chinese Configuration

The above-listed anomalies are not exhaustive but even this brief list suggests that perhaps an alternative viable reality exists.

It was because of the need to unlock these riddles that the author was compelled to seek alternative explanations and conceptualizations. This new conceptualization takes on a configuration form because individual elements of the Chinese Business System, when examined in isolation, were not able to provide fruitful comparative insights because one could always identify similar instances in other economies. Every economy has small firms. Every economy has entrepreneurs. Every economy has family firms. Every economy experiences employee disloyalty. It is only when all the relevant elements are considered in interactive relationships with each other that a coherent and consistent pattern is found. It is this collective patterning of variables, not the individual fragments of reality, that is being considered here.[3]

What is presented below is the logical reconstruction of the configuration. Two new labels have been created, firstly for convenience of discussion, secondly for the purpose of alerting the reader to the unit of analysis adopted for this paper. The unit of analysis is not a firm, but groups of firms. The term used for the Chinese case is the 'Chinese Business System', and its correspondent reality, the 'Japanese Business System'.

It is proposed to present this new perspective in terms of the following components:

1. Structure: Form of co-operation
2. Actors: Major actors and their relations in the System
3. Process: Major processes leading to renewal
4. Behaviour: Group dynamics of firms
5. Culture: Ideology

---

[3] I enjoyed much stimulus from discussion of the configuration concept with Professor Richard Whitley.

*Component 1: Structure of the Chinese Business System — Unlocking the
first anomaly — Industrial power released by atomistic firms*

While it is relatively easy to comprehend the industrial might of the
Japanese Business System, being composed of juggernauts like *sogo shosha*,
heavy industrial combines, huge banks and ministries, it is more difficult
to understand why the export machinery in Hong Kong is also so powerful.
For after all, the average manufacturer has only 18 employees and the
average size of a trading company is 5.69 persons (1984 figures).

These statistical figures are deceptive and are based on a legal definition
of the firm. Also it is easy to read into the Western concept of the firm an
image of an organization composed of marketing, production, purchasing,
finance, personnel, distribution and other forms of horizontal division.
Each of these units will be structured into layers of hierarchical positions
until at the top of the pyramid, the CEO reports to the shareholders who
own the enterprise.

If that is the usual image, then there are reasons to adjust these concepts
when one approaches the Chinese Business System. Each of the aforemen-
tioned functions is divided and subdivided into numerous units, with each
unit having the legal prerogatives of an independent firm but performing
only a very small part of the total task which normally is done within one
enterprise in the U.S. The functional equivalent of a large corporation in
the West is a constellation of firms in Hong Kong. The functional equivalent of a section supervisor in the West is an entrepreneur in Hong Kong.
The task of co-ordination, however, is not done by hierarchy, its equivalent
in Hong Kong is the network (Redding and Tam 1985). Networks are
mostly built up by family, kin or friendship ties.

On the surface, it is quite similar to the Japanese industrial system. On
closer inspection, however, the Hong Kong system is immensely more
flexible. The rigidity of the Japanese system is built into the structure itself:

1. Their industrial groups tend to have a marketing arm which normally
   has substantial control over the market. This is denied to Hong Kong
   enterprises which normally export to importers and distributors in other
   economies in which they have limited control. Market fluctuation is a
   given in Hong Kong and is built into the expectation psyche of the
   entrepreneur. Without a stable market base, shifts in product-market
   requirements are met by shifting constellations of production units, that
   is: firms.
2. The relative permanency of relations within enterprise groupings in
   Japan does not encourage rapid switching of subcontractors. The relative transience of such bonding between enterprises in Hong Kong
   gives more flexibility.

Transactions of different magnitude and technical difficulty can be absorbed by the Chinese system, which can be conceived as being composed of numerous shifting constellations of firms ready to serve the market. With a total of 280,000 establishments in Hong Kong crowded into close proximity, almost unlimited combinations and permutations of capacity mobilization can be formed. There are pragmatic limits to the number of firms one could bring into formation such as the extensiveness of the organizers' network, industrial and technological differences across companies, the kind of capacity each company is already committed to, etc. Even after taking these constraints into account, the size of constellation one could form at one time is still formidable.

For any firm in the system there is no definite correlation between its size in terms of numbers of employees and its potential and variable capacity. In the course of one year a trading firm was found to have engaged the services and capacity of over sixty establishments and directly facilitated the formation of five enterprises, and yet all it employed was a staff of 17.

Taken as a whole, this system is both flexible and powerful, because collective strength can be easily mobilized in different combinations and permutations. Individual firms, however, are constantly embedded in a context of uncertainty and insecurity. The layers of the safety net found in the Japanese situation are generally absent. Long-term orientation is largely redundant, economic ties and interdependence within and between firms are transient and temporal.

Component 2: Actors in the system — Unlocking the second anomaly: The untrained excellent performers

Given the structural features of the Chinese Business System, an abundance in the supply of well-equipped, well-rounded entrepreneurial talent is absolutely essential. And indeed, Hong Kong is famous for its businessmen. However, the VTC survey reported that they are undertrained.

Field research has discovered an entrepreneurial development system in Hong Kong, very different from the way managers are trained in the West and also different from the way company managers are trained in Japan (Redding 1990, Tam 1987).

1. They are not trained, they develop themselves, with or without facilitators. Learning is not firm-centred, although it might appear to be so on the surface. Learning for entrepreneurship is essentially self-directed, self-structured, goal-driven, exploratory, experientially based and continuous throughout life. It therefore transcends individual firms' boundaries and existence.

2. This is in contrast to the Japanese model, where human resource development performs, among other functions, an integrative function. Entrepreneurial development in Hong Kong is achieved by divisive and rebellious acts, judged from the perspective of maintaining the integrity of the firm. True to the character of entrepreneurship, the successful learner either breaks away from the employing firm to establish a firm of his own or assumes the steering position of the original firm with a new vision.

Essentially, Chinese entrepreneurs are produced by two routes: (a) the nurtured route; (b) the self-made route.

These routes correspond to the bifurcation of managerial career pathways commonly found within a Chinese firm. Firms are seen as family property in the Chinese universe, and this proves to be an insurmountable barrier for integrating the employer and the employees. The nurtured route is reserved for those who are related in one way or another to the owning family whereas the self-made route is trodden by those who are not. Those who are related will be on a fast track, ending up eventually in the ownership echelon. Those who are not related are given limited career movement, and they face an upper ceiling barring them from the top.

Corresponding to the bifurcation of managerial career routes is the existence of two layers of management development activities in a Chinese firm. One is openly endorsed, the other closely concealed. There are thus the overt learners and the covert learners. The covert learners in Chinese firms must be the ultimate self-developers. A substantial proportion of entrepreneurial development activities are actually conducted without the awareness of the owner-manager. It was this covered-up layer that the economywide survey by the Vocational Training Council failed to tap, thereby bringing forth an image of grossly untrained owner-managers.

An analysis of the career histories of some 300 entrepreneurs, drawn from a variety of industries, indicates that some 71% of them had gone through the second route, that is, moving from employee to employer status. Only 29% took the first route, and they included second generation children of the owning groups, spouses, kin and trusted friends. This finding is supported further by a much bigger survey over five major industries in Hong Kong, which discovered that some 80% of the entrepreneurs were once employees themselves (Sit and Wong 1988).

For those treading the second route, the most critical transition is the jump from employee to employer. Given their limited resources for setting up a firm, highly ingenious mechanisms have developed to ease the transitional trauma. The ultimate vehicle for learning entrepreneurship is, of course, the firm. Again, hundreds of ingenious ways to form a firm with extremely modest resources are being discovered.

Contrary to the Japanese human resource system, the entrepreneurial development system in Hong Kong produces its heroes by fission, by outward radiation rather than by integration and indoctrination. The Chinese Business System provides a seedbed for learning and experimentation, given the constant ups and downs of market changes, the tendency for opportunities to spill over and the readiness of the underground entrepreneurs to take chances. Mechanisms have evolved which enable the learners to get into the act in low-cost, low-risk and high-reward fashion, providing significant learning opportunities. In comparative terms the existence and viability of alternative human resource development systems have diametrically opposite effects on the form of cooperation one could practice in Japan and Hong Kong.

Component 3: Process — Unlocking the third anomaly: Constant renewal of conservative firms

With the owner exercising tight control and human resources lacking in commitment and loyalty, one might suppose that the chance for a firm to renew itself were low, but if one were to look at the system as a whole, a different view emerges.

The system is continually given new leases of life because of fission and refusion. The source of dynamism, in complete contrast to the Japanese case, lies not in the strength of solidarity, but in the creativity of divisiveness.

With the key actors in the system constantly evolving into fully-fledged entrepreneurial status, constant breaking up of firms in Hong Kong is a daily affair. The development of entrepreneurship could not be done by standardization of behaviour and subjugation of the learner to the organization's needs but is mostly achieved when the learner breaks away from the straitjacket of the company and strikes out on his own.

Again this requires a new concept: that fission and re-fusion of the firms in the Chinese case is a virtuous cycle. It is virtuous because it constantly revitalizes the system as a whole and it prevents ossification. It also weakens the possibility of building bureaucracies. In many respects this is the only viable renewal mechanism available to the system because:

1. radical change in small firms is likely to affect them very deeply and will thus be resisted;
2. the mental configuration of successful entrepreneurs in control is so very well established that a major re-configuration is unlikely.

Whereas fission might be harmful to the individual firm, taking the view of the bubbling vitality constantly available to the system as a whole, it becomes a positive force sponsoring renewal. The force further triggers the system to adjust in the following ways:

a. The chance for a serving employee to strike out on his own comes when an opportunity to improve the business situation occurs but remains unseized or unperceived by the existing employers. This could be a buyer ill-served, technological advantage unrealized, product unimproved, market niche not occupied, costs not reduced, etc. If resources permit, a new firm is immediately formed.
b. The newly constituted firm is founded because the opportunity for improving the business situation exists. Should this new firm become successful, it will erode the survival base of the original firm, forcing it either to adjust or stay out of the game. And then the cycle repeats itself.

There is another side to the picture which ensures that the fission and re-fusion cycle will be perpetuated within the system. This concerns the role of the fissioned firm in causing a chain reaction. A newly fissioned firm is struggling for existence in a highly interdependent network which had previous commitments and bondage. In order to build up its own network, longitudinal research by the author has uncovered their tendency to actively promote the formation of newer firms which depend on them, thereby in the long run enabling themselves to be surrounded by a ring of dependable units. Again this process produces system effects, because most of these new firms will be formed by fission, that is, by faciliting employees to become employers. The act of increasing security and stability in one firm actually creates insecurity and instability for others in the system.

This chain reaction runs on a logic reversing the trend we saw earlier in the Japanese enterprise group formation process. But this captures only the tendency for employers and employees to go their seperate ways and split the firms. It is, therefore, only part of the story, albeit the major part. What remains to be seen is how the owning group itself displays a tendency to split up, thereby adding the ultimate impetus to the centrifugal tendency.

For those firms with family members as owners the answer is to be sought in the equal inheritance rule. The Chinese customarily view the firm as family property and Chinese custom requires the property to be divided equally amongst the children. There is thus an inbuilt divisiveness in any Chinese family-owned firm. In Japan, by contrast, inheritance has traditionally been by primogeniture.

Those firms run by partners without blood ties are also very unstable. Wong, in his study of thirty-two cotton spinning mills incorporated by partners, found only four remaining under partnership control at the time of his investigation (Wong 1986). The balance had turned into sole proprietorships. My field research into firms of diverse industries confirms this observation. Long-term cooperation amongst partners cannot be taken for granted. Where it continues to exist, these are rare cases. In a sense, there is an inherent paradox built into the partnership situation. In order to be a successful entrepreneur, one needs to develop a unique approach to business. A partnership arrangement attempts to bind two or three independent thinkers together, each of them ultimately needing to walk his own way. This somehow explains the difficulty of maintaining long-term partnership relations. The tendency of working towards one family — one business has led to a lot of break-ups between partners. The net result of this is the individuation of ownership in Chinese firms. It is customary in Hong Kong to associate a firm with the owner by family name. For the sake of convenience, we could call this the single-family-enterprise syndrome. In no way can one take for granted ease and continuity in cooperation of owners within a Chinese firm.

The impact of equal inheritance within these single family enterprises need not wait until the senior generation passes away to take effect. The splitting up process, both covert and overt, starts long ahead of its date of maturation, in some cases going back decades.

Component 4: Culture — Unlocking the fourth anomaly: The disloyal, uncommitted but motivated and effective work-force

Unlike the Japanese organization, which attempts to practice total and egalitarian inclusion for its members, the Chinese organization practices differential and discriminatory inclusion. Reward differentials between owner and employee are high, career opportunities are reserved, development efforts are concentrated, decisions are centralized, dismissals are arbitrary and, in fact, the firm is seen both by the owner and the employee as belonging to the owning family or families. This is different to the Japanese version on every count.

But the workforce in both places works hard. The Japanese work hard amid a context of security; the Chinese work hard in a context of insecurity. The Japanese work for their 'family', as which they see the firm. The Chinese work for their family, which is not the firm. Even for the owning group, the firm is just an instrument for the service of the family. The locus of primary loyalty lies outside the firm. It is the persistence and aggrandizement of the family tradition, not the firm, which commands loyalty and commitment.

In a secure context the Japanese employee has learned to depend on the company. In an insecure context the Chinese employee has learned to be self-reliant. In many ways the Chinese are motivated to work *in* the company but not *for* the company. This explains their high rate of inter-firm mobility, learning intensity and the sense of urgency in equipping themselves for the setting-up of their own business. In-depth interviews also uncovered a tendency for clique formation as a measure of protection against insecurity. Here, a firm is not a common fate entity, as the Japanese are led to believe.

The surface harmony of a Chinese firm has a hidden dimension: the tendency to polarity between the owning group and its employees. Given the centrifugal tendency, owners are forced to centralize, delegation is a risky affair and direct supervision becomes neccessary. Employees are difficult to depend on, and there are many cases in which this belief has been confirmed. The employees can not cross the barrier into the board-room and are led to the belief that the only way is to take fate in one's hand and have a firm of one's own. But it is seldom realized that being an owner in the Chinese context is to lock oneself into another context of insecurity.

The difficulty in relying on employees has pushed many Chinese firms to externalize their operational and administrative functions, in the belief that the market is more reliable than their employees. As an consequence of this tendency, more specialized businesses find their way into the market and Hong Kong has evolved its own *KanBan* System. Not only does one find many firms to have their basic productions stages subcontracted out, but there are many who let part of their administrative function be catered for by the market. Maintenance, accounting, personnel recruitment, con-sultancy, delivery and canteen services are obvious candidates for exter-nalization. One of our sample companies actually farmed out a whole business project because of the difficulty of obtaining trust from employees.

The balance of these forces produces a drive towards more businesses being set up, a reduction in the internal complexity of firms and greater determination in employees to become their own boss.

Component 5: System Behaviour — Unlocking the fifth anomaly: The econ-omies of de-scaling

Fission and refusion as a dominant mechanism for firm formation has brought in train a series of system behaviours which are perhaps unique to the Chinese system:

a. given the atomistic organizational format, it is actually quite impossible for a firm to dominate a market, unless the protection is by non-market means.

b. the fact that there is always an army of potential entrepreneurs on watch for opportunities, and given the lack of market domination, means that market entry takes on a rapid and easy form, very much like crowd behaviour.

c. the tendency for the fission process to evolve from within existing enterprises makes it highly unlikely that secret recipes and exclusive approaches to business can be kept for long.

The way Chinese firms are co-ordinated is very different from the bureaucratic form, or the community form, and can therefore be regarded as a unique system with certain properties not found elsewhere. The pursuit of scale efficency is probably beyond question. What appears to be a key strength of this system can be termed innovation efficiency:

1. the system provides a favourable context for innovation diffusion.
2. the system is conducive to fostering cross-fertilization and new combinations, which can be regarded as nurturing grounds for innovation.
3. it is conducive to innovation adoption, given the entrepeneurial inclination.
4. it is conducive to rapid entry into and exhaustion of business opportunities.

As an indicator of this, in the first year the wig industry was founded in Hong Kong, there was one factory. In the second year there were over three hundred. This happened in many industries such as plastic flowers, watches, telephone set manufacture, etc.

The rigidity of the organization in the West and Japan, in relative terms, can lead to a polarization of the objectives of efficency and innovation (Lawrence and Dyer 1983). In Japan product innovation had to be done by task forces, outside the main-stream organization (Imai 1984). These are not necessarily polar opposites in the Hong Kong system. Specialization and co-ordination are done on a different basis from elsewhere, the details of which are still to be uncovered by research.

The Overall Configuration

Major elements of the Chinese Business System have now been covered in terms of its structure, actors, process, culture and behaviour. The anomalies identified earlier are perhaps less puzzling in the light of the configuration presented in this chapter.

It seems appropiate at this point to discuss the interrelations of the various components.

a. The exclusive nature of the family ownership system appears to account for many of the discriminatory practices that are prevalent within Chinese firms. This strong familism exerts its influence as powerfully over the employers as it does over the employees, resulting in a mutually reinforcing situation. On the one hand, A does not wish to be integrated into B's family; on the other hand, B does not wish to integrate A, C or D into his own family.

b. Fission, re-fusion and familial exclusiveness reinforce each other. Familial monopoly over ownership and control blocks the career aspirations of employees, leaving fission as the major means of gratifying entrepreneurial ambitions. The more prevalent the practice of fission, the more dangerous it is for the family to loosen its control.

c. Persistent fission and re-fusion continually creates and re-creates the network and molecular structure.

d. The existence and viability of atomistic organizations reduces career progression possibilities and eases the way to firm formation.

e. Ease of firm formation encourages entrepreneurial development.

f. Entrepreneurial development causes fission and re-fusion, in addition to network readjustment.

g. Persistent fission and the resulting lack of trust amongst employers and employees has led many firms to externalize their functions, thereby creating more business opportunities.

All these elements are mutually reinforcing and are internally consistent. Collectively, they stabilize the configuration, producing and reproducing it over time.

The underlying tendency over the years has continued to be centrifugal.

Contrasting Ideal Types
These two systems in ideal-typical form are presented in Table 2.

Conclusion

As a conceptual tool, this ideal-typical construction does much to explain Chinese business behaviour, even if it does not add greatly to what we already know about the Japanese system. It illuminates why the typical Chinese firm becomes locked into the familial mode, why leaders in Chinese firms are forced to centralize, why a typical Chinese firm in Hong Kong

Table 2 Ideal-Typical Form of the Two Systems

	Hong Kong Business System	Japanese Business System
Overall developmental tendency	Centrifugal	Centripetal
I. ENVIRONMENTAL LEVEL		
Political context	Apathetic, hostile	Supportive, protective
Market context	Limited control	Greater control
II. ENTERPRISE GROUP LEVEL		
Inter-organizational clustering	Shifting constellation	Based on enterprise group strategy
Inter-organizational bondage	Transient, unstable	More permanent, stable
Stability & security of individual firm in system	− Lower − Limited back up	− Higher − Multiple back up system
Developmental context of firms	The game of small scale	The game of large scale
Relationship between individual firms	Instrumental, utilitarianistic,	Interdependent, mutual prosperity
III. ENTERPRISE LEVEL		
Fundamental goals in firms	− Firm as instrument of family − Opportunistic	Continuation & prosperity of firms
Fundamental attitude to human resource in a firm	Differential & discriminatory inclusion	Homogeneous egalitarian inclusion
Impact of human resource development	More divisive	More integrative
Product of h. r. development	Entrepreneurs	Salary man
RELATIONSHIP BETWEEN INDIVIDUAL & ENTERPRISE		
Perception of the firm	− Firm as belonging to one family − Fate should be in one's hands	− Firm as one family − Common fate entity
Employee attitude to firm	Disloyalty	Loyalty
Locus of primary loyalty	Family	Firm
IV. INTERPERSONAL LEVEL		
Fundamental interpersonal orientation	− Self-reliant − Dependence avoiding	− Collectivistic − Interdependability
SYSTEM LEVEL		
Basic structure	Network & molecular organization	Enterprise groups
Basic process for system renewal	Fission & fusion	− Crisis excitement − Collective action
Key actor	Entrepreneur	Collectivity
System strength	Innovative efficiency	Size & collectivistic

is unlikely to grow very big by international standards, why there are so many entrepreneurs in Hong Kong and where Hong Kong might have advantages when compared to Japan.

Should this ideal type prove to be descriptively accurate, then there are wider theoretical implications:

a. commitment and loyalty is not a universal recipe;
b. the bureaucratic organization form is not universally appropiate;
c. management development might take on a disintegrative form and still succeed;
d. divisiveness and segmentalism could be conducive to innovation and adjustment.

Given the fact that this is an exercise in ideal-typical construction, it is subject to all the limitations common to this method. There may be a need to review aspects of this largely abstract model in the light of further empirical research. There are conditions and moderating factors which might facilitate or frustrate the underlying processes, which need to be explored. For example, it will be theoretically important to study how firms manage to grow in this centrifugal context and to explain why some firms have grown to an appreciable size, albeit still small in international terms.

References

Caves, R. and M. Uekusa (1976): *Industrial organisation in Japan*, Washington, D. C.: The Brooking Institution.

Clark, R. (1979): *The Japanese company*, New Haven, Conn.: Yale University Press.

Cole, R. E. (1971): *Japanese blue collar*, University of California Press.

Doi, T. (1973): *The anatomy of dependence*, Tokyo: Kodansha, International Ltd.

Dore, R. (1973): *British factory, Japanese factory*, Allen and Unwin: University of California Press.

Hage, J. (1980): *Theories of organisations*, New York: Wiley Interscience.

Handy, C. (1987): *The making of managers*, London: British Institute of Management.

Hirschmeier, J. and T. Yui (1981): *The development of Japanese business*, London: George, Allen and Unwin.

Hsu, L. K. Francis (1963): *Clan, caste and club*, Princeton, N. J.: van Nostrand & Co.

Hsu, S. S. (1979): *Strategy of Japanese Zaibatsu*, Taipai: Dailim Press (in Chinese).

Hsu, F. L. K. (1981): *Americans and Chinese*, Honolulu: University of Hawaii Press.

Imai, K., I. Nonaka and H. Takeuchi (1984): Managing the new product development process: How Japanese companies learn and unlearn, Hitotsubashi Discussion Paper No. 118.

Kagono, T., I. Nonaka, K. Sakakibara and A. Okumara (1983): An evolutionary view of organisational adaptation: US vs Japanese firms, Hitotsubashi Discussion Paper No. 117.

Kono, T. (1984): *Strategy and structure of Japanese enterprise*, London: McMillan.

Lau, S. K. (1978): Utilitarianistic familism, Chinese University of Hong Kong Occasional Paper, No. 74.

Lawrence, P. R. and Dyer, D. (1983): *Renewing American industry: Organizing for efficiency and innovation*, New York: The Free Press.

Lockwood, W. W. (1968): *The economic development of Japan*, Princeton, N.J.: Princeton University Press.

Marsh, R. M. and H. Mannari (1976): *Modernisation and the Japanese factory*, Princeton, N.J.: Princeton University Press.

Morishima, M. (1982): *Why has Japan 'succeeded'?* Cambridge: Cambridge University Press.

Nakane, Chie (1970): *Japanese society*, London: Weidenfeld and Nicholson, Penguin.

Redding, S. G. (1986): Developing managers without 'management development': the Overseas Chinese solution, *Management Education and Development* 17, 3: 271 – 281.

Redding, S. G. (1990): *The spirit of Chinese capitalism*, Berlin: de Gruyter.

Redding, S. G. and G. L. Hicks (1985): The smaller the better: the declining size of the Hong Kong manufacturing firm, Working Paper: The Mong Kwok Ping Management Data Bank, University of Hong Kong.

Redding, S. G. and S. Tam (1985): Networks and molecular organisations: an exploratory view of Chinese firms in Hong Kong, in: K. C. Mun and T. S. Chen (eds.), *Proceedings: inaugural meeting of the Southeast Asian Region Academy of International Business,* 129 – 142, Hong Kong: Chinese University of Hong Kong.

Redding, S. G. and G. Y. Y. Wong (1986): The Psychology of Chinese Organisational Behaviour, in: M. H. Bond (ed.), *The psychology of Chinese people,* 267 – 295, Hong Kong: Oxford University Press.

Rohlen, T. P. (1974): *For harmony and strength,* Berkeley, California: University of California Press.

Sato, I. (1984): *A sketch of the Sanwa Group,* Shanghai: Translation Press. (in Chinese)

Sit, Victor F. S. and S. L. Wong (1988): *Changes in the industrial structure and the role of small and medium industries in Asian countries: the case of Hong Kong,* Tokyo: Institute of Developing Economies.

Tam, S. (1987): The making of Chinese managers in Hong Kong, Paper at the Tenth Anniversary Conference, 1987, Hong Kong Institute of Personnel Management.

Vocational Training Council (1983): *Committee on management supervisory training report on a survey of training and development of owner-managers and management staff,* Hong Kong: Vocational Training Council.

Vogel, E. (1979): *Japan as Number One,* New York: Harper and Row.

Wong, G. Y. Y. (1988): Interlocking directorates in Hong Kong, Mong Kwok Ping Management Data Bank Working Paper, 1986, University of Hong Kong.

Wong, S. L. (1979): Industrial entrepreneurship and ethnicity: A study of the Shanghainese cotton spinners in Hong Kong, D. Phil. Dissertation, University of Oxford.

Wong, S. L. (1985): The Chinese family firm, *British Journal of Sociology* 36, 1: 58 – 72.

Yonekura, S. (1985): The emergence of prototype of enterprise group capitalism – the case of Mitsui, *Hitotsubashi Journal of Commerce and Management* 20, 1: 1 – 2.

Yoshihara, K. (1982): *Sogo Shosha*, Tokyo: Oxford University Press.

Yoshino, M. Y. (1968): *Japan's managerial system*, Cambridge, Mass.: MIT Press.

Part II
Regulation and De-Regulation

Corporate Governance: A Ripple on the Cultural Reflection

Robert I. Tricker

I have taken a simple theme, in relation to the scope of this volume: the governance of corporations and its possible cultural significance.

In many countries corporate governance is rooted in Western practices and ideologies — and in most cases is based on Anglo-American common law tradition (e. g. Australia, Canada, Hong Kong, India, Malaysia, New Zealand, Philippines, South Africa, Singapore, the USA and the U. K.). The approaches to corporate governance are less similar in the Roman law tradition countries of Western Europe and quite dissimilar in Eastern Europe, Russia, China and elsewhere.

Culture reflects a society through its language, beliefs, customs and self-perceptions. Corporate governance is part of that cultural reflection. But what happens when a Western orientated form of governance is superimposed on business in non-Western cultures, for example in Hong Kong, or with multi-national companies in many locations? That is the theme of this chapter; perhaps too little attention has been paid to date to the implications of this ripple on the cultural reflection.

Recognizing that some readers may not be familiar with the literature of corporate governance, Part 1 of the chapter comments on the nature of the concept, the body of knowledge, the current interest in the topic, and the evolution of the practice, as a lead into Part 2, which rehearses the cultural implications.

Part 1 — The Concept of Corporate Governance

The Nature of Governance

All human societies need governing. Wherever power is exercised to direct, control and regulate social activity, affecting people's legitimate interests, governance is necessary.

Governance identifies rights and responsibilities, legitimizes actions and determines accountability. It is concerned with the derivation, use and limitation of power.

Governance is necessary whether the society is a nation state, a town community, a professional body, an Oxford college, a charity or a business corporation. Each has its governing body and governance activities.

Corporate governance is concerned with the processes by which corporate entities, particularly limited liability companies, are governed; that is, with the exercise of power over the direction of the enterprise, the supervision of executive actions, the acceptance of a duty to be accountable and the regulation of the corporation within the jurisdiction of the states in which it operates (Tricker 1984).

Primarily, corporate governance is concerned with the board of directors – its structure, style and processes, their relationships and roles, the linkages and activities – also with the roles of the company's members, auditors and others.

Some find it useful to distinguish the functions of the board from the processes of management (Eilon 1974). In the main stream of management literature management is typically depicted as being about the organizing and running of a business efficiently and effectively, within the boundaries of the corporate entity. By contrast, governance is not about the processes of running the business, per se; rather it is concerned to see that it is well run – giving overall direction, monitoring and supervising executive actions and with satisfying the legitimate expectations for accountability and regulation, by interests beyond the corporate boundary.

In other work (Tricker 1987) the author has found it helpful to differentiate the board and management roles, as in Figure 1, superimposing the board structure on the top management hierarchy. The outside, non-executive directors' relationships with those directors who also hold managerial responsibilities are delineated.

The notation of the board circle superimposed on the management organization can highlight alternative board structures, varying from the totally executive director board to the German and French model of a supervisory board totally independent of management with no common members. Within the managerial hierarchy, whatever the organizational style and climate, there lies an authority structure: by contrast, within board circles consensus is necessary; all directors have equal powers and responsibilities; there is no hierarchy of authority.

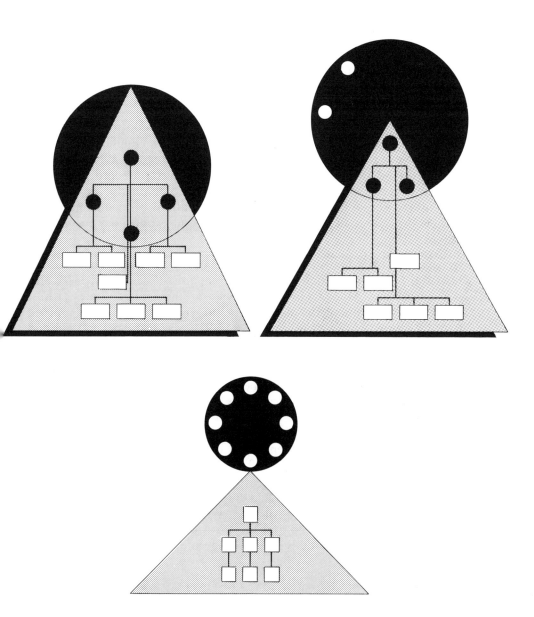

Figure 1 Alternative structures for boards and management

The Knowledge of Corporate Governance

Writing in 1969, Nichols observed that in sociological circles, the director had remained a much neglected creature. Despite his own contributions (Nichols 1969) on the value systems and social experience of British directors, the comment is still apt, and not only in sociological circles.

The tendency towards a separation of ownership and control in the public corporation has been extensively explored and the implications much debated (Keynes 1931, Berle and Means 1932, Dahrendorf 1959, Burnham 1962, Crosland 1959 and 1962). The effect, however, on board power (for example in terms of board structures, the right to nominate, the power of election and the domination and 'self-perpetuation' of incumbent elites) remains the source of anecdote, speculation and exhortatory recommendations.

Spencer has made one of the few attempts to get at the reality of roles 'behind the boardroom door' in British companies (Spencer 1983, see also Aris 1986), and Mace's pioneering work in the United States, whilst attacking a few shibboleths of conventional wisdom about boards, posed more questions than it answered (Mace 1971, see also Tricker 1978 and 1984 and Herman 1981).

In definitive studies of organizational power Pfeffer (1981) devotes two pages to boards of directors; Mintzberg (1983) has a chapter, which draws an important message: 'The board may be an influential or a powerless body, an agent for the control of management, or a tool that can be used by management, or simply a facade'. Data on board structures and processes, such as the use of independent outside directors, with audit or nominating committees to separate functions of executive and supervision, are more plentiful: for example, Mautz and Neumann (1977), annual studies by Korn Ferry International and occasional reports by, inter alia, The Conference Board, Booz-Allen & Hamilton, The MSL Group, The Corporate Consulting Group and the Institute of Directors. But the implications that might be derived from the data remain at the pragmatic level.

Wider discussion of alternative forms of governance can be found in the American Law Institute studies (American Law Institute 1984), the Bullock Report (Bullock 1977) and various exploratory papers on EEC draft directives on corporate governance and company law harmonization.

Other components of the body of knowledge about corporate governance stem from jurisprudence (see, for example, Hadden 1972), financial accounting and control (see, for example, Midgley 1982, ASSC 1975) and anecdotal and autobiographical comment by board members.

This brief survey of the literature is not definitive, but demonstrates the widespread focus, but lack of penetration, in the arena of debate on corporate governance.

Until five or ten years ago interest in the field of corporate governance was restricted to legislators, company lawyers and the occasional commentator concerned with accountability and financial disclosure. More recently, interest has escalated, which poses the question 'why'. Of the many reasons which can be cited, the following are listed as of particular significance.

a. The increasing scale, complexity and international activities of major corporate groups

Corporate structures for the purposes of limiting liabilities, facilitating tax planning internationally and corporate reporting, may not map onto organizational structures created for effective management. Moreover, the relationship of subsidiary and associated company boards to holding company boards (on issues such as resource allocation, cash flow, transfer prices, performance measures and strategy formulation — particularly if there are outsider minority interests in the subordinate company), can raise fundamental issues of rights, responsibilities and powers. Some jurisdictions insist on local board representation, others impose demands for corporate conformity accompanied by appropriate disclosure of information.

b. Greater power and activities of institutional investors

In many stock markets the institutional investors now account for more than half of the market capitalization and even more of the market activity whilst retaining the right to 'vote with their feet' — selling stocks to avoid a disadvantageous position and the danger of becoming locked in. These institutional investors, particularly in the United States and Britain, have shown a greater tendency to influence boards through formal participation in company meetings, even to the point of litigation and, informally, through direct contact with directors.

c. The activities of predator companies

Hostile takeover bids have been a feature in the United States and the U.K., with other European countries, Australia and elsewhere, now following suit. Scale is no longer a defence against predators, and recent years have seen some huge re-groupings.

An entire vocabulary has arisen around the takeover manoeuvres — junk bonds, dawn raids, concert parties — and the attempts to counter them

– golden parachutes, 'B' shares, poison pills, white knights! Each of these notions reflects a panoply of schemes and devices.

d. The activities of regulatory authorities

Company law changes and new securities trading regulations in various parts of the world, have proposed new responsibilities and powers to the regulatory authorities such as the Securities & Exchange Commission in the USA, new regulatory bodies in the U.K. embodied in the Financial Services Act 1986, the SEC in Australia and the Securities Review Committee in Hong Kong.

e. Recent disclosures and rethinking on insider trading

The 'Boesky revelations' on Wall Street practices and the 'Guinness scandal' in Britain have provoked a rethink of acceptable behaviours, particularly in contested bid situations, where individuals and companies act to protect or promote a bid with privileged price sensitive information.

In some jurisdictions (e.g. Japan, Hong Kong), where insider dealing is an unacceptable but not illegal act, consideration is being given to criminalization.

One result of public debate about unacceptable business practices has been a spate of business ethics course proposals in business schools.

f. Demands for independent supervision of executive actions

The EEC 5th draft directive, which called for independent supervisory boards to monitor executive boards' activities, was a forerunner of this debate. Bullock (1977) in a U.K. response proposed a unitary board, but with equal representation from capital and labour.

Although neither of these proposals has been well received by business, conventional wisdom has now embraced the notion of non-executive, outside directors to serve on boards, as a check to the power of executive directors (see Institute of Directors 1982, PRONED 1987).

The notion of independence has also been debated, arguing that non-executive directors, with vested interests or representing vested interests in the business, or past executive officers of the company may have a legitimate and valuable role on the board, but may not be considered independent and objective.

Other approaches to preserving a separation of function between executive and supervisory roles have included the audit committee, the nomination committee and the remuneration committee of the main board with independent members; also the proposal to separate the Chief Executive Officer function from that of the Chairman of the Board.

An audit committee of independent outside directors is required for a listing on the New York and American Stock Exchanges.

g. Calls for greater accountability by companies and their boards

Better use of the annual meeting of the members as a vehicle of accountability has been proposed, together with many other ideas to make significant corporations more 'democratic' and socially responsible (see Nader and Green 1979; Public Citizens Congress Watch 1980).

h. Developments in the audit profession

The major accountancy practices have become, in recent years, very large multi-national enterprises, with significant consultancy and other interests outside audit practice. In view of this, the Metcalf Committee (1977) in the USA and the EEC 8th draft directive have questioned the independence of auditors and the need for state involvement, as against a self-regulating profession (for a detailed analysis, see Tricker 1983).

In the U. K. proposals currently under review would enable audit firms to incorporate and attract outside equity capital, under stringent controls.

i. Developments in accounting standards and corporate regulation

The development of accounting standards by bodies such as the Financial Accounting Standards Board (USA) and the Accounting Standards Committee (U. K.), plus the harmonizing activities of the International Federation of Accountants world wide, has led to the incorporation of such standards into the required company reporting by many jurisdictions (see Zeff 1972).

j. An increasingly litigious environment

Finally, it has to be observed that a major determinant of the increasing interest in corporate governance lies in the propensity of people to bring actions through the courts alleging damages for breaches of trust and duty or negligence, against companies, their boards, individual directors and firms of auditors.

The Evolution of Corporate Governance

In the context of this chapter it is important to appreciate the historical and ideological development of the subject. It is significant to the case to be argued that the concept of the joint-stock, limited liability company is rooted in mid-nineteenth-century English ideology, which to this day exercises an influence in business affairs around the world, sometimes in sympathy with, but often contrary to, the norms and mores of a given society. Moreover, given the pressure to harmonize accounting standards of financial reporting, this significance is being heightened.

Prior to the mid-1800s

The dramatic evolution of the company concept in Britain stems from the mid-nineteenth century, in particular from the Companies Acts of 1855 and 1862. At the beginning of the century, limiting the liability of businessmen for the debts they incurred seemed immoral and separating ownership from management control foolhardy. By the end of the century both had become commonplace.

The developments that led to the corporate concept are threaded far back through the evolution of British trade and industry, indeed back to medieval England, with the importance of individualism, freedom and self-regulation contrasting with the more prescriptive rule of law in continental European countries. These contrary precedents become important in understanding some of the difficulties in harmonizing company law today between member states of the European Community.

For the first half of the nineteenth century there were four basic forms of corporate business activity:
— Sole proprietorships: the sole trader contracting personally.
— Partnership: business proprietors working together and sharing profits, losses and liabilities.
— The unincorporated company, operating under a trust deed and perhaps having non-executive 'sleeping' partners providing finance. All members, however, bore a liability for corporate debts.
— The incorporated company, operating under Royal Charter or an Act of Parliament, under which it was incorporated and which may well have limited the liability of members for corporate debts.

1844—1862

Sole trader, partnership and unincorporated companies remained the dominant organizational forms for the first half of the century. In 1844 a Joint-Stock Companies Act was passed which required the registration and regulation of all unincorporated companies. This was an act of intervention on the part of government to protect the investor from the unscrupulous and fraudulent company promoter. 970 unincorporated companies were registered and over the next fifteen years a further 910 were added to the register. Predominantly the companies were in insurance, shipping and public utilities such as water and gas undertakings and market halls. Manufacturing business accounted for less than 10%.

The 1844 Act called for the directors to 'conduct and manage the affairs of the company', to appoint the secretary, clerks and servants, to hold meetings periodically of the company (that is of the members) and to appoint a chairman to preside at such meetings. Account books were to be kept and balanced. A balance sheet was to be produced by the directors to the shareholders. Auditors were to be appointed by the company and the appointment registered with the Registrar of Joint-Stock Companies. These auditors were to report to the members on the balance sheet. A register of shareholders was to be kept, which could be inspected.

Thirty pages long, the 1844 Act laid the foundation for the registration, incorporation and regulation of companies that has survived to this day. But the liability of members was still unlimited.

Full incorporation, with the liability of members limited to their initial equity stake, was not pursued vigorously in the first half of the nineteenth century, although the interest had been kindled in the late eighteenth century. Businessmen still tended to associate incorporation with Royal Charters and trading under monopoly power and privilege — ideas quite inconsistent with the self-help norms of Victorian England. Experience of unscrupulous company promotions also raised doubts about the propriety, indeed the morality, of taking business risks whilst limiting personal responsibility.

Then, dramatically, in the middle years of the nineteenth century, between 1855 and 1862, there was a volte-face. Exactly why is unclear. Cottrell (1980) argues that the granting of the right to incorporate and to limit the liability of all members for the debts of the enterprise thus created was due to confusion and a mistaken attempt to create a continental European type of corporate structure in which the liability of financial, non-management members was limited, but in which the owner-directors who ran the business remained totally liable themselves. Jeffreys (1938), on the other hand, advances a more economic view that investors were seeking outlets for accumulating wealth, without staking their personal fortunes on the future of an unincorporated company.

Whatever the reasons, in August 1855 an Act for limiting the liability of members of certain joint-stock companies was passed. Now any joint-stock company, with a capital divided into shares of a nominal value not less than Pds. 10 each, may obtain a certificate of complete registration with limited liability upon complying with the following conditions:

1. the promoters state that the company is proposed to be formed with limited liability.
2. the word 'Limited' shall be the last word of the company name.
3. the deed of settlement shall state that the company is formed with limited liability.
4. the deed of settlement shall be executed by at least 25 shareholders holding at least three-quarters of the normal capital and at least 20% paid up.

Further amending Acts followed in 1857 and 1858, then in 1862 there was a Consolidating Act.

The 1862 Act laid down the mode of forming a company — seven or more people by subscribing their name to a Memorandum of Association could form an incorporated company with or without limited liability. Where the liability was to be limited, the Memorandum should contain the name of the company with the word 'Limited' at the end, the address of the registered office, the objectives for which the company was to be formed, the declaration that the liability of the members was limited and the amounts of capital which the company proposed to have registered. This underlying principle of incorporation has not changed since.

Experiences in Other Jurisdictions

Comparisons with company law developments in other jurisdictions are illuminating.

In France the *société en commandite par actions* had existed since 1807, but in 1856 the regulations were tightened. This form of incorporation involved unlimited directors but limited shareholders. Minimum share values were stipulated which had to be fully issued and 25% subscribed. The *société à responsabilité limitée* was created in 1863 for companies up to 20 m francs, a ceiling subsequently removed. But the basis of the legislation was the Napoleonic code of 1807, which was essentially prescriptive and regulatory, as opposed to English law based on common law evolved from statute and case.

German law, like French, followed the prescriptive pattern of Roman law, lacking the flexibility of English practices. The formation of limited companies, though permitted in 1884, was tightly regulated. A board of supervision, quite separate from the company's management board of directors, was mandatory to represent and protect the shareholders' interests. Annually it examined and reported on the accounts prepared by the directors for the members, of whom it could call meetings if necessary. Company promoters and the directors who subsequently ran the business were, thus, subject to greater scrutiny and their affairs to more visibility than their English counterparts. The difference in approach survives to this day: here is the basis for the two-tier supervisory board of the draft 5th directive.

Company law developments in the United States followed the British path more closely. Individual states passed legislation to facilitate the incorporation of companies, typically in the later years of the nineteenth century. Governance was through the members' meeting which had the power to nominate and elect the directors and to require accountability from them. Federal incorporation was not, and is still not, available. The concept has been transferred around the world.

The Advent of the Private Company

For the first fifty years or so, of incorporated, limited liability companies they were mainly public: incorporated for the purpose of attracting external capital. Today less than 1% of all registrations are public companies.

Since the liberalizing of company law in the mid 1800's, a few companies had been incorporated which did not, in fact, seek public subscription to their capital. In the later years of the century the number of such companies had become important: 560 were registered in the five years from 1880 to 1884. These 'private' companies tended to be family businesses and/or trading partnerships, often in manufacturing, led by entrepreneurs. Their growth came from the plough-back of profits and the owner's funds. For them incorporation achieved limited liability, the separation of the business from its owners and the transferability of shareholdings — very useful on inheritance and succession.

It was suggested, in evidence to the Royal Commission, that such private companies, being closely held, need not publish balance sheets. Thus emerged the idea of different types of company — the private and the public.

The private company was formally recognized in the Companies Act of 1907 for the first time. It must not have more than fifty members, not invite the public to subscribe for its shares and, by its Articles of Association, the right to transfer its shares must be restricted. Such private companies were then exempted from much of the disclosure requirements laid on the public company.

The Significance of Corporate Governance

The classical ideas of the limited liability company, created in the mid-nineteenth century, remain unaltered in principle to this day.

The essential concepts are:

1. the creation of an autonomous legal entity, quite separate from the owners, under the law,
2. limitation of liability of members (that is the owners) for corporate debts,
3. ownership as the basic of power, through the ability to nominate and elect the directors, and to require accountability,
4. the meeting of members as the vehicle for exercising such power,
5. regulation under the Acts, requiring the keeping of records and disclosure and filing of specific matters,
6. supervision of executive actions through the board and with auditors, appointed by the members, or in the USA by the directors, to report whether the accounts provided by the directors show a true and fair view,
7. transferability of the shares in the corporate entity,
8. perpetuity outside the natural lives of the founders.

The nineteenth-century notion of the corporate entity was elegantly simple and superbly successful. For a century and a half it has been the basis of capital formation, business growth and wealth creation — not only in North America and the United Kingdom, but wherever common-law based, company legislation has percolated. The idea of the corporation, legally separated from its owners, who nevertheless retained powers, was one of the great innovations of the Victorian era. The details of company legislation and the practices of corporate governance inevitably have diverged between jurisdictions over the years. Nevertheless, the underlying concept remains intact.

But, could it be that the very simplicity and success of the original conception contained the seeds of subsequent malaise? Companies have proliferated, corporate groups have become highly complex and the realities of governance in practice can appear far removed from the original idea. The second part of this chapter will discuss divergencies in practice between countries, to illustrate the ideological, culturally dependent aspects of corporate governance.

Part 2 — The Reality of Corporate Governance

In this part of the paper we contrast what might be styled 'North Atlantic' with 'North Pacific' practices of corporate governance: specifically drawing on data from studies of U. S. and U. K. companies, compared with material on overseas Chinese businesses, particularly in Hong Kong.

The three specific aspects of corporate governance to be reviewed are:

1. Ownership patterns
2. Sources of authority to govern
3. Group structures

This will lead to the central argument that the concept of corporate governance is ideologically rooted and that perceptions of the corporate entity differ between cultures. Various implications flow from these contentions.

Ownership Patterns

In the leading public companies in the United States and Britain the majority of the voting equity is quoted on stock exchanges and spread among individual, corporate and institutional investors without any one person or group capable of exercising a dominant interest (see Berle and Means 1932, on separation of ownership from control and Dunning and Pearce 1981, Thompson 1988, for more recent data).

Exceptions to this broad generalization are found where a government holds a dominant stake, for example Britoil, U. K., where another, even larger, entity owns a controlling interest, for example Esso Petroleum, U. K. owned by Exxon, USA, or in jointly held groups, for example, Shell Transport & Trading as part of the Royal Dutch Shell Group. However, with the exception of the government supervision, there is typically an ultimate governing body recognizing accountability to a group of shareholders.

Academic debate continues about the significance of the institutional investors in the mix of investors in leading public companies. In most cases it would appear to be a significant (i. e. greater than 50%) proportion.

Further down the league table of public companies, examples occur of large proportions of equity in the hands of individuals or coalitions of interest, who are thus able to influence board membership, even to the point of dominating control.

In the venture capital markets, such as Chicago, Vancouver or the London Unlisted Securities Market, continuing control by the founder or owner-manager group is widespread, with the publically floated element of the equity being insufficient to allow control to pass from the dominant interests. (See also Jordan on leading private companies.)

We may now compare these 'North Atlantic' practices with those of mainly Chinese firms in the 'North Pacific'.

Overseas Chinese businesses are typically family centred and small. In Hong Kong, for example, in the manufacturing sector, there are over 45,000 enterprises with fewer than 100 employees; whilst less than 150 firms have more than 500 employees, accounting for some 10% of the total workforce in the sector (Hong Kong Monthly Digest of Statistics, June 1987).

Nevertheless, despite their family-capitalism, many of the more successful family enterprises in Hong Kong have created public companies, obtained a Stock Market quotation and attracted funds from individual and institutional investors; similarly in Singapore.

Typically, in inviting outside equity participation, the Chinese-run family business offers a minority stake in a public company within the network of family firms. Control of this public company is maintained within the family by:

1. direct investment in the equity by other family companies,
2. direct investment in the equity by individual family members,
3. cross holdings with related companies associated with the family group,
4. cross directorships with related companies,
5. transactions creating an element of control with related parties.

An example of the interconnectedness of such groups is shown in Figure 2, also of intergroup transactions in Figure 3.

It should be noted that nominee holdings are permitted in Hong Kong without disclosure of beneficial ownerships: also that non-public companies do not have to file accounts.

One might legitimately wonder why anyone would invest, as a minority outside shareholder, in such a family firm.

The answer may lie in the attitude of the (largely) Chinese investor. It may be that appreciation of the nature of a public company is not widespread, nor are there significant expectations of disclosure, regulation or independent supervision. Rather the investor equates the public company, in which he can buy a share, with the family group of which it is part. The

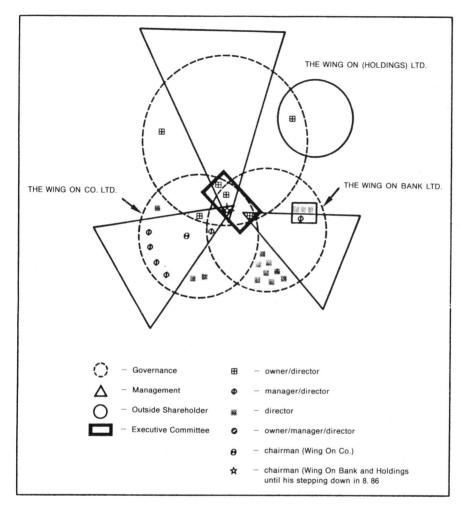

Figure 2 Structure of the Wing On (Holdings) Ltd.

investment is not so much in the specific public company as in the reputation of the owner-entrepreneur, the network of family businesses and the future good-fortunes of that family. The exact legal entity, in which the public invest, is less significant.

By contrast, the Anglo-American expectation of disclosure and regulation for the protection of investors and, ultimately, of the power of these shareholding owners to determine the state of affairs, are rooted in the concept of the joint-stock, limited liability company itself.

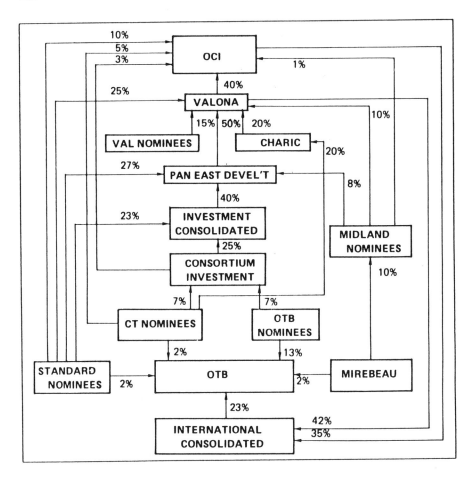

Figure 3   OTB Group Ownership Network (Simplified)
Other investors in the companies not shown.

In the overseas Chinese-led public company great care is taken to maintain
control in the hands of the owner-manager and thus, it is argued, of
succeeding generations of the family. A classic example of this thinking is
given in Dr. An Wang's autobiography (Wang 1986). Having built up the
Wang Computer Company to international dimensions, with a minority
public floatation on the New York Stock Exchange, he was faced with the
loss of control if the company issued further capital essential to sustain
the growth. He proposed to issue some 'B' class shares, giving disproportionate voting power to the (family) holders. The NYSE refused this
request, arguing that each equity share must carry equal rights. Dr. Wang

switched the entire listing to the smaller (and more speculative) American Stock Exchange, where he was allowed to issue the 'B' shares and maintain control.

Two alternative interpretations of the different behaviours depicted here, between the North Atlantic and North Pacific experiences can be posited:

1. that the wish to preserve the right to dominate the enterprise is inherent in the Chinese conception of family and business (for a discussion of the origins of this, see Redding 1989);
2. that the Chinese-owned companies described here are at a particular stage of their evolution, comparable to owner-managed family businesses in the North-Atlantic sector at the turn of the century; or venture capital, entrepreneurial companies today. They are still at the relatively small, first- or second-generation state, and longitudinal studies will ultimately reflect a similar evolution to that in the West. It should be recognized that the overseas Chinese public companies being considered are small by comparison with the international giants in the 'North Atlantic' sector.

The Sources of Authority to Govern

As we have seen, at law the Board of Directors has the power to govern delegated to it by the members. This is a fundamental tenet of the corporate concept.

Nevertheless, in the literature there are frequent observations that reality sometimes differs (Ingersoll 1986; Kesner and Dalton 1985 and 1986; Kramer 1986; Waldo 1985). Sometimes directors fail to act in the owner's interests, with complaints of acting more in their own interests as a self-perpetuating oligarchy of power.

Hence the emphasis in the 'North Atlantic' literature of the importance of a separation of function between executive and independent directors; the use of independent board committees; and the separation of CEO and board chairman (Dalton and Kesner 1987).

Studies by Korn/Ferry (annually) show that the boards of the leading public companies in the United States predominantly have a majority of outside directors, while those in the U.K. (with the exception of banks and insurance companies) tend to have about a third non-executive directors. A recent study by Dalton and Kesner (1987) suggests that the proportion of outside directors in British public companies is close to the

American pattern, but the sample was limited to 50 companies and their size not disclosed.

Board structures and processes in Overseas Chinese enterprises are quite different.

Power and prestige in the Chinese business lies with the owner-manager. Responsibility for day-to-day activities of production and operations may be delegated to managers, but even then with frequent rearrangements and what would be considered, by Western executives, interference in delegated responsibilities. Responsibility for financial and personnel matters typically remains with the owner (Deyo 1983, Redding and Wong 1986, Silin 1975).

Writing about the larger Chinese firms, Deyo (1983) comments:

Unlike their more bureaucratic Western counterparts, with extensive reliance on formal rules and written procedures, Chinese managers rely on highly centralised finance and budget decision-making, and on personnel practices which enhance trust and control.

In the Chinese culture there is a ready acceptance of authority and the essential rightness of hierarchy. The father of the family is respected and his sons will follow his directions. It is quite normal, for example, for a son who has been highly successful in business abroad, to return at this father's bidding to contribute to the family enterprise. Such an occurrence would be much less likely in a Western setting, where individuals expect independence once they 'leave home'.

With the Chinese respect for authority comes a natural acceptance of hierarchy. By contrast, the Western mind has a preference for egalitariarism, reflecting the individual-centred perception.

The Chinese devoutly believe that a large gap should exist between the entrepreneur – owner and the manager. They see this as a strong incentive to their young people to become entrepreneurs (Limlingan 1983).

The contrast between Eastern and Western tolerance of societal power-distance (that is the degree of acceptance of social hierarchy) is strikingly shown in the well-known study by Hofstede (1980).

Far from the conception of a board, with independent membership for supervision and accountability, in the overseas Chinese business there is:

an admiration for the owner who seems to be in control, who orchestrates every-thing, who defines the rules and regulations, without being subject to them (Lim-lingan 1983).

Loyalty is expected from the employee, matched by a paternalistic concern, often rooted in economic dependence. Little, if any, effort is made to provide management training (Redding 1986), partly because of the low level of authority given to managers, and partly to reduce the risk of investing in someone who thereupon leaves to set up his own business in competition.

Recruitment decisions in Chinese firms emphasise trustworthiness and loyalty to a far greater degree than in Western firms. Well known is the tendency to hire kinsmen or closely trusted persons for top level positions, rather than to search more widely for person of the best qualifications (Deyo 1983).

In a society whose social fabric is dependent on networks of relationships social harmony is likely to be a prerequisite. As Redding and Wong (1986) comment: 'A great deal of ritual behaviour takes place in the Chinese organization in an effort to maintain the social harmony which is so highly prized'.

By contrast, Western society is likely to emphasize the 'tough-minded, open and frank' discussion in its business dealings. Prepared to risk confrontation for the sake of clarity and to move towards a unequivocal outcome, the Western manager avoids the ambiguity and lack of directness needed in the East. His Chinese counterpart would have to employ far more subtlety in the exchange, to avoid putting anyone in the position of risking loss of 'face'.

Furthermore, the notion of a board of directors with the responsibility to direct, that is be involved in the formulation of strategy, the allocation of resources and the crucial long-term business decisions is contrary to the rubric of Chinese business thinking. The underlying perception of business in the Chinese mind is as a series of ad hoc deals, a succession of contracts or ventures, rather than a dominant strategy to provide a product and create a market. There is a close parallel with the attitude of a trader.

Consequently, Chinese manufacturing companies in Hong Kong have often been dependent on a handful of customers for whom they manufacture to order. There is seldom a research and development function, a marketing function or significant expenditure on product or market development.

Referencing Limlingan (1983), Redding (1986) describes '[...] the special nature of the Chinese management system which is oriented more to deals and resulting streams of cash flow than to balance-sheet accountability and systematic long-term control'.

There is an element of intuition and hunch, a reliance on good fortune and superstition (accompanied by a tough-minded business bargaining stance), which is less apparent in the Western strategic planner who relies, at least overtly, on more analysis and quantitative planning.

Table 1 Number and levels of subsidiary companies (U. K. top 100 industrials)

Number of companies in the sample	Rank order	Total number of subsidiaries	Average per group	Range
44	1 – 50	10,127	230.16	5 – 858
39	51 – 100	4,083	104.69	2 – 259

1 — Numbers of subsidiary companies in top groups

		Levels of subsidiary										
		1	2	3	4	5	6	7	8	9	10	11
44	1 – 50	2291	3381	2085	1255	721	254	127	8	2	2	1
39	51 – 100	1099	1521	1025	292	80	26	37	3	–	–	–

2 — Numbers of subsidiaries by level

| 43 | 1 – 50 | 52 | 77 | 47 | 28 | 16 | 6 | 3 | 1 | 1 | 1 | – |
| 39 | 51 – 100 | 28 | 39 | 26 | 7 | 2 | 1 | 1 | – | – | – | – |

3 — Average number of subsidiaries by level

Source: The Times 1,000 U. K. industrial companies 1983 Corporate Policy Group, Oxford (Tricker 1984).

Group Structures

The nineteenth-century originators of the corporate concept failed to foresee one outcome of giving the corporate entity many of the legal rights of a natural person: by permitting it to own assets, it acquired the right to own other companies.

For the first half century of 'North Atlantic' experience this right was seldom exercised. Where there were amalgamations, the existing companies were wound-up after their assets and liabilites had been acquired by the new company.

By contrast, the leading companies today operate their activities through large groups of subsidiary and associated companies. The scale of group activity is shown by the U. K. data presented in Table 1, demonstrating the large number of subsidiaries held at multiple levels (Tricker 1984).

The data suggest a hierarchical ordering of subsidiaries below the parent holding-company. Most subsidiaries are wholly owned, and minority interests are relatively unusual.

Data on Overseas Chinese enterprise structure are quite different. The holding-company is not found at the apex of the ownership pyramid. As we have already seen, the business interests are more likely to reflect a network of interdependent holdings. The public company, often floated on the collateral of a property interest, is likely to be within the network of, and dominated by, other family enterprises. The business context is family-centred.

The family is the traditional context of the Overseas Chinese enterprise. The head of the family fulfils the dominant owner-manager role. Close relatives are employed in key positions. More distant relatives can join in when needed; and long-serving employees may acquire an 'honorary membership' of the family circle. The boundaries between business and family are not clear, as they might be in a modern Western company (Baker 1979, Hsu 1981, Lai 1978, Silin 1976).

In the event, Overseas Chinese organizations are virtually all family businesses, and even the largest of them, having appeared to go public, have rarely become professionally managed bureaucracies of the Western kind, and commonly still display heavy family influence, if not absolute dominance (Redding and Wong 1986).

The family-centric view of enterprise extends into the business environment. Leeming (1977) found that 'overseas contacts are usually based on uncles and cousins living overseas. Business contacts are friends, and virtually all business is based on personal contacts'.

The family-business networks are held together, not by formal organization structures or well-articulated performance measures, but by informal obligation networks.

Social stability and socialization based on the family unit, promoting sobriety, education, the acquisition of skills and a sense of responsibility to contribute in tasks, job and other obligations, is a primary trait of post-Confucian ideology (Kahn 1979, Redding and Wong 1986).

The significance of this family-centric culture goes much deeper than the outward signs of social behaviour: it is inherent in the Chinese view of self. The Chinese person perceives himself inseparably from his networks. He is a being insofar as he connects (Hsu 1971).

It is perhaps not unreasonable to say that in the West we see the family as an institution which exists to provide an environment in which the individual can be conveniently raised and trained to go out into the world as a full member of society [...]. But the emphasis in the traditional Chinese situation was reversed — it was not the family which existed in order to support the individual, but rather the individual who existed to continue the family (Baker 1979).

Western thought recognizes the primacy of the individual.

Since the 13th century [...] England has been inhabited by a people whose social, economic and legal system was in essence different, not only from that of peoples in Asia or Eastern Europe, but also in all probability from the Celtic and Continental countries of the same period (Trevelyan 1944).

Recognition of rights of the individual, enshrined in Magna Carta, the approach to personal ownership of property, and power based on such ownership, suggest that ideas in England had been evolving, emphasizing the individual for nearly a thousand years.

As Macfarlane (1978) comments:

When Jefferson wrote, 'We hold these truths to be sacred and undeniable: that all men are created equal and independent, that from that equal creation they demand rights inherent and inalienable', he was putting into words a view of the individual and society which had its roots in thirteenth-century England or earlier.

The Anglo-Saxon concept of the individual is deep-rooted and needs to be contrasted with the even older Chinese view of man. The English word 'man' with all its overtones of separateness, free-will and individualism does not overlap in meaning with the Chinese word *yan* with all its overtones of connectedness and reciprocal relations (Hsu 1971, Redding and Wong 1986).

Herein lies the core argument of this chapter. In the original Western concept of the corporate entity the company in law takes on many of the attributes of a person. It has a legal persona. It is a separate, bounded entity. Thus, differing perceptions of the nature of man entail correspondingly different expectations of the corporate entity.

Conclusions and Implications

The classical paradigms of corporate governance have been shown to be rooted in Western thought. What is often treated as unassailable fact is in truth culturally determined.

The corporate entity notion does not readily relate to Chinese cultural expectations. To separate management from ownership appears foolhardy to the Chinese entrepreneur; whilst to remove personal liability for debts incurred might seem immoral, just as it did to the Anglo-Americans at the start of the nineteenth century.

Of course, Chinese family businesses in the Pacific Region have adopted Western practices, incorporating companies and raising capital on the stock market through public companies. However, the mismatch of cultural attitudes could explain a number of phenomena in Chinese companies which are unexpected to the Western observer. For example:

1. the public company, with only a non-controlling minority interest in public hands, enmeshed in a complex network of family business interests.

If there is little distinction in the businessmen's minds between business entities and family business interests, then inter-company trading, related party transactions, cross-holdings and cross-directorships all become common-place. There need be no devious intent; rather this would be a natural result of a failure to separate company from family interests. Chinese shareholders might well share such a view of the indivisibility of company and family.

2. the attitudes to outside shareholders in a public company, particularly a company which is in financial difficulty.

Whereas in the West the attitude might well be to exercise limited liability and for the company to be allowed to become insolvent and wound-up; there are well-charted examples in Hong Kong of such companies being supported by the family — even to the extent of committing additional funds which are in effect gifts to the minority, outside shareholders.

In the Western concept of the company ownership is the basis of power over the enterprise. All members, that is the shareholders, meeting together in a properly convened meeting, exercise the rights to nominate and elect the directors of the company.

The directors, on their part, accept a responsibility to exercise stewardship over the company's assets and to run the business for the benefit of the members. Further they recognize a duty to be accountable to the members, rendering regular accounts and directors' reports in accordance with the company law.

The Chinese business community has shown its ability to utilize joint-stock companies. However, if in one's mind there is no real separation between family and company interests and if the corporate boundaries are unclear or moveable, then stewardship and accountability acquire different meanings. For example:

1. the concept of members' rights, exercised in a member's meeting, presupposes an egalitarian, democratic meeting of members: in a centrally controlled company, dominated by the family head, such a perception is irrelevant.
2. similarly, in a public company, if both the managers and minority public shareholders coincide in viewing minority shareholdings as permission to participate in the company to share in the family fortunes, concepts of stewardship for the benefit of the members are inappropriate.

3. where secrecy about business matters is the norm, disclosure and reporting for accountability are likely to be kept to the absolute minimum
demanded by legislation or Stock Exchange rules.

These arguments give rise to some interesting implications. Firstly, the
need for an awareness of the cross-cultural differences in the perception
of corporate governance. There is a tendency for Western commentators
to argue that what is appropriate for governance in New York or London,
ought to be appropriate anywhere there is a claim to financial sophisti-
cation (e. g. Lord Benson during the Carrian Company committal proceedings). The opposite might be the case. The success of the 'North
Pacific' nations, as observed by Kahn (1970) in his post-Confucian hypothesis, may reflect cultural antecedents owing more to early Chinese
philosophers than nineteenth-century forms of corporate governance.

Secondly, a case can be made for rethinking corporate governance to
reflect the reality of governance in dominated companies. Instead of seeking
to circumvent such dominant power-bases by the devices of outside directors, separation of functions, audit committees, more disclosure, tighter
regulation etc., a category of dominated company could be added to the
typology of public and private company.

Such an extension to the fabric of corporate governance might also be
directly relevant to the governance of entrepreneurial, venture-capital firms
elsewhere. The North Pacific cultures might then contribute to the North
Atlantic practices of governance.

References

ASSC [Accounting Standards Steering Committee] (1975): *The corporate report,*
London: ASSC.
American Law Institute (1984): *Principles of corporate governance,* 3 volumes,
Philadelphia: American Law Institute.
Aris, Stephen (1986): *Non-executive directors: their changing role on UK Boards,*
Economist Intelligence Unit; Report 244, March 1986, London: Economist
Intelligence Unit.
Baker, H. R. D. (1979): *Chinese family and kinship,* New York, Columbia University
Press: Macmillan.
Berle, Adolf A. and G. C. Means [1932] (1968): *The modern corporation and private
property,* New York; Macmillan; revised edition 1968 Harcourt, Brace & World.
Bullock, Lord (1977): *Report of the committee of inquiry on industrial democracy,*
Cmnd 6706, London: HMSO.
Burnham, James (1962): *The managerial revolution,* London: Penguin [first edition
1941, New York].

Cottrell, P. L. (1980): *Industrial finance 1830–1914*, London: Methuen.

Crosland, C. A. R. (1959): The private and public corporation in Great Britain, in: E. S. Mason (ed.), *The corporation in modern society*, Cambridge, Mass.: Harvard University Press.

Crosland, C. A. R. (1962): *The conservative enemy*, London: Jonathon Cape: Oxford University Press.

Dahrendorf, R. (1959): *Class and class conflict in industrial society*, London: Routledge & Kegan Paul.

Dalton, Dan R. and I. F. Kesner (1987): Composition and CEO duality in boards of directors, *Journal of International Business Studies.*

Deyo, F. C. (1983): Chinese management practices and work commitment in comparative perspective, in: L. A. P. Gosling and L. Y. C. Lim (eds.), *The Chinese in Southeast Asia: Vol. II; Identiy, culture and politics*, Singapore Maruzen Asia.

Dunning, John H. and Robert D. Pearce (1981): *The world's largest industrial enterprises*, Farnbourgh: Gower Publishing.

Eilon, Samuel (1974): Board-functions and structure, *Management Decisions* 12: 2.

European Economic Community (1983): *Proposals for draft directives*, No. 5 on supervisory boards, No. 9 on governance in gorups and the 'Vredling' draft on employee participation, Brussels: European Economic Community.

Hadden, Tom (1972): *Company law and capitalism*, London: Weidenfeld & Nicolson.

Herman, Edward (1981): *Corporate control, corporate power*, Cambridge: University of Cambridge Press.

Hoftede, G. (1980): *Culture's consequences*, Beverly Hills, Cal.: Sage Publication.

Hsu, F. L. K. (1971): Psychosocial homestasis and Jon – conceptual tools for advancing psychological anthropology, *American Anthropologist* 73.

Hsu, F. L. K. (1981): *Americans and Chinese: passages to differences*, Honolulu, University Press of Hawaii.

Ingersoll, B. (1986): One-share, one-vote controversy come to head in SEC hearings, *Wall Street Journal* December 16: 29.

Institute of Directors (1982): *A code of practice for the non-executive director*, London: Institute of Directors.

Jeffreys, J. B. (1938): *Trends in business organization in Britain since 1856*, London: University of London.

Jordan (Annual): *Britain's top private companies*, London: Jordan and Sons Ltd.

Kahn, H. (1970): *World development: 1970 and beyond*, New York: Croom-Helm.

Kesner, I. F. and D. R. Dalton (1985): Antitakeover tactics: management 42, stockholders O., *Business Horizons* October: 17–25.

Kesner, I. F. and D. R. Dalton (1986): Boards of directors and the checks and (im)balances of corporate governance, *Business Horizons* October: 17–23.

Keynes, J. M. (1931): *Essays in persuasion*, London: London University Press.

Korn Ferry International (Annual): *Boards of directors studies*, London and New York: Korn Ferry International.

Kramer, D. (1986): Big trouble at Allegheny, *Business Week* August 11: 56–59.

Lai, P. W. H. (1978): Nepotism and management in Hong Kong, Unpublished Dip MS dissertation, University of Hong Kong.

Leeming, F. (1977): *Street studies in Hong Kong,* Hong Kong: Oxford University Press.

Limlingan, V. (1983): *The Chinese Walkabout: a case study in entrepreneurial education,* Manila: Asian Institute of Management.

Mace, Myles L. (1971): *Directors: myth and reality,* Boston: Harvard University Press.

Macfarlane, Alan (1978): *The origins of English individualism,* Oxford: Blackwell.

Mautz, R. K. and F. L. Neumann (1977): *Corporate audit committees — policies and practices,* New York: Ernst & Ernst.

Metcalf Committee (1977): *Subcommittee on reports, accounting and management of the Senate Committee on Governmental Affairs,* Washington, D. C.: U. S. Govt. Pub.

Midgley, Kenneth (ed.) (1982): *Management accountability and corporate governance,* London: Macmillan.

Mintzberg, Henry (1983): *Power in and around organizations,* Englewood Cliffs, N. J.: Prentice-Hall.

Nader, Ralph and Mark Green (1979): Public citizens' congress watch, editorial *The New York Times* 28 December 1979.

Nichols, Theo (1969): *Ownership, control and ideology,* London: George Allen & Unwin Ltd.

Pfeffer, Jeffrey (1981): *Power in organizations,* Boston, Mass.: Pitman Publishing.

PRONED (1987): *Promotion of non-executive directors: code of recommended practice on non-executive directors,* London: PRONED.

Public Citizens Congress Watch (1980): *The case for a Corporate Democracy Act,* Washington, D. C.: PCCW.

Redding, S. G. (1982): Western and Chinese modes of reasoning — their implications for engineering management, *Hong Kong Engineer* March 1982, HKIE paper 14 April 1982.

Redding, S. G. (1984): Two cultures and the managerial revolution: inaugural lecture, *Hong Kong University Gazette* 31, 4 (30th April).

Redding, S. G. (1986): Developing managers without 'management development': the overseas Chinese solution, *Management Education and Development* 17, 3: 271 – 281.

Redding, S. G. (1989): *The spirit of Chinese capitalism,* Cambridge: Cambridge University Press.

Redding, S. G. and M. Ng (1982): The role of face in the organization perception of Chinese managers, *Organization Studies* 3/3.

Redding, S. G. and G. Wong (1986): The psychology of Chinese organizational behaviour, in: M. H. Bond (ed.): *The psychology of Chinese people,* 267 – 295, Hong Kong: Oxford University Press.

Silin, R. (1976): *Leadership and values,* Cambridge, Mass.: Harvard University Press.

Slater, Paul (1986): Seatrade Hong Kong conference, *South China Morning Post* 18 November.

Spencer, Anne (1983): *On the edge of the organization — the role of the outside director,* Chichester: John Wiley & Sons.

Thompson, Louis M. (1988): *The changing role of the institutional investor in corporate governance*, Southern Californian Chapter NIRI, 13 January 1988.

Trevelyan, G. M. (1944): *English social history*, London: Penguin.

Tricker, R. I. (1978): *The independent director*, London: Tolley.

Tricker, R. I. (1983): *Governing the Institute — a study on the direction, control and regulation of the Institute*, London: Institute of Chartered Accountants in England & Wales.

Tricker, R. I. (1984): *Corporate governance*, Aldershot: Gower Publishing Co. Ltd.

Tricker, R. I. (1987): Improving the Board's Effectiveness, *Journal of General Management* 12, 3.

Waldo, C. N. (1985): *Boards of directors: Their changing roles, structure, and information needs*, Westport, CT: Quorum Books.

Wang, An (1986): *Lessons*, Reading, Mass.: Addison Wesley.

Zeff, Stephen A. (1972): *Forging accounting practices in five countries*, Edinburgh: University of Edinburgh.

Accounting: The Private Language of Business or an Instrument of Social Communication?

Peter E. M. Standish

Introduction:
Perceptions of Financial Information and Reporting

This chapter is concerned with contemporary conditions that affect the production of financial information on the performance of enterprises. Every society, capitalist or communist, developed or less developed, in which there is extensive separation of ownership of financial or real assets from management of those assets has a need for periodic reporting of enterprise financial performance. In the OECD nations, especially in the English-speaking world, the conditions for production of financial performance information, chiefly in the form of audited annual accounts, have in the past generation become more complex and far more visible. There is now considerable tension in the process, as attested by media attention, political and bureaucratic intervention, disciplinary sanctions and civil lawsuits. Although the annual accounts of companies, to name the most prominent category of enterprises, are in law the accounts of the directors, most of the public odium and penalties associated with grossly misleading accounts fall upon the accounting profession and its members, especially registered auditors.

The complexity and visibility of the financial reporting process are associated with a remarkable growth in the size of the accounting profession, particularly in the English-speaking world, and of the principal firms of public accountants and auditors. If the term 'industry' is taken to connote a major economic activity, in which there is substantial employment, investment and turnover, then public accounting meets those criteria. Public accounting practice internationally is increasingly dominated by what are known in the world of accounting as the Big-8 firms, namely:[1]

---

[1] As these firms are not listed public companies, they are not obliged to make their annual accounts public. Most of them issue material of a public relations character giving some indication of their size. No systematic survey has been undertaken of this material but indications are that the gross annual worldwide fee income of each firm is now to the order of US$ 1.5 billion and upwards.

Arthur Andersen
Arthur Young
Coopers & Lybrand
Deloitte Haskins + Sells
Ernst and Whinney
Peat Marwick McLintock
Price Waterhouse
Touche Ross

Public accounting firms, whether one of the Big-8 or a small local firm with a handful of partners, are not concerned solely with the production of financial information. Nevertheless, a major part of professional practice directly or indirectly relates to financial reporting and compliance with relevant laws and regulations, whether in the development and operation for clients of accounting systems and controls, in carrying out the statutory audit, or in tax advising with effects on the recorded financial position and exposure to tax. Moreover, these services of public accounting firms to enterprises constitute only one side of the coin of financial information production. On the enterprise side there is need for specialist accounting staff and financial accounting systems to comply with statutory reporting obligations, to determine tax liability, and to deal with financial relations between holding and subsidiary companies, especially for the purpose of consolidation of accounts, as the basis for obtaining an overall group view of performance.

The domain within which financial reporting takes place in advanced capitalist nations is shaped by the following major factors:

1. Laws and regulations for financial disclosure of annual accounts to owners or for filing of accounts with regulatory authorities, varying principally between nations in which:

a. a general statute applies to all companies, regardless of size (though in some jurisdictions the provisions relating to annual accounts and audit are simplified or waived for small companies), e. g. Australia (*Companies Code*), Britain (*Companies Act*);

b. statutory financial disclosure requirements are primarily directed at listed public companies, e. g. USA (Securities and Exchange Commission, *Regulation S-X*);

c. a general commercial statute applies to all enterprises whether incorporated or not, e. g. France (*Code de commerce*).

2. Laws and regulations for filing income tax returns relating to financial performance, varying principally between nations in which:

a. the procedures required to be followed in rendering an annual declaration for business income tax purposes and in estimating taxable income are not closely connected with the accounting basis for the annual accounts (a state of affairs that generally applies to the English-speaking world);

b. the procedures for rendering the annual business enterprise tax return and for estimating taxable income are closely related to or imposed upon the accounting basis for the annual accounts (a state of affairs that applies in many non-English-speaking nations).

3. Recommendations and statements of accounting standards issued by national or international institutions of the accounting profession, the following being important examples in their respective spheres of influence:

a. Accounting Standards Committee (ASC) (Britain, a composite of the six professional accounting bodies);

b. Financial Accounting Standards Board (FASB) (USA, established by the American Institute of Certified Practising Accountants and various para-professional bodies with an interest in financial reporting and its analysis);

c. *Ordre des experts comptables et des comptables agréés* (OECCA) (France);

d. International Accounting Standards Committee (IASC) (established and adhered to by a large number of national accounting bodies).

In less-developed nations and in the communist world financial reporting is a less open process, for such reasons as the higher proportion of competitive economic activity in the hands of smaller privately-owned enterprises, simpler or more discretionary tax regimes, or financial reporting by state-owned enterprises directly to their controlling ministries and without public disclosure of their performance.

Many constructions have been put upon the processes of production of financial information and their outcomes. An obvious dichotomy is between regarding financial reporting as an activity intended to serve the assumed mutuality of interest between managers on the one hand and owners and financiers of the enterprise on the other, and regarding it as an instrument of state surveillance and control. There is frequently an assumed ideological division between these two interpretations. The former may be characterized as seeing financial reporting driven by competitive forces in the market place and their needs for adequate information. The latter sees financial reporting as necessary to prevent abuse, to protect the fiscal base of the state and to maintain public confidence in the working of the securities markets. Nevertheless, arguments for and against the standardization and control of financial accounting and reporting can be, and at times are, stood on their heads. State intervention in this domain has been justified as necessary to improve the informational base used by the private sector for its own decision-making purposes, by countering a Gresham's Law effect in which unrestrained competition drives out fuller and more accurate financial disclosure through fear of revealing too much. In contrast, those wishing to roll back the boundaries of state economic activity and make it behave more in accordance with the canons of the private sector can point to the frequently deplorable and obscure financial information available on the performance of state enterprises, all of which needs to be addressed (so it may be claimed) through application to the public sector of accounting ideas and techniques worked out in the private sector.

This chapter therefore enters into a well-contested arena. As ever, the forces at work are in motion. Even as the whole world seems set on a path of greater accountability (associated with *glasnost, perestroika,* and so forth), the excesses of Wall Street and insider trading scandals suggest that Gresham's Law is after all not dead, and that the private sector and accounting profession may not effectively be able to maintain order for purposes of the political domain as well as the market place. The objective of the chapter is to counterpoise these two broadly opposed ideas about the role of accounting and financial reporting and to draw attention to an importantly different model for accommodating them both, namely the national accounting code developed in France. The discussion is presented in five sections. First, attention will be paid to the perceptions that accountants bring to their tasks of financial accounting, shaped by the historical conditions of *laissez-faire* capitalism under which the accounting profession developed. Those original perceptions have been further shaped by ideas drawn from economic theory and by a growing awareness by accountants that the setting of accounting standards, to which much professional energy is now devoted, takes place in a context of conflict and tension among interest groups. Ideas drawn from sociology and political theory are therefore relevant to an understanding of these perceptions. In the second section a comparison is made between English-speaking and French approaches to accounting standardization. The former are well-known, even dominant, internationally. The latter are little known outside France and those nations that have chosen to follow the French model for their purposes. What distinguishes French standardization of financial accounting is its national accounting code and broadly based national accounting council, both operative since shortly after the Second World War. In the third section, attention is given to the social forces affecting standardization of financial accounting and enterprise annual accounts. Those forces are viewed in terms of public sector imperatives for information, economic management and revenue raising, and in terms of private sector strategies for gaining advantage, managing risk and using information. In the fourth section there is an examination of models of social order as related to financial accounting, introduced so that the observed differences between national arrangements for dealing with this issue may be more clearly understood. Finally, in the fifth section the policy implications of the preceding sections are considered in terms of the demands for professional accounting skills in advanced capitalist nations and in developing or Third World nations where the accounting profession is less well organized.

A Comparison of Perceptions from Different Fields of Enquiry

The form of production of financial accounts is a matter of perceptions about financial representation of economic activity and its disclosure. Those perceptions create the possibility of discourse. This section briefly establishes the roots and nature of perceptions about financial reporting and its institutional framework associated with important categories of actors and thinkers.

Accountants

The basis of the perceptions held by accountants and collectively by their professional institutions were laid down in the circumstances of the origin and development of modern capitalism, especially in Britain. The 19th-century dominance of *laissez-faire* liberal ideas created conditions in which the emergent craft of the accountant was put firmly at the service of the entrepreneur. Even though much of the demand for the services of the accountant was grounded in liquidation work on behalf of creditors and audit on behalf of shareholders (Armstrong 1987: 419 – 423), there were no state agencies for supervising standards of the keeping of accounts or financial reporting.

In any event, action is impossible without ideas. Accounting was not considered a worthy subject of study in the universities (and has only become so in the past 20 years) and there was little or no theorizing about accounting as that would be understood today. In short, accountants were practical men who learned their craft as apprentices of practitioners (frequently by being articled in a manner comparable with law clerks), had at their disposal instructional texts of both a descriptive and prescriptive character and might at best attend evening classes in some college where they would be coached in necessary knowledge for the passing of professional examinations. In Britain the profession was organized entirely on a voluntary basis by practitioners, commencing with the formation of the Edinburgh Society of Accountants in 1854. Following establishment of The Institute of Chartered Accountants in England and Wales in 1880 and the granting of its Royal Charter in 1882, we see firmly in operation the processes of credentialism and social closure by exclusion (Parkin 1979; on the history of the English profession, see Stacey 1954).

The 19th-century professionalization of accounting accordingly occurred in a theoretical vacuum. Even though there was an emerging body of economic theory, possibly capable of interpretative application to financial measurement (Tinker 1985: Part III), accountants were not in any corporate sense organized to take note of it, nor is it likely that many individual accountants thought deeply about such matters. The original financial data base of the enterprise comprised its recorded revenues and expenditures and, at balance date, the amounts owing to creditors and owed by debtors. At heart, the transaction data provided a natural base from which to determine costs of operation and associated revenues. In other words, there were conditioning factors predisposing the accountant to determine financial performance on an historical cost basis, to use the general term of art still employed in the accounting literature (Hendriksen 1982: Ch. 2, Lee 1985: Ch. 4). The historical basis of financial accounting came, however, to be overlaid with various conventions of practice. The need to recognize that expenditures on capital equipment and facilities do not secure resources of immutable value meant that the accountant had to think about how to track changes in values over time. Further, the exigencies of trading might lead to stocks at year-end having a value below their cost, as well as to irrecoverable trade debts and loans. Issues of valuation, to be considered in a more deliberate and conscious way, crept into accounting. Even though this created the possibility of writing assets up in book value above their cost, the basic cast of financial accounting was, until recent times, prudent and conservative[2]. Prior to the U. K. *Companies Act*, (1948) it was not necessary for companies to disclose transfers to and from reserves and provisions. In those conditions it was easier for a company to follow a financial reporting strategy in which undisclosed transfers, together with associated adjustments to asset and liability values, would enable it to

---

[2] A statement made with some caution. There have been many spectacular exceptions in the famous fraud cases much quoted in accounting instruction, e. g. Baxter and Davidson 1962: Section on 'Outside the Law'.

maintain a fairly constant relationship between reported profit and dividends. In other words, financial reporting practices enabled dividend policy to drive profit measurement, rather than the contrary. All this was of great use in creating a corporate image of solidity and reliability, and in reducing apparent risk[3].

Changing times and social expectations about corporate performance have made accounting vastly more complicated. Persistent inflation in the 1970s and its associated phenomenon of changing currency exchange rates, huge increases in the value of positional goods (e. g. prime city real estate), new contractual forms of financing (e. g. leasing), and more complicated possibilities for business organization and control (e. g. trading trusts; significant but non-controlling equity investments) have been factors in pulling accountants here and there between adherence to a fairly strict historic cost basis for financial accounting and current valuation models of accounting (e. g. the much-debated proposals for current cost accounting, set out in the U. K. Sandilands Report [1975] and the subject of a long and finally unsuccessful attempt by the British accounting profession to convert those proposals into standard accounting practice; see Thompson [1987]).

The palette of the accountant enables him to paint the picture to be portrayed in the annual accounts with many choices of colour[4]. In interpreting its mission, financial accounting has hovered uncertainly between measurement based on historic cost and on valuations reflecting possible future outcomes (Tinker et al. 1982). In part, this reflects the epistemological dilemmas of the task, as related to the field under observation. In part, it denotes the desire of the accountant and his master, the manager or board of directors, to embed financial reporting in a zone of ambiguity or, in other words, to create a decision space in which management can control as far as possible the formation and content of the message it wishes to transmit to the world outside. Symbolizing this, the final incantation uttered by directors and auditors that the annual accounts are true and fair has little or nothing to do with common-sense interpretations of those words. Indeed, the accounting profession has repeatedly been at pains to argue that the words should be construed as having a technical, not a natural meaning (National Companies and Securities Commission 1984: 20–21, Wolnizer 1987: Ch. 5).

---

[3] Although the equity shareholders of a company are the ultimate risk bearers, it seems that many a shareholder really wants to be a rentier enjoying a fixed income but at a higher level than if merely a debtholder.

[4] Somewhat tongue in cheek, Chambers (1965) showed that there were hundreds of thousands of alternative combined possiblities for determining annual profit. It is hard to know whether accountants were shocked by this academic revelation or pleased to see that they had managed to be so inventive.

Economists

Economists are the high priests of theorizing about matters concerned with pricing and allocation of scarce resources, whether at the macro level (as pertains to a nation or national grouping) or at the micro level (as pertains to the individual household or firm). Given that money is the numeraire for expression of prices and values, and that there is a large body of economic theory expressly devoted to the creation and management of the money supply, economists have been remarkably silent about the financial information base for the testing and application of much of their theorizing. National agencies for the production of economic statistics are, of course, designed to provide necessary economic data but, for purposes relating to analysis to the business sector, little direct interest has been shown in the data produced by the accountant. In part, this may reflect frustration with the interminable debates within the accounting profession on fundamental matters of income measurement and asset valuation, reinforced by the known complexities of financial statement interpretation (Foster 1978). But in part it reflects a lack of conviction that accounting theory has anything of particular value to offer to the foundations of economic theory (Boulding 1962). It is only when the economist enquires into the wealth of nations and measures national income that the contribution of the accountant becomes potentially relevant. Until or unless the accountant can come up with more tractable and standardized data, however, the economist has perforce to skirt around what is on offer in enterprise annual accounts.

Accountants have, on the other hand, drawn from the economists though the effects have been primarily on theorizing by academic accountants rather than on practice. These have been twofold:

1. Theories of value have entered into the search by academics for meanings that could be attached to financial accounting consistent with economic theory and that could securely insert financial information into models of rational decision making. If achieved, this would be more glamorous than the rather humdrum and unfashionable explanation of financial reporting as connected with (mere) concepts of stewardship of the managers on behalf of owners (Littleton 1953: ch. 2) and has been marked in the literature by an emphasis on the entity concept of accounting, wherein the enterprise becomes the focus of accounting interest in its own right (Paton and Littleton 1960: ch. 2). This in turn lead to the elaboration of theories of capital maintenance, where the goal of preservation of entity capital (however defined) becomes effectively an end in itself (Edwards and Bell 1961: Part One). It is not hard to imagine that this is potent with consequences for dividend policy and distribution of enterprise income, especially

in times of general inflation or rapid technological change (Thompson 1987).

2. The rise of monetarist economics and positivism as a methodology for empirical testing has been powerful in reconstituting our view of what questions in relation to financial reporting and its regulation are answerable or even worth asking. Despite claims of objectivity by the most ardent accounting positivists, the value basis of what is on offer can plainly be seen. This is a belief in the power of unregulated markets to maximize possiblities of consumer choice and, through the effects of competition, to achieve economic growth and enhance consumer welfare (Tinker 1984). Translated into the domain of accounting, this reads as follows:

a. The effect of market forces will deliver such reported financial information as its users, actual or potential, may require, especially through the monitoring requirements imposed by principals (e. g. major lenders) on performance by their agents (viz. managers) (Watts and Zimmermann 1986: ch. 8). Given this, there is no need for the state to intervene (Benston 1981); moreover, in instances when it has done so, there has been no clear benefit to users of accounts (Chow 1983[5]).

b. There is no point in thinking normatively about grand schemes for the standardization of financial reporting. If there were a perceived demand for radical changes in institutional arrangements, market forces would bring this about. In any event, there is little empirical possibility of showing that a proposal for change having widespread social implications would produce sufficiently worthwhile economic benefits to outweigh the costs of change involved. (In passing, it is unclear how an empirical methodological limitation can be used to support a normative conclusion that questions about possible directions of social change should not be asked [Tinker 1988; Whittington 1987].)

Sociologists and Political Scientists

The contribution of sociology and political science to the evolution of perceptions about financial reporting is of a different nature and relatively recent. Scholars in those fields have not been interested in accounting theory as such, nor about whether economic theory is relevant to account-

---

[5] The work of Chow is cited for its philosophical orientation toward the distributional superiority of market forces, rather than for its empirical findings, which have been sharply questioned (Merino et al. 1987).

ing measurement. Ironically, Watts and Zimmerman (1978, 1979), as the most frequently cited accounting theory positivists, helped raise the eyes of accountants from their ledgers by pointing out that the process of arriving at agreed accounting standards is one owing little to the discovery of accounting truth but much more to political bargaining among interested parties. For them, the point of this observation seemed partly to be an epistemological one, aimed at dethroning deductivist approaches to an understanding of possibilities for financial reporting (as argued in Christenson 1983, Schreuder 1984), and partly an ideological one, reflecting a belief in the social superiority of market deregulation (Whittington 1987).

For academic accountants to realize that processes of accounting standardization are highly politicized has been a wrenching experience, since it requires understanding that such matters are not decided on the basis of their intrinsic technical merits. Although it would hardly be news to partners of Big-8 firms or boards of directors that accounting standards on some issues are worth bargaining about, given their power to change perceptions of profitability, taxability and income distribution, it is potentially dangerous for this to come clearly into view. Once that happens, general public attention is more pointedly directed to the nature of sectional interests, whereas formerly, in the era of deductivism, it was possible to mask those interests behind accounting debates of a technical character. Even so, the case for location of socioeconomic interests as related to financial accounting has not been made to any marked extent by social scientists from outside the domain of accounting. For all the weight of Marxist criticism of capitalism and implicitly of capitalists, Marxist theorists have paid hardly any attention to the financial information base that is maintained by capitalist bookkeepers. One can only marvel again at the success with which accountants have conveyed an image of dependable if somewhat boring neutrality and have mystified accounting to a degree beyond the ability of most non-accountants to penetrate[6]. Chua (1986: 594) remarks:

Within techne, accountants speak of profitability, growth and the benefit of accounting reports without a clear knowledge of how those notions are created and politicized in organisational and social life. Little is mentioned of the people who

---

[6] Lenin wrote extensively on the need after the revolution for standards of management to be strengthened and for workers to become more involved in managerial processes (whilst at the same time trying to skirt round the political dangers for his position of syndicalism) (Fischer 1964: chs. 35 and 36). I believe he stated at one point that, 'After the Revolution we shall all become bookkeepers', though I have not as yet succeeded in verifying this. Needless to say, it did not happen, in that financial reporting within the Soviet Union is extremely primitive by Western standards.

suffer or those who gain, at times intentionally and at times not. Neither is there much discussion of the manner in which accounting numbers value people, machines and time via an all-pervasive instrumental rationality which makes human beings more countable and accountable.

Accounting theorists have, however, started to recognize a need to look across discipline boundaries into theories about social structures and processes if they are better to comprehend the social context of accounting and the role it plays in national life. We may briefly note some emerging ideas and perceptions, categorized as follows (Standish 1988 b):

1. A broadly Marxist or labour process approach

This lays stress upon concerns about financial measurement and reporting as manifestations of the class relations and interests implicated in the structure of advanced capitalist societies, driven by inherent contradictions within that social system. The inherent problem with this characterization of accounting is its arbitrary or ideologically driven focus on capitalist societies. There is unlikely to be any disagreement with the universal proposition that accounting is intimately linked with ideas about control of scarce resources, a matter which concerns all complex societies whatever their political stripe.

2. Identification of interest groups and agency theory

The quest to identify the nature of interests bearing upon financial reporting and the ways in which particular groups seek to extract value from other groups, e. g. through monitoring contracts, is not in any obvious way culture-bound. Nevertheless, much of the so-called agency theory literature has to be interpreted against a positivist, market deregulation stance (as noted previously). This has, quite unnecessarily, come to import a bias against a consideration of alternative social arrangements for the regulation of financial reporting and, in particular, to denigrate the possibility for the state having a role of any significance in this arena.

3. Theories of social structure and change

These theories direct attention to the dynamic processes by which societies and their component groups react to pressures for change, especially intrusive events from outside the society, and to the need to establish how social groups are focalized by those pressures and events, as they adapt to change or seek to shape it to their advantage. (For a study which illustrates the application of these ideas to an analysis of financial reporting in Japan, see McKinnon [1986].)

4. Theories of discipline, authority and power

Considering that accounting practices are so intertwined with the idea of control, little attention has been given to the notion of accounting control as a way of structuring social relationships. In much of the standard management accounting and auditing literature, control is what the controllers (i. e. the managers, especially the accountants) do to the controlled (i. e. all other employees than the controllers). The controlled are, for want of any specific consideration of the matter, inert creatures whose sole duty is either to be controlled or face punitive sanctions. Now the idea is being looked at more closely. Miller (1987) has particularly drawn from the ideas of Foucault in this connection and, with O'Leary, has characterized the mission of accounting in a way arrestingly conveyed by the very title of their contribution, 'Accounting and the construction of the governable person' (Miller and O'Leary 1987).

Another source of ideas coming more recognizably from political theory concerns ways of regarding mechanisms for social order. Notable is the identification of an associative model (Streeck and Schmitter 1985), drawing attention to possibilities for a concertation of the state and organized interest groups for purposes of developing and giving effect to policies that might otherwise be beyond the power of the state or of interest groups operating outside this structure. These ideas are connected with corporatism (Grant 1985, Schmitter 1985) and are in many ways consonant with Olson (1982), as regards the social gains achievable under some circumstances from the emergence of encompassing (i. e. multi-interest) organizations (see cross-references in Streeck and Schmitter 1985, and Grant 1985, to the work of Olson 1982).

A Comparison of English-Speaking and French Approaches to Accounting Standardization

In all the advanced capitalist nations there is broad political agreement that a degree of standardization of financial measurement and reporting is required so that the messages in annual accounts become comprehensible through being based on more uniform representations of financial performance. The broad instruments for achieving this were noted in the introduction to the chapter. Although there are many ways in which these elements combine to form national arrangements for standardization of financial accounting and reporting, those arrangements can be clustered on the basis of some strongly differentiating characteristics. Broadly speaking, a distinction can be drawn between nations in which the private sector dominates accounting standardization and the state does not intervene for the purpose of integrating financial accounting and reporting with matters central to its mission, and nations in which the state actively seeks to shape financial accounting for state purposes as well as for the general public welfare. On that basis, there is a divide between English-speaking nations and most non-English-speaking nations. Of the latter, it appears that France has gone furthest toward accounting standardization, particularly as related to the primary recording of accounting transactions and organization of the entity accounting system. For that reason, a comparison will be offered in this section between the English-speaking world and France. As there is an extensive literature on the nature and operation of national arrangements in the English-speaking world, only a few salient points will be made here (see also Nobes and Parker 1985).

Australia, Britain and the USA

Of the major English-speaking nations, Britain stands out as having least intervention by the state in matters of financial accounting. Despite company frauds and scandals of impressive magnitude and number (e. g. consider the dramas in recent years affecting Lloyds of London, widely reported in the media; e. g. see annual index references, for *Accountancy* 1985, 1986), the ideological power of self-regulation, at least in the City, remains undented. The British Government is not in any way a party principal in the working of the Accounting Standards Committee (ASC), the body charged with developing statements of standard accounting practice and which aims to speak for the whole accounting profession and the business sector, or at least the larger corporate end of it. There is no government regulatory agency for the supervision of the securities industry and corporate compliance with the *Companies Act*, comparable to the U. S. Securities and Exchange Commission (SEC) or the Australian National Companies and Securities Commission (NCSC). Instead, the Securities Industry Board appears to wish to achieve its objectives as far as possible through encouragement of self-regulation, which may be regarded as yet another instance in life of the triumph of hope over experience (see annual index references for *Accountancy* 1987). Although public companies are required to file annual accounts with the Department of Trade, there is no systematic surveillance of compliance with statutory financial disclosure requirements. Finally, ASC statements of accounting standards do not have the force of law and enjoy only a somewhat indeterminate relationship to the specific disclosure requirements of the *Act* or its overriding requirement that annual accounts show a true and fair view (see Sutcliffe and Patient 1984: especially Appendix 1).

In both Australia and the United States the position differs importantly from Britain. As a general position, the SEC requires that companies subject to its jurisdiction (i.e. listed public companies) present annual accounts drawn up in accordance with Financial Accounting Standards Board *Statements of Financial Accounting Standards*. In Australia the Accounting Standards Review Board, a government agency, issues what under the *Companies Code* are termed approved accounting standards. These are to be the basis on which company annual accounts are drawn up except in those instances where the directors are of the opinion that it is necessary to depart from them in order that the accounts show a true and fair view. In that event, there are various requirements for disclosure of the financial effects (Standish 1985). The SEC and NCSC, respectively, exercise considerable discretionary power over listed public companies, especially in relation to mergers and takeovers. In neither Australia nor the USA is the state directly implicated in the specification of accounting standards. Neither are accounting standards and the basis of drawing up the annual accounts connected in any systematic way with such major concerns of state as protection of the fiscal base.

France

Accounting standardization in France differs from the English-speaking world in a number of major respects (examined in greater detail in Scheid and Standish 1989).

1. Standardization of the financial accounting system and presentation of the annual accounts.

This has been achieved by the following means:

a. Promulgation of a national accounting code, the *Plan comptable général*, operative since 1947.

   The *Plan comptable général* is essentially a standardized chart of accounts, issued under the authority of a government agency, the *Conseil national de la comptabilité*, and required to be used as the basis for structuring the accounting system of the individual organization. Accounts are grouped into seven classes, of which five are for different categories of accounts typically giving rise to year-end balances and hence amounts in the balance sheet. For example, Class 1 groups all the owner's capital accounts and Class 4 all accounts dealing with debtors and creditors. Two classes of accounts deal with the components of the profit and loss account, viz. revenues and costs respectively.

Accompanying the chart of accounts is an extensive list of defined financial terms and explanation of permissible bases of income measurement and net asset valuation. The full text of the *Plan*, including explanatory material, runs to nearly 400 pages (Conseil national de la comptabilité 1987).

b. Adoption of fixed formats for the annual accounts.

The *Plan* includes fixed formats for the balance sheet, profit and loss account, and the various financial schedules required to be included in notes to the annual accounts, e. g. statement of sources and uses of funds, schedules of fixed assets and associated depreciation. Thus the standardized layout of the annual accounts builds upon the broadly standardized structure of the underlying accounting system[7].

2. Application of the *Plan comptable général* across the economy.

Since 1947 application of the *Plan* has been extended more and more widely across the economy, initially to public enterprises and certain categories of private sector businesses receiving public subsidies. Later, there were fiscal inducements for commercial enterprises to adopt the *Plan*. It now applies via the *Code de commerce* to all companies and unincorporated enterprises established under the commercial code (Dalloz 1987: Article 8), to almost all categories of public enterprises and institutions other than central administrative departments of state (for which there are other standardized accounting requirements), to non-profit organizations and to local government.

3. Adaptation to particular industries, sectors and organizations.

Provision exists for adaptation of the *Plan* to the needs of particular industries in the private sector on the submission of a variant of the *Plan* by any recognized industry association on behalf of its members. In practice, the approved adaptations show variations from the basic *Plan* primarily in terms of account titles, but in some instances with modifications to the generally prevailing approved bases of financial measurement. There are also adaptations to a number of economically important sectors, such as agriculture, and within the public sector, to major undertakings and authorities, e. g. the national railways, electricity authority and forestry service with details of approved adaptations set out in the *Document* series

---

[7] Fixed formats for the annual accounts had for many years been contained in the law of other European countries as well, notably West Germany. The outcome of bargaining between the EEC member states on a basic financial disclosure law, the Fourth Directive, adopted in 1978, was that fixed formats have since become law in all the member states, including Britain (Nobes and Parker 1985: ch. 3).

issued by the *Conseil national de la comptabilité*. Any organization may at its discretion further subdivide the various classes and sub-classes of accounts in the *Plan* as a way to adapt it to its particular informational needs.

4. Meshing of the *Plan* with other needs of the state.

As it now operates, the Plan meshes closely with needs of the state for fiscal administration and tax assessment of business income, as well as for statistical information on enterprise performance. Thus the standard forms for the annual enterprise tax return, *Impôt sur les sociétés*, issued by the *Direction Générale des Impôts* (DGI), and the annual enterprise statistical return forms, *Enquête Annuelle d'Entreprise*, issued by INSEE (the national statistical office), both use the same terminology in relation to financial items as is employed in the *Plan comptable général* and require information taken straight from the annual accounts in a form corresponding to the accounts. Moreover, the relationship between the *Plan* and the fiscal authority (DGI) in essence requires all transactions of an organization that are properly assessable or deductible to be entered into its accounting records.

5. Creation of an all-encompassing authority for accounting standardization.

From the outset, the *Plan* has been the responsibility of a broadly based agency. Now entitled the *Conseil national de la comptabilité*, and under the control of the Ministry of Finance, the *Conseil* has a membership of 105 persons, drawn from all major private sector associations and professional institutions, as well as from government ministries and agencies interested in the reliability of financial accounting and its suitability for the needs of users.

The combined effect of these measures for accounting standardization has been to diffuse awareness widely throughout France of what is required of enterprises as regards financial accounting and reporting. In effect, the French have created a national accounting language, an achievement which could not by any stretch of imagination be said to exist in the English-speaking world. For the French, this has had the following significant effects (explored further in Scheid and Standish [1989]):

1. enabling the economy and state to function with comparatively fewer professional accountants than, for example, is the case in Britain;
2. raising standards of practice in the basic keeping of accounts, especially by small- and medium-sized enterprises, both as regards systematized documentation of invoices and other transaction records, and in terms of a known structure for the chart of accounts;

3. reducing risk to the auditor by structuring in a more predictable manner the tasks of assessment of enterprise accounting controls and compliance of the annual accounts with the law;
4. facilitating inter-firm financial comparison and in promoting development of software incorporating a standardized chart of accounts.

The operation of the *Conseil* accords well with the Olson (1982: 47 – 53) conception of an encompassing organization as an instrument of social decision making and co-ordination, with important consequences for forcing its constituent lobbying groups to behave differently toward each other than if they were not brought together in this context. Indeed, it is this structure that gives to accounting standardization in France its character, rather than indigenous cultural factors, though those factors are relevant to an explanation of why the French were amenable to adopting a national accounting code and establishing the *Conseil* in the first place (Standish 1988 a).

It is to be noted, in passing, that the French model for accounting standardization and adoption of a national accounting code has been implemented in varying degrees in Belgium, Spain, Greece and a number of Third World countries in Africa.

Social Forces Affecting Accounting Standardization

Enough has already been said to identify the existence of diverse and at times conflicting perceptions about whether and in what form accounting should be standardized. In this section explicit attention will be drawn to these issues, dealing separately with ideas relating to state and enterprise, to governance and the relationship of the enterprise with the state.

Public Sector Imperatives

The issue of what are the proper concerns of the state on behalf of its citizenry has become so embattled that we may well wish it could be avoided. At every point, government seems perverted by the insistent demands of special interest groups (including its far from disinterested functionaries). To taxpayers with higher incomes, it often seems incapable of doing anything other than in a wastefully inefficient way. All this makes it difficult to think dispassionately and imaginatively about what government can best do or can alone do in a modern state. This is especially so in the domain of relations between business and government, where big business chiefly wants the state to fade away or to see things its way (including protecting its economic interests through subsidies, profitable government contracts, absence of tedious regulation, etc.). Nevertheless, an act of reconsideration and imagination is what will now be attempted.

a. General Economic Welfare

It has become a matter of high fashion for politicians, even those who are somewhat to the left, to speak of the proper role of government as creating a level playing field for the various competitive interests that make up the community. Securing a flow of well-structured and interpretable financial information about the achievements and condition of organizations and enterprise, whether public or private, is an essential condition for achieving that objective. For the state to imagine that it could secure this simply by exhortation or by leaving the matter to the unrestrained expression of self-interest is too foolish for words, given the historical evidence of financial reporting abuses when regulation is ineffectual or non-existent. The metaphorical idea of a level playing field in this regard is taken to conform with the position adopted by Parkin (1979: 112):

[...] that the relation between classes is neither one of harmony and mutual benefit, nor of irresolvable and fatal contradiction. Rather, the relationship is understood as one of mutual antagonism and permanent *tension*; that is, a condition of unrelieved distributive struggle that is not necessarily impossible to 'contain'.

b. Knowledge of the Private Sector

Drawing upon Foucault for ways of thinking about the nature of the state and its role and actions in the political management of society, Miller (1987): 208) refers to *reasons of state* and the *theory of police*, explaining that the former is to be regarded as an art intended to strengthen the state through knowledge and for which *'Political statistics or arithmetic* was to become indispensable for correct government'. Ideas about *Police*, as Miller (1987: 208) remarks, referred in the 17th and 18th centuries to the processes of government applied to the domains, techniques and objects on which the regulatory power of the state should bear: "The relationships between men and things, their coexistence on a territory, what they produce, how they live, the diseases and accidents that befall them" but with the overall objective of enabling the people to live, survive and do better than they would otherwise do.

The gathering of national statistics on enterprise financial performance reflects the continuing concern of the state to know more of the private sector. Procedures for this purpose in the English-speaking world, not being closely coupled with enterprise financial accounting, are bedevilled by the multiplicity of accounting measurement and valuation bases in use, as well as differences in account terminology and classification. The idea of state concern with the well-being of enterprises points to the desirability of its exhibiting a conscious interest in the conditions of financial accounting as an instrument for learning more about the well-being of enterprises and the normality of their financial behaviour. On this view, the state would not be discharging its mission by leaving this matter to the determination of the very parties about whom the knowledge of financial condition is required.

c. Intervention in the Private Sector

The free-market insistence that governments abstain from seeking to influence economic choices at micro- or industry-level through interventionist policies for setting subsidies, tariffs and other non-tariff barriers to trade, etc., distracts attention from the continuing reality that governments do intervene in the private sector and are not likely under any conceivable circumstances to refrain altogether from doing so. Indeed, the evidence of economic consequences flowing from government intervention does not obviously favour either intervention or non-intervention, when one compares the economic condition of nations having a more *dirigiste* tradition of government (e. g. France, Japan) with those that do not (mainly the English-speaking world nations). Leaving equity considerations aside, the present argument is that governments will be better fitted for interventionist decisions if their knowledge base relating to the private sector includes appropriately standardized financial information permitting robust cross-sectional comparisons of performance. For example, if steel-making companies, an industry dogged by excess capacity, want taxpayers' money to aid corporate reconstruction and plant closure but turn out to have underprovided depreciation comparatively with other technologically changing industries and to have over-distributed profits (i. e. effectively distributed capital), one would not want government to be particularly moved by their plight, at least not on financial grounds. But effective financial data is a precondition for assessing such matters in the first place. For reasons already indicated, the conditions for achieving this are less well realized in the English-speaking world. This may be contrasted with the position in France where standardization achieved through the *Plan comptable général* has facilitated development of major cross-sectoral data bases of financial performance, notably the collection maintained by the Banque de France (the *Centrale de bilans,* Banque de France 1980, 1982).

A more general issue than the matter of data available as a decision aid for instances of specific state intervention is the issue of the grounds on which regulation, as a systematic form of state intervention, might be justified. Lev (1988: 4) characterizes the case for regulation of financial reporting in terms of equalizing of *ex ante* opportunity to investors in securities in these terms:

> [...] inequality of opportunity is present when investors are endowed with different information about securities or market mechanisms, a situation known as differential, or asymmetric, information.

Although his argument is coloured to a degree by the importance of the securities markets in the USA as an instrument for raising capital (whereas in a number of other OECD countries, the banking system plays a relatively greater role in providing long-term finance), Lev (1988) points to high transaction costs, restricted trading volumes ('thin markets'), low liquidity and, in general, decreased gains from trade as adverse private and social consequences resulting from inequity in the capital markets. At the same time, he points to the international pervasiveness of regulation of financial reporting. This may be taken to support the view that unless government intervenes in this arena, there will be no other basis for a solution to the problem of reducing informational asymmetry.

d. Protection of the Fiscal Base

In any political theory that attributes essential functions to the state, there is an inescapable role for government to act so as to determine and maintain the fiscal base required for the harvesting of necessary tax revenues. It is widely recognized that the taxation of consumption (e. g. by a value-added tax) is less problematic than the taxation of income. Moreover, taxation of business profits presents greater difficulties than personal taxation, where the latter is largely garnered through withholding taxes on wages and salaries, interest payments, dividends, and welfare or any other payments determined by law (if subject to taxation). Corporate tax collection is beset by problems associated with transfer pricing across national frontiers and arbitraging between different tax regimes, especially tax havens.

Governments that do not take effective steps to arm themselves with adequate information about corporate financial performance are risking erosion of the corporate tax base. The response of many governments has been either to move heavily away from corporate taxation (as occurred in Britain during the 1970s) or to incur substantially higher tax administration costs in a battle of wits with the corporate sector. The latter task, from a government perspective, is by no means guaranteed of success. Corporations can outrank government any day in terms of their ability (and motivation, given what is relatively at stake for them) to hire the best brains and, in the limit, to move financial assets offshore. It is therefore little short of astonishing that the major English-speaking world governments have allowed themselves to be brain-washed ideologically into accepting the accounting profession viewpoint that financial accounting must be decoupled from the determination of taxable income. This has been a case of the tail of a technical dog, whose pedigree comes from the professed search for accounting truth and 'good' accounting, wagging the body politic and, as it happens, protecting the economic interests of the corporate sector. Matters do not so have to be arranged, as the French system of meshing financial accounting with tax assessment shows.

Private Sector Strategies

To date, it could be said that the promise of accounting standardization in the English-speaking world has been considerably greater than the performance. The reason is that policy-makers have insufficiently addressed the operation of possibly countervailing private sector strategies toward standardization. Added to this is the fact that those private sector strategies are in many ways in conflict with each other. The accounting profession, once it has come to accept that pressures for standardization must somehow be accommodated, has learned to use a rhetoric that gives promise without substance. For example, the U.S. FASB conceptual framework project (expressed in the FASB *Statements of Financial Accounting Concepts*) is essentially an exercise in establishing the moral authority of the private sector to deal with financial accounting standards and to keep government away from this domain. As a catalogue of vaguely defined fundamental concepts, the framework institutionalizes rather than eliminates many possibilities of differences in accounting practice.

In this section the nature of those private sector countervailing strategies is considered.

a. Extraction of Surplus Value

It is assumed that the central objective of actors in a market-based competitive economy is the extraction of surplus value from others, be it from employees, customers having to pay prices higher as a result of monopolization of conditions of supply, or from taxpayers via government intervention in support of particular activities. In this context, individual actors having the economic power or, which amounts to the same thing, the possibility of operating social and political networks for their own ends, are not likely to favour accounting standardization if that carries the prospect of reducing excess returns from superior access to information. The most celebrated manifestation of excess returns is from insider trading, which is a particularly problematic issue for government or the exponents of self-regulation. But there are many other conditions for the achievement of excess returns short of crossing into the zone of illegal insider trading. Lev (1988: 18) cites studies showing that observed return differentials achieved by U. S. taxpayers from investment in traded securities are sufficiently different across income groups to suggest that wealthy investors enjoy systematic excess returns even within the current U. S. regulatory environment. Those investors are unlikely to see advantage in public policies aimed at reducing their chances of achieving these excess returns.

b. Risk Avoidance and Location

Another way to characterize the process of extraction of surplus value is to consider the matter of location of risk among actors, or classes of them. It is well understood, for example, that the adverse financial consequences of corporate fraud fall far more heavily upon auditors, as a result of professional negligence suits, than upon directors, especially directors who are employees without substantial personal fortunes rather than major owners of the company. In other words, each group has an incentive to shift possible adverse risk effects onto other groups while retaining for itself expected favourable effects.

Thus auditors have been happy to achieve what appear to be the excess returns associated with monopolization of the supply of statutorily mandated audit, but have seen some attractions in accounting standardization as a means of defence against negligence suits. This is most evident in the USA where the auditor works in a highly litigious environment and where, among the English-speaking nations, accounting standardization has proceeded the furthest. Insofar as standardization reduces the range of possibilities for lawsuits against auditors, the financial risks of fraud are then thrown back onto shareholders and creditors.

c. Access to Information

There are many circumstances of private sector decision making in which access to reliable financial reporting accounts is well-nigh essential. It is not, however, a simple matter to infer from that proposition how well private sector interests would be served by accounting standardization. Monitoring agreements between investor/lender and investee/borrower can largely bypass the problems posed otherwise by non-standardized information. Moreover, the private sector need for standardized information may depend in part on the national financial system. Historically, there have been differences in the relative importance for capital raising in particular nations of the stock market vis-à-vis the banking system. As securities markets develop, however, possibilities for redeployment of capital extend to takeovers and mergers of other companies of which the bidder often has no close operational knowledge. In these circumstances differences between the accounting practices of companies constitute a further element of risk to the general investment community for which there are no obvious compensating advantages.

Even so, it is striking to see to what little extent financial analysts and portfolio fund managers in Britain and the USA (to name the two countries with the most highly developed securities markets) have sought to standardize financial accounting. This most likely reflects an expectation that they can extract excess returns through the development of superior insights into complex, unstandardized information (incidentally giving rise to the high transaction costs referred to by Lev [1988]). In France the existence of standardized financial information has presented analysts with a different situation in which there are possibilities for gaining economies of scale through standardized analysis of annual accounts and calculation of financial ratios (e. g. as seen in the publications of the major French private sector financial information service, DAFSA [1985]). In contrast to their English-speaking peers, French financial analysts seem satisfied that the standardized annual accounts delivered by the *Plan comptable général* are to their benefit (Mériaux 1986).

Models for the Operation of a Standardizing Process for Financial Accounting

Much of the effort expended nationally and internationally to arrive at effective accounting standards has perforce been directed at developing a process of standardization. If there are no ultimate accounting truths discoverable at a technical level and if accounting standards are likely to redistribute economic welfare, then it needs be recognized that the process is implicated in an interactive social context. Clearly, the various accounting professional bodies that were first to embark on the setting of accounting standards had no real idea of what they were letting themselves in for. The profession supposed that to arrive painlessly at technical solutions, it had only to form a technical committee and have its members sit around a table behind closed doors (partly because accountants are habituated to secrecy, partly because it would have surprised the profession to discover that anybody else might find such matters interesting). But every step proved to be a step into a quagmire, with committees set up, abandoned, bypassed, reconstituted and so forth (Leach and Stamp 1981: chs. 1, 2, 4, Zeff 1972).

Using the Streeck and Schmitter (1985) models of social order, this section considers the approaches that have been taken to constituting processes for pursuing accounting standardization.

Community

The early stages of development of financial reporting in the English-speaking world, in the 19th century, conform with the attributes of a community model of social order. The accounting profession sought social closure through statutory monopolization of its key functions but with enforcement and disciplinary issues to be left to the profession (and, in practice, ignored). The way forward was to achieve social respectability. The British profession in particular developed strong values associated with notions of membership, status and solidarity (Willmott 1985). In many ways this is still the dominant model underlying processes of accounting standardization in Britain but, for reasons already indicated, it is creaking at the seams. Moreover, a model of this type, having a community (i.e. national) particularity, finds it difficult to cope with the opening up of accounting standardization to international influences. The more important of the EEC Directives on Company Law have all posed considerable headaches for the British profession, by introducing ideas from Continental Europe requiring more formalized specification of key elements in the determination of financial performance, presentation of the annual accounts, and qualifications required of the statutory auditor. Though the British profession has been reluctant to abandon its affinity for a community model for the social ordering of accounting, the profession in other nations of the Commonwealth, notably Canada and Australia, has done so to a greater extent (on Australia, see Standish [1985]).

Market

The United States provides an example of evolution of its accounting profession and standards of practice conforming more closely to a market model of social order. Its federal political structure permitted an element of competition in the conditions of company legislation, which is a responsibility at state level, with the result that the state 'blue sky' company laws, as still known, imposed little on companies by way of financial disclosure. At the same time, the wide geographical dispersion of population, industry and commerce, not to mention the social dynamics of immigration and internal movement of people, meant that there never was much chance for the emergence of communitarian ideas of self-regulation along British lines. Although the Federal Government took powers to intervene in the regulation of financial reporting of listed public companies with the creation in 1934 of the Securities and Exchange Commission and passage of related legislation, it has exercised those powers rarely and only on limited issues (Chatov 1975), such as the mandating in 1976 of disclosure of certain indicators of financial performance measured on a replacement value basis (Tweedie and Whittington 1984: ch. 7) and overriding the accounting profession in relation to the treatment of fixed asset investment tax credits (Zeff 1984).

In this, considerable influence has been exerted in recent years by the Rochester school (see earlier references to Benston 1981, Watts and Zimmerman 1978, 1979, 1986) in providing intellectual backbone for minimizing the regulatory influence of the state. Lev's (1988) discovery of the case for financial reporting regulation is of more interest for the evident need to present this argument in the USA than for what it says, none of which would provoke surprise in practically any other country. A purely market-determined basis for a system of financial reporting was only ever an ideal, a normative underpinning for the much-vaunted rigour of the positivist theorists in accounting (Tinker et al. 1982).

Etatisme

It is not for nothing that the term used to denote a conception of the state as the great animator of national life should be French. Some commentators have gone so far as to opine that France is the only true example of a functioning state. Whether or not this is too extreme, the state in France created the institutions of the accounting profession, the *Plan comptable général*, and the *Conseil national de la comptabilité* (Scheid and Standish 19898). These moves reflected particular circumstances in modern

French history, especially the perturbations of World War II and the early post-war period, an acute conviction at political and bureaucratic levels that France had to be forcefully modernized and rendered better able to face international competitive pressures, notably from the English-speaking world, and a belief in the possibilities of national economic planning (Fourquet 1980, Kuisel 1981).

But France is not an island unto itself, and the apparatus of the state does not have limitless capacity to discern, ordain or procure. The maintenance of the *Plan comptable général* is not simply a bureaucratic exercise and cannot in the end function without the cooperation of the accounting profession and the business sector. As France becomes more firmly drawn into a wider international context, in which its leading enterprises wish to play a prominent part, the pressures on the state to loosen up on detailed control of financial reporting are intensifying. Thus the state has conceded a degree of freedom from some of the requirements of the *Plan* normally applicable to the individual enterprise for the purpose of preparation of consolidated group accounts, notably in accounting for provisions for tax and the treatment of long-term leases (Conseil national de la comptabilité 1987: II, ch. IV). *Etatisme* may have been possible in the conditions of establishment of the *Plan*, but it no longer appears that the French state can alone control the process of accounting standardization.

Corporatist

A model of an associative or corporatist social order draws attention to possibilities for binding interest groups into processes that force them to confront the reality of variant or opposed interests. An analysis of characteristics of this social order is shown in Streeck and Schmitter (1985: Table 2). In brief, this draws attention to structures and processes leading to mutual recognition of status and rights of access, to the making of pacts, to satisficing in the interest of gaining greater certainty and to avoiding complete rejection of sectional objectives. This social order is characterized in the following terms (Streeck and Schmitter 1985: 16):

Devolving state functions to the *community* amounts to an attempt to marshal *collective other-regarding interests* for social purposes; its underlying premise is that people hold solidaristic values and communitarian identities that, just as their self-interests, can contribute to social order directly and without state coordination.

A strictly associative model is likely to face problems of cohesion and legitimation of authority. The label 'private interest government' used by Streeck and Schmitter (1985) points to some of the political tensions that might be quickly engendered by excessive devolution by the state of quasi-authority in matters of widespread import. It is to be doubted that establishment of an associative model of private interest groups to deal with accounting standardization would stand much chance of success, for all the reasons and circumstances identified earlier. But it is not clear why we cannot contemplate an arrangement that lies somewhere between a model operated solely by the state, i. e. a bureaucratic process, and an associative model that includes representation of state as well as private interests. As noted, this is exemplified in the structure of the French national accounting council, the *Conseil national de la comptabilité*, constituted as follows:

1. Office-holders:
   1 President (in practice, a senior state functionary)
   5 Vice-Presidents (each responsible for a *Commission*, e. g. financial accounting, public sector accounting
   1 Secretary-General (a bureaucrat)
2. Representatives from the following categories:
   22 Government ministries and agencies
   19 Organizations and commissions specializing in accounting and financial matters
   27 Professionally qualified accountants drawn from public practice and major enterprises
   10 National employers' federation, the chambers of commerce and industry, and of arts and crafts
   5 Trade unions
   5 Civil service
   10 Persons of standing in accounting, law, economic affairs and finance

In the case of the *Conseil* the question of legitimation of authority does not arise, given its statutory basis of operation and the ongoing presence in its deliberations of key state interests, notably the fiscal authority (*Direction Générale des Impôts*). In what sense then can it be said to have elements of an associative process? Participation in its affairs is not obligatory, but nevertheless there is no suggestion of bodies with the right to representation refusing involvement or withdrawing at critical junctures. Moreover, many members have experienced long terms on the *Conseil*, indicating a degree of stability in the functioning of its processes.

Another issue is whether the constituent groups making up the *Conseil* consider that their interests have been sufficiently addressed to make involvement worthwhile. Beyond noting stability of involvement, no clear answer is available. It is said that the influence of the fiscal authority is considerable and that many key decisions of the *Conseil* reflect compromise between it and the national employers' federation (*Conseil national du patronat français*). The institutions of the French accounting profession (*Ordre des experts comptables et des comptables agréés* and *Compagnie nationale des commissaires aux comptes*) clearly do not have the same influence on standardization as their English-speaking counterparts.[8] It is an arrangement that evidently suits the French, for social and cultural reasons explored in Standish (1988 b).

Policy Implications

The public policy implications of the ground traversed are considerable. In this section some of the elements and consequences of choice are addressed.

Advanced Capitalist Nations

There is a remarkable difference between the number of professionally qualified accountants and statutory auditors in the various advanced capitalist nations, as may be illustrated by comparing the English-speaking world, confined here to Britain and France. Comparison of the relative size of the accounting profession in various nations is not simple, given the different structures of the profession and ways in which the law reserves the designation of accountant. In brief, there are six professional bodies in Britain, embracing accountants in public practice, in commerce and industry, and in state and local government. To complicate matters, many British accountants work abroad, while one body (the Chartered Association of Certified Accountants) has a history of admitting to membership nationals of Third World countries. The bodies which particularly represent practising accountants and statutory auditors are the three Institutes of Chartered Accountants (of England and Wales, Scotland and Ireland), having a combined membership of approximately 100,000. Of those persons, a substantial proportion is not in public practice. In France mem-

---

[8] The *Conseil national de la comptabilité* does not operate in open session as, for example, does the U.S. Financial Accounting Standards Board. There has been no reported study of its process or analysis on the basis of socially grounded theory. The observations in the text are based on personal enquiry of over 50 persons at high levels of responsibility in the accounting domain in France in 1986, and include many hours of interviews with all senior office-holders of the *Conseil*, as well as its Secretary-General and a number of its professional staff.

bership of the two professional bodies is restricted to those in public practice, and a high proportion of members belong to both bodies. Membership of OECCA is currently at 11,000. Assuming only 50% of British Chartered Accountants to be in public practice and given the closely similar population of the two nations (both some 56 million), it follows that Britain has nearly five times as many accountants in public practice as France, absolutely and per head of population. Since there is no professional body in France catering on a large scale for accountants in commerce, industry and government, it is likely that there is a far lower number of persons working in those sectors than in Britain with skills and tasks that would attract the designation of accountant in the English-speaking world.

How is it possible for the French to conduct their national economic life, which delivers a living standard to its citizens little different in terms of national income measures from Britain, with so few accountants? As yet, nobody has seriously addressed this type of question, whether for this pair of nations or any other grouping of countries. Some tentative explanations for the elevated number of accountants in Britain must include factors such as the more ubiquitous requirements for companies to be audited, the fact that rendering income tax returns is decoupled from the basis for preparing the annual accounts, and the lack of basic standardization of enterprise accounting systems, which means that for every separate enterprise there is the distinct possibility that a new accounting wheel may be invented. In Britain, and more generally the English-speaking world, the whole matter of accounting seems to be a major production. The French have not found it necessary for this to be so. Whether one or the other nation is better off for this state of affairs is beyond current speculation. What is certainly true is that the fivefold number of British accountants are not working for nothing and that their gainful employment, together with a large retinue of support staff and apprentice accountants, constitute an oncost to the British way of doing things, compared with the French way.

Developing Nations

Advanced nations can afford the luxury of having lots of accountants, along with lawyers, social workers, public relations experts and all the other groups that draw on the superabundant productivity of present-day technology and its consequent production of surplus value. Matters are different in much of the Third World where, if anything, indigenous accountants with foreign training are likely to be lured away by opportunities in London, Paris and so forth. The problem for those nations is to stretch their usage of accounting skills and, when the matter is considered with any degree of disinterest, to simplify the accounting tasks that are truly essential. Those tasks are to create a stable fiscal base, without which the state will be hard pressed to extract surplus value for the needs of the community at large, and to enable enterprises to design and operate accounting systems of a straightforward kind.

Within the nations of the Francophone the existence of the *Plan comptable général* is well known and has sparked interest in the development of national accounting codes. The most notable outcome is the *OCAM Plan* (*Organisation commune africaine et mauricienne*), largely based on the 1957 French *Plan comptable général*. At present, national accounting codes are in course of development for other of these nations, notably Morocco (Perochon 1988). Associated with the development of these codes has come recognition of the interlinkages between accountability and issues of public policy already traversed, as well as the creation of national accounting councils (for extended review and analysis of the experience of African nations, see Kinzonzi Mvutukidi Ngindu 1984). Third World nations that are largely unaware of the concept of a national accounting code obviously have to cope with their needs in other ways. Those developing countries without a national accounting code but which tolerate or encourage private enterprise are likely to find their indigenous accounting arrangements shaped along the lines of the English-speaking world. This will tend to produce the effects noted earlier, namely a relatively larger number of accountants, a greater extent of individual enterprise design of accounting systems, higher audit costs and a reduced degree of usefulness to the state of enterprise accounting information. In the interface between national economic activity and international trade and investment the Big 8 firms can be expected to play an increasing role. As yet, we await studies to compare achievements in the domain of financial accounting and reporting under different social arrangements and of the degree to which the various needs of the private sector and the state are satisfactorily met.

Conclusion

The original question posed by the chapter was to consider the extent to which accounting and its informational outcomes are primarily to be regarded as constituting a private language for business and therefore, as knowledge and a source of power, or under what conditions its role might be more broadly recast as an instrument of social communication. The mission of the accounting profession in advanced capitalist nations has historically been to view that role as subservient to private interests. The profession has not sought to enlarge the domain of consideration. Even so, nations do have choices about how they wish to arrange for the discharge of accountability though in practice this generally proves difficult to deal with, given the range of opposed sectional interests and tensions between them. To understand what the choices are and to make them in an informed way requires conditions of possibility for discourse and perhaps a random conjunction of facilitating circumstances. Such, at any rate, was the case with France which took a different path from its English-speaking neighbours and which shows a model for the process and objectives of accounting standardization of considerable influence in other nation states of the EEC and various developing countries. Whether that model should or will have influence elsewhere is another question. It might be better answered if there is a greater social awareness of what is at stake and of the experiences of different nations in shaping financial accounting to their public and private needs.

References

Armstrong, Peter (1987): The rise of accounting controls in British capitalist enterprises, *Accounting, Organizations and Society* 12/5: 415–436.

Banque de France, Centrale de bilans (1980): Les ratios de la Centrale de Bilans de la Banque de France, *Note d'information* 43: Paris: Banque de France.

Banque de France, Centrale de bilans (1982): *Méthode d'analyse et présentation des résultats,* Paris: Banque de France.

Baxter, William and Sidney Davidson (eds.) (1962): *Studies in accounting theory,* London: Sweet & Maxwell.

Benston, George (1981): Are accounting standards necessary? in: Sir R. Leach and E. Stamp (eds.), *British accounting standards: the first 10 years,* 201–214, Cambridge: Woodhead-Faulkner.

Boulding, Kenneth (1962): Economics and accounting: the uncongenial twins, in: W. Baxter and S. Davidson (eds.), *Studies in accounting theory,* 44–55, London: Sweet & Maxwell.

Chambers, Raymond (1965): Financial information and the securities market, *Abacus* 1/1: 3–30.

Chatov, Robert (1975): *Corporate financial reporting,* New York: Macmillan.

Chow, Chee (1983): The impacts of accounting regulation on bondholder and shareholder wealth: the case of the securities acts, *The Accounting Review* 58/3: 485–520.

Christenson, Charles (1983): The methodology of positive accounting, *The Accounting Review* 58/1: 1–22.

Chua, Wai-Fong (1986): Theoretical constructions of and by the real, *Accounting, Organizations and Society* 11/6: 583–598.

Conseil national de la comptabilité (1987): *Plan comptable général,* Paris: Conseil national de la comptabilité, 4th edition.

DAFSA (1985): *Fiche DAFSA d'analyse financière: manuel de l'utilisateur,* Paris: DAFSA.

Dalloz (1987): *Code de commerce,* Paris: Dalloz.

Edwards, Edgar and Philip Bell (1961): *The theory and measurement of business income,* Berkeley, Cal.: University of California.

Financial Accounting Standards Board (1986): *Statements of Financial Accounting Concepts,* Stamford, Conn.: Financial Accounting Standards Board.

Financial Accounting Standards Board (1986): *Statements of Financial Accounting Standards,* Stamford, Conn.: Financial Accounting Standards Board.

Fischer, Louis (1964): *The life of Lenin,* New York: Harper & Row.

Foster, George (1978): *Financial statement analysis,* Englewood Cliffs, N. J.: Prentice-Hall.

Fourquet, François (1980): *Les comptes de la puissance,* Paris: Encres.

Grant, Wyn (1985): Introduction, in: W. Grant (ed.), *The political economy of corporatism,* 1–31, London: Macmillan.

Hendriksen, Eldon (1982): *Accounting theory,* Homewood, Ill.: Irwin.

Inflation Accounting Committee [the Sandilands Report] (1975): *Inflation accounting,* London: HMSO, Cmnd 6225.

Kinzonzi Mvutukidi Ngindu, K. (1984): *Normalisation comptable: facteur d'accélération de développement économique,* Paris: Foucher.

Kuisel, Richard (1981): *Capitalism and the state in modern France,* Cambridge: Cambridge University Press.

Leach, Sir Ronald and Edward Stamp (1981): *British accounting standards: the first 10 years,* Cambridge: Woodhead-Faulkner.

Lee, Tom (1985): *Income and value measurement: theory and practice,* Wokingham, Berks.: Van Nostrand Reinhold.

Lev, Baruch (1988): Toward a theory of equitable and efficient accounting policy, *The Accounting Review* 63/1: 1–22.

Littleton, Ananias (1953): *Structure of accounting theory,* Ann Arbor, Mich.: American Accounting Association.

McKinnon, Jill (1986): *The historical development and operational form of corporate reporting regulation in Japan,* New York: Garland.

Merino, Barbara, Bruce Koch and Kenneth MacRitchie (1987): Historical analysis – a diagnostic tool for 'events' studies: the impact of the Securities Act of 1933, *The Accounting Review* 62/4: 748–762.

Mériaux, Jacques (1986): L'information comptable 1984: la cassure, *Analyse Financière* (1er trimestre) 65–73.

Miller, Peter (1987): *Domination and power,* London: Routledge & Kegan Paul.

Miller, Peter and Ted O'Leary (1987): Accounting and the construction of the governable person, *Accounting, Organizations and Society* 12/3: 235–266.

National Companies and Securities Commission (1984): *'A true and fair view' and the reporting obligations of directors and auditors,* Canberra: Australian Government Publishing Service.

Nobes, Christopher and Robert Parker (eds.) (1985): *Comparative international accounting,* London: Philip Allan.

Olson, Mancur (1982): *The rise and decline of nations: economic growth, stagflation, and social rigidities,* New Haven: Yale University Press.

Parkin, Frank (1979): *Marxism and class theory: a bourgeois critique,* New York: Columbia University Press.

Paton, William and Ananias Littleton (1960): *An introduction to corporate accounting standards,* Ann Arbor, Mich.: American Accounting Association.

Perochon, Claude (1988): L'influence hors Europe de la IVème Directive: le projet marocain de normalisation comptable, Paper presented to the Congress of the European Accounting Association.

Sandilands Committee (1975): *Inflation accounting: report of the Inflation Accounting Committee under the chairmanship of F. E. P. Sandilands,* London: HMSO (Cmnd 6225).

Scheid, Jean-Claude and Peter Standish (1989): Accounting standardization in France and international accounting exchanges, in: A. Hopwood (ed.), *International pressures for accounting change,* 162 – 186, London: Prentice-Hall U. K.

Schmitter, Philippe (1985): Neo-corporatism and the state, in: W. Grant (ed.), *The political economy of corporatism,* 32 – 62, London: Macmillan.

Schreuder, Hein (1984): Positively normative (accounting) theories, in: A. Hopwood and H. Schreuder (eds.), *European contributions to accounting research: the achievements of the last decade,* Amsterdam: Free University Press.

Stacey, Nicholas (1954): *English accountancy 1800 – 1954: a study in social and economic history,* London: Gee.

Standish, Peter (1985): Financial reporting in Britain and Australia, in: C. Nobes and R. Parker (eds.), *Comparative international accounting,* 44 – 74, London: Philip Allan.

Standish, Peter (1988 a): The origins of the *Plan comptable général:* a case study in cultural intrusion and reaction, Sydney: Fifth World Congress and Exhibition of Accounting Historians.

Standish, Peter (1988 b): The *Plan comptable général:* a case study in cultural contingency', Manchester: Second Interdisciplinary Perspectives on Accounting Conference.

Streeck, Wolfgang and Philippe Schmitter (1985): 'Community, market, state – and associations?: the prospective contribution of interest governance to social order, in: W. Streeck and P. Schmitter (eds.), *Private interest government: beyond market and state.* 1 – 29, London: Sage.

Sutcliffe, Charles and Matthew Patient (1984): *Tolley's accounting problems of the companies acts,* London: Tolley.

Thompson, Grahame (1987): Inflation accounting in a theory of calculation, *Accounting, Organizations and Society* 12/5: 523 – 544.

Tinker, Tony (1984): Theories of the state and the state of accounting: economic reductionism and political voluntarism in accounting regulation theory, *Journal of Accounting and Public Policy* 3: 55 – 74.

Tinker, Tony (1985): *Paper prophets,* New York: Praeger.

Tinker, Tony (1988): Panglossian accounting theories: the science of apologising in style, *Accounting, Organizations and Society* 13/2: 165 – 190.

Tinker, Tony, Barbara Merino and Marilyn Neimark (1982): The normative origins of positive theories: ideology and accounting thought, *Accounting, Organizations and Society* 7/2: 167 – 200.

Tweedie, David and Geoffrey Whittington (1984): *The debate on inflation accounting,* Cambridge: Cambridge University Press.

Watts, Ross and Jerold Zimmerman (1978): Towards a positive theory of the determination of accounting standards, *The Accounting Review* 53/1: 112−134.

Watts, Ross and Jerold Zimmerman (1979): The demand for and supply of accounting theories: the market for excuses, *The Accounting Review* 54/2: 273−305.

Watts, Ross and Jerold Zimmerman (1986): *Positive accounting theory,* Englewood Cliffs, N. J.: Prentice-Hall.

Whittington, Geoffrey (1987): Positive accounting theory: a review article, *Accounting and Business Research* 17/68: 327−336.

Wolnizer, Peter (1987): *Auditing as independent verification,* Sydney: Sydney University Press.

Willmott, Hugh (1985): Setting accounting standards in the U. K.: the emergence of private accounting bodies and their role in the regulation of public accounting practice, in: Streeck, Wolfgang and Philippe C. Schmitter (eds.), *Private interest government: beyond market and state,* 44−71, London: Sage.

Zeff, Stephen (1972): *Forging accounting principles in five countries: a history and an analysis of trends,* Champaign, Ill.: Stipes.

Zeff, Stephen (1984): Some junctures in the evolution of the process of establishing accounting principles in the U. S. A.: 1917−1972, *The Accounting Review* 59/3: 447−468.

Deregulation and Degradation in Managerial Work

Malcolm Lewis and Alan MacGregor

Introduction

The banking industry in the Western world has undergone rapid restructuring in the recent past, especially with regard to economic and financial deregulation. This has given rise to perceived increases in competition. The effect of this has been that banks are concentrating on marketing, that is, to sell a wide variety of services in order to maintain or increase market share. In line with this, rapid changes in technology, especially the development of electronic data processing (EDP), have lead to the re-structuring of work. In Australia and New Zealand such changes have been late in coming but the election of right-wing (economically at any rate) governments in both countries has seen a push for wholesale deregulation of many sectors of their economies. For the banking industry this has resulted not only in change, but a very high rate of change. It is our contention that the effects of this have been felt most by branch managers and that these effects are detrimental to them.

Our purpose in this chapter is to examine, given the above context, the deskilling thesis within labour process theory, using for our analysis bank branch managers rather than clerical workers so as to examine the extent to which work is changing higher in the bureaucratic structures. In doing this, we will examine the efficacy of the deskilling thesis for our task and attempt, by building on earlier criticisms of deskilling, to extend the viability of the labour process framework for the analysis of change.

Method

The analysis of technological change in terms of how technology deskills manual craft labour has also been applied to clerical work, '[...] although the tools of the craft only consisted of pen, ink, other desk appurtenances, and writing paper, envelopes and ledgers' (Braverman 1974: 298). Nonetheless, Braverman tells us that it represented a total occupation. This analysis of technological change has gained considerable support. Even the most ardent of Braverman's supporters, however, have not accepted the deskilling thesis unconditionally and, in recent years, there has developed a considerable literature which has sought to extend and refine this analysis of the labour process. In this chapter we seek to apply and extend a number of items in the post-Braverman debate to an analysis of the perceptions of bank branch managers in New Zealand in early 1987. The chapter is based upon a continuing research project which began in Western Australia in 1986, which involved in-depth interviews with branch managers, senior management and staff below the level of branch manager, with trade-union officials, technical experts and others associated with the industry. These interviews were followed up with further interviews in New Zealand in 1986. Our findings here are based on a national survey.

To determine how changes are affecting the perceptions of branch managers, we sent questionnaires to all of the managers of three banks, the Australia and New Zealand bank (ANZ), the Bank of New Zealand (BNZ) and Westpac in New Zealand; this was in early 1987. There were 354 respondents to the 90-item questionnaire which represents a response rate of 60%. Although the questionnaire had 90 questions, most questions allowed respondents to include an unspecified number of items. All responses were usable although some questions were not answered on some questionnaires. The questionnaire was constructed following in-depth interviews with branch managers in Western Australia, where we perceived that the rationality of change discussed by senior management was not necessarily reflected in the responses of branch managers.

The respondents came roughly equally from each bank (BNZ 35%, ANZ 38%, Westpac 27%). Respondents were mainly middle aged (40+ years, 88%), male (99.5%) and married (95%). These percentages were stable across the banks except for age where the BNZ had only 2% of managers under 40 years of age. Respondents came from branches of diverse sizes and geographical locations.

Theoretical Background

In what follows we seek to examine the basic notion of Braverman's deskilling thesis and to examine aspects of the criticism which have arisen of that analysis which will form a framework for our examination of branch management. In particular, we wish to deal with the problems which develop out of Braverman's use of the Marxian two-class model based on ownership and non-ownership of property. We recognize that this is an analytically useful model, especially in organizational analysis where it highlights the relationship between a dominant class which largely benefits from the work done by a subordinate class which sells its labour-power to organizational employers. It is our belief however, that although the critics of Braverman's work draw our attention to the simplicity of his analysis in relation to deskilling and the question of control, they do not draw sufficient attention to the complexity of the relationships existing among elements of the environment, bureaucratic control, technical control and the workers' own perceptions of these.

Braverman suggests that management staff must be considered as a part of the labour process. This means that at the corporate level in industrial capitalism, managerial work forms part of the collective labour process open for further development. Thus managerial work must be analysed within the same conceptual apparatus used by Braverman and others in their treatment of the development of manual and clerical work (Teulings 1986). Knights and Willmott (1986) take the view that although management occupies a position of corporate material and symbolic advantage it is still a labour process 'analogous to the process of production' (Braverman 1974: 267). Management consists of a set of practices and positions that arise to secure a transfer of control over the production of goods and services from the hands of the worker into the hands of the professional manager who applies his specialist expertise in the interests of capital.

The question of how management affects this control forms the central core of Braverman's work and revolves around Taylorism and deskilling, but recent writers, notably Edwards (1979), suggest that forms of management control have evolved from simple control though terminal work-flow control to the current situation where management in large organizations depend mainly upon a complex bureaucratic system in which a battery of unobtrusive controls play a central role. Knights and Willmott (1986) suggest, however, that the most recent research in the area indicates that the development of strategies of control is explained exclusively in terms of their version of a functionally appropriate solution for each new crisis in capitalism. The fundamental flaw in such a formulation is that management practice is either 'mechanically, fatalistically determined by the functional needs of the capitalist system; or that it involves the conscious, premeditated omniscient identification of strategies that most consistently satisfy the processes for accumulation' (Knights and Willmott 1986: 5).

It follows from this that it cannot be assumed that management is, or could become a homogeneous, unambiguous phenomenon whose actions are programmed by a single, well defined objective — such as the achievement of profitable growth (Burawoy 1985, Reed 1984, Tomlinson 1982). Numerous factors and forces mediate the relationship between the capitalist imperative of accumulation and the control of work production (Cressey and MacInnes 1980). In large corporations, such as banks, management controls and associated ideologies are directed at a wide range of concerns, including the pricing and supply of raw materials, the penetration of product markets and the planning and siting of future capital investment (Teulings 1986), any of which may exert greater influence than capital per se on the organization of the labour process at the point of production (Child 1985, Kelly 1985).

The relationship between technology and management control, especially the introduction of new (computerized) technology has been central to the discussion of the labour process (Child 1972, 1985, Kelly 1982, 1985). John Storey (1986) in a comparative study of three regional centres within different insurance companies found that management did not use the potential for control the technology offered. Storey argues that this is because the insurance companies are paternalistic and the soft-pedalling approach to new technology fosters cooperation from employees and, within this, employees maintain a positive attitude to new technology. This is especially important where in strategic terms it is essential to maintain cooperation and goodwill in the use of new technology in securing a competitive advantage: a point to which we will return later in the chapter.

Buchanan (1986) found in his study of technical change involving new technology that management does not form a homogeneous group, in that managers differ in their aspirations. More importantly, he found that management is not preoccupied with control since commitment and effort is willingly made by the workforce. In this chapter we suggest that such commitment is very high in branch management. However, where Storey found that limits were placed on management choice and action imposed by their 'ultimate structural control' within capitalist relations of production, Buchanan finds scope for autonomous rule bending. He argues that their disregard for capitalist imperatives shapes the longer-term trends in the structural organization of their relations. Our perceptions are that limits are imposed, but that rule bending may occur as elements of resistance but, within branch management at least, the rule bending does not impinge directly on the relations of production. In examining such issues, it would seem that the outcome depends on the conditions in which the problem is set. As Teulings (1986) has found, within large multi-national corporations (such as banks) management is seen to become differentiated into a number of loosely coupled activities, each with its own separate labour process. In what follows we will examine the operation of control more closely.

The Question of Control: Levels and Circuits

In addressing the question of control, we have suggested that there have been many critiques of Braverman's (1974) analysis (Beechey 1979, Burawoy 1979, Elger 1979, Littler 1982, Stark 1980, Wood 1982), and it is considered not to be adequate as an explanatory framework (Couchman 1984: 177). These criticisms have revolved around several themes. Storey (1985), in an attempt to summarize the inadequacies, has suggested 'monism' as a label. By this he means that there appears to be a 'single-track search for the definitive modes of work control which are assumed to exist wherever employment occurs'. Such an approach he sees as essentially functionalist in that

[...] capital must and can devise coherent systems of control to ensure the structurally necessary extraction of surplus value. Capital's requirements are depicted as always being met. There is an absence of contradiction in the institutions devised (Storey 1985: 194).

Storey correctly argues that '[...] the diversity and complexity of social control processes within work organisations are not sufficiently accommodated'. Thus, "[...] managers are regarded as unproblematic agents of capital who dispatch their 'global functions' in a rationalistic manner" (Storey 1985: 195). In order to resolve these issues, Storey proposes to shift the central problematic from looking for general types or strategies of control, to viewing control configurations as 'the temporary outcomes' of a dialectical process generated by managers with ranging degrees of rationality in negotiation among different management groups as well as workers, and within limits set 'by market competition, the commodity status of labour and the apparatus of the modern state' (Storey 1985: 200).

We support Storey's contention thus far, in that it moves us away from a simplistic two class model. We concur with Storey that the result is a variety of means of control and with his suggestion that this variety of means of managerial control takes the form of 'levels and circuits' of control (Storey 1985: 198). Circuits of control here means instances where supplementary forms of control operate alongside each other, that is, they co-exist. 'Levels of control' refers to circuits of control which exist in a 'vertically-reinforcing fashion'.

The means of management control approach, Storey claims, has the advantage of not being structurally deterministic in that multiple control devices 'oscillate, are activated, deactivated, merge and are constituted anew'. The problem 'for capital' is that 'this process does not occur systematically and functionally because multiple forms occur out of struggle between managers and workers' (Storey 1985: 207−208). We would content that struggle occurs between levels of mangement also. Storey here, then, develops a notion of resistance within a dynamic, dialectical process. We consider, however, that such a scheme still implies rational management in terms of strategy commitment. Storey considers that the means of control are subject to continual experimentation, 'a striving towards a logical incrementalism' (Storey 1985: 203).

It would appear that Storey is saying that managers at corporate level formulate strategy based on evaluation of alternative broad paths. Choices, such as 'what business are we in' once made, result in commitment to certain courses of action and cut out others. Once the broad path is chosen, structure and style patterns are devised, though Storey says that they are likely to emerge without intent to construct a 'strategic campaign plan'. Instead, the process occurs by 'muddling through', by dealing with short-term issues as they occur. Thus logical incrementalism allows

time to broaden political support and legitimate new perspectives and configurations. It also permits structural flexibility and creates opportunities to monitor
developments and where appropriate, reward key thrusts (and presumably penalise
any other!) (Storey 1985: 202).

This is supposed to mean that monistic coherence has been replaced by a logical incrementalism which somehow suggests mediation through or by resistance. We have considerable problems with this because, despite Storey's argument to the contrary, his own analysis still suggests rationality on the part of management however achieved; it also suggests an omnipotent managerialism.

We would argue from the outset that the evidence to support the contention that strategy is based on evaluation of alternative broad paths is thin indeed. Bass (1983) in his empirical analysis of decision making suggests that choices, where made, result from inadequate information, personal whim, the opinions of non-expert friends, etc. This within a functionalist framework. If we consider decision making from a power perspective, then the issues are clouded further, in that decisions may be made to serve the interests of power brokers rather than those of the particular organization. Further, ideologies which may be prevalent at any given time (for example, those of the New Right) may move corporate managers not to act in the best interests of the organization. As Child (1985) has suggested, the notion of a strategy need not imply rationality or coherence or effective implementation.

A second aspect of this is that management itself does not operate at one level, nor is it necessarily a coherent group. Labour process theory tends to consider management as a single entity. We consider this to be misleading. Thus, within bureaucracies, Weber draws our attention to the problems associated with the contradiction between means and ends, between formal and material rationality (Albrow 1970). Corporate management and so-called middle management are involved in different aspects of this contradiction which, we will argue, makes for irrationality which limits the notion of logical incrementalism as depicted by Storey.

Totality

Burrell and Morgan (1979) in their discussion of radical structuralism state that the basic dimensions of this paradigm include notions of totality, structure, contradiction and crisis (Burrell and Morgan 1979: 358–359). This follows from the work of the later Marx. Totality is, however, an extremely difficult concept. Labour process theory has, for the most part, not dealt adequately with totality. Storey insists that the concept needs to be included in a proper dialetical analysis of the means of management control. He sees totality as an expression of wider political, economic and ideological structures. He considers that social institutions should be looked at "relationally [...] 'separate' behaviours in fact constitute parts and these reflect the totality which in turn is a reflection of the parts" (Storey 1985: 197). The point here is, that if we are to examine these constituent parts in relation to the totality, we require more information on how this is to be done. On this, Story is vague. How are we to know the relationships which may exist among the political, economic and ideological structures, let alone how these reflect on the parts? He specifically states that " 'Totality' should not be taken to imply a deterministic relationship between parts" (Storey 1985: 199), but he does not tell us how they may relate nor how limits are imposed on the parts by the totality.

We can take as an example Friedman's (1987) reply to Storey's attack on him for being deterministic in relation to market forces, identifying singular topics of control characteristics of particular market forces. Friedman argues that in his *Industry and Labour* (1977) he brings considerable evidence to bear to show that increasing competition in product markets and oversupply in external labour markets push managers to *direct control* types of strategies, and that the opposite conditions encourage *responsible autonomy*. He says both these types of strategies have characterized management throughout the history of capitalism (Friedman 1977: 78–79). This is in reply to Storey's charge that Friedman is a monistic commentator who seeks a definitive singular type of control (e. g. Taylorism) which may be characteristic of a particular period, country, sector, company, production market etc. (Storey 1985: 207). Friedman then, links particular types of control to the economic environment. Tight competition and unemployment gives rise to conditions which permit direct control, though contingency theory might suggest that he turbulent environment created by competition would require more responsible autonomy (Burrell and Morgan 1979).

Irrespective of the rights or wrongs of Storey's argument, we can identify in Friedman's writing a shift from a two- to a three-class model. He suggests that it is "top managers' who seek to use the two types of strategies to exercise authority" (Friedman 1977: 78). This implies a middle class as well as a working class. Watson (1980) has explicitly linked Friedman's framework to a three-class model. Following Fox (1984), he suggests that middle-class workers tend to have a relatively *diffuse implicit contract*, and are required to use *discretion* in their work and are involved in a *high-trust* relationship with their superiors (Watson 1980: 207). (One assumes this would be typical not only of middle-class workers but also of craftworkers.) This work results in relatively high levels of reward in the form of cash, status, opportunity for intrinsic satisfaction and career advancement. It might be expected that bank branch managers would typify such workers. The high-trust relationship is reciprocated on the part of the employees with a willingness to comply with organizational requirements on their own initiative. Responsible autonomy, however, gives rise to 'insidious control' (Blau and Schoenherr 1971), which has the potential to erode real individual autonomy. "Organisational norms are […] 'internalised' and individuals […] control themselves (as well as their subordinates) on behalf of their superordinates" (Watson 1980: 207).

Routine work is characterized by a *restricted type of implicit contract*. Hence *low-trust* relationships with superiors (Fox 1974) are associated with generally lower levels of reward. Work tasks are more closely prescribed and the execution of work is separated from its conception (Braverman 1974). The contractual commitment is specific rather than diffuse, giving rise to a hourly or weekly wage, tighter specification of job requirements and by the lack of inducement in the form of potential career promotion. Direct control typically treats workers as though they were machines, removing responsibility and submitting them to close supervision (Friedman 1977). Friedman and Ikegami (1987), in their analysis of the work of computer programmers, found that direct critical and responsible autonomy provided a broad range of strategies for control and that control is not a simple dichotomy. Further, that the combination of actual strategies used is a matter of strategic choice mediated by resistance and that decisions, once made, are proponent to other decisions (Friedman and Ikegami 1987: 17). Thus a decision once made must have important consequence for those that follow.

A major aspect of our research is to consider the extent to which these two types of control overlap. Storey's notions of levels and circuits of control lead us to expect that branch managers would be subjected to both types of control and that the application of New Right philosophy would mean that greater direct control would be more effectively exerted, which in turn would subvert the diffuse contract, high-trust relationship bank managers might have come to expect. As Cressey et al. (1985) indicate, such subversion would lead to a loss of legitimacy on the part of senior management (i. e. head office). In effect, any moves toward direct control would mean the deskilling of work, because a major element of skill involves discretion (Cooper 1974). The loss of discretion might not result in higher levels of resistance however, for the internalized organizational norms may mediate against any direct action.

Friedman's (1977) analysis relates types of control to changes in the economy. The political philosophy which has been associated with the contraction of the market economy through a so-called relaxing of the controls over the economy by the modern state is that of the New Right. Nowhere is this more prevalent than in New Zealand. We consider that this philolsophy has consequences for the notion of rationality in relation to increased efficiency through control in organizations, and takes the analysis of the totality beyond that of the economy alone. In addition, that totality consists also of technological change which is moving office control to greater automation.

First-Wave Technology

Couchman (1984) considers that two waves of technological change have moved office work from craftwork to the automated office. The first wave of technological change involves mechanization. Within the New Zealand banking system this move entails the telephone, the typewriter and adding machine. It takes place slowly with electric adding machines, introduced in 1935, giving way to the electronic machines in 1950 (Brocklesby 1984: 197). Because the cheque handling process remains a manual function, the banks are still labour intensive. Nonetheless, these machines led to a technical division of labour which facilitated the separation of 'mental work' from 'manual work' in the office (Couchman 1984: 179). Glenn and Feldberg (1979) consider that this gave rise to

1. an *administrative hierarchy* whose work centred on conception and
2. a hierarchy of *detail workers* concerned with execution.

Thus, within office work, mechanization leads to direct control. Couchman reminds us that it also coincided with the introduction of women into clerical employment. This feminization of the workforce meant that relatively cheap labour was now available. The first female staff were employed by the BNZ in 1915. By 1938 a third (1000) of the staff were females. These numbers then declined but, by 1943, of approximately 2,000 staff 713 were females (Brocklesby 1984: 201). A second important aspect of this is that women provided a pool of reserve labour, and career opportunities for women were considered limited. Typically women 'assisted the men' (Brocklesby 1984: 201) and were confined to secondary positions. Male clerks on the other hand were locked into a relationship of structured dependency, built upon a system of upward mobility reinforced by the absence of any external banking labour market. Males would expect to move from direct control to one of responsible autonomy.

Second Wave Technology

Computers began to be introduced into offices in the 1950s and 1960s. With the advances in microelectronic technology, computers became much smaller and more cost effective; the 1970s saw the advent of first minicomputers, then microprocessors and word processors (Guiliano 1982). The BNZ opened two computer centres in 1966. Other banks joined in 1967, and nationwide coverage was fully operational by the end of 1969 (Brocklesby 1984). Owned by the member banks, the new system was set up as a separate organization called Databank Systems Ltd.

Databank is a computerized clearing system, which details the net flow of capital between each bank. Similarly, the system performs traditional ledger functions; calculating interest and charges, as well as providing management with information on customers, accounts, personnel and so on. Increasingly this system bypasses expensive manual labour in one form or another. This includes automatic payment of regular transfers, direct credits and debits. In addition, automatic teller machines (ATMs) provide direct links from the customer to the computer to bypass the bank teller. The most recent move is to have direct terminal access to the computer's customer information files.

This system allows tellers to record transaction details directly into the terminal, eliminating the processing and movement of money makers and other paperwork. It provides automatic branch cash control and credit card authorization functions, and the programmed terminals have the capacity (not yet in use) to approve or reject loan requests. This system allows for a significant reduction in services provided by middle-level staff, towards one in which most branch work is handled by front-line tellers.

The 'second wave' of technological change is leading towards a complete restructuring of the bank branch system when lower-level staff may make decisions, but only according to principles elaborated by senior management (for a discussion of this, see Crompton and Jones 1983). What is important for us here is that low control 'decision making' is becoming increasingly common at all levels in the industry. Not only do the computers have the capacity to process transactions through their direct link with the customer, but they also apply standard procedures which effectively remove decision-making functions from the operator and the more senior officer who would have used background knowledge and experience to arrive at an appropriate decision (Brocklesby 1984).

For branch managers, the loss of processing functions to the computer means that branch performance can no longer be explained as a result of branch efficiency or the calibre of the staff. Databank requirements and deadlines impact upon internal branch organization and the whole processing function has been standardized. Many personnel functions and marketing campaigns are established by head office. Managers feel a sense of loss; this is deskilling of a different kind. Their control is being eroded because business which departs from routine is referred to the specialists and, at the same time, routine decisions are being handled by the computer.

Friedman considered that types of control depended upon particular kinds of markets. Here we see that technological change, which occurs slowly over time and is not a function of fluctuations in market forces, leads to increasingly greater erosion of conditions of work. We concede that in other industries this may not be the case. Attewell (1987) argues persuasively that there are practical limits to the use of computer surveillance. He contends that the critical mechanisms in place prior to computerization were sufficient to retain as much control as was necessary. Less convincingly, he says Human Relations philosophy has led both Citibank and Prudential Insurance in the USA to programme for "redesigning 'assembly-line' clerical jobs into more complex and varied skillful jobs" (Attewell 1987: 94). On the face of it this seems to reflect a lack of historical context and the kind of research reminiscent of American managerialism.

Both the technological and economic aspects give rise to various kinds of layers of control. They interact and are acted upon. The long-term technological development is not the same in all industries. Clerical work, and here we include banking, because of its highly routine procedures lends itself to a high degree of technological control. At the same time, for bank managers this permits a shift towards more direct control which may be accelerated by what is happening in the economic sector. Both of these, however, are powerfully affected by the political; the use and misuse of power.

Politics and the Philosophy of the New Right

Our contention is that New Right philosophy produces a rhetoric about competition and the importance of market forces; organizations must work harder and be more efficient in this competitive environment. Within the banking industry in New Zealand this drive for efficiency tends to move the bureaucracy towards greater technical centralization in order to increase control over the organization in a changed environment.

To analyse this we will examine firstly the effects of deregulation on the banking industry in New Zealand. In so doing we will use, where appropriate, information from our previous studies of the banking industry in Australia (Bowles and Lewis 1988). Banking is a multi-national operation and the similarities in banking around the world are remarkably consistent within and among banks (see for examples, Bowles and Lewis 1988, Child and Tarbuck 1985, Crompton and Jones 1983, Griffin 1985, Hill et al. 1986, MacDonald and Lamberton 1983). In this paper we will pay particular attention to the perceptions of bank branch managers concerning deregulation and especially increased competition, which, following the Australian example, is leading to increasing computerization and massive restructuring of the bureaucracies. In discussing these issues it is essential that we describe, if only briefly, those aspects of the New Right philosophy which determine the direction which New Zealand organizations are taking, following of course, similar directions in other Western Capitalist countries, although it seems we may be going further faster. In describing New Right philosophy we will draw on a recent analysis put forward by Lauder (1987).

Lauder argues that the New Right considers human nature to be concerned fundamentally with the pursuit of self-interest and is primarily directed towards the acquisition of wealth, status and power. The system which is most consistent with this view is capitalism which allows for the pursuit of self-interest by the accumulation of personal wealth. Within this, poverty is a spur to success, thus the welfare state must be abolished or at least minimized.

Lauder considers that the logic underlying this attack on the welfare state rests on eighteenth-century individualism combined with nineteenth-century social Darwinism. Thus

Individualism linked to competition, under conditions of unrestrained free market capitalism leads to the survival of the fittest (hence the ubiquitous metaphors about economies and companies becoming 'leaner'); which in turn produces material progress (e. g. economic growth) (Lauder 1987: 5).

We find that these notions are given expression in the comments of senior bank management as quoted at the beginning of the paper and in professional journals which the corporate sector is likely to read. In the October 1987 issue of the *Accountants' Journal* an article on competition in banking was entitled *Surviving*. This article argues that the granting of licences to create new banks will lead to increased competition and that the banks will have to become aggressive and more innovative to survive (MacLennan 1987: 30).

As a part of becoming lean and hungry, the Australia and New Zealand Bank (ANZ), for example, has reorganized its management structure so that the bank, rather than having a pyramid structure, is now divided into separate business units, retail banking being only one division in a network which includes treasury (foreign exchange, etc.) and corporate and commercial units. Within the retail sector this restructuring is paralleled by changes in the organization of labour in which lower-level employees, especially young people and women part-time workers, will staff the *front desk* and deal with the customers. The second level will be largely drawn from graduate recruits and groomed for higher things. The old career path to typical branch managers is unlikely to continue as we know it (Bowles and Lewis 1988).

The move from lending to competitive selling is changing the *culture* of branch banking (Bowles and Lewis 1988), bringing a narrowing of task boundaries (deskilling), greater monitoring of performance and changes in the internal labour market. The effect has been to alter the status and reward systems, the patterns of recruitment and nature of the employment relationship.

The rhetoric of the New Right is such that the reorganizing of the economy, organizations and work is seen as essentially rational so that if organizations are to be competitive they must be lean and hungry, must be efficient in a strictly economic sense, costs must be cut, people must work harder and technological changes are inevitable if competitors are to be outflanked. If the competition have new technology, then we must have it. There is an inevitability about it all. Rationality determines direction.

We see then, that the political ideology of the New Right seems to have severe consequences for the way in which the economy is run, regulation gives way to full market forces. This in turn justifies the actions of senior management to themselves and legitimizes actions to subordinates. The contraction of the economy leads to a tightening of organizational control, which is seen as essential if the organization is to 'survive'. In Friedman's (1977) terms the pressure leads to direct control, particularly where there is a large pool of unemployment. We argue that the control experienced by middle management also becomes tighter and more direct. Such control is many layered.

The tightness of control is, perhaps, less obvious than it might be in other industries because bank managers are, firstly, already used to tight control; secondly, unaware of the control aspects of computer technology and thirdly, committed to the notion of developing a mean, lean organization and see changes to more direct control as necessary.

The Branch Manager and the Banking Labour Process

Banking may be divided into traditional, in terms of first wave technology, and modern, following the recent introduction of sophisticated technology in the second wave. Traditional banking may not have been a 'craft' industry, but Brocklesby (1984) considers that it contained certain elements of craft control, there being a wide range of non-routine tasks, knowledge and control over the production process in that control over data was not relinquished and there was the exercise of considerable autonomy (Brocklesby 1984: 200). Chappell (1961) has described banking as a profession in which the banker is 'master of his own house'. Nowhere is this skill more obvious than in the granting of credit. Chappell says of the branch manager:

In fact he remains the most skilled purveyor of credit in the community. It is a life-long study. The ability to gauge the difference between a satisfactory and an unsatisfactory banking proposition is achieved only after a long apprenticeship. No officer of less than 20 or 25 years experience would be sufficiently qualified to authorise the granting of advances (Chappell 1961: 380).

Table 1 Managers' Reasons for Wanting Future Promotion

Reason	Frequency	%
Self-esteem	202	57.0
Job related	37	11.0
Uncertain if wanted	30	8.0
Don't want	73	21.0
No reply	8	2.0
Other	4	1.0
Total	354	100.0

In fact, in New Zealand branch managers have for years been instructed to be very tight in the granting of advances and, unless customers had the best possible credentials, they were unlikely to receive an advance. This situation has changed markedly in the past few years and managers are now expected to sell the credit facilities of the bank. The freeing up of the economy has changed the manager's role from gatekeeper to salesman. Many managers find selling difficult. As one senior branch manager stated, 'I did not join the bank to become a Hoover salesman'. There is a loss of status implied here. See Table 1.

Table 1 shows that managers are extremely concerned about self-esteem, and 57% give this as their main reason for wanting promotion. We consider that this may be considered so important because managers perceive a sense of loss of status deriving from the changes to their work.

Brocklesby (1984) reports that during the 'craft' period of bank development, considerable initiative was requested even of the lower status clerk. Following Stickler (1949), he tells us that a clerk would have knowledge of the whole production process and the opportunity to influence internal organization and work procedures. He says that several (now retired) bank managers commented that, during the immediate pre-computerization period, branch autonomy enabled different recording and processing systems to be used from one branch to another (Brocklesby 1984: 200).

On the other hand, the work of the branch and of the clerk within it, even with knowledge of the procedures, could be 'numbingly monotonous'. Stickler puts it this way:

[...] the duties of the bank (have) been so reduced to routine that the difficulty is to find work which calls for intelligence in sufficient quantity to keep engaged those member of the office staff who have demonstrated their ability to perform such work [...] many men feel that the vast majority of the tasks that they do for the first 25 years of their service are numbingly monotonous (Stickler 1949: 25 as quoted in Brocklesby 1984: 200).

This implies that when men become branch managers this changes. Certainly it would appear that managers felt that they had some control over their branches. Data was kept at the bank (files on customer's accounts etc.) and to some extent this still exists in the New Zealand banks. In Australia moves have been towards centralized administration, moving files and typing facilities etc. to area offices so that branches are left with a 'front desk' and a branch manager. All the administrative and control functions normally carried out by the 'back office' have gone. This has not happened in New Zealand yet, but there have been moves in this direction.

All of this means that branch managers are finding that they have reduced control. They do not have the authority to hire and fire the staff in their branches and, increasingly, they have fewer senior clerks below them. Files are being removed and routine functions are being absorbed by the computer. The emphasis of head office is on selling, and managers are expected to find customers (even to the extent of cold selling − on the knocker) and to extend the packages customers already have, that is, to extend the range of accounts any customer may have. Larger (commercial) accounts are, however, being transferred to regional offices.

Bank managers have come through the bureaucratic system, moving through the bank hierarchy to secure middle-class positions. They could not, however, apply for promotion. They have had to demonstrate their ability and motivation by obtaining favorable annual reports from their senior officers. Their training was gained on the job and in the past was controlled by the manager and accountant who would take note of work-flow requirements, as well as the needs of staff to gain experience of branch activities. Now, however, branch managers are allocated personnel by head-office and have little control over what they do. Junior staff are moved from branch to branch to suit the convenience of the personnel departments.

The highly bureaucratic career structure and operation of the banks structured dependency upon the bank, fulfiling the implicit control functions described by Friedman. The expectation of lifetime employment, coupled with a policy of internal promotions in this internal labour market, creates an employment relationship of commitment and dependency. Bank managers are, then, socialized and strongly induced to perform as the bank requires. Obviously, any withdrawal of cooperation and goodwill would have a potentially serious impact upon future career prospects and hence self-esteem.

Table 2 Managers' Perception of the Effect of Computers on Promotion

	Frequency	%
Promotions will be effected	53	15
Promotions will not be effected	273	77
Uncertain	28	8
Total	354	100

The Question of Deskilling: Technology

Our discussion has shown that computers have enormous potential for control, both in terms of the centralization of activities and in the restructuring of the bureaucracies so that managers are moved to the periphery of banking. Their main function being to sell and not control. Yet it appears that few managers perceive technology as a threat.

Table 2 shows that most managers do not perceive that computers will affect promotion. Interestingly, however, bank policies are moving increasingly towards the use of graduates as future managers. Such people will not be required to know much about banking as such, for these activities will be centralized. Graduates will be trained on the 'fast track' and can expect to be managers before they are 30 years of age. We consider, too, that computers are regarded in a neutral vein. They fulfil a function, they act as a tool and the full implications of their uses remain unseen. On the other hand, managers do perceive graduates as a threat to promotion. Our survey showed that 80% of managers were aware of the problem they presented, but did not see the technological changes as a part of the same problem. The routinization of this technical rationalization in practice forms the basis for non-reflection in which the 'iron-cage' is no longer exterior but internalized into the constitution of rational action based on 'objective knowledge' (Wilson 1983). In terms of control, bank managers still see the prime form of monitoring as being through the annual audit; despite constant surveillance through the computer, 79% of respondents gave the audit as the first form of monitoring.

Furthermore, technical rationalization gives rise to confused perceptions, not only in terms of threats to promotion but in how managers perceive their world, for in the case of branch managers not only is deskilling occurring through a loss of control, but within the bureaucracy through the separation of the execution of work from its conception (Braverman 1974). Many managers seem to be unaware of the extent of the changes

Table 3   Managers' perceptions of the Extent to Which They Set Their Own Branch
          Goals

	Frequency	%
Few or none	92	22
All or most	134	33
Setting of goals is not supported	4	1
Personal goals only	20	5
Related to business volumes — yes	101	25
Marketing — yes	26	6
Other	32	8
Total	409	100

Table 4   Features That Managers Most Like About the Banks

	ANZ %	Bank BNZ %	WESTPAC %	Total %
Linked features				
Challenge, autonomy or status	3.4	7.6	7.4	18.4
Conditions	6.5	7.7	6.8	21.0
People	17.3	19.5	23.8	60.6
Total	27.2	34.8	38.0	100.0

n = 353

which are occurring and are likely to occur. Head Office, it seems, is not inclined to keep them informed. The matter is vividly illustrated in Table 3.

Despite the notion of trust and diffuse control, managers are very confused as to what extent they set their own goals. When asked how managers receive their goals, 45% stated that they received such information by general newsletter and not by direct communication.

The Question of Deskilling: Bureaucratic Control

Control, as discussed above, is a central function of bureaucracy and management would expect to exercise a high degree of responsible autonomy based upon a diffuse implicit contract. This high-trust relationship would lead us to expect that management would like the work itself. Table 4, however, indicates that in each of the banks, people aspects (e. g. meeting people) featured as what managers most like about the banks.

Table 5 Features That Managers Most Dislike About the Banks

Disliked features	ANZ %	Bank BNZ %	WESTPAC %	Total %
Structure factors	15.5	22.6	25.5	63.6
Work load	2.0	5.2	6.3	13.5
Other	9.7	6.6	6.6	22.9
Total	27.2	34.4	38.4	100.0

n = 349

Table 6 Managers' Perceived Degree of Control Related to What They Dislike About the Banks

Perceived degree of control	Head office related %	Job related %	Disliked features People related %	Nothing %	Total %
High	49.6	18.0	10.5	2.0	80.1
Partial	4.7	0.6	0.0	0.6	5.9
Little	2.6	0.6	1.2	0.0	4.4
Other	7.6	1.5	0.5	0.0	9.6
Total	64.5	20.7	12.2	2.6	100.0

n = 343

What managers most disliked about the banks relates to structural features, which means head office, that is, they dislike the control which is imposed on them. This may not be new, of course, and indeed those managers also felt that they had a high degree of control themselves, but still disliked head office (see Table 6). The perception of a high degree of control relates perhaps to the question of perceived self-esteem in that managers would not wish to see themselves without control despite the problems of that control being more direct and from head office. A cross tabulation to check the extent to which more senior managers felt antagonistic about head office revealed no difference to those less senior managers. Seriority relates to the number of people working in each branch; the people being called 'hands'. Large metropolitan banks have up to 200 hands, small branches only 2 or 3.

Table 7 indicates how managers feel about computers in relation to what they dislike about the banks. A large percentage (62%) of those that disliked head office saw computers as necessary.

Table 7 Managers' Feelings About Computers Related to What They Dislike About the Banks

Feelings about computers	Head office related %	Job related %	Dislike the banks People related %	Nothing %	Total %
Necessary, good	30.1	10.1	6.4	1.7	48.3
Acceptable	15.7	4.4	2.6	0.6	23.3
Depends	7.8	1.8	0.6	0.0	10.2
Dislike adjustment	4.0	2.3	1.2	0.0	7.5
Other	7.0	2.3	1.4	0.0	10.7
Total	64.6	20.9	12.2	2.3	100.0

n = 345

This confirms the insidious nature of computer control. Indeed, most managers accept computers. They do realize the 'numbing monotony' of earlier times, and computers make figures available relatively quickly, though not always in the form that managers like. There may be a felt practical need for the computers because they make the banks appear more efficient in line with the push for efficiency.

Bureaucratic Versus Technical Control

A cross-tabulation of how managers view monitoring against the forms of monitoring, see Table 8, shows that 80% see the audit as the most important form of monitoring and that of these, 43% see it positively. Given Friedman's thesis, we might expect to find this insidious control operating. Of those few who see MIS reports as the most important form of monitoring (1.4%), nearly all have negative or mixed feelings about it. Those people see control through computers and dislike this form. As the use of computers becomes more developed (i. e. their potential for control is realized), more managers may see them in negative terms. This could lead to increased resistance.

Table 9 takes this point further in that those who see monitoring through MIS reports feel that monitoring will increase direct control.

More managers saw control increasing rather than decreasing which may reflect increasing pressure to perform. Those who see monitoring decreasing may see the pressure to sell leading to reduced control. It is important to note here that we are discussing perceptions of changes in control. The

Table 8 Managers' Views of Monitoring Related on the Form of Monitoring

| Views of monitoring | Form of monitoring | | | |
	Audits %	MIS %	Other %	Total %
Positive feelings	43.3	0.3	8.3	51.9
Negative feelings	12.0	0.2	3.7	15.9
Mixed feelings	19.9	0.9	6.8	27.6
Other	4.6	0.0	0.0	4.6
Total	79.8	1.4	18.8	100.0

n = 349

Table 9 Managers' Perceptions of Control Trends Related to the Form of Monitoring

| Perception of control trends | Form of monitoring | | | |
	Audits %	MIS %	Other %	Total %
Decreased	17.1	0.0	3.7	20.8
Unchanged	33.3	0.9	7.1	41.3
Increased	29.4	0.5	8.0	37.9
Total	79.8	1.4	18.8	100.0

n = 351

picture is not straightforward, but the figures indicate that, although technical monitoring (direct) is increasing, few are aware of it, but many are aware that monitoring is increasing overall.

The Question of Resistance to Selling

The long experience of the branch managers surveyed relates to loan allocation. The situation as described earlier indicates that they are not conditioned to selling, yet the rhetoric of the New Right suggests strongly to the managers that they must sell for the good of the banks. The rhetoric to sell within the banks is very strong indeed. Table 10 indicates that nearly 60% report a positive attitude to selling, but that only 6% spend a considerable amount of time doing it (hours not specified).

Table 10   Managers' Feelings About Selling Related to Time Spent Selling

Feelings about selling	Time spent			Other %	Total %
	Large amount %	Moderate amount %	Small amount %		
Positive feelings	6.0	24.8	19.4	9.1	59.3
Mixed feelings	1.1	5.1	5.2	2.0	13.4
Negative feelings	1.7	5.7	7.4	4.0	18.8
Other	0.3	4.0	2.8	1.4	8.5
Total	9.1	39.6	34.8	16.5	100.0

n = 351

Table 11   Managers' attitudes to Selling Related to Their Responsibility for Selling

Responsibility for selling	Attitudes to selling			Other %	Total %
	Positive feelings %	Mixed feelings %	Negative feelings %		
Responsible over	41.4	9.1	12.6	5.4	68.5
Personal selling	12.9	3.7	4.0	2.0	22.6
Other	5.4	0.6	2.0	0.9	8.9
Total	59.7	13.4	18.6	8.3	100.0

n = 350

Similarly, of those who have a positive attitude only 13% are involved in personal selling, see Table 11.

If we combine the tables for the type of selling that managers do with the time they spend doing it, we find that only 1.4% spend a large amount of time in personal selling. For the rest, a small to moderate amount of time is spent supervising or being responsible for motivating others, see Table 12.

Combining the type of selling with subordinates selling, see Table 13, we find that in practice no-one seems to be selling to any extent.

We consider this to be a complex issue. It seems that the banks, in order to be efficient in what appears to be a competitive environment, are moving, through the restructuring of their bureaucracies (e. g. moving control away from managers) and through increased direct control (through computer technology), towards a situation in which bank managers are becoming

Table 12 Mangers' Responsibility for Selling Related to the Time They Spend in Selling

| Responsibility for selling | Time spent in selling | | | | |
	Large amount %	Moderate amount %	Small amount %	Other %	Total %
Responsible over	6.9	25.2	24.9	11.5	68.5
Personal selling	1.4	10.6	6.3	4.3	22.6
Other	0.9	4.0	3.4	0.6	8.9
Total	9.2	39.8	34.6	16.4	100.0

n = 349

Table 13 Managers' Responsibility for Selling Related to Time Spent by Subordinates in Selling

| Responsibility for selling | Subordinates' time spent in selling | | | | |
	Large amount %	Moderate amount %	Small amount %	Other %	Total %
Responsible over	0.9	7.3	49.3	11.0	68.5
Personal selling	—	2.9	16.9	2.6	22.4
Other	—	1.2	6.4	1.5	9.1
Total	0.9	11.4	72.6	15.1	100.0

n = 343

proletarianized. They are no longer required to practice the skills they have accumulated. This leads to a sense of loss which is real in that those elements of work which make up the total task are being eroded. This finds expression in a wish for self-esteem and in confusion as to what is happening.

Storey (1985) and others have stated that monism and the 'panacea fallacy' — that capital always finds the solution to its problems (Nolan and Edwards 1983) — derive from a concern to show a long-run trend towards deepening management control. Thus, in labour process theory resistance does not seem to have much effect in stemming the tide. Yet the dialectical process as discussed by Marx brings Storey to insist that resistance must exist. A major problem, it seems to us, is that resistance is less well analysed than the methods for control. It would seem that this stems from an inability to define or to analyse resistance adequately.

Traditionally, resistance has been considered in terms of absenteeism and labour turnover. The problems with these, however, relate to their limited use in times of economic decline and their non-specificity in relating to the particular issues which may cause dissatisfaction. Labour turnover is reported as being very high among new recruits in the banking industry in Australia and New Zealand, especially in the metropolitan areas. This turnover may relate to any number of issues, but one which has importance for the analysis of resistance among managers is that new recruits are not yet 'locked-in' to the system.

Littler has noted that the most crucial dimension of the employment relationship is dependency (Littler 1982: 44). Once employees accept that they are tied a particular employer, they are more likely to accept company policies. In the case of branch managers the dependency dimension is extremely strong. They are tied to the employer by an internal labour market, low mortgage rates and superannuation schemes. They have no skills outside of banking and in our survey we fond that managers had little education which would equip them for alternative occupations.

A second aspect of resistance is collective action, through union activity in particular. The literature on this is ambivalent as to its success. Within those studies concerned with banking, the impression given is one of limited success in gaining benefits from the introduction of new technology. For the most part, however, management has not been inclined to concede its managerial prerogative to the workforce in terms of negotiating technology changes, nor have the new systems been opposed altogether (Brocklesby 1984: 208). There is scant evidence to support the view that management has altered its plans as a result of the opposition offered so far (Bowles and Lewis 1988).

Bank managers are not supposed to belong to unions, after all, they are management. Nonetheless, a number of managers are still members of the New Zealand Bank Officers' Union, giving as a major reason for retaining membership the benefits which accrue to staff being passed on to them. Branch managers are members of the managers association which relates to their own bank; rather like a staff association for bank managers. These in-house associations seem to serve the function of disseminating head office information to branch managers on a less formal basis, rather than serving the needs of managers per se.

Our evidence suggests that resistance among managers takes a different form. Unable to leave or to take collective action, managers resist in individual terms by not fulfiling the required demands of head office, namely selling. We see it as an outcome of structural changes in the bureaucracy and the moves to more direct control through the technology.

More direct control has meant a felt loss of control by branch managers. They have less control of their own branch, of information, of customers. They carry responsibility if things go wrong, but have no authority to put things right. They cannot hire or fire; if the computers break down and they do so quite frequently, great stress is placed upon the branch. Mistakes occur with increasing regularity and the branch is not in a position to put them right. In moving to more direct control, the banks produce contradictions.

At the same time, branch managers are faced with a situation where they are expected to be competitive. They see the changes as necessary in order to compete. New technology is an essential part of the prescription and is viewed as essential for success. We consider that the high profile given to the New Right philosophy within New Zealand aids in the acceptance of change. The lean, efficient organization in a competitive environment forms a part of the rhetoric which reduces resistance by giving the impression that more direct control is inevitable and *essential* (Lewis and MacGregor 1987). Whether or not there is real competition among the banks is not the issue here.

Branch managers are under pressure and report that their jobs are becoming more stressful. They feel loyalty to their organizations, yet they work in organizations which are increasing control and confusion; they cannot walk out, nor can they take collective action. They reduce their stress by not selling. In discussion, some have stated that they do not have time to sell, but one senior manager said that time and motion studies had led to a prescription for managers to organize their day (in classic Tayloristic fashion) so that they could sell. It was only the disorganized manager who could not do so.

The power of the individual branch manager as a participant in the division of labour of the management process has decreased. An increasing rationality of the labour process of management is achieved by its differentiation and hierarchical corporation of functions. But, at the same time, this makes the inner contradictions more manifest. Rationalization of management as a labour process results in a politicization of the relations between levels of management (Teulings 1986: 164). This development leads to feelings of incapacity by the individual manager, for the rules which lead to success in his own labour process no longer appear to apply. The power of the individual branch manager and, in particular, his sense of power, lags behind the power of management as a whole. The branch manager forms part of an extensive machinery of power, without being able to derive from it any real sense of sharing that power.

Conclusion

We would contend that labour process theory and the deskilling thesis are still useful. However, in our view, the two classic models in which it has been couched do have limitations. Our analysis of bank branch management shows that deskilling is moving into the ranks of management in this industry. Further, it is our belief that management beyond the branch level is affected by the forces of capital. Choices are limited. It is not as though senior managers, who have themselves come up through the ranks, wish to act to the detriment of their branch managers.

The introduction of computer technology has been inevitable. The technological imperative is such that senior managers believe they will be severely disadvantaged if they do not have the latest and that they will not be able to compete. Thus, choice is limited and decisions emerge as to how things will be done. An examination of a number of banks shows that the same outcome has been derived for all of them. They use the same technologies, the same marketing techniques, the same strategies. Limitations are imposed. We are left with the impression that even if senior management wanted to change they could not do so.

It is central to an appreciation of our argument that we are taking a broad historical perspective. We accept that at any particular historical moment instances that run counter to long-run trends may be found. The state of the economy as presented by the New Right reduces resistance and makes the acceptance of technological innovation inevitable, but we argue that technological change has been a long process which over the past fifty or so years has slowly been reducing control for the workforce and moving it towards the centre. We belive that Gramsci's (1971) notion of ideological hegemony here explains the importance of New Right philosophy in the acceptance of market conditions which themselves justify moves to more technological control.

If we were to remove the deskilling thesis from this analysis, it would not be possible to examine the interface between labour and control, but this interface cannot be examined only in terms of a simple two-class system, nor by looking at deskilling simply in terms of what people do. Work is changing for everybody and within the banking industry we see moves to direct control shifting up the hierarchy. At the same time, choices for senior management become more limited. How branch managers perceive the changes is linked to a complex set of relationships which combine technology with diffuse and direct notions of control within particular industries at given historical moments. Changes in political philosophy may affect how changes are accepted, and the question of resistance must be examined in terms of all of these.

Resistance may take many forms and cannot be tied to simple cause and effect relationships. Contradictions are complex and diverse. It is our view that these contradictions can only be examined in terms of the context of the organization. Of course, collective action through union activity may indicate resistance, but in the cases where this is hard to find it may be thought that there is no resistance at all. It is only through the analysis of contradictions within the organization that subtle forms of resistance will be revealed. In this study we have found contradiction in confusion and non-selling. We are convinced more subtle forms of analysis would reveal more.

References

Albrow, M. (1970): *Bureaucracy*, London: Macmillan.

Attewell, Paul (1987): Big brother and the sweatshop: computer surveillance in the automated office, *Sociological Theory* 5 (Spring): 87–99.

Bass, B. M. (1983): *Organizational decision making*, New York: Irwin.

Beechey, V. (1979): Labour and monopoly capital – notes towards a Marxist feminist critique, University of Warwick, Sociology Department (mimeograph).

Blau, P. M. and A. Schoenherr (1971): *The structure of organizations*, New York: Basic Books.

Bowles, M. H. and M. Lewis (1988): Threats and opportunities for middle management: the impact of new technology and competitive banking, *Journal of Industrial Relations* 30, 87–96.

Braverman, H. (1974): *Labour and monopoly capital*, New York: Monthly Review Press.

Brocklesby, S. (1984): Technological change and the labour process – towards an analysis of computerisation in the New Zealand trading banks, *Journal of Industrial Relations* 26, 4: 195–210.

Buchanan, D. A. (1986): Management, critical strategies and inter-professional competition: the cases of accountancy and personnel management, in: Knights, D. and H. C. Willmott (eds.), *Managing the labour process*, 21–56, Aldershot: Gower.

Burawoy, M. (1979): *Manufacturing consent: changes in the labour process under monopoly capital*, Chicago: University of Chicago Press.

Burawoy, M. (1985): *The politics of production*, London: Verso.

Burrell, G. and G. Morgan (1979): *Sociological paradigms and organisational analysis*, London: Heinemann.

Chappell, N. M: (1961): *New Zealand bankers hundred*, Wellington: Bank of New Zealand.

Child, J. (1972): Organisational structure and performance: the role of strategic choice, *Sociology* 6: 1–22.

Child, J. (1985): Managerial strategies, new technology, and the labour process, in: D. Knights, H. C. Willmott and D. Collinson (eds.), *Job redesign: critical perspectives on the labour process,* 161 – 180, Aldershot: Gower.

Child, J. and M. Tarbuck (1985): The introduction of new technologies: managerial initiative and union response in British banks, *Industrial Relations Journal* 16, 3: 19 – 34.

Cooper, R. C. (1974): *Job motivation and job design,* London: Institute of Personnel Management.

Couchman, Paul K. (1984): Towards the automated office: technological change and office work in the New Zealand public service, *Journal of Industrial Relations* 26, 4: 177 – 195.

Cressey, P. and J. MacInnes (1980): Voting for Ford: industrial democracy and the control of labour, *Capital and Class* 11: 5 – 33.

Cressey, P., J. Eldridge and J. MacInnes (1985): *Just managing: authority and democracy in industry,* Milton Keynes: Open University Press.

Crompton, R. and G. Jones (1983): *White collar proletariat: deskilling and gender in clerical work,* Philadelphia, Penns.: Temple.

Edwards, R. C. (1979): *Contested terrain: the transformation of the workplace in the twentieth century,* New York: Basic Books.

Elger, T. (1979): Valorisation and 'deskilling': a critique of Braverman, *Capital and Class* 7 (Spring): 58 – 99.

Fox, A. (1974): *Beyond contract, work power and trust relations,* London: Faber.

Friedman, A. L. (1977): *Industry and labour,* London: Macmillan.

Friedman, A. L. (1987): The means of management control and labour process theory: a critical note on Storey, *Sociology* 21, 2: 287 – 194.

Friedman, A. L. and Ikegami, I. (1987): Measuring and identifying managerial strategies, Working paper, Department of Economics, University of Bristol, Jan. '87.

Glenn, E. M. and R. L. Feldberg (1979): Proletarianising clerical work: technology and organisation in the office, in: Zimbalist, A. (ed.), *Case studies on the labour process,* 84 – 109, New York: Monthly Review Press.

Gramsci, A. (1971): *Selections from the prison notebooks of Antonio Gramsci* (eds. Q. Hoare and G. Nowell-Smith), London: Lawrence and Wishart.

Griffin, G. A. (1985): *White collar militancy,* Sydney: Croom Helm.

Guiliano, V. E. (1982): The mechanisation of office work, *Scientific American* 247, 3: 124 – 134.

Hill, J. O., R. J. Birrell and J. P. Cook (1986): The industrial attitudes of Australian private bank employees, *Journal of Industrial Relations* 27, 3: 310 – 329.

Kelly, J. E. (1982): *Scientific management, job redesign and work performance,* New York: Academic Press.

Kelly, J. E. (1985): Management's redesign of work: labour process, labour markets and product markets, in: Knights, D., H. Willmott and D. Collinson (eds.), *Job redesign: critical perspectives on the labour process,* 30 – 51, Aldershot: Gower.

Knights, D. and H. C. Willmott (eds.), (1986): *Managing the labour process,* Aldershot: Gower.

Knights, D., H. C. Willmott and D. Collinson (eds.) (1985): *Job redesign, critical perspectives on the labour process,* Aldershot: Gower.

Lauder, H. (1987): The New Right and educational policy in New Zealand, *New Zealand Journal of Educational Studies* 22, 1: 3–23.

Lewis, M. and A. MacGregor (1987): Bureaucracy and the New Right: perceptions from within, paper presented at the SAANZ Conference, July, Sydney.

Littler, C. E. (1982): *The development of the labour process in capitalist societies,* London: Heinemann.

MacDonald, S. and D. Lamberton (1983): Tradition in transition: technological change and employment in Australian trading banks, *The Australian Computer Journal* 15: 128–139.

MacLennan, C. (1987): Surviving, *Accountants Journal* October 30–35.

Marx, Karl (1967): *Capital,* Vol. 1, New York: International Publishers.

Nolan, P. and P. K. Edwards (1983): Homogenise, divide and rule, in: *Segmented work, divided workers,* Social Science Research Council: Industrial Relations Unit, University of Warwick, U. K.

Reed, M. I. (1984): Management as a social practice, *Journal of Management Studies* 21, 3: 273–285.

Stark, D. (1980): Class struggle and the labour process, *Theory and Society* 9: 89–130.

Stickler, J. C. (1949): The human element in the banking machine, *The New Zealand Banker* 15 (10): 24–31.

Storey, J. (1985): The means of management control, *Sociology* 19: 193–211.

Teulings, A. W. M. (1986): Managerial labour processes in organised capitalism, in: D. Knights and H. C. Willmott (eds.), *Managing the labour process,* 142–165, Aldershot: Gower.

Tomlinson, J. (1982): *The unequal struggle? British socialism and the capitalist enterprise,* London: Methuen.

Watson, T. J. (1980): *Sociology, work and industry,* London: Routledge and Kegan Paul.

Wilson, H. T. (1983): Technocracy and late capitalist society: reflections on the problems of rationality and social organisation, in: S. Clegg, G. Dow and P. Boreham (eds.), *The state, class and the recession,* 152–238, Sydney: Croom Helm.

Wood, S. (1982): *The degradation of work?* London: Hutchinson.

Part III
Blockages and Breakthroughs in Organizational Adaptation

Efficiency, Ideology and Tradition in the Choice of Transactions Governance Structures: The Case of China as a Modernizing Society

Max Boisot and John Child

The development of nations involves the mobilization of resources and their effective combination through the transactions of production and exchange. The level of effectiveness achieved is most usually assessed by economic measures of gross national product which refer to the aggregate value or volume of transactions. This resort to simple aggregative measures of transactions has tended to favour economic over other forms of analysis. Thus the concept of efficient markets is held up as the standard against which other structures for governing transactions are assessed. Classical economics assumes that 'in the beginning there were markets' (Williamson 1975: 20). Students of organization, however, have taken the existence of hierarchies as given and social anthropologists the presence of communities, whether communes, clans or feudal fiefs (cf. Butler 1983, Radcliffe-Brown 1950). Institutional economists such as Coase (1937) and Williamson, together with business historians such as Chandler (1977) and Daems (Chandler and Daems 1980), now pose hierarchy as the stable alternative governance structure to market contracts.

There is no a priori reason to believe that in practice the choice between transaction modes is made in the light of purely economic considerations. For one thing the definition, let alone measurement, of transaction costs becomes shrouded in considerable uncertainty once one moves outside the market place. Moreover, alternative structures for governing transactions affect the distribution of economic gains, and this may be regarded as an important social criterion for favouring one over others. As institutional forms embodying social relations, such structures are also subject to criteria of acceptability in the light of the values and norms which derive from the political and cultural character of the country concerned. The choice of transactions governance structures cannot be abstracted from the social context in which transacting occurs.

In this chapter we shall take one problem of modernization to be that of finding socially appropriate governance structures which only subsequently define a scope for economic transactions. The contingencies relevant to the efficiency of alternative transactions governance structures are seen to include their acceptability to the parties concerned on cultural and ideological grounds. More fundamentally, their very possibility is likely to depend on how far they align with the institutions and structures of power which are extant in the society. It is for these reasons that societies such as Britain, West Germany, Japan and the United States achieved modernization through structures for governing transactions which contrasted in the degree of their reliance on market, hierarchical and community-type modes (Littler 1983). The approach adopted here builds upon the informal analysis of Dore (1973), refined by Boisot (1983), concerning the modernization of Japan. Dore's own conclusion, through comparing a Japanese and a British firm, that Japan is organization-oriented and Britain market-oriented, helps to articulate but does not move beyond the markets and hierarchies paradigm. Boisot's re-analysis of Dore's study concluded that there were further ways in which transactions could be governed, and in a recent paper he has argued that these options are rooted in cultural predilections (1986).

Development, seen in this light, may be *constrained* by economic considerations including the efficiency with which transactions are conducted, but it remains both socially *driven* and *patterned*. It is socially driven because modernization involves social construction and reproduction. Values shape transactional preferences, as Williamson recognized in his brief discussion of 'atmosphere' (1975: 37–39). They work for the promotion of given types of social and economic relations as intrinsically desirable outcomes. Economic development is socially patterned because the modernization drive finds expression in a configuration of social and institutional arrangements that are in continuous interaction with a society's physical and technical endowments.

Values legitimate certain styles of transaction and forms of their governance. A distinction is usefully drawn between values of an ideological kind which express a political preference for a particular set of socio-political arrangements, and those of a cultural kind which derive from tradition. The dominant paradigm of ideological differentiation today is that distinguishing socialism from capitalism. Kornai (1985) has identified four 'ethical principles of a socialist economy'. The first is 'socialist wage-setting', according to which everyone should be rewarded according to their work. The second is solidarity, in which the weak are assisted rather than penalized for their weakness. The third principle is security, including the guarantee of employment. The fourth is the priority of the general interest over the partial or private interest. Kornai delineates the conflicts between these principles and definitions of efficiency as offered by theories of the beneficial effects of decentralized markets. Their preservation requires suspicion of the individualistic opportunism encouraged by profit-seeking market transactions. All the principles justify the external regulation of transactions, and the fourth in particular appears to require that this be a centralized regulation over the total configuration of transactions and their outcomes. In contrast, capitalist ideology claims the benefits of fostering an efficient and innovative response to social requirements through private initiatives in the market place. It is suspicious of any bureaucratic regulation which it sees as distorting markets and reducing their efficiency as systems of transactions. Although in practice this has not prevented the development of regulatory bodies such as the American Securities and Exchange Commission, 'he governs best who governs least' remains capitalism's core value.

The other category of values are cultural in the sense of having their roots in a society's traditions. Their effect is to mould preferences in favour of certain forms of governance for transactions and of the style of conducting transactions which accompanies these. Cultural dimensions of this kind include the 'pattern variables' which Parsons and Shils (1951) suggested would distinguish a traditional from a modern orientation, as well as dimensions such as 'power distance', 'uncertainty avoidance' and 'individualism' which Hofstede (1980) found to differentiate among the employees of a corporation with plants located in different countries. Tradition is also sedimented into those institutions which can either establish initial conditions for the patterning of transactions, such as kinship groups and networks, or actually regulate transactions directly, such as the law.

It is argued, in short, that an adequate understanding of modernization, when regarded as a problem of attaining viable structures for governing economic transactions, requires that we look beyond a narrow cost-based analysis of these transactions and instead consider transaction modes as expressive of socially based preferences. Thus the ecology of a country's transactions governance structures is a socially constructed one and needs to be analysed in terms of its local options and preferences. The material conditions of a country, namely its physical and technical contingencies such as population size, and area, ease of communication, natural resources, educational and skill attainment, will of course exercise an influence over what are viable options, but the diversity of transactional arrangements adopted by countries of comparable physical and technical endowments suggests that these are not of overriding significance to the choice of governance structures.

A country that lends itself to this kind of analysis is the People's Republic of China (PRC). China, the world's largest developing nation, decided in 1978 to accelerate its modernization process through a series of economic reforms and an 'open door' policy intended both to increase the scope given to market forces internally as well as the country's exposure to external economic and technological influences. Both imply significant shifts of transactional patterns and style, and have even been viewed by some as a deliberate break with existing traditions and ideologies in the attempt to improve material conditions.

In what follows, we attempt to interpret both the intentions that underlie current reforms in the PRC and their progress to date within the 'culture space' conceptual framework developed by Boisot (1986). The framework takes transactions as social strategies with economic consequences rather than the other way round, although no strong determinism is claimed here. Since the framework has been described in detail elsewhere (Boisot 1983, 1986), it will only be briefly outlined below. Then the basic objectives of the current economic reforms, as set out in a number of recent official Chinese documents and speeches, will be presented. At this point some empirical evidence drawn from the authors' work into Chinese state-owned enterprises is injected into the discussion in order to assess the actual progress of the reforms on the ground. This evidence reflects the position as of the Autumn of 1985 and not necessarily the current one in view of the speed of transformation in China. In the last section the conceptual framework is used as an interpretative tool and applied to an analysis of the material presented.

An Introduction to the Culture-Space (C-space) Framework

Over the past forty years, definitions of culture have been numerous and varied, yet few have really strayed very far from Kroeber and Kluckhohn's (1952) basic insight that culture has something to do with the way that social groups structure and share information across space and over time. Our typology accordingly takes the structuring and sharing of information as the key dimension around which to develop an interpretative framework and, like Oliver Williamson (1975), identifies the transaction in which information is produced and exchanged as a unit of analysis.

The structuring of information is a coding process in which both information compression and loss takes place (Brunner 1974). Uncertainty is reduced and conceptual and perceptual stability is achieved at the cost of perceptual texture and richness. When the process is a social rather than an individual one, we may speak of *codification*, and since information sharing forms a constituent part of our analysis, we shall prefer the latter term to coding. Codification is a matter of degree that could in theory be placed on a scale from 0 to 1 with zero representing the mystical experience that cannot be given any structure at all, and one representing whatever

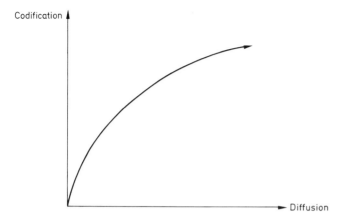

Figure 1   The Codification-Diffusion (C − D) Curve

can be compressed into a single binary digit. Clearly the amount of information to be structured is all-determining, so that with a message of infinite length we end up with the ineffable: $\frac{1}{00} = 0$, and with a message consisting of just one binary digit we obtain $\frac{1}{1} = 1$, the general formula for our codification scale being $\frac{1}{n \text{ bits}} = $ degree of codification, where n represents the number of bits contained in any potential message. The greater the codification, the greater the information compression and the fewer the number of bits, and by implication also, the shorter the transmission time.

The sharing of information for our purposes can be described by the percentage of a population that possesses it, expressed as a coefficient. Since the sharing of information is achieved by a diffusion process, we shall construct a *diffusion* scale that measures the extent of information sharing within a given population. The codification and diffusion dimensions then create a *culture space* (C-space) in which information structuring and sharing − the cognitive and communicative strategies of individuals and groups − can be studied as a pattern of transactions in which information is produced and exchanged.

The culture space would offer little more than a transaction taxonomy, were it not for the fact that the codification and diffusion of information are functionally related (Figure 1). The more information that can be

Table 1 Transactional Structures and Modes

Codified	2. *Bureaucracies* — information diffusion limited and under central control — relationships impersonal and hierarchical — submission to superordinate goals — hierarchical coordination — no necessity to share values and beliefs		3. *Markets* — information widely diffused — no control — relationships impersonal and competitive — no superordinate goals — each one for themself — horizontal coordination through self regulation — no necessity to share values and beliefs
Not Codified	1. *Fiefs* — information diffusion limited by lack of codification to face to face relationships — relationships personal and hierarchical (feudal/charismatic) — submission to superordinate goal — hierarchical coordination — there is a necessity to share values and beliefs		4. *Clans* — information is diffused but still limited by lack of codification to face to face relationships — relationships personal but non hierarchical — goals are shared through a process of negotiation — horizontal coordination through negotiation — there is a necessity to share values and beliefs
	Not Diffused		Diffused

compressed into codes, the more quickly and widely it can be transmitted. It may take half a lifetime for an acolyte to master the arcane practices of his Zen master — and then only if they live together — but it takes only a few seconds for Tokyo to register share price fluctuations on the Dow Jones. The curve in Figure 1 has to be empirically derived, yet it creates an information environment for transactions located in different parts of the space. The characteristics of these transactional environments and the transactions to which they give rise are described in Table 1.

Three points are worth mentioning at this juncture. The first is that our table locates hierarchical processes on the left and market processes on the right so that the Williamsonian approach essentially confines itself to locating transactions along the diffusion dimension as a function of the monopolistic possession of information. Although the codification dimension is occasionally hinted at in discussions of 'atmosphere', it is not taken on board in Williamson's analysis. The second point is that cultural anthropologists such as Edward Hall, in distinguishing between 'high context' and 'low context' cultures, have focused on the codification dimension with, again, only elliptical reference to the implications for

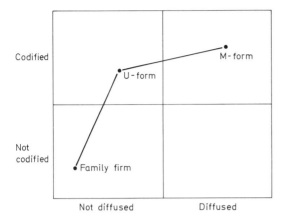

Figure 2   Firm Level Transactions

information sharing. Thus, one is holding the trunk of the elephant, and the other the tail. It is high time they met. Finally Tonnies, in his distinction between *Gemeinschaft* and *Gesellschaft* cultures, alights on the differences in transactional styles, but with no simple theory to underpin them.

The flow of knowledge in a social system is constantly posing the problem of transactional reassignment by redistributing the relative costs and benefits of transacting in different parts of the C-space. The problem can be analysed at different levels:

— At the level of the individual firm it describes the process of organizational growth from the fief-like transactional style of the highly-personalized small family firm to the more bureaucratic structure of the U-form organization and thence to the more competitive culture of the M-form (Figure 2). With the move from quadrant to quadrant, both a firm's social and physical technologies and its managerial technologies need to adapt, first to each other and then to their new information environment.

— At the societal level it describes a process of institutional development that legitimates and channels broad shifts in aggregated transactional patterns — i.e. in the case of Europe a move from the charismatic institutions of feudalism, firstly to the bureaucratic structures of the absolute state and subsequently to the market institutions of competitive capitalism (Figure 3).

At both levels the path of development follows the codification-diffusion curve (C-D curve). Does this suggest some kind of development law, operating both at the macro and the micro scale, and information-driven?

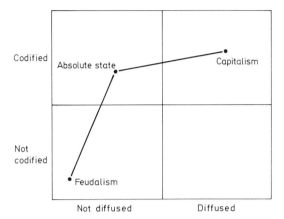

Figure 3   Societal Level Transactions

Such a development law, albeit one not explicitly linked to the information environment, has already been proposed in the guise of a *convergence hypothesis*. As currently formulated, it suggests that technology acts upon organizations and social institutions in a way that forces the adoption of similar solutions to similar problems. The forces of production ultimately impose upon the relations of production. Thus, to the extent that social development pushes for a greater codification of transactions — Tonnies' move from *Gemeinschaft* to *Gesellschaft* — a greater diffusion of information takes place in a way that ultimately favours the growth of transactional infrastructures in the market quadrant. The invisible hand shapes the international economic order.

This functional view of the transaction structures suited to development positively relates diffusion to codification. However, comparative research also indicates the presence of cultural and ideological preferences for the structuring of transactions and cultural differences in society's information-sharing behaviour. A conscious and collective social effort is involved in building such structures. The curve of Figure 1 implies the existence of zones in the C-space in which information must be actively manipulated to achieve given diffusion objectives: bureaucracies in which barriers to uncontrolled diffusion, such as an organization's structure, must always be maintained; clans in which inherently undiffusible information must be actively pushed on to a larger population over a protracted period through, for example, a process of socialization. Where these cultural preferences are weakly expressed, we should expect a greater degree of transactional scatter in the C-space than where they are not. Ideological pluralism, for instance, would lead to scattered transactions whereas ideological purity would create more focused ones, targeted in that region of the C-space most supportive of the given belief system.

Having set out the essentials of the culture-space framework, we can now employ this to assist an examination of recent social and economic developments in the PRC and their implications for the governance of transactions.

The PRC in Transition

This section examines the programme of economic structure reform which has been underway in China since 1979. In the industrial sector the programme is an attempt to improve the performance of enterprises by decentralizing responsibility to their managements and by delegating powers from central to local authorities. The role of local authorities is intended to shift gradually from direct involvement in enterprises to one of servicing and monitoring them. A greater recourse to market transactions (structured through a greater diffusion of codified data) is envisaged as the result of granting enterprise managements more freedom to set prices, market products, secure supplies, and enter into direct cooperation with other enterprises. The intention is for a correspondingly reduced involvement of the bureaucratic hierarchy in the governance of economic transactions, and for a diffusion of economic transactions beyond the confines of local city or provincial preserves.

The Chinese economic reform is progressing within a set of contextual conditions which may be expected to affect its implementation and outcome. Significant factors in this context are the country's cultural and institutional inheritance, and the issues of ideology and government which have been prominent in its socialist development. It is not unusual for contemporary Chinese writers to note the legacy of these previous social conditions, as did an editor of the official *Beijing Review* who referred to 'a land of prolonged feudal rule and distorted proletarian dictatorship' (6 January 1986: 5). The country's material and technical situation is also relevant. We therefore begin with a brief outline of these contextual features.

The Context

China, enjoying the world's oldest unbroken civilization, has conferred on its present generation a distinctive cultural legacy (Domenach 1986, Knutsson 1986, Lockett 1985a, Pye 1985, Qian 1986). Its predominant features are (1) respect for hierarchical position and leadership, (2) a group or collective orientation directed particularly to family and local community but which co-exists with a strong sense of national identity and respect for the national leader, and (3) importance attached to personal relationships and connections. It is also part of Chinese tradition that behaviour is regulated by Confucian appeals to good conduct, with any issues being resolved by persons of standing and virtue within the community. Recourse to the impersonality of the law was not favoured, and was indeed taken as a sign of failure in personal conduct. The Chinese did not therefore have a well-developed legal code or a tradition in which law is closely followed.

Cultural values of this kind will favour a certain transactional mode. They imply a preference for informal transactions of a face-to-face kind which are based upon personal trust and mutual obligation. The most enduring and reliable transactional ties in this cultural milieu are likely to be those within families and communities. These are predominantly local, but may extend to more dispersed family-based clans. Relatively low value will be placed upon formal transactions based upon contract rather than upon status and trust. Within these groups, the relationships on which particular importance is placed in the Confucian tradition are all hierarchical except for those between friends. Entrepreneurial or other opportunistic behaviour on the part of individuals is likely to be discouraged since it can readily appear to be at variance with hierarchical deference and the interests of the group. We have noted the reluctance to take issues outside the group and to have recourse to legal authorities.

There is an obvious tension between these transactional preferences and those involved in market relations (of other than a purely local kind) which rely substantially upon impersonal communications and the force of legal contract (i.e. a diffused codification of rules). Local loyalties are likely to place impediments in the way of wider market relations. There is also the implication that the operation of hierarchical transactions will be governed more by inter-personal accommodations than by the formal specification of objectives, duties and procedures, and that factional or departmental allegiances will be a salient feature of organized life.

The apparent cultural paradox of local family and community loyalties combining with a strong sense of national identity reflects an important institutional legacy in China. The two focuses of loyalty were personal ones which could co-exist because they were not tightly coupled. National loyalty was historically to the Emperor as the embodiment of Confucian virtues, and was reciprocated by 'the conviction that the welfare of the subjects was dependent upon the charisma of the ruler' (Weber 1958: 441).

The Chinese saying points out, however, that 'the Heaven is high and the Emperor is far away'. Symbolically and administratively China has been a centralized state but one that has operated with limits to the downward extension of its powers (limits greater than Pye's [1985] analysis of Chinese centralization allows). It was generally averse to interfering in economic affairs, except at times of famine, and in any case faced formidable natural barriers to communication. Chinese bureaucracy was centralized in an inward and personalized direction, catering primarily for the requirements of the monarch and his court. "This left the countryside largely free of direct rule and control by superior authority, since, in Reischauer's words, 'the government thus was a relatively small, highly centralised body that floated on a sea of isolated peasant communities'" (Rodzinski 1984: 48). In other words, China was a cellular society of low complexity in terms of the transactions to be managed. It held together through loyalty to the Emperor and with the aid of a relatively simple bureaucracy.

The relationship between centralized leadership and localized communities has become more of a problem in modern times, as transactions have become more complex. With this apparently in mind, Domenach (1986) has expressed the view that China's social texture is not yet ready for economic modernization. In his assessment there is still too much individualism at the top and collectivism lower down. Collectivism creates a reluctance to assume responsibility and recent Chinese history suggests that uncertainties generated by idiosyncrasy at the top have added to such reluctance.

The leader-collective, central-local issue has understandably been prominent in debates on how China should develop as a socialist society. Schram (1984) identifies as one of the major ideological concerns in China, the 'patterns of rule or dialectics of leadership'. Pye (1985: 208) has described 'the basic rhythm of Chinese politics as an alternation between the tightening of authority and the relaxing of controls'. Solinger (1984) has identified a clash in Chinese socialist politics between three 'visions', namely (1) the bureaucratic one of central administrative planning, (2) the Maoist vision of social mobilization and a mass movement orientation which is anti-bureaucratic, and (3) a restrained form of market socialism. The present economic reform programme, guided by the last vision, is therefore set within a field of ideology and practice which has been particularly contentious during China's socialist history.

The role of bureaucracy in economic and social transactions is bound up with this dilemma of leadership. The pre-revolutionary 'Yanan Period', which Edgar Snow (1972) has described in rich detail, was one in which the gap between leader and followers was closed without recourse to administrative hierarchy. Mass loyalty to the charismatic revolutionary leaders could be cemented through direct contact and identity in a shared proletarian cause and lifestyle. Once the revolution encompassed the nation as a whole, the transactions to be managed became much more complex. A centralized planning system was set up that attempted to be comprehensive and to bridge the gap between central and local levels. This interposed administrative levels − provinical and county or city − to connect central planning with the point of production. The essentials of this structure remain in place today and it contributed to substantial advances in heavy industrial output during the 1950s. It was nevertheless an important one reflecting Soviet practice, and the Chinese have never been entirely happy with it. Within industry, this centralized approach coexisted with the indigenous 'Shanghai system of management' involving a major role for the collective leadership of the Party Committee and significant participation by shop-floor work teams. Its stress on single-line downward executive authority ('one-man management') came under increasing criticism (Littler 1983, Xie 1985).

After reforms in 1956 and 1961 intended to address this problem, enterprise organization was caught up after 1966 in the Cultural Revolution. While the motives behind this movement are still a matter of debate, it is apparent that Mao Zedong was aware of the limitations placed on his personal leadership both by the aftermath of the disastrous 'Great Leap Forward' and by the steady development of a bureaucratic administration which routinized his charisma. His strategy referred back to that developed during the anti-Japanese and civil wars in the revolutionary bases of the Yanan period, namely the mobilization of a mass nationwide movement combining local direct workers' control with loyalty fostered by an exclusively personal leadership style. This kind of mega-clan structure (relying on a limited diffusion of non-codified information) was intended to discredit and remove intervening layers of bureaucracy and industrial administration. Lockett's (1985 b) study of the Beijing General Knitwear Mill − officially regarded as a model factory during the Cultural Revolution − suggests, however, that radical changes to previously-established managerial structures and reductions in the numbers of bureaucratic staff were in practice short-lived.

Chinese bureaucracy has therefore never conformed to the rational-legal Weberian ideal-type, whether in imperial or socialist times. Its structure and operation rests rather more upon relations, gradations and mutual obligations of a fieflike nature than upon codified rules designed to impart rational conduct oriented towards defined economic or social objectives. Insofar as China nevertheless relies on its bureaucratic apparatus as the chief means for governing economic transactions, these limitations on its utilitarian rationality are liable to present a serious obstacle to the country's modernization. Pye (1985: 209) has summarized the problem and its cultural roots as follows:

It has always been easy for the Chinese to establish bureaucratic hierarchies because they have an instinct for recognising fine status differences and their social order is a continuum of rankings from the lowest person to the highest official. Yet, once the hierarchy has been established, so much energy is expended on the interplay of relations between superiors and subordinates that at times there is little left over for accomplishing anything else.

In its attack on bureaucracy and the 'unhealthy tendency' of seeking personal privilege through it, the cultural revolution also re-affirmed the principle of 'equity' which Qian (1986) argues has its roots in the thinking of the Chinese peasantry as well as modern socialism. Weber (1958) noted that the mandarins were also averse to the development of too sharp a social differentiation arising from the creation and acquisition of wealth through market exchange. Although Chinese social thinkers now stress the distinction between equity and egalitarianism, the principle reflects a deep-seated antipathy towards differential opportunities for private material advancement. It poses a potential constraint on the resort to market forces, given the social inequalities these tend to promote.

Despite temporary aberrations, then, the communist regime has so far attempted to govern transactions through multi-layered bureaucratic hierarchies. This has not, however, proved very successful in integrating across the local community or departmental loyalties which the country's cultural system is always likely to bring into prominence. While the balance between the two has shifted dramatically, China has relied overall on a combination of central directives and local collective self-regulation as the procedures for governing transactions. Until recently, this approach has substituted for the development of the legal and contractual systems which are necessary to support the development of diffused market transactions.

The material and technical conditions of the country further serve to constrain the operation of a more market-based transactional mode. Their relevance has been brought out clearly by the World Bank's (1985) Report on *China: Long-Term Issues and Options*. In particular, the under-development of the communications and transportation systems inhibits the development of wider internal markets and the potential rationalization of production. These physical limitations reinforce those which by tradition already serve to separate regions and municipalities. Other manifestations of the country's developing status also tend to encourage local economic autarchy, including the desire not to risk employment by exposure to interregional competition and the dependence of industry on the local generation of scarce electricity supplies. A further scarcity is that of the management skills required at enterprise level if there is to be a successful transition from top-down planning and hierarchical resource allocation to a system of decentralized planning and market transactions.

The Economic Structure Reform Programme

In December 1978 the Third Plenum of the Party Central Committee decided on a major programme of reform for the structure of the Chinese economy. This programme became identified with the 'Four Modernizations' of agriculture, industry, science and technology, and defence. While more immediately it was an attempt to rebuild the economy after the depletions of the Cultural Revolution, the reform programme represented a reaction both to the perceived shortcomings of that period and a desire to transcend the limitations of the Soviet-style centralized system developed between 1950 and 1957. There were to be moves towards decentralized market socialism, akin to the Hungarian model which Chinese experts studied closely, and away from both the mega-clan of the Cultural Revolution and the command bureaucracy of the early socialist period. The principle of socialist planning was, however, to be retained.

The Cultural Revolution was seen to have dissipated incentive and responsibility for economic performance through egalitarianism, the weakening of management, the general devaluation of expertise and the claim that ideological fervour and inspired leadership could substitute for technical knowledge. The mass mobilization of workers against the authority structures upon which central direction depended led to chaos and destructive factionalism. The older Soviet-style system was not, however, regarded by the 1978 reformers as an appropriate model to which to return. Although this was acknowledged to have played a role in establishing a base of heavy industry, it was now viewed as too rigid. Its heavily administrative approach confused the functions of government and enterprise, imposed undue uniformity and suppressed initiative, failed to adapt to changes in market demand and did not link rewards to economic performance (Huan 1985).

So the search began, through a series of experiments, for a structure of economic management which combined incentive and responsiveness with the maintenance of overall central planning and control, combining market and bureaucratic transactions. This is the so-called 'dual structure'. The stages through which the reform developed have been detailed by Oborne (1986) and only the key developments are mentioned here. The first reform experiments in agriculture and industry were instituted in Sichuan, home province of both Deng Xiao Ping and Zhao Ziyang, the Prime Minister. The agricultural reform was based on the household 'responsibility system', whereby land is contracted to peasants, and on various incentive policies linked to permitting higher levels of commodity production for the market. This raised production significantly and spread rapidly.

As is continually stressed by the Chinese, urban industrial reform is a much more complex matter. It has developed through a longer process of trial and error which still continues. The key elements have been the administrative delegation of powers to the provinces and municipalities, the decentralization of responsibility for performance to enterprise managers, and a controlled receptivity to foreign capital and technology.

By mid-1979, over 100 provincial-level enterprises in Sichuan were authorized by the central government to assume new powers over production and the marketing of products. A system allowing some retention of profit was introduced to create a link between enterprise performance and reward. There were new forms of investment financing, and opportunities for enterprises to use depreciation funds were improved. By 1980, most provinces had initiated pilot experiments in enterprise management covering a total of some 6,600 state enterprises.

In 1981 there was a recentralization of decision making with respect to the allocation of inputs and the distribution of products, especially in heavy industry which had suffered a 5% decline in output that year. A drain on foreign exchange reserves also led to the centrally imposed postponement or cancellation of many contracts for foreign equipment. The government now decided to keep more direct administrative control over key allocative and distribution decisions, but at the same time to apply a form of the responsibility system which had been successful in the agricultural sector. This was intended to clarify responsibility for success and failure at all levels of the industrial hierarchy down to factory workers. It was complemented by a contract system allowing for direct inter-enterprise transactions. By the end of 1982, this reform was being tried out in over 3,000 state-owned enterprises.

Although governmental planning and control of state-owned industry were retained, the bureaucratic apparatus was streamlined at this time. There was a reduction from 98 to 52 in the number of ministries and commissions. The State Planning Commission and the State Economic Commission were given more direct responsibility for enterprise planning and control, with many decision-making powers, including finance and investment, being delegated to provincial authorities. The local branches of foreign trade corporations were given wider powers to negotiate directly with overseas trade partners. In March 1982 selected cities were designated to pioneer urban economic restructuring, particularly to decentralize enterprise mangement and create conditions for more effective market transactions.

Throughout the reform period since 1979, an 'Open-Door' policy designed to encourage economic and technical contracts with foreign investors and partners has been pursued, primarily through the four Special Economic Zones, fourteen coastal cities and three 'Open Economic Zones' where there are special incentives for foreign investors. This policy both opened a portion of Chinese industry to world-market competition and reflected the trend to delegate powers to local authorities.

In October 1984 the Party Central Committee adopted a major policy document on 'China's Economic Structure Reform' (Communist Party of China 1984). This document was an attempt to build upon experience with the economic reform programme, to reaffirm its 'pressing necessity' and to expound a 'systematic' and 'all-round' policy to be applied generally through the industrial sector. The most important focus in this blueprint is on enterprise management reform allied to a greater role for market forces and complementary reforms in the fiscal and pricing systems. The main themes of this important document are now summarized (page numbers refer to the English version given in the references).

The document views the main requirement for injecting vitality into enterprises as an extension of their decision-making power so that they can respond to market forces. The major defects of the existing economic structure are seen to lie in its combination of bureaucracy and featherbedding:

No clear distinction has been drawn between the functions of the government and those of the enterprise; barriers exist between different departments or between different regions; the state has exercised excessive and rigid control over enterprises; no adequate importance has been given to commodity production, the law of value and the regulatory role of the market; and there is absolute egalitarianism in distribution. This has resulted in enterprises lacking necessary decision-making power and the practice of 'eating from the same big pot' prevailing in the relations of the enterprises to the state and in those of the workers and staff members to their enterprises. The enthusiasm, initiative and creativeness of enterprises and workers and staff members have, as a result, been seriously dampened and the socialist economy is bereft of much of the vitality it should possess (pp. 5–6).

The new policy envisaged an extension of enterprise decentralization within a system of governmental planning in which the mandatory element was reduced in favour of guidance plans and where control was exercised through economic regulators rather than administrative fiat. Enterprises would become 'independent and responsible for their own profit and loss and capable of transforming and developing themselves [...] [acting] as legal persons with certain rights and duties' (p. 11). Their directors would assume full responsibility for their performance under a unified management system.

The document particularly stresses the need for city governments not to interfere in enterprise management or to create barriers to inter-enterprise contracting (p. 21). All government organs were enjoined to see their role as providing services to enterprises rather than treating them as their private fiefdoms (p. 23). They also had to 'eliminate such bureaucratic maladies as organisational overlapping, over-staffing, vague delimitations of fuctions and endless wrangling' which handicapped the effective operation of enterprises (p. 23).

The document envisages the continued opening of China to external market transactions and even more the removal of barriers to such transactions within the country (p. 31). Internal market barriers are seen to hamper the growth of production and its rationalization. Exposure to market competition would 'lay bare the defects of enterprises quickly and stimulate enterprises to improve technology, operation and management' (p. 22). It is recognized that efficient markets operate through the price mechanism, and that the system of centralized price control should therefore be relaxed (p. 17).

In May 1984 the central government decided to expand enterprise decision-making powers over ten areas including production, finances, bonuses, pricing for non-quota products and personnel. In October 1984 a directive was issued increasing enterprise autonomy, releasing certain enterprises from central ministry control and permitting some prices to float. Enterprises could now charge market prices for production achieved in excess of their plan quotas. At the same time, a decision to make enterprises responsible for profits and losses was accompanied by a fiscal reform under which they would be allowed to pay taxes on profits rather than have to remit all profits to the central government. Retained profits could be used to pay bonuses and/or pay for new construction or renovation, which increased the incentive for profit maximization. Proposals were also announced for a law under which enterprises could be declared bankrupt and experimental sales of shares in enterprises began.

At the level of declared policy, the Chinese economic structure reforms, express a firm belief that efficient and rapid modernization requires a decentralized management system that is exposed to market forces and is capable of adapting to them. They retract bureaucracy from a directly controlling to a guiding and ring-holding role, and require the dissolution of local fieflike preserves which create internal market barriers.

The Progress of Reform on the Ground

As the reform unfolded through 1984 into 1985, China faced mounting macro-economic problems, notably inflation, excessive growth, wasteful investment, a fall in grain production and a drain on its foreign exchange reserves. Price rises were particularly steep in the cities following the large measure of de-control in October 1984 and the abolition of food subsidies in May 1985. Income differentials increased between more and less well-endowed farming areas and in the cities between different groups of workers, between workers and independent traders, and between those in employment and those 'waiting for work'. All this created social strains which were manifested inter alia by student unrest and a go-slow among Beijing bus drivers. An increasing amount of corruption and fraud also came to light, with the biggest scandals occurring in the areas least subject to central economic control and most exposed to the international market, such as Hainan Island and Shenzhen.

These major problems could be readily associated with the reform pro-gramme's shift from central bureaucratic control to decentralized market socialism. This association was in fact made in September 1985 by senior conservative Marxist cirtics within the Party, particularly Chen Yun, who had been an architect of the 1950s system of central planning. They attacked the economic muddle and the normal evils which they alleged had been introduced by economic reform and the open-door policy. Senior government reformers now admitted that the progress of decentralization to enterprises depended on an ability to regulate the macro economy — as Vice-Premier Tian Jiyun put it in a speech of January 1986, 'It is not proper to employ with haste flexible policies for the micro-economy before good management measures are adopted to bring the macro-economy under control' (*Beijing Review*, 10 February 1986: XIV).

Nevertheless, government leaders have reaffirmed that the reform pro-gramme will still go forward, albeit with stronger central management of the economy. Reform seems likely to remain official policy for the fore-seeable future, and this lends continuing relevance to investigations into its progress. Indeed, attention has concentrated on macro-economic prob-lems and much less is understood about the progress which has actually been achieved in applying reform where it was really intended to have results, in the enterprise itself. The question here is how far internal transactions, and those between the enterprise and its environment, have been modified by the reforms. For even if the problem of macro-economic control is solved, there may still be difficulties in actually implementing changes locally. Both the general experience of managing top-down change and the peculiarities of the Chinese context lead to the expectation that the implementation of decentralization and engagement in market transactions will be subject to severe constraints, even when backed strongly by central government. Some of these constraints are likely to reflect enduring cultural and institutional factors bearing upon economic transactions and will tend to persist even if macro-economic equilibrium is regained.

We now examine experience of the economic reform at the level of enterprise transactions from evidence collected in the state sector of industry. The most detailed source of information available to us comes from studies we conducted with the aid of industrially experienced Chinese MBA students within six enterprises located in Beijing. Shorter visits were also made to other enterprises and additional interviews conducted with Chinese managers, researchers and management education faculty. Further information about these enterprises and the method of research is given in Child (1987).

The reform envisaged that enterprises would become responsible for their profit and loss, and that this responsibility would be accompanied by the decentralization of authority permitting their managements to establish strategic plans within the guidelines of state plans and policies. This assumption of strategic powers would be formalized by a 'responsibility contract' between the enterprise director and higher authority. A government regulation issued in September 1985 on 'Strengthening the Vitality of Large and Medium-Sized State Enterprises' confirmed this procedure, stated that enterprise plans should be drawn up with reference to market conditions, and urged that 'enterprises should change from production oriented operation to production *and* marketing oriented production' (*People's Daily*, 20 September 1985).

When studied in the autumn of 1985, all six of the Beijing enterprises reported that there had been some relaxation in control by their higher (municipal) authorities. Three were now given profit rather than output targets, and the others had increased the non-quota proportions of their output which could be marketed, and in some cases priced, with a degree of managerial discretion. A detailed analysis of decision-making authority in each enterprise indicated that engagement in market transactions had been facilitated by the decentralization of authority to enterprise management in certain areas. Four of the six enterprises were now able to set prices within limits for at least some of their output and one other, manufacturing a national brand electrical product, could vary its discounts on non-quota sales. All were able to select their own suppliers for non-strategic items, and five could determine procedures for purchasing including the terms of the contract. Although they did not enjoy powers to alter their overall employment establishment or total wage and salary bill, enterprise managements could vary bonus levels within prescribed limits. With one exception they also enjoyed greater control over the selection of new workers. In four of the enterprises directors were now formally able to initiate the return of unsatisfactory workers to the 'labour market' through dismissal, although in a workers' state this is a delicate matter, on which they would in practice still secure the approval of the enterprise Party Committee, if not a higher authority.

These changes had allowed enterprise managements to extend their market place transactions, up to a point. Nevertheless, two major limitations remained in force. The first was that higher-level authorities still retained control over key strategic decisions on investment, marketing and production planning. The second was that the practical operation of market transactions remained severely inhibited even where there had been some *de jure* decentralization.

It was officially claimed, for example, that fiscal reform would provide for a significant increase in decentralization by allowing enterprises to retain their post-tax profits. Official statistics indicate that in 1985 81% of state enterprises adopted the system of substituting tax payments for profits delivery (*Beijing Review*, 24 March 1986: 29). However, the great bulk of investment is still financed out of the state 'investment fund', leaving little to the responsibility of enterprise management. For once taxes have been paid to the state and municipality, there may be no more than 15% of pre-tax profits left to be retained by the enterprise. This retention has to finance bonus payments and welfare provisions in fixed proportions, leaving possibly around 5% for investment expenditure at management's discretion. A regulation restricts the per annum allowance for depreciation to 5%, half of which has to be remitted to the supervising bureau or holding company. There are also restrictions on the purchase of equipment requiring foreign exchange. The enterprise's ability to enter into investment transactions is therefore severly limited.

In the area of marketing restrictions on pricing were re-imposed in 1985 following worsening inflation. Managers in the Beijing enterprises which could officially vary product prices reported that in practice municipal price bureaux were making it increasingly difficult to raise them. Although an increasing number of enterprises (including four of the six studied) had begun to form their own policies on market coverage and priorities, these suffered from poor information. Market information was not being gathered and analysed on a systematic basis in the six enterprises. Where the system of quotas which have been agreed with the higher authority has been retained, this means that a substantial proportion of production (usually over 50%) remains out of the strategic control of enterprise management and is located within the realm of bureaucratic rather than market transactions so far as inputs and outputs are concerned.

The moves towards decentralized market transactions envisaged by the reform were also being inhibited by the contextual conditions of Chinese society identified earlier. Particularly salient, in addition to the limitations inherent to the Chinese bureaucratic system and those arising out of material and technical development, where the fieflike dependence of enterprises on their municipality of other local authority.

In an interview published in *China Daily* (12 April 1986: 4), Tong Dalin a deputy minister of the State Commission for Restructuring the Economic System called upon municipal authorities to facilitate the improvement of enterprise performance. He noted that now 'provincial governments are prevented from directly meddling in enterprise affairs, the municipal level seems to be the main stumbling block at the moment'. He called upon municipalities to allow effective decentralization to enterprise managements and to simplify the higher administrative structure with which enterprises have to deal. 'At present, he said, no Chinese manager seems to feel that he or she has been given enough decision-making power, and that most of the problems are indeed associated with the large number of local bureaux'. This view was echoed by an official of the State Economic Commission who, addressing the National People's Congress early in 1986, complained that 'there are too many authorities lording it over the enterprises' (*Beijing Review*, 14 April 1986: 27). Several enterprise directors expressed their frustration to the Congress over the lack of progress towards decentralization.

This criticism pinpoints one of the major constraints that have operated upon the implementation of the reform, but it is more deep-seated than just a matter of administrative structuring. At the local level there exists a web of diffuse multiple dependencies between the municipality and the enterprise. These represent an historical continuity with the local Chinese communities in which primacy was accorded to local networks of personal obligation and trust.

Local enterprises are the main source of a municipality's or county's tax revenues secured in part through a 'regulation tax' designed to equalize the profits of individual enterprises and negotiated bilaterally with each one. This tax may well absorb 35% of an enterprise's profit. Since there is a regulation by which enterprises are not allowed to pay more than 15% of retained profit out as bonus, negotiations with the municipality over the regulation of tax had a direct effect upon management's ability to offer incentives. Moreover, the enterprise is required to provide housing, schooling, medical and other welfare facilities for its workers, so taking on responsibilities which in western countries would be handled by the municipality itself or by the state. In return, the municipality has protected 'its' enterprises by making it difficult for outside competitors to enter the local market. Enterprises remain largely dependent upon the supervising municipal bureaux for their resource allocation, particularly for investment. More recently, they have been encouraged to approach banks for some of their investment funds, but these are unlikely to lend without informal approval from the supervising bureau.

The intensity of these local Chinese community networks was dramatically demonstrated by the Hainan Island scandal concerning the illegal resale to the mainland at inflated prices of tax-free imports which came to light in 1985. According to an official report released in July that year, 872 enterprises and 88 government departments on the island participated in the racket, along with party officials, bank branches and even schools and kindergartens! (*Beijing Review*, 12 August 1985: 8 – 9). A number of other well-publicized cases of corruption have also illustrated the high level of local administrative and business interdependence that prevails.

The continuing dependence of enterprises on the municipality places major obstacles in the way of their engagement in wider market transactions. Most enterprises have relatively few direct links with markets. The distribution of their products tends to be carried out by municipal or state agencies. Local protectionism creates barriers to an extension of markets and, in the prevailing conditions of shortage, municipal bureaux place pressures upon enterprises to supply local customers in preference to ones further afield even though the latter will often be prepared to pay higher prices for good products. This also means that although enterprises have to find many of their own supplies, they can be forced to purchase locally. The underdevelopment of communication and transportation facilities further discourages market transactions on a national scale, and in any case what information there is about wider market opportunities tends to be held (and retained) by municipal departments. Even within the municipal area, weaker producers may be protected at the cost of limiting the expansion of superior producers, as was happening with manufacturers of heavy electrical plant in one major city.

Enterprises effectively enjoy no access to the labour market. They have to request the local labour bureau for permission to change their labour establishment and are obliged to accept the quota they are given. They can face difficulties in selecting individuals from within that quota, and some managements reported that they were faced with all-or-nothing choices so far as the quality of recruits is concerned. The operation of quasi-market forces within the firm is inhibited by the absence of effective performance evaluation and the persistence of egalitarianism in the distribution of bonuses within job categories. The continuing influence of tradition in labour allocation is also manifest in the tendency for children to work where their parents do. For example, in one engineering enterprise visited 50% of new recruits are children of existing workers. Children want to work, and therefore live, close to their parents, since by tradition they are duty bound to support them.

These limitations on the operation of market transactions seriously inhibit the intention of economic reform to improve enterprise performance by decentralizing responsibility. They constrain management's ability to select the best available supplies of inputs and they prevent an effective expansion of output. Together with the fact that the municipal price bureaux still fix or at least set limits to the prices of most outputs, this means that a production-oriented cost centre mentality still predominates rather than the market orientation encouraged in official pronouncements. Over the country as a whole, the rationalization of production and achievement of scale economies is inhibited by local restrictions, as the World Bank Report emphasizes. The combination of local economic autarchy with the failure of municipal authorities to decentralize economic decisions to enterprises has led to some very wasteful expenditures on investment and imports, approved, according to a Chinese ministry study, on grounds other than business judgement (Thomson 1986a). This helps to account for government criticism of municipal authorities and the withdrawal by the centre of some powers it had previously delegated.

Our analysis suggests that the progress of reform on the ground is being slowed *inter alia* by local administrative attitudes and institutions which have traditional roots. It would be foolhardy, however, to generalize for all urban areas. Official accounts indicate that progress has been made towards the creation of more efficient local market structures for products, supplies, technology, labour and finance to which enterprises have access, by those cities specially designated by the central government to experiment with urban economic structure reforms (e. g. *Beijing Review*, 2 December 1985). The extent to which those cities have lowered barriers to trade with other localities is not obvious. However, official sources also tell of a rising number of cooperation agreements made directly between enterprises located in different regions and/or industries, and of the spread of contracting and subcontracting arrangements.

Should the Centre Promote Codification and Diffusion?

From the assorted evidence that is available, the lesson seems to be that local inertia and restriction is more likely to be overcome when the central government gives reform a push through special designation or other focused means, including the creation and provision of codified data for diffused transactions. In the light of the problems which have arisen at both macro and micro levels, the Chinese government will probably feel obliged to heed the World Bank's (1985) advice that 'reform in China must also involve strengthening the state's ability to direct the future course of economic and social development' (para. 10.135). Insofar as some of this central direction will have to rely upon bureaucratic means, the present weaknesses in the government apparatus need to be remedied. This may not be easy to achieve since they derive partly from the fact that the bureaucracy also operates within a Chinese cultural context. Insofar as a system of indirectly regulated market socialism is favoured, this will require the development of formal legal-rational codes, particularly in the areas of law and accounting. Deficiencies in both these spheres of codification have constrained the implementation of the reform programme.

One problem lies in the system of governing industry by administrative regulation. The system has created ambiguities and inconsistencies. Some regulations, such as that of September 1985 cited earlier, are couched in general, rather exhortatory terms. As the cancellation of its provisions a few months later illustrates, uncertainties have also arisen because regulations are frequently countermanded. The result is contradiction. One regulation, for instance, states that enterprises are not subject to an upper limit on the bonus payments they can make out of profits, but another regulation imposes a tax on bonuses that exceed certain proportions of wage levels. Both regulations were issued by the State Council. Enterprises have often found themselves subject to conflicting guidelines issued respectively by their industrial ministry and their municipality. For example, a truck enterprise based its plans on the long-term capacity programme of the national automobile corporation (an ex-ministry) giving rise to a particular investment requirement. This was, however, inconsistent with the lower investment quota for the enterprise allocated by the municipality in the light of its own industrial development plan which had been approved by another state ministry. The effect of these ambiguities and inconsistencies is clearly to make enterprise planning much more difficult.

The system of Chinese bureaucratic regulations has another unhelpful feature in that they are intended to apply generally irrespective of the requirements that derive from the specific tasks and circumstances of enterprises. The stated intention of the economic structure reform was to not impose a standard uniform model upon enterprises, yet this is the continued effect of some regulations. For example, there is a regulation stating that every managerial position should have a vice-manager reporting to it, which can lead to a redundant level of authority in a small department. The formal organization structures of Chinese state enterprises are far more uniform than would be expected from contingency-related organizational design principles. The result is to encourage 'mock bureaucracies' (Gouldner 1954) in which formal structures and procedures imposed from above are mostly circumvented or disregarded altogether. Thus two plans may be drawn up by the enterprise, one being the official plan which has to be approved by higher authority and provides for the lowest possible level of quota production, and the other being the one which management intends to follow. Many job descriptions are 'honoured in the breach' and do not derive from any systematic evaluation of tasks within the enterprise itself.

The government bureaucracy has been the subject of considerable criticism from within the country, and has been identified as a factor inhibiting economic reforms (Xinhua 1986). Indeed, one of several articles carried by the *Beijing Review* in mid-1986 on the theme of overcoming obstacles to reform was a 1980 speech by Deng Xiaoping which castigates bureaucracy as 'a major and widespread problem in the political life of our Party and state', and identifies many of its problems with both Chinese tradition and over-centralized administration under socialism (11 August 1986: 15−19). Despite the simplification of the governmental structure in 1982, enterprise managements still have to deal in a time-consuming way with many bureaucratic departments which have been reluctant to permit the decentralization envisaged in the reform programme. Chinese critics claim that staffing in the bureaucracy persists at a high level and that administrative employees naturally resist the redundancy of their pre-reform functions. The likelihood of conflicting decisions and regulations is enhanced by the strong emphasis placed upon vertical departmental lines within the bureaucracy, which makes for poor co-ordination, duplication of effort and factional loyalties. This problem of segmentalism is reflected downwards into the enterprise. In all six of the Beijing enterprises the hierarchical loyalty of functional departments to their counterparts within the municipality aggravated serious problems of integration.

In addition to improving the formal rationality of hierarchical transaction governance through the bureaucracy, there is also a need to develop formal rules and conventions which will provide the framework necessary for market transactions. One problem here lies in the uncertainties and incompleteness of Chinese commercial law. For example, a foreign businessman was recently quoted as telling how Chinese officials have occasionally cited new laws affecting his joint venture, yet when challenged to produce these, have claimed that they were not yet published or that their access was restricted to senior officials (Thomson 1986 b). The underdevelopment of financial conventions for matters such as credit are also inhibiting to market transactions. Standard accounting conventions as well as a less distorted price system will be required for comparative assessments of enterprise performance and worth to be conducted.

The continuing cultural significance attached in China to hierarchical relations and informal connections is clearly likely to affect the operation of formal systems and structures. We have suggested that within the bureaucracy it bolsters vertical tendencies and segmental loyalties, and that it also makes it difficult for enterprises to escape from dependence on local administrations. Traditional transactional modes have substituted for codification in ways that are inconsistent with economic rationality and market transactions. For instance, the underdevelopment of accounting conventions means that proposals for investment cannot be subject to comprehensive financial calculations and the transaction therefore remains largely uncodified. This is, however, quite consistent with a social process whereby the chance of obtaining investment funds depends importantly upon the enterprise's relationships with higher authority, and, in particular, on personal connections to persons of higher standing. We noted earlier how the resort to law has in Chinese Confucian tradition been regarded as an admission of failure in social relationships. Many dealings between firms therefore rely upon the traditional force of mutual personal obligation as gentlemen's agreements, and are not enforceable by law. It is estimated that there are at any one time about one million people travelling on China's railway system to make business transactions in person, and that about half a million travel in and out of Beijing each day for the same purpose. Reaching such agreements can incur considerable costs in time and the special favours associated with what the Chinese accurately call 'personal relationship expenses'. A codified legal framework is necessary if the scope of market transactions is to extend beyond the limits of local and other face-to-face dealings where personal obligation can be relied on. This has been recognized by the government, which has promulgated a number of economic laws recently as well as moving to develop a legal code (cf. *Beijing Review*, 21 April 1986, 5 May 1986 and 2 June 1986).

The reform programme is intended to speed up modernization, but the constraints on its implementation are in turn exacerbated by China's lack of a developed material and technical infrastructure. While the problem of material shortages may be hightened by both planning deficiencies and distortions arising from traditionalistic behaviour, they basically stem from a condition of economic underdevelopment. The presence of a sellers' market distorts transactions away from a marketing emphasis and towards an inflation of purchasing activities. The overloaded transport system constrains the growth of national marketing and so reinforces the tendencies towards localism. In the absence of a national electricity grid, local power shortages reinforce the need for enterprises to oblige their municipal authorities if they are to receive a due allocation of power. Systems for communicating information, particularly telecommunications, also remain limited. While communications at a distance do not satisfy present Chinese norms for closing economic transactions (you cannot clinch a deal over the telephone in China), they do place constraints on the exchange of information necessary if the scope of market transactions is to be widened and technical development hastened. For example, the country lacks a nationwide system for exchanging technological information, and trade fairs remain almost the only venues at which new technology is displayed.

We have reviewed problems which have inhibited the implementation of economic reforms in the Chinese industrial sector, and which are likely to persist if and when the thrust of reform is renewed. They are seen to lie in the constraints imposed by the bureaucracy both as an entrenched institution threatened by a shift from hierarchy to markets and very importantly as a transactions governance structure whose rationality is compromised by elements of traditionalism. However, if the popular cry to retrench the bureaucracy were heeded, the influence of traditional practice reflecting the dominant value system might well pull transacting back even more into the realm of municipal and provincial fiefdoms rather than promoting the development of unrestricted markets. For there has as yet been insufficient codification to underpin market calculations and contracts, while the development of wider markets remains constrained by infrastructural underdevelopment.

Conclusion

We have sought to describe the salient difficulties attending China's modernization programme. The effective mobilization and organization of resources through appropriate transactional structures is taken to be the key to modernization, and China has been examined in terms of the aspects of transactions governance consistent with its traditions, socialist ideology and recent moves towards market regulation. The 'culture-space' framework was advanced as a basis for distinguishing between these transactional modes in terms of information codification and diffusion. This is an analytical scheme that lends itself *inter alia* to the thesis that development requires progression along the codification-diffusion curve such as to imply a particular set of transitions between transactions governance structures.

Contemporary Chinese governmental thinking implicitly appears to accept this thesis, seeking to reject traditional transactional modes and to reduce the reliance on bureaucratic ones. In particular, the Chinese leadership has taken the view that any shift towards the market quadrant of the culture-space framework (see Table 1) implies a disinvestment in the bureaucratic quadrant. As noted, 'get rid of the bureaucrats' is a populary cry. Our analysis suggests, however, that, for the most part, transactions removed from the bureaucratic quadrant will find their way back into the fief quadrant (localized, relatively uncodified transactions), *where the dominant traditional value system still resides*, and not into the market quadrant.

The evidence of a somewhat informal kind presented in this paper points to a continuing cultural preference for the local, face-to-face transaction, and involving the obtaining of informal social hierarchical approval for action. 'Atmosphere' and shared values are all important in this mode of transacting. We have stressed that Chinese 'bureaucracy' is itself culturally distinct. From a western Weberian perspective, it is arguable that the investments made in the bureaucratic quadrant during this century, and especially in the 1950s, never really took root. The mirage of a monolithic rational-legal bureaucracy might effectively hypnotize outsiders located at a suitable distance or over the horizon. But those who work in the system's bureaux or in joint ventures with it, can never afford to be fooled for an instant into abandoning their 'back door' and *Guanxi* connections as a pre-requisite for getting things done. They are still in the world of what Weber himself termed a 'patrimonial bureaucracy', one that hails from the fief quadrant.

China's present problem, in other words, is not that she has overinvested in the bureaucratic quadrant at the expense of the market quadrant, but rather that she has not invested enough in bureaucracy to achieve a shift into markets. This is perhaps best understood in terms of the distinction between delegation and decentralization. Delegation occurs when subordinates are given the means to pursue superordinate goals. It presupposes the existence either of trust or of a viable hierarchical structure that ensures compliance. Decentralization, by contrast, occurs when actors are free to pursue their own goals. It presupposes neither trust nor a hierarchical control structure, but rather the existence of horizontal information flows that underpin a self-regulating process. So far in human experience, beyond a certain scale of organization, delegation has required that trust and interpersonal relations be replaced by vertical control structures that are the essence of the large Weberian modern state and corporate bureaucracies. Where these structures are absent or cannot cope with conditions of complexity and/or rapid change (such as are entailed with entry into unprotected markets), control loss occurs and subordinates pursue their own goals (Williamson 1970). In effect, decentralization takes over. The question is then whether such decentralization is functionally creative for the organization or society as a whole, or whether it degenerates into the prosecution of local interests at the expense of the totality. In the absence of diffused horizontal codified information flows, decentralization leads not into the market quadrant but into the clan quadrant. This is what happened during the Cultural Revolution, and it is happening today when cities and provinces go their own way, conspire with their local enterprises to avoid paying taxes to the central government, and re-assert the feudal vassal relationship wherein the enterprise offers 'loyalty' and obedience to its urban master in exchange for protection from both the central government and from non-local competitors. We might term this phenomenon 'industrial feudalism'.

Thus it would appear that only on the back of a properly functioning bureaucratic structure, in which information is already being codified and selectively diffused, can an *efficient* decentralization towards markets occur. Even the stock market needs its Securities and Investments Board or its Securities and Exchange Commission. This is the logic of the codification-diffusion process as it has emerged in the development of western economies. It does not say that you move *out* of the bureaucratic quadrant and *into* the market one, but rather that in order to build up a transactional infrastructure in the latter, a major prior investment is required in the former which has to be maintained and not run down. Bureaucracy is required to regulate conduct in order to ensure that markets do not become inefficient through the withholding of information from some of the players. Seen in this light, China's bureaucracy is too weak to sustain its current reform programme rather than too strong. Both the country's forces of production (its technical and communication infrastructure) and its relations of production (organizational and institutional infrastructure) are still too underdeveloped (i. e. uncodified) for a trouble-free shift towards the market quadrant.

Are we to conclude pessimistically from this analysis that China's modernization will be vitiated because cultural forces will continue to prevent it developing an impersonal codified framework to underpin the growth of market transactions, and instead retain it within the fief quadrant which remains congenial as a transacting mode? An unqualified adherence to this position would rely upon the questionable assumption that the same codification-diffusion curve which appears to have been functional for western modernization will necessarily become an imperative for any late developer. Late development carries the advantage of being able to utilize more advanced techniques and the knowledge of other nations' experiences so as to formulate a system of transactions which is culturally more congenial and yet at least as effective. Thus it has been argued that Japanese industry has successfully preserved larger, fieflike enclaves both inside and outside the firm, and that it has been able as a late developer to indulge in technological leap-frogging with a less than wholehearted commitment to the market quadrant (Boisot 1983, Littler 1983). Could China, then, not follow suit and find a solution that built positively upon its traditions rather than find its modernization hampered by them?

We shall preface our answer with a brief description of a recent visit to some remote villages three hours north of Baotou in Inner Mongolia. The villages could only be reached by jeep, driving a good part of the way along a river bed, as no roads existed. Yet in the villages themselves, almost every dwelling sported a television antenna and most had colour television. A good number of the younger villagers were wearing fashionable 'gear'. Modern telecommunications had diffused market-relevant information to communities as remote as these. If modernization in Europe and America was powered by the railway and the telegraph wire, then in China it is likely to be powered by satellite-based telecommunications and new information technologies. China had already launched eighteen satellites by August 1986.

The key characteristic of these new information technologies relevant to our analysis is that their vastly increased data transmission capacity permits the extensive diffusion and rapid exchange of information in forms, such as the audio-visual, which can be transmitted at a *lower level of codification* than earlier technologies allowed. For example, whereas previously commercial communication over long distances may have had to take the relatively impersonal form of standardized letters, it may in the future proceed by a more personalized audio-visual interaction. This would enable both the vertical and horizontal transactions upon which respectively delegation and decentralization depend to follow a mode that is better suited to the existing transactional preferences of Chinese culture — namely face-to-face but now over a distance. At the same time the greater freedom of access to information, much of it, such as prices, necessarily coded, should allow for a more efficient national market place. This would mean in terms of the culture-space framework that new information technologies have the potential *to alter the shape of the codification-diffusion curve itself* (Figure 4). While we earlier argued that under present technological conditions China needs to strengthen its bureaucracy in a legal-rational direc-

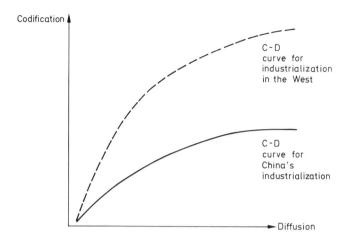

Figure 4   The Potential Modification of the Codification-Diffusion Curve for China's Modernization with the Aid of Information Technology

tion in order to encourage market transactions, in the longer term under new technological conditions it should find it possible to rely for a policing of market behaviour upon the greatly improved access to information available to all the participants interacting in a more personalized, less codified mode.

Technological leap-frogging by late developers in the twenty-first century therefore offers a prospect of information diffusion and access sufficiently powerful as to reduce significantly the level of bureaucratic underpinning previously necessary for the achievement of efficient markets. Information technology transcends the physical time and space barriers to the choice of transactional mode. In so doing, it offers the best opportunity for China to integrate efficient modernization with its traditional preferences for less codified and personalized transactions. The electronic village or commune, reflecting an ever-widening scatter of transactions in the culture-space as its inhabitants discover that the technology imposes few transactional restrictions, is potentially both *Gemeinschaft* and *Gesellschaft* at the same time — i.e., both clan and market. Moreover, it may provide China, which has already assumed the mantle of pathbreaker in the development of socialism, with the opportunity not only to dissolve the informational barriers to achieving efficient markets, but also to achieve to progressive withdrawal of the state from transactions both in line with Marx's prediction for communism and with the Chinese State's already limited historical role in the country's governance. 'Socialism with Chinese characteristcs' would then take on its full meaning.

References

Beijing Review (12 August 1985): Officials sacked for car import racket, 8 – 9.
– (2 December 1985): Shenyang: old city takes on new look, 20 – 27.
– (6 January 1986): 1985, 1986 and beyond, [Editorial] 4 – 5.
– (10 February 1986): On the present economic situation and restructuring the economy, [Speech by Tian Jiyun] III – XV.
– (24 March 1986): Communique on the statistics of 1985 economic and social development, 27 – 33.
– (14 April 1986): Reform guarantees fulfilment of new plan, 26 – 28.
– (21 April 1986): New progress in China's legislation, 16.
– (5 May 1986): China adopts law on foreign enterprises, 14 – 17.
– (2 June 1986): Legal guarantee for foreign investors, 4 – 5.
– (11 August 1986): Reforming leadership system, [Speech of 1980 by Deng Xiaoping] 15 – 19.
Boisot, M. H. (1983): Convergence revisited: the codification and diffusion of knowledge in a British and a Japanese firm, *Journal of Management Studies* 20: 159 – 190.
Boisot, M. H. (1986): Markets and hierarchies in a cultural perspective, *Organization Studies* 7: 135 – 158.
Brunner, J. S. (1974): *Beyond the information given*, London: Allen and Unwin.
Butler, R. J. (1983): Control through markets, hierarchies and communes: a transactional approach to organisational analysis, in: A. Francis, J. Turk and P. Willman (eds.), *Power, efficiency and institutions*, 137 – 158, London: Heinemann.
Chandler, A. D. (1977): *The visible hand*, Cambridge, Mass.: Harvard University Press.
Chandler, A. D. and Daems, H. (1980): *Managerial hierarchies*, Cambridge, Mass.: Harvard University Press.
Child, J. (1987): Enterprise reform in China – progress and problems, in: M. Warner (ed.), *Management Reforms in China*, 24 – 52, London: Pinter.
China Daily (12 April 1986): Economic agencies in some cities face reform of functions [Report of Speech by Tong Dalin]: 4.
Coase, R. H. (1937): The nature of the firm, *Economica* 4: 386 – 405.
Communist Party of China (1984): *China's economic structure reform – decision of the CPC Central Committee, October 1984,* Beijing: Foreign Languages Press.
Domenach, J.-L. (1986): Chinese culture: collective values in the Chinese industrial environment, Paper given to conference on 'Chinese culture and management', organized by *The Economist*, Paris, January.
Dore, R. (1973): *British factory – Japanese factory,* London: Allen and Unwin.
Gouldner, A. W. (1954): *Patterns of industrial bureaucracy*, New York: Free Press.
Hofstede, G. (1980): *Culture's consequences*, Beverly Hills, Cal.: Sage.
Huan Xiang (1985): On reform of Chinese economic structure, *Beijing Review* 20 May: 15 – 19.
Knutsson, J. (1986): Chinese commercial negotiating behavior and its institutional and cultural determinants, Paper given to conference on 'Chinese culture and management' organized by *The Economist*, Paris, January.
Kornai, J. (1985): *Contradictions and dilemmas*, Budapest: Corvina.

Kroeber, A. L. and C. Kluckhohn (1952) *Culture: a critical review of concepts and definitions*, Cambridge, Mass.: Peabody Museum of American Archaeology and Ethnology, Harvard University.

Littler, C. R. (1983): A comparative analysis of managerial structures and strategies, in: H. F. Gospel and C. R. Littler (eds.), *Managerial strategies and industrial relations*, 171–196, London: Heinemann.

Lockett, M. (1985 a): Cultural revolution and industrial organization in a Chinese enterprise: the Beijing General Knitwear Mill 1966–1981, *Templeton College Management Research Papers* 85/7, Oxford.

Lockett, M. (1985 b): Culture and the problems of Chinese management, *Templeton College Management Research Papers* 85/8, Oxford.

Oborne, M. (1986): Industrial organisation in China, Paper given to conference on 'Chinese culture and management' organized by *The Economist*, Paris, January.

Parsons, T. and E. Shils [eds.] (1951): *Towards a general theory of action*, New York: Harper and Row.

People's Daily (20 September 1985): Regulation on strengthening the vitality of large and medium size state-owned enterprises.

Pye, L. W. (1985): *Asian power and politics*, Cambridge, Mass.: Harvard University Press.

Qian Bing Hong (1986): Social values that influence Chinese organizational behaviour, unpublished paper, Shanghai Academy of Social Sciences, February.

Radcliffe-Brown, A. R. (1950): Introduction, to A. R. Radcliffe-Brown and D. Forde (eds.), *African systems of kinship and marriage*, Oxford: Oxford University Press.

Rodzinski, W. (1984): *The walled kingdom*, London: Fontana.

Schram, S. R. (1984): *Ideology and policy in China since the Third Plenum 1978–84*, University of London: School of Oriental and African Studies.

Snow, E. (1972): *Red star over China*, Harmondsworth: Penguin.

Solinger, D. J. [ed.] (1984): *Three visions of Chinese socialism*, Boulder, Col.: Westview.

Thomson, R. (1986 a): Chinese report criticises imports, *Financial Times* 11 July: 4.

Thomson, R. (1986 b): Chinese joint ventures reach a watershed, *Financial Times* 20 June: 7.

Weber, M. (1958): The Chinese Literati, in: H. H. Gerth and C. W. Mills (eds.), *From Max Weber: essays in sociology*, 461–444, New York: Galaxy (Oxford University Press).

Williamson, O. E. (1970): *Corporate control and business behavior*, Englewood Cliffs, N. J.: Prentice-Hall.

Williamson, O. E. (1975): *Markets and hierarchies*, New York: Free Press.

World Bank (1985): *China: long term issues and options*, Washington, D. C.: World Bank.

Xie Yu Jao (1985): Interviews with Mr. Xie, Enterprise Administration Bureau, State Economic Commission, Beijing, 30 September and 5 October.

Xinhua [New China News Agency] (1986): Report of 1 April summarized in *Mainichi Daily News* [Japan], 3 April: 2.

Organizational Change and Stability in Japanese Factories: 1976—1983

Robert M. Marsh and Hiroshi Mannari

Introduction

Japanese organizations' success can and should be interpreted through the 'normal' science of organization theory. In the 1985 APROS conference Donaldson (1986) examined whether the generalization about size and bureaucratic structure holds true across all societies and demonstrated that the variation in organization structure in the East and the West can be explained in terms of certain situational factors of context. Our study focuses on causal relations between organizational structures and contextual variables in Japanese manufacturing organizations. We try to explain Japanese organization structure and its performance in terms of relatively universal, rational, structural properties. A key component in an efficient 'economic culture' is flexible, responsive adaptation to the changing contingencies of the environment. We propose to show how our longitudinal analysis enables us to understand what makes Japanese 'economic culture' work in practice and also, how our analysis should lead us to revise organization theory.

This chapter[1] reports the research results of organizational change and stability for 48 manufacturing units concerning various industries in a large industrial community in Japan. The research was conducted in 1976 and again in 1983. In using Aston measurements, we measured systematically their organizational variables in input, throughput and output and explored empirically what aspects of our Japanese factories changed and what aspects did not during the seven-year period. It is a short period for organizational change but the time covers two oil crises in 1973 and 1979 following prolonged economic recessions and subsequent industrial restructuring. The research results make it possible to evaluate Japan's organizational structure and functioning in adapting to environmental conditions and adjusting internal features of their management.

---

[1] The entire research results of this study have been published by Robert M. Marsh and Hiroshi Mannari, *Organizational Change in Japanese Factories*. 1988, Connecticut: JAI Press.

The Japanese Economy in the 1970s and Early 1980s

In viewing the changes that affected industries and the strategies of particular firms in those industries in the 1970s and early 1980s, it is important to distinguish two kinds of adjustments. One consists of adjustments that are part of the general process of structural modernization in industry from pre-World War II days to the present. The other set of changes are responses to external shocks, most especially the oil shocks of 1973 and 1979.

The first, or modernization-related adjustments, include such trends as labour-saving, reorganization of the work process, computerization, increased attention to marketing and the competition from new industrial exporting countries like Taiwan and South Korea that could increasingly undersell Japan's textile and machine industry products. Resources were shifted away from textiles and other labour-intensive consumer goods industries and toward capital-intensive and high technology industries. Japan's overall increasingly favourable international trade balance caused its exports to face greater friction with other advanced countries and this negatively affected such Japanese industries as steel and autos.

These trends reflect changing market demand profiles and technological modernization and would have occurred even without the oil shocks of the 1970s. Moreover, the steep rise in energy prices affected some industries less than others. Electronics, fine chemicals and machinery and equipment that utilize numerical control (NC) machine tools actually expanded during the 1970s.

Nevertheless, the 1973 oil shock is widely believed to have signalled an end to Japan's period of high economic growth of 10−12%. Prior to 1973 the oil Japan had to import was relatively cheap. After 1973 rising prices for energy and other goods combined with a falling growth rate. Japan experienced its worst recession in the post-war period (Sato 1980: 9). Steel and other basic industries' demand declined as a result of the falling growth rate. Industries found themselves variously in situations described as structural recession or depression. Industrial production fell and only slowly recovered.

These challenges called for a more drastic restructuring of industry after 1973 than would have been required had only general modernization been operating. Management, with the cooperation of regular employees, sought ways to economize in oil consumption and to improve productive efficiency. Anticipating lower growth rates, investment in new equipment was restrained and employment was reduced through the buffers of being able to lay off temporary employees, reduce orders to subcontracting firms and by not replacing those who retired or offering attractive severance pay to those who would voluntarily retire early or accept jobs elsewhere. The fixed capital and labour costs inherited from the period of high expected growth were a great burden to firms: they raised the point at which firms could break-even, thereby reducing profits. Declining profits were another incentive to find more efficient uses of existing assets and to reduce costs. Successful efforts to reduce these fixed costs drove the break-even point down again by 1979. Wage demands were moderated, dropping from an annual increase of 4.6% before 1973 to 1.9% in 1974–76 (Allen 1981).

As a result of these successful readjustments, labour productivity in manufacturing, which fell in 1973–75, rose rapidly and by 1979, when the second oil shock hit Japan, was 35% higher than the 1973 level (Allen 1981).

Method and Data

In 1976 we conducted a field survey of 48 industrial manufacturing establishments each employing 100 or more persons in a city in southwestern Japan. The focus was on the interrelationships between properties of these factories as organizations – their products, technology, size, internal organizational structure and performance. The city studied had manufacturing firms in 13 of the 21 two-digit industries classified in Japan's 1972 Establishment Census of Manufacturing. Our sample has one or more firms in each of these 13 industries.

In 1983 we re-studied the same 48 firms with the same set of questions, intending to examine and explain changes over the seven-year period since 1976. Data collection in each factory in both 1976 and 1983 consisted of a tour of the production plant, an interview with one or more key informants (senior officials) and a questionnaire filled out by these key informants.

Organizational Change and Stability

As open systems, our Japanese factories had to respond to the unusual shocks of the oil price increases, the resulting energy crisis and the worst recession in Japan since World War II. These challenges called for more than usual amounts of restructuring of industry after 1973.

To understand the extent of this restructuring in the factories we studied, we can make some statistical comparisons. Which variables had significant change in their means between 1976 and 1983? This tells us something about change and stability at the aggregate level, across all our factories.

Consider the variables that show significant differences in their intertemporal means.

1. Factory size had an average increase of 12.6% between 1971 and 1975, but declined 9.1% between 1976 and 1983. The difference in means for these two period rates is significant.
2. Factory output performance increased significantly over the seven-year period, relative to the rate of inflation.

	$\bar{X}$% Increase, 1975 to 1982
Labour productivity (value-added per employee)	123.3%
Sales productivity (sales per employee)	99.8%
Yen value of factory production per employee	71.2%
Inflation[2]	41.8%

3. Factory production technology became more advanced in several respects. The mean automaticity score (including both the automation of the bulk of the production equipment and that of the single most automated piece of equipment) rose significantly. Woodward technology scores, which register which of five types of technology an organization most fully uses, increased significantly in the direction of the more advanced levels of production continuity. The Khandwalla technology scores, which measure the degree to which a factory uses each of Woodward's five types of technology, increased significantly in the direction of a greater diversity of advanced types of technological rationalization. Thus, technological rationalization is unmistakable in all these respects, even during this relatively short seven-year period.
4. Although our firms are mostly in mature, 'smoke stack' industries, they adapted to the increasing knowledge complexity of work by significantly increasing the percentage of personnel who are university graduates.
5. The percentage of firms that have added a job classification system (*shokumubunrui*) to the seniority wage system increased significantly from 57.5% in 1976 to 70.2% in 1983.

---

[2] The inflation rate was estimated by comparing gross national expenditure in 1975 and 1982 (a) at constant 1975 price and (b) at current prices. The former increased by 38.8%, the latter by 80.6%, and the difference between these two percentage increases, 41.8%, is the estimated increase in inflation between 1975 and 1982. Sources: The Bank of Japan, 1981: 327 – 330, 1983: 181 – 182.

6. Factory product diversification, as measured by the six-digit MITI classification, significantly decreased. Firms adapted to the poor economic conditions by becoming more product specialized.
7. As overall factory size declined, the number of production workers fell at a more rapid rate than the number of supervisory and managerial personnel. As a result, first-line foremen were supervising significantly fewer workers, on the average, in 1983 than in 1976, and administrative intensity — the overall A/P ratio — had increased significantly.
8. There was a significant decline in the number of horizontal units — subsections (*gakari*) — in the factories from a mean of 18.3 in 1976 to 13.3 in 1983. There was no significant change, however, in the mean number of hierarchic levels: the response to declining size was a narrowing of the organizational pyramid, not a flattening. The factories' rank structures were as tall in 1983 as in 1976.
9. The gender composition of the workforce showed a significant decline in the percentage of women personnel, from 31.9% in 1976 to 27.6% in 1983.

Explaining Change: The Important Causal Variables

The empirical analysis was carried out in terms of the Input-Throughput-Output (ITO) systems model. As we moved through the ITO system, we sought to explain one after another of the dependent variables.

It is useful now to organize our reassessment of the findings by the independent variables. Which independent variables had significant net effects over the range of dependent variables in the ITO systems model? We shall discuss the effects of each independent variable in the order of its location in the ITO model. In Marsh and Mannari (1988) we classify the main variables as follows in the ITO model:

Inputs: environmental and contextual variables: origin, goal, product diversification, borrowed capital, environmental uncertainty, task variability, dependence on customers, internal dependence and autonomy, number of company sites, age.

Throughputs: differentiation of management from ownership, technology, size, labour inputs by types of personnel, size versus technology, structural complexity, centralization of authority, spans of control, administrative intensity and administrative costs, research and development.

Outputs: market share, labour productivity, profit, absenteeism.

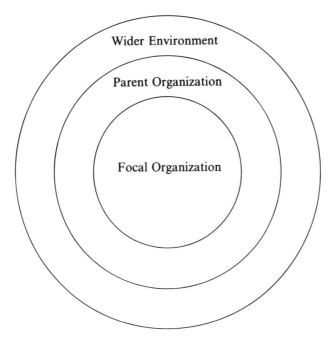

Figure 1   Nested Dependence of Organizations

The organizational literature is replete with lists of cross-sectional, bivariate relationships. What follows is not another such list. Instead, in each of our propositions there is typically a seven-year lag between the independent and the dependent variable, and the relationship is significant net of the lagged dependent variable. Such relationships can be taken more seriously as causal inferences.

Organizations have a nested dependence (see Figure 1). A focal organization — here, a factory on a particular site — is more or less dependent on its parent organization, i. e. the ultimate owning group. The parent organization in turn is more or less dependent on the wider environment, consisting of the industry of the firm's product line(s), including the market and customer taste, suppliers, the government and the general public. Our Input-Throughput-Output systems model starts with this idea of nested dependence, what the Aston group partly conceptualized as internal and external dependence.

The basic assumptions driving our ITO systems model are that 'the development of an organization proceeds from its individual founding and capitalization in response to market opportunities, through its design based on copying and modifying an existing technology, on to the design of the organization's structure, and finally to the employment of a work force to staff the nearly completed organization' (Aldrich 1972: 34).

Effects of Production Technology

1. The more automated a factory's production technology, the more it relies subsequently on mechanized rather than personal means to evaluate the quality of production.
2. The more automated a factory's production technology, the larger its subsequent R & D budget.
3. Net of the earlier percentage of factory personnel with university educations, the more advanced the Woodward type of technology, the less the increase in university-educated personnel between 1976 and 1983.
4. The more diversified a factory's advanced (Khandwalla) technology, the less the interdependence between workflow segments. Thompson's reciprocal type of interdependence is most likely when the factory relies on one main type of technology.
5. The more mechanized the quality evaluation of production, the greater the later factory sales per employee.

Effects of Size

The great attention given to size as a cause of organizational phenomena is wholly justified. In our data, size is in a class by itself as the most frequent cause of other aspects of organizations. Controlling for each lagged dependent variable, we have found that the larger the size of the factory (number of employees),

1. the greater the interdependence of workflow segments;
2. the higher the overall level of computerization in the factory;
3. the greater the differentiation of the organization into horizontal and vertical structural components;
4. the greater the number of job titles;
5. the larger the span of control of first-line foremen;
6. the more likely that the firm recognizes a labour union.

The rate of change in factory size between 1976 and 1983 had two significant net effects:

1. The more factory size grew, the greater was the increase in the yen value of production.
2. The more factory size grew, the lower was the subsequent voluntary quit rate.

Company size had the following significant net effect:
The larger the size of the company, the more likely it had differentiated management from ownership.

Kimberly (1976) proposed that different configurations of the size – structure relationship may hold depending on whether one uses number of employees or some other measure of scale. Aldrich (1972) suggested that scale, e. g. sales volume, is theoretically more justifiable than number of employees as a cause of structure. The economies of scale realized through a high sales volume can affect structure. Forecasted sales are usually the starting point of most operations' planning and capital budgeting, and these in turn may lead to modifications in organizational structure (Khandwalla 1974). In our Japanese factories, the log of size and the log of scale (sales) were highly collinear, their effects on other variables were very similar and parallel, and there is no evidence that scale is a better predictor of these variables than is size. We thus remain unpersuaded by Kimberly's and Aldrich's preference for other measures of size. Most of the literature uses number of personnel. We find no basis for using scale rather than size as a major causal variable.

Our findings on the numerous causal effects of size support Blau and the Aston group. Indeed, it strengthens their work by demonstrating that the relationships hold up when longitudinal data and controls for the lagged dependent variables are used. However, we have also found that some of the causal effects attributed to size in cross-sectional studies by Blau, the Aston group and others, are misspecified. In our causal model some, or all, of the apparently significant impact of size in the following instances was in fact due to (a) the historical effect of the dependent variable on itself over time or (b) the effect of one or more variables omitted in the theories of Blau, the Aston group and others.

First, more than one causal model provides an equally good explanation of the number of hierarchic levels in the factories. Net of the number of levels in 1976, one model has number of levels in 1983 as a positive function of size and of a personal, enterpreneurial origin of the factory. A second model shows number of levels to be a positive function of the number of subsections (horizontal differentiation causes vertical differentiation) and a negative function of the centralization of authority. When number of levels is regressed on the prior number of levels, size, origin of the factory, number of subsections and centralization of authority, it is the factory's entrepreneurial origin and its number of subsections, not size, that cause the later number of levels.

Second, a factory's structural complexity is explained equally well by two alternative models. One is Blau's theory that increasing size generates increasing structural differentiation. The other is that as a factory increases its range of products, it adds new horizontal units to house their production; this in turn necessitates the creation of new hierarchic levels due to the cognitive limits imposed on spans of control. The result is a higher degree of structural complexity.

In the third place, size is not the main cause of administrative functional specialization. Rather, the sources of specialization are increased product diversification and a decentralization of authority. Under those two conditions, administrative functions previously carried out in a centralized way by the boss become assigned to functional specialists whose work is geared to the more diversified products of the firm.

Fourth, size is a significant cause of formalization only when the more important dimension of authority and control is omitted from the causal model. Though larger organizations tend to be more formalized than smaller ones, it is the distribution of authority between headquarters and the plant, and within the plant, that is the more decisive cause of formalization. Factories that must refer more decisions to company headquarters are directed by headquarters to become both more centralized internally and more formalized. The principal cause of formalization is not that a factory becomes large, but that it lacks autonomy: its parent organization is the source of its greater centralization of decision making and its higher formalization at the plant level. A factory that is an independent firm or one that has greater autonomy from company headquarters can become large with less accompanying centralization and formalization. This is because the factory's top officials decentralize authority within the factory more and rely less on extensive formal written communications and rules.

Fifth, in their New Jersey factory study, Blau et al. (1976) found that, net of structural complexity, size had a significant negative effect on the CEO's span of control. But this purely cross-sectional relationship did not control for the effect of the CEO's span at an earlier time. In our data, size is a cause of structural complexity which in turn has a positive effect on the CEO's span of control. Size has no significant direct effect on the CEO's span; its effect is only indirect, via its tendency to increase the organization's complexity. Thus, controlling for prior CEO span, increasing the number of people who report to the CEO is mainly a response to the increasing structural complexity of the organization, not the sheer growth in size.

The more differentiated parts the organization has, the more managers report directly to the CEO. A larger organization that does not become as structurally differentiated will not have as many managers and others reporting to the CEO.

Sixth, Blau's middle range theory of size, complexity and administrative intensity (A/P ratio), receives some support in our data. We do find that the economies of scale in managerial overheads exceed the costs of complexity such that the negative effects of size on A/P exceed the positive effects of complexity of A/P. The net effect of size on A/P is thus negative, meaning that larger Japanese factories have a smaller proportion of managerial and supervisory personnel than do smaller factories. However, Blau's theory explains only between 2% and 13% of the variance in administrative intensity in the various tests made with our data, both cross-sectionally and over time and, when prior levels of the A/P ratio are held constant, neither size nor structural complexity has a significant net effect on the A/P ratio. Once again, Blau's theory suffers from misspecification.

In summary, the core of Blau's theory is the relationship of size to the various ways in which organizations become structurally differentiated. This by no means exhausts the phenomena in which students of organizations have been interested. But we have shown that even on its home ground, Blau's theory is misspecified in important respects. Cullen, Anderson and Baker (1986) have shown that Blau's theory explains structural differences in scale across organizations at one point in time rather than structural change over time within organizations. It is our conclusion that by ignoring the prior levels of each structural differentiation dependent variable and by omitting certain other theoretically important prior variables, such as product diversification, whether the organization was founded entrepreneurially or bureaucratically, and the autonomy of the focal unit in relation to the parent organization, Blau has exaggerated and over-generalized the importance of organizational size. At the same time, when we find that size is a main causal variable, net of the lagged dependent variable and other hypothesized causes, the theoretical case for size is strengthened since the panel data support the earlier cross-sectional findings.

Our longitudinal data also enabled us to go beyond Blau and ask whether the effects of changes in size are symmetrical in growing and declining size organizations. Managers and supervisors increase more rapidly in growing factories than they decrease in declining size factories. Production workers decrease more rapidly when size declines than they increase when factory size is growing. The result is increasing administrative intensity in declining size organizations. Japanese factories are not immune to the 'ratchet effect' (Freeman and Hannan 1975, Inkson, Pugh and Hickson 1970). Changes in declining size factories are not simply a mirror image of the growth of each personnel component in growing factories.

Why can managers and supervisors resist the elimination of their positions more effectively than production workers? The fashionable explanation is that managers and supervisors have more power. Considerations of formal structure and efficiency make us unwilling to accept the power explanation. In the case of supervisors the lag before structure responds to a decline in the number of workers may reflect the fact that a supervisor must be retained as long as he or she still has any remaining subordinates who cannot be re-assigned to another supervisor, who may still have as many subordinates as can be effectively handled. In the case of managers their normal role is to cope with the external environment and they are more likely to be retained than workers because the need to find new adaptations to environmental conditions — the reason for declining size in the first place — devolves upon them. We submit that until more research can test the competing power and efficiency explanations, a healthy scepticism is in order.

The Size Versus Technology Issue

Organizational sociologists for years have struggled with the problem of 'the relative causal effects of size versus technology' and this problem continues to vex us. Different studies continue to provide evidence for the causal superiority of size or technology and theoretical schools are defined as the 'size school' (Blau, the Aston group) or the 'technology school' (Woodward, Perrow, Aldrich, Blauner, Zwerman).

Having already summarized the relative effects of size and technology on other variables, we tried to resolve the 'size versus technology' debate in two as yet untried ways: first, by considering the reciprocal effects of technology and size on each other and second, by integrating the effects of technology and size in a single production function as a capital/labour ratio.

First, instead of evaluating the relative influence of technology and size by how much each influences variables in other domains, e. g. structure and performance, we asked: if there are reciprocal causal effects of technology and size on each other, is causation greater in one direction than in the other? Simultaneous equations and two-stage least squares analysis with instrumental variables enabled us to examine the effects of 1983 automaticity on 1983 size and vice versa, net of the effects of the other prior variables that influence automaticity and size, respectively. We found no evidence of any significant net reciprocal effects of size and automaticity on each other. That is, net of other variables in the model, 1983 automaticity exerts no significant effect on 1983 size; nor does 1983 size significantly influence 1983 automaticity. This outcome provides no support for Aldrich's (1972) argument that automaticity is causally prior to size. Lacking any evidence that technology in general is causally prior to size or the reverse, we reaffirm our own position: both technology and size are a result of managerial strategy decisions, as constrained by environmental and other inputs into the organization. Technology and size belong in the same causal 'column' in the ITO systems model diagram; their position is parallel, rather than one in which technology (or size) is logically and generally the prior causal variable. This does not contradict our earlier point that with respect to particular ITO dependent variables, size may be causally more important than technology, or vice versa.

Second, we sought a fresh perspective on the size versus technology debate through the theory of the firm in micro-economics. There, in the short run, capital equipment (technology) is assumed to be given, and the decision on the number of personnel to employ depends on the relationship between marginal, variable costs and price. In the longer run, technology is variable. Elasticity of substitution between capital and labour may be assumed in a well-behaved production function. This suggests that instead of trying to differentiate the causal effects of capital (technology) and labour (size), as sociologists have typically done, we should integrate their causal effects by considering the capital/labour (i.e. technology/size) ratio. Does the variable capital-versus labour-intensity of a factory have stronger and more extensive causal effects than the separate effects of technology and size?

The effect of this ln K/L variable — the log of the value of factory fixed assets in million yen per employee — was compared with the effects of the separate ln size and technology variables, always controlling for each lagged dependent variable[3]. The results are negative. Among the 27 successive dependent variables considered in our larger study (Marsh and Mannari 1988), the ln K/L variable had a stronger causal effect than any of the

---

[3] As expected, in 1976, ln K/L was significantly positively related to all the size and technology variables. Its Pearson r was .81 with automaticity, .69 with Woodward technology, .39 with Khandwalla technology, .67 with ln scale and .25 with ln size.

technology or size variables only three times. More capital intensive firms in 1976 had, by 1983, (a) a larger span of control at the CEO level, (b) more sales per employee and (c) lower voluntary quit rates. But in each instance, the regression coefficient for ln K/L was only marginally larger than that of size or technology. Thus, we must conclude that the microeconomic production function approach of integrating the effects of technology and size into a single K/L ratio does not resolve the continuing controversy over the relative effects of size and technology on organizational phenomena. Knowing a factory's degree of capital- or labour-intensity provides a good explanation when size and/or technology variables also provide a significant explanation, but is not helpful when size and technology fail to provide a significant explanation. It does not improve the explanatory situation in the sense of carrying our understanding farther than when size and technology are used separately as independent variables.

Despite the popularized image in the West that Japanese managers' main preoccupation is with generating and maintaining happy, loyal, committed workers, it was our observation in both 1976 and 1983 that a more compelling managerial concern was for the need to substitute more automated technology for workers. We have seen that on the average our 48 factories did become more technologically advanced and did reduce the size of their workforce during this period. But it is misleading to say that at the level of individual factories the substitution of automation for workers was the main trend. Our data do not generally support the technological unemployment thesis. Firms whose automation increased were in fact much more likely to increase their number of employees (than those whose technology either did not change or became less automated). It was 'standing pat' in technology, not becoming more automated, that led to a decline in the number of personnel. Where size did decline, it was more a result of recession-based decline in demand for the firms' products than of the increases in automation.

In short, managers who told us their firm 'would have gone under without technological rationalization' had not necessarily actually cut their workforce. Advances in technology generally made for a net increase in the number of jobs in our factories. One mechanism accounting for this is that net of labour productivity in 1975, the greater the rate of increase in automaticity between 1976 and 1983, the greater the increase in labour productivity by 1983. The higher labour productivity lowered unit production costs and could allow the prices of the firm's products to be reduced. This could increase demand and thus require a larger workforce to operate the more advanced technology.

Conclusion

Some texts on organizations are remembered as One-Big-Idea approaches, each carrying the message 'Take X into account!' The parade of X's over the years has included scientific management (Taylor 1911); human relations (Roethlisberger and Dickson 1939); conflict (Gouldner 1954); technology (Woodward 1965); environmental contingency (Lawrence and Lorsch 1967); size (Blau and Schoenherr 1971); matrix or task force organization (Kingdon 1973); ambiguity (March and Olsen 1976); design (Mintzberg 1979); population ecology (Aldrich 1979); power (Pfeffer 1981); and taxonomy (McKelvey 1982).

Our approach is not in terms of One-Big-Idea. It grows out of a set of choices concerning the best ways to study change and stability in organizations. The first choice was the unit of analysis. At the micro-boundary of the field, individuals and sub-units within an organization are the unit of analysis. We treat organizations as the unit of analysis because we believe the interrelationships between elements of organizations are of sociological interest in their own right, apart from their effects on individuals and groups within an organization. We also eschewed the most macro approach in the field, where whole populations of similar organizations are the unit of analysis. Population ecology is a valuable perspective for answering a certain range of questions. But it tends to reify the environment — to make the environment a kind of secular version of Calvin's God — selecting some organizations for survival, others for death. It also tends to treat intra-organizational processes as a black box and to virtually deny any proactive role for managerial choice. These features made the macro approach of population ecology less useful for what we wanted to do in studying change in Japanese factories.

Second, we chose to break with the long-standing practice in the field of making causal inferences on the basis of cross-sectional data. How organizations remain stable or change over time can only be inferred from static data with the heroic assumption that organizational relationships are in equilibrium. Unwilling to make that assumption, we collected longitudinal data so that causal inferences could be based on panel regression analysis. This had led to the modification of several earlier theories.

Third, we adopted a position that combines structural contingency theory and input-throughput-output systems theory. Contingency theory sensitizes us to the ways in which managers manipulate their strategy variables — goals, technology, size, etc. — and design the internal structure so as to satisfy performance expectations of various constituencies, e.g. the ultimately owning group, suppliers, customers and workers. Some writers interpret these adaptations as a result of power interests and class struggle rather than as means to performance efficiency. We do not deny the influence of power and class interests, but argue that organizations cannot be indifferent toward performance in terms of sales, labour productivity, market share, profit, absenteeism and turnover: some of their strategic choices and structural redesign are directed at these performance goals. To say 'directed at performance goals' does not, of course, mean equally successful results: our firms vary on each dimension of performance and that is one of the key things we have tried to explain.

Systems theory can be made to yield much more than the truistic proposition that the subsystems of an organization and its environment are interrelated in a dynamic way. We have tried to extend systems theory to specify which inputs initiate what changes in throughputs; which inputs and throughputs cause what changes in which outputs; and which outputs have feedback effects on what later inputs? Previous studies of these questions have often been unduly restrictive in one or more of the following ways. They considered only some of the important contextual, input factors as independent variables; they analyzed only a few organizational dependent variables; they showed the effects of context, size and/or technology on internal structure, but failed to explore the independent effects of some aspects of structure on other aspects of structure, net of context, technology and size.

To overcome these restrictions, we have deployed more organizational-level independent variables and sought to explain a greater range of organizational-level dependent variables. We have also been able to demonstrate that, net of the lagged dependent variable and net of context, technology and size, specific organizational structure variables have significant effects on other structure variables. For example, the number of levels is a function of the number of horizontal units; functional specialization and formalizeation are both a function of the centralization of authority; and the span of control at the CEO level is a function of the degree of structural complexity. In short, a fuller explanation of variations in the ways organizations are designed can be achieved when not only contextual variables, technology and size, but also related aspects of structure itself are included as independent variables.

Although our propositions have been tested with data from Japanese factories, our approach has been more 'structural' than 'cultural'. This will disturb those readers who are culture vultures and believe that the only reason one would study Japanese organizations is to reveal their distinctive embeddedness in Japanese culture. Studies that have done this by taking a culture-specific approach outnumber the kinds of study we have done, which searches for cross-cultural structural universals. We have tried to move the study of Japanese organizations out of the realm of cultural exotica and into the mainstream of comparative structural organizational theory. The major difference is that instead of talking about how 'typical Japanese organizations' differ from 'typical American' or 'typical British organizations', we have inquired into a quite different set of problems: how do Japanese organizations vary and to what extent can these variations within Japan be explained by relatively universal, structural, system properties of any organization?

References

Abegglen, James (1958): *The Japanese factory: aspects of its social organization*, Glencoe, Ill.: Free Press.

Abegglen, James (1984): *The strategy of Japanese business*, Cambridge, Mass.: Ballinger.

Aldrich, Howard E. (1972): Technology and organization structure: a re-examination of the findings of the Aston group, *Administrative Science Quarterly* 17: 26–43.

Aldrich, Howard E. (1979): *Organizations and environments*, Englewood Cliffs, N. J.: Prentice-Hall.

Allen, G. C. (1981): *The Japanese economy*, New York: St. Martin's.

Amber, George H. and Paul S. Amber (1962): *Anatomy of automation*, Englewood Cliffs, N. J.: Prentice-Hall.

Azumi, Koya, David Hickson, Deszo Horvarth and Charles McMillan (1979): Nippon no Soshiki Kozo (Structure of Japanese organizations), *Soshiki Kagaku* (Organizational Science) 12. 4: 2–12.

Azumi, Koya, David Hickson, Deszo Horvath and Charles McMillan (1984): Structural uniformity and cultural diversity in organizations: a comparative study of factories in Britain, Japan and Sweden, in: Sato Kazuo and Yasuo Hoshino (eds.), *The anatomy of Japanese business*, 101–120, Armonk, N. Y.: Sharpe.

The Bank of Japan, Research Statistics Dept. (1981): *1983 Annual reports of economic statistics*, Tokyo: The Bank of Japan.

The Bank of Japan (1983): Economic Statistics Monthly, No. 440.

Blau, Peter M. and Richard A. Schoenherr (1971): *The structure of organizations*, New York: Basic Books.

Blau, Peter M., Cecilia M. Falbe, William McKinley and Phelps K. Tracy (1976): Technology and organization in manufacturing, *Administrative Science Quarterly* March 21: 20–40.

Blauner, Robert (1964): *Alienation and freedom*, Chicago: University of Chicago Press.

Caves, Richard E. and Masu Uekusa (1976): *Industrial organization in Japan*, Washington, D. C.: Brookings Institution.

Cullen, John B., Kenneth S. Anderson and Douglas D. Baker (1986): Blau's theory of structural differentiation revisited: a theory of structural change or scale? *Academy of Management Journal* 29. 2: 203–229.

Donaldson, Lex (1986): Size and bureaucracy in East and West: a preliminary meta analysis, in: Stewart R. Clegg, Dexter C. Dunphy and S. Gordon Redding (eds.), *The enterprise and management East Asia*, 67–92, Hong Kong: Centre of Asian Studies, University of Hong Kong.

Evan, William M. (1976): Organization theory and organizational effectiveness: an exploratory analysis, in: S. Lee Spray (ed.), *Organizational effectiveness: theory–research–utilization*, 15–28, Kent, OH: Kent State University Press.

Freeman, John H. (1973): Environment, technology and the administrative intensity of manufacturing organizations, *American Sociological Review* December 38: 750–764.

Freeman, John H. and Michael T. Hannan (1975): Growth and decline processes in organizations, *American Sociological Review* 40: 215–222.

Gouldner, Alvin W. (1954): *Patterns of industrial bureaucracy*, New York: Free Press.

Hannan, Michael and John Freeman (1984): Structural inertia and organizational change, *American Sociological Review* 49: 149–164.

Hannan, Michael and Alice A. Young (1977): Estimation in panel models: results on pooling cross-sections and time series, in: David R. Heise (ed.), *Sociological methodology*, 52–83, San Francisco: Jossey-Bass.

Inkson, J. H. K., D. S. Pugh and D. J. Hickson (1970): Organization context and structure: an abbreviated replication, *Administrative Science Quarterly* 15: 318–329.

Khandwalla, Pradip N. (1974): Mass output orientation of operations technology and organizational structure, *Administrative Science Quarterly* 9: 74–97.

Khandwalla, Pradip N. (1977): *The design of organizations*, New York: Harcourt, Brace Jovanovich.

Kimberly, John R. (1976): Organizational size and the structuralist perspective: a review, critique and proposal, *Administrative Science Quarterly* 21: 571–597.

Kingdon, Donald R. (1973): *Matrix organization: managing information technologies*, London: Tavistock.

Kono, Toyohiro (1984): *Strategy and structure of Japanese enterprises*, Armonk, N. Y.: Sharpe.

Kosai, Y. and Y. Ogino (1984): *The contemporary Japanese economy*, Armonk, N. Y.: Sharpe.

Lawrence, Paul R. and J. W. Lorsch (1967): *Organization and environment*, Homewood, Ill.: Irwin.

Lincoln, James R. and Arne Kalleberg (1985): Work organization and workforce commitment, *American Sociological Review* 50: 738–760.

March, J. G. and J. P. Olsen (1976): *Ambiguity and choice in organizations*, Bergen: Universitesforlaget.

Marsh, Robert M. and Hiroshi Mannari (1976): *Modernization and the Japanese factory*, Princeton, N. J.: Princeton University Press.

Marsh, Robert M. and Hiroshi Mannari (1981): Technology and size as determinants of the organizational structure of Japanese factories, *Administrative Science Quarterly* 26: 33–57.

Marsh, Robert M. and Hiroshi Mannari (1988): *Organizational change in Japanese factories*, Conn.: JAI Press.

McKelvey, B. (1982): *Organizational systematics*, Berkeley, California: University of California Press.

Meyer, Marshall W. (1968): Expertness and the span of control, *American Sociological Review* 33. 6: 944 – 951.

Meyer, Marshall W. (1972): Size and the structure of organizations: a causal analysis, *American Sociological Review* 37: 434 – 441.

Mintzberg, Henry (1979): *The structuring of organizations*, Englewood Cliffs, N. J.: Prentice-Hall.

Nakane, Chie (1970): *Japanese society*, Berkeley, Cal.: University of California Press.

Norbeck, Edward (1978): *Country to city: the urbanization of a Japanese hamlet*, Salt Lake City: University of Utah Press.

Pascale, Richard T. and Anthony G. Athos (1981): *The art of Japanese management*, New York: Simon and Schuster.

Perrow, Charles (1967): A framework for the comparative analysis of organizations, *American Sociological Review* 32: 194 – 208.

Perrow, Charles (1979): *Complex organizations: a critical essay*, Dallas, Tx.: Scott, Foresman.

Pfeffer, Jeffrey (1981): *Power in organizations*, Cambridge, Mass.: Ballinger.

Pugh, D. S. and D. J. Hickson (1976): *Organizational structure in its context: the Aston Program I*, Lexington, Mass.: Lexington Books.

Roethlisberger, F. J. and W. J. Dickson (1939): *Management and the worker*, Cambridge, Mass.: Harvard University Press.

Sato, Kazuo (1980): The Japanese economy at the crossroads, Unpublished paper presented at the Columbia University Seminar on Modern East Asia: Japan, April 11.

Scott, W. Richard (1977): Effectiveness of organizational effectiveness studies, in: Paul S. Goodman and Johannes Pennings (eds.), *New perspectives on organizational effectiveness*, 63 – 95, San Francisco: Jossey-Bass.

Scott, W. Richard (1981): *Organizations: rational, natural and open systems*, Englewood Cliffs, N. J.: Prentice-Hall.

Shimada, Haruo (1977): The Japanese labor market after the oil crisis (1), *Japan Labor Bulletin* 1. 16: 7 – 10.

Taylor, F. W. (1911): *The principles of scientific management*, New York: Harpers and Brother.

Thompson, Victor (1961): *Modern organizations*, New York: Knopf.

Tracy, Phelps K. and Koya Azumi (1976): Determinants of administrative control: a test of a theory with Japanese factories, *American Sociological Review* 41: 80 – 94.

Williamson, Oliver E. (1970): *Corporate control and business behavior*, Englewood Cliffs, N. J.: Prentice-Hall.

Woodward, Joan (1958): *Management and technology*, London: H. M. Stationery Office.

Woodward, Joan (1965): *Industrial organization: theory and practice*, London: Oxford University Press.

Zwerman, William L. (1970): *New perspectives on organization theory*, Westport, Ct.: Greenwood Press.

Japanese Influences on British Industrial Culture

Barry Wilkinson and Nick Oliver

Introduction

This chapter examines the activities of Japanese manufacturers in the U. K., in particular their forms of work organization and patterns of industrial relations, and explores their impact on British industrial culture. The term 'industrial culture' is used in preference to 'economic culture' as our emphasis is on social and industrial relations within manufacturing companies. Aspects of the wider context, such as the nature of relationships between the state, manufacturing and finance capital, are raised, however, on the grounds that what is occurring within organizations cannot be sensibly divorced from the context within which they are operating. The chapter draws heavily on our own survey evidence (Oliver and Wilkinson 1988) plus the survey evidence of colleagues at the Cardiff Business School (Gleave 1987, Morris 1988 b, Pang 1987). In combination, these surveys cover 31 (63%) of the Japanese manufacturers operating in the U. K. at the end of 1987. In addition to this survey evidence, the chapter draws on case study and anecdotal evidence to illustrate our arguments. Although the number of Japanese manufacturing companies with operations in the U. K. is small at present, we would argue that these small numbers belie their importance, not only because the numbers are increasing rapidly but, more importantly, because Japanese companies are serving as a model which many British and other Western manufacturers operating in the U. K. are trying to emulate.

Japanese Direct Investment in the U. K.

Japanese direct investment began in the U. K. on a significant scale only in the mid-1970s, and the most recent figures show a sharp acceleration in investment in the mid-1980. The recent rapid growth is part of a trend on the part of Japanese investors to increase overseas investment worldwide due to trade friction and political pressures, as well as the effects of a strong yen.

The Japanese Ministry of Finance calculated direct investment overseas (cumulative total since 1951) to have increased from US $ 4.7 billion at the end of 1973 to US $ 22.3 billion by 1979. By the end of 1986 the figure stood at almost US $ 106 billion, of which US $ 28.2 billion was accounted for by manufacturing industry. US $ 34.5 billion of the total at the end of 1986 was committed during the previous two years alone, and 1986 saw an 82.7% rise in overseas spending over 1985 (Anglo-Japan Economic Institute 1987).

The Finance Ministry further calculated that in the U. K. direct investment from Japan reached a cumulative total (since 1951) of US $ 4.1 billion at the end of 1986, almost US $ 1 billion of which was committed in 1986 alone. The figure of US $ 4.1 billion represents around 4% of the total investment overseas by the Japanese. The U. K., up to now, has been the recipient of almost a quarter of the total Japanese investment commitment in the EEC. The *Financial Times* (24 April 1987) reported that Japanese investment in the U. K. was worth G. B. Stirling 3.2 billion and involved the direct employment of over 17,500 people. During 1987, further investment decisions were made and many Japanese companies already established announced expansion plans which would increase investment commitments and employment levels. Nissan alone announced a plan to add G. B. Stirling 250 million to its present commitment of G. B. Stirling 350 million, creating an additional 1,400 jobs by 1992 and, during 1987, Japanese companies invested G. B. Stirling 560 million in the U. K. (*Western Mail* 22 January 1988).

The 49 Japanese manufacturing companies accounted for 13,557 of the total employed by Japanese companies in the U. K. at the beginning of 1987 (Morris 1988 a), which means that although manufacturing investment is still a small proportion of total Japanese investment, it accounted for 77% in terms of numbers employed. This contrasts with the situation at the end of 1983 (just over three years earlier) when Japanese manufacturers accounted for less than 6,000 employees – around 38% of the total employed in Japanese companies (Dunning 1986).

There are at least three reasons to expect an increase in the significance of Japanese direct investment. One is the expected inflow of suppliers to the major Japanese corporations – 'follow my leader'. A second is that (at least until Nissan arrived) manufacturing investment commitment has been heavily concentrated in the electronics sector – it is possible that other sectors could follow. Indeed, the big Japanese construction companies, already well established overseas in the Far East and Australia, are now looking further afield – including to Europe (*Financial Times* 18 May 1987). Thirdly, many of the existing Japanese companies in the U. K. are in the process of rapid expansion as their 'toeholds' in the U. K. become major manufacturing concerns.

It must be emphasized that Japanese direct investment and employment in Japanese companies in the U. K. are still low in comparison to, for example, American companies, and how long the conditions supportive of substantial Japanese commitments — the strong yen, trade friction and so on — will continue is debatable. Nonetheless, the long-term commitment of the inwardly investing Japanese companies appears to be there, as is indicated in the following quotation from a speech made by Takao Negishi, European director of Japan's Electronic Industries Association:

We are in a transition period, at the infant stage, and we need time and understanding [...] in the second stage we will be picking up the best brains in the country.

The speech was made at the launch of a pamphlet describing the Japanese contribution to Britain. The pamphlet was sent to all 633 British Members of Parliament.

Japanese manufacturers in the U. K. tend to be more concentrated in the economically depressed regions of the North East and South Wales — over a quarter have chosen Wales alone — though some have preferred investment in new towns such as Livingston in Scotland, Milton Keynes and Telford. Morris (1988 a) noted that all 20 companies in his survey had received grant aid from government sources.

We will now turn attention to the practices these Japanese companies are introducing in the U. K. and address their implications for British industrial culture.

Japanese Practice and Work Culture

Working in a Japanese company appears to be distinctly different from working in a traditional British company. Virtually all the Japanese companies in Britain on which we have evidence share their parent companies' obsessions with keeping quality high whilst minimizing costs due to waste and inefficiency. In practice, this often means the use of total quality principles of responsibility, accountability, flexibility and teamwork, sometimes backed up by systems of production based on a just-in-time approach (Schonberger 1982), which may extend to bought-in parts as well as those made in-house. Typically, work is organized around 'teams' of flexible, multi-skilled workers, with responsibility for their own inspection, routine

maintenance, materials handling and so on — responsibilities which traditionally (in typical British companies) would be those of specialist groups.
Distinctions and demarcations between occupations are hence blurred.

Systems of reward are typically designed to encourage flexible working.
At Toshiba in Plymouth, for instance, there are 18 recognized production
skills, and increments are paid for each one mastered. A formal assessment
of each employee is carried out annually. Other Japanese companies use
systems of performance appraisal, in which employees are evaluated against
a range of criteria. At Komatsu, this procedure is particularly sophisticated
and goes well beyond on-the-job performance. Empolyees are assessed on
their flexibility, teamwork and communications skills, and activities 'beyond the contract' (Komatsu Employee Handbook 1987).

'Bell-to-bell' working and close attention to detail are also characteristic
of Japanese companies operating in the U. K. As a senior official from the
EETPU, who had negotiated a number of agreements with Japanese firms,
remarked to the authors:

> The Japanese believe in bell-to-bell working. They cannot understand the mentality
> of the British people where they have to go to the toilet at times other than their
> natural break because they have conditioned themselves to do that. They can't
> understand why they are not prepared to co-operate with the company and give
> back to the company the two and a half minutes washing time before the end of
> the bell because the Japanese say, 'Well it's our company and that two and a half
> minutes, if added up throughout the week is 70 television sets'. Whichever way
> you look at it they are absolutely right.

In some cases, bell-to-bell working is written into union agreements. The
Nissan-AEU agreement, for example, states 'Employees will be prepared
for work at the start and end of their normal working day/shift' (Wickens
1985). At Nissan, employees typically arrive 15 minutes ahead of start-up
time to don the company uniform, and each shift begins with a meeting
between production teams and their supervisors to discuss yesterday's
achievements, mistakes and problems and the new day's targets (*Independent* 11 February 1988). A supervisor from Komatsu quoted in a recent TV
documentary also felt that such discipline was important in Japanese
companies' success, going so far as to say that:

> All that the British worker has got to do to work to the Japanese system is to
> work during the time he is paid [...] once the British worker has done that he has
> fulfilled the Japanese system (BBC 1987).

White and Trevor (1983) noted much greater attention paid to minor
details in the production process. Takamiya (1981), contrasting British and
Japanese practice in printed circuit board assembly, stated that while the
British strategy to safeguard quality was to buy an extremely sophisticated

and expensive testing machine, the Japanese approach was to organize assembly into three-worker teams, with two workers inserting components and one visually checking and correcting. He recounts:

Every movement of the operators is closely watched and constantly improved upon. Every mistake they make is constantly and individually fed back to them verbally by supervisors, formally by tables and graphs displayed in front of them and visually by supervisors taking them to the other production section where their mistake is causing trouble (Takamiya 1981: 8).

Many accounts suggest that discipline on the shopfloor is much tighter, which manifests itself in a variety of ways. Reitsperger (1986) found that Japanese TV companies in Britain exacted much stricter work discipline, discouraged social interaction of semi-skilled workers on the assembly line and meticulously enforced work standards and procedures in comparison to equivalent British and American companies. Takamiya (1981: 9), also comparing Japanese with British and American firms, noted:

While both British and American companies allow eating, drinking and smoking on the shopfloor, the Japanese strictly prohibit such activities even during breaks. Sometimes chatting can be cause for a warning.

Many Japanese companies utilize public displays of individual and group performance, the effect of which might be to intensify peer pressure to produce up to standard. For instance, at Mitsubishi's electronics plant at Livingston new town, the weekly performance ratings of operators are displayed on charts above their heads, and charts at the end of assembly lines show the performances of work teams with regard to attendance, housekeeping and defect rates (*Financial Times* 18 January 1988).

Hence while work organization in Japanese companies entails an 'enrichment' of work for many operators because of job rotation and multi-skilling, the salience of craft skills is reduced, and an intensification of work takes place with a heightened accountability for all.

Of course, because Japanese companies tend to push responsibility and authority for output and quality away from specialists and downwards from middle management to the level of the work team, their dependence on workers is heightened. Mere absenteeism or lack of cooperation regarding task allocation or tea breaks could potentially cause major problems. It is not surprising, therefore, that the Japanese take serious consideration of the 'cultural supports' necessary for this reliance. Their approach to industrial relations and trade unions is obviously important here, and this will be considered in detail below. Japanese companies also pay attention to creating the 'right attitudes' through careful selection, offering high job security, creating direct communication channels and deliberately avoiding real and symbolic distinctions between 'them and us'.

Morris (1988 b) noted that 15 out of 20 Japanese companies approached in his survey recruited young, unskilled labour — generally school leavers — to perform production jobs. The commercial director of Livingston Development Corporation refers to a preference on the part of newly-investing companies for 'uncontaminated' labour (*Financial Times* 18 January 1988). Pang (1987) found a similar preference for raw recruits in 7 out of 11 companies surveyed, although there was a marked tendency for managerial talent to be 'bought in'. This emphasis may be partly explained by the generally low skill levels required in many of these companies, but also, we suspect, due to a desire to have a reasonably compliant and flexible workforce. For instance, NEC's personnel manager, responsible for the employment of 280 operators whose average age is 18.5, argued that the company needed a young workforce willing to undergo frequent training. As he put it: 'We cannot offer them a long-term job. But we are guaranteeing them long-term employment'.

It is possible that the emphasis on raw recruits at all levels may increase as Japanese companies establish themselves and have to rely less on externally acquired professionals and skilled workers. Certainly a strong internal training capability is being developed within these companies (Gleave 1987, Pang 1987). One exception to the 'raw recruit' policy is Takiron, a Japanese company established in Wales with a single union agreement with the Transport and General Workers Union (TGWU). Their policy is to recruit young married men because of their ability to work shifts (Gleave 1987).

Whether or not Japanese companies have this in mind, the effect is to take on a workforce with little previous work experience, and hence free from 'unsuitable' working habits which might not fit the company culture. Neither is it likely for such a workforce to have any previous experience of, or involvement in, trade union activity of any kind. Hence recruits are more easily socialized into the ways of the company and, if the company does have a trade union, more easily socialized into cooperative union-management relations. Some companies, of which Komatsu and Nissan are examples, make use of a variety of attitude tests in their selection procedures.

Following recruitment, a company-organized induction programme typically awaits the candidates in Japanese companies in Britain (Gleave 1987), the length of which varies from company to company. At Matsushita's Panasonic plant in Cardiff the formal induction lasts only one day, for instance, whereas at Komatsu in Sunderland there are 10 full day sessions spread over the first ten weeks at work, including Japan familiarization courses. Further initial socialization is typically given with immediate on-the-job training in a variety of tasks or jobs. At Mazak, the Japanese machine tool plant in Worcester, this involves the trainee submitting weekly reports on progress, serving to impress the importance of flexible working on the recruit.

Out of 22 companies on which we have the information, 73% offer high job security to their core workers although, as in Japan, this is a matter of policy rather than a contractual obligation. At the same time about one third of Japanese companies in Britain (out of the 21 on which we have the information) make substantial use (10% plus) of temporary workers. Interestingly, Nissan was the first company in the U. K. to use temporary workers on automobile assembly lines since the 1940s (*Financial Times* 16 February 1987). Nissan's policy is to develop a 'reservoir' of trained temporary labour — about 8 − 9% of the total workforce — to be used from May to July during the run-up to peak demand in August (*Financial Times* 10 February 1988). In Japan such peripheral workers provide 'rings of defence' for the core workforce, and it appears that at least some Japanese companies utilize this practice in the U. K.

In-company communications (described in the section on unions below), single status facilities and the provision of staff benefits for blue-collar workers may further contribute to the sorts of attitudes desired by Japanese companies in the U. K. The available evidence suggests widespread usage of these practices. Companies regard these practices favourably according to our survey evidence, although other evidence suggests the picture is a little more mixed lower down the organization. Single status appears to have been generally welcomed by direct employees and by trade unions, although some of its trappings — for example the wearing of uniforms — have not always been wholeheartedly appreciated. At Matsushita in Cardiff, for example, some of the female administrative workers were reluctant to wear uniforms as they considered them unflattering and, at Hoya, the managing director was reported as having a problem convincing a lorry driver that he was in fact the managing director, on account of the uniform he was wearing (Gleave 1987).

Single status is generally welcomed by those who would otherwise be well down the status hierarchy, but what about those who would traditionally be at an advantage status-wise? In general, this does not appear to have caused many problems, although there are signs from some of the longer established Japanese companies that the homogeneity generated by single status tends to be eroded over time, partly due to the existence of status differentials in the wider industrial environment. Commenting on the situation at a TV manufacturer, a trade union official remarked to us:

When senior management are taken on they ask 'What's the pension scheme? — Is there a special incentive scheme?' They are told that it's the same as the guy on the shopfloor. So there is a little bit of change and resentment about the old British type of understanding about perks creeping back into the company.

The case of a newly appointed supervisor at Komatsu, ruefully reflecting on how he used to dream about the day he would come to work in a suit and tie (BBC 1987), provides another example of this sentiment and, at Mitsubishi, managers have 'quietly' ceased wearing uniforms (*Financial Times* 18 January 1988). We have no information on managerial turnover in the Japanese companies, but one might expect it to be relatively high unless the lack of status-related rewards is compensated for by more pronounced salary differentials. Pang and Oliver (1988) found that 7 Japanese companies out of a sample of 11 offered salaries and wages greater than those offered by comparable local firms; the other four all claimed to offer rates which were the same.

To summarize, Japanese manufacturers operating in the U.K. provide a different experience of work to that found in traditional U.K. manufacturing organizations. Work is bell-to-bell, more intense than in traditional British companies, and workers are expected to be dependable, flexible, dedicated and loyal to the company rather than the union or craft or professional specialism. Rigorous selection emphasizing 'attitudes', together with induction programmes, training in a variety of skills, single status conditions, permanent employment and frequent and direct communications all contribute towards the new work culture.

Of course, management-union relations must also be in line with the demands of such a work culture, and it is to these which we will now turn.

Trade Unionism

According to Takao Negishi, European director of the Japanese Electronic Industries Association, management and workers in Japan

have a fundamentally different attitude. They believe they are all on the same ship and if it runs into storms they all fight them together. Maybe this sense should be formed, slowly but steadily, in the frame of manufacturing in Britain (quoted in *Western Mail* 22 January 1988).

Of the 31 Japanese companies on which we have information, 21 (68%) recognize trade unions. This indicates a unionization rate similar to that for British manufacturing as a whole. Union densities — on average around 60% — are also similar to those in companies long established in Britain. A third point of similarity relates to the fact that newly investing Japanese companies tend to recognize unions in areas with union traditions (9 out of 11 in Wales for instance) but to avoid trade unions when locating in new towns such as Milton Keynes, Telford and Livingston. However, the conditions attached to recognition are stringent, and the management-union relation typically stands in marked contrast to anything seen in U.K. manufacturing previously. The implication is the emergence of a different form of trade unionism in British manufacturing industry.

The first point to note is that Japanese companies, when they do allow unionization, invariably go for single union deals, mostly with the 'new realist' Electricians (EETPU) and Engineers (AEU) unions. An exception is one Japanese company which recognizes seven unions, though in this case the company 'inherited' its industrial relations after a takeover. With trade union power and membership on the decline in the 1980s (Beaumont 1987), Japanese companies have been able to take advantage of bitter inter-union rivalry over membership and gain deals with single unions which stipulate conditions conducive to the effective operation of Japanese-style production and working practices. In an interview with the authors a GMB officer commented:

This (membership problem) is what leads trade unions to sign these sorts of agreements − the chase, the desperate need for membership − but then the Nissan's and Hitachi's make them a waste of time altogether.

At the turn of the decade the EETPU found itself offering the sorts of union relationship desired by Japanese companies, and the pioneering deal was that signed by Toshiba and the EETPU in 1981 (Gregory 1986). Since then other Japanese companies have achieved similar deals, mostly with the EETPU, but notably also with the AEU, the General and Municipal Workers Union (GMB) and even the antagonistic Transport and General Workers Union (TGWU).

Reports by the TGWU (1987) and Kelly (1987) suggest that union power will be enhanced with the use of flexible work practices − a mere refusal to be flexible becoming a significant power resource in bargaining. However, it is exactly such a possibility that the deals typically address. A single union representing all employees rather than multiple unions representing craft and occupational groups, for instance, is aimed at enabling flexibility and preventing demarcations. In most agreements (indeed in all the agreements we have seen) flexible work practices are actually stipulated and agreed by the union. A typical statement in this regard is the one found in the agreement between Komatsu and the AEU. This agrees:

Complete flexibility and mobility of employees; changes in processes and practices will be introduced to increase competitiveness and that these will improve productivity and affect manning levels. To achieve such change employees will work as required by the company and participate in the training of themselves or other employees as required; Manning levels will be determined by the company using appropriate industrial engineering and manpower planning techniques.

Such an establishment of managerial prerogatives over labour deployment precludes the threat of withdrawal of cooperation over flexible working as a bargaining tactic — at least at an official level.

The deals are also remarkable for their unitarist ideological prefaces which appear to redefine the role of trade unions as *partner in commercial success* rather than *company adversary*. Toshiba's agreement with the EETPU, for instance, reads:

The company [...] and the trade union [...] in reaching this agreement wish to establish and operate policies and procedures which will ensure that the company and its employees enjoy a harmonious relationship to their mutual benefit. Both parties recognize, in this joint approach, that the security of employment and advancement of all employees can only be through the company's commercial success and through the common purpose and involvement of all employees in the company's activities.

'Harmony', 'mutual beneficence' and 'commitment to company success' feature prominently in all the recognition agreements signed by Japanese companies which the authors have seen. The EETPU and MATSA (the GMB's white-collar section) actually emphasize 'realism' and 'mutuality' in the model agreements which they offer to potential companies.

The most contentious aspect of the deals is the procedures which make strike action — at least official action — unlikely. Indeed, at least 9 agreements signed by Japanese companies have a provision for *binding arbitration* which explicitly rules out strikes or any other form of official industrial action. Since the first strike-free deal was signed by the Japanese company Toshiba in 1981, there has not yet been a case where a dispute has led to arbitration. Nonetheless, it is this agreement to abandon strike action as a weapon which has led to most criticism of the deals within the trade union movement, some trade union leaders referring to 'loathsome alliances' and 'yellow deals' between 'crawling unions' and 'samurai managements' with the blessing of Mrs Thatcher and in the context of the creation of a 'coolie economy' where democratic rights are on the wane.

Important as it is, it seems to the authors that probably the most fundamental problem facing unions signing agreements with Japanese companies is not the binding arbitration clause, but the insistence on the establishment, recognition and acceptance of extensive and direct management-worker communications, and in particular the Company Advisory Board (CoAB). 11 out of 20 Japanese companies in Britain on which we have the information have CoABs, and 8 of these are also unionized. In some cases

CoABs may be deliberately being used to prevent trade union penetration. At Mitsubishi, for instance, approaches for recognition by the EETPU were rebutted by the company on the grounds that its elected staff consultative committee eliminated the need for union recognition (*Financial Times* 18 January 1988). More often, however, CoABs and unions co-exist.

The CoAB appears under a variety of names such as company council (Nissan), company members board (Hitachi), advisory committee (Orion), staff council (Kyushu Matsushita), or advisory council (Komatsu). What they share in common is that first, unlike the Joint Consultative Committee (JCC), its elected employee representatives (elections are normally by secret ballot) are not necessarily shop stewards, nor necessarily trade union members, and are chosen by non-union employees as well as union members. Second, also unlike Britain's traditional JCCs which normally limit themselves to non-collective bargaining issues (Marchington and Armstrong 1986), CoABs typically go beyond 'tea and toilets', providing a forum for negotiations on pay and conditions. Hence they break down the traditional distinction between consultation and bargaining. For instance, the EETPU's agreements with Hitachi, Inmos, Yuasa Battery, Orion and Kyushu Matsushita, all place responsibility for the first stage in collective bargaining on the CoAB. If agreement is achieved, then the union and the company consider the CoAB's recommendations, and union involvement in negotiation begins only if either party do not accept the recommendation. Provision for secret ballots is typically made towards the latter stages of procedure and, as described, procedure often ends with binding arbitration.

In these circumstances the role of the trade union representative is called into question. The Toshiba agreement with the EETPU makes this clear in stating that:

The function of the (union) representative will be *to represent trade union members on those issues which cannot be resolved through the Company Advisory Board* and to represent individual members of the trade union in cases of individual grievances, discipline or other related matters. [Emphasis added.]

Toshiba also request new union representatives to sign a form, together with the trade union official and personnel manager, stating:

It is recognized that the Company Advisory Board is the best and first means of resolving all collective issues between the company and its employees, and *the representative fully supports and encourages the role of the Company Advisory Board* in the conduct of relationships between the company and its employees. [Emphasis added.]

The shift of important responsibilities from shop stewards to CoABs which is typical of the new realist deal has been the subject of criticism. Crowther and Garrahan (1988), in describing Nissan's deal with the AEU, claim that

it allows virtually no independent role for shop stewards, and whilst it appears that the company does not intend to actively obstruct union activities, the mechanisms for representation are highly supportive of non-union participation.

This is one explanation, they suggest, for the low membership density at Nissan, claimed by some to be no more than 10% and at most to be 30%. On the other hand, membership densities are normally much higher, and it should be pointed out that, in signing single union deals with various companies, the EETPU has often persuaded managements to encourage union membership. This is achieved largely through managements offering union membership forms and displaying positive attitudes to the union to new recruits, and through the provision of 'check-off' arrangements. (A check-off facility means that union subscriptions are automatically deducted from union member's pay until the member gives written notice that it should cease — this makes withdrawal from union membership due to allowing subscriptions to lapse impossible and eases the burden of the shop steward as money collector.) A commitment to company encouragement of union membership is actually written into the deals with Yuasa, Hitachi and Orion, and Kyushu Matsushita state that they will provide check-off facilities.

Linn (1986: 28), in a detailed study of the new realist deal between the TGWU and Norsk-Hydro in Humberside (a company attempting to emulate Japanese industrial relations practice), concisely summarizes the problems for trade union organization:

[...] should the TGWU change its stewards' constituencies to correspond with those of the advisory council? Should it persist in putting up candidates for the advisory council or should it play a very low profile in that arena, to effectively allow the 'supervisory types' that the ex-TGWU convenors believe will dominate the employee constituencies to do so, and thereby discredit it in the eyes of the workforce? Is the union organization equipped to counter the arguments of those who will start to question why they should join the union when they can have a say in collective issues through their representative on the advisory council?

A defence of the CoAB often posited by the 'new realist' camp in the trade union movement is that it is a consultative mechanism which makes available company information on important matters which companies in the U.K. have tended to keep secret. Kyushu Matsushita state in their agreement that the staff council is to be used for the provision of information and consultation on 'company investment and business plans' and 'company operating efficiency and manpower plans' as well as terms and conditions, pay and benefits, and health and safety. A high level of access to information normally the sole preserve of managements is, like single status arrangements, considered quite a coup by EETPU leaders, and further justification for the new realist deal. (Critics point out that the seriousness and extent of information provision remain dependent on the goodwill of management.)

The existence of company advisory boards is particularly problematic for unions because ignoring them could lead to marginalization, while attempting to use them to increase union influence (by seeking election of union representatives to the board), implies incorporation. From the point of view of the company seeking avoidance of adversarial labour relations, this situation is ideal, for in effect the union becomes *voluntarily* incorporated — even if the option is marginalization.

Such deals have been defended by 'new realists' in the trade union movement, and particularly by leaders of the EETPU, on the grounds that the alternative might be no union at all, and also that there are positive benefits in the form of open and extensive consultation, single status terms and conditions, and a company commitment to training in a range of skills (Bassett 1986, Bevan 1987). The debate, of course, continues. What is clear is that the form of trade unionism implied by the deals is one radically different to traditional British trade unionism, one which is company-based, which denies fundamental conflicts of interest between labour and capital, and which implies an erosion of union independence.

Relations with External Agencies

Our survey evidence shows that Japanese companies in the U.K. have mostly attempted to implement what Dore refers to as 'obligational contracting'. In return for long-term contracts with their primary suppliers Japanese companies expect low prices, high quality and reliability. This contrasts with the typical British use of multiple-sourcing, price competition and heavy goods-inward inspection as strategies for handling supplies. The Japanese strategy implies close collaboration with suppliers. As a spokesman for a company supplying Komatsu commented:

The Japanese tend to camp out on your doorstep. We've got English firms that we see once or twice a year [...]. It's nothing for the Japanese to turn up two, three, four times a day (BBC 1987).

This close relationship comes with buyer influence over policies on pricing and operations, and, some have suggested, an influence over personnel management and industrial relations. A company requiring goods of assured quality (perhaps also delivered just-in-time and single sourced) is obviously highly dependent on its suppliers, so such attempts at influence are to be expected. McFadden and Towler (1987) claim that Nissan lists in its criteria for selection of primary suppliers industrial relations, working practices and strike record. The implication is that Japanese direct influence over industrial relations could go beyond the immediate organization.

By the same logic, it makes sense for such organizations to seek predictability from *all* constituents or 'stakeholders'. Crowther and Garrahan (1988) suggest that Nissan took advantage of its ability to influence the local authority in the North East and thereby secure, at low cost, the land necessary for the creation of a 'spatially concentrated' production arrangement facilitative of just-in-time supplies. They claim there was

a concerted effort by local 'power brokers' (regional government officials, elected local councillors, the Washington New Town Development Corporation, private sector firms, regional trade unionists and the media) to conform with the pattern *determined by* Nissan (Crowther and Garrahan 1988: 52. Authors' emphasis).

The authors' own interviews with representatives of the Wales TUC, the Welsh Development Agency, the Welsh branch of ACAS and the Wales CBI also revealed an orchestrated effort to create the conditions for the attraction of Japanese capital to Wales. In one glossy publication targeted at inward investors, the Wales TUC general secretary writes:

[...] from the basis that industrial disruption is contrary to the interests of management, the workforce, the company as a whole [...] I would ask you to consider myself and my trade union colleagues as potential allies should you be considering investment in Wales, a country within the U.K. where industrial relations are making a positive contribution towards securing economic success (ACAS/WINvest 1986).

In the same publication the Wales CBI and ACAS make remarks encouraging potential inward investors and in another WINvest (1986) publication (WINvest is the Welsh inward investment agency), a Sony representative is quoted as saying:

It is possible to have access to top government officials, both in business and socially, on an almost day-to-day basis. Good relations can be built up very easily.

And another Japanese manager says: "South Wales is similar to Japan in some ways as regards the people and the environment."

The extent of influence of Japanese companies over local 'power brokers' is unclear, though certainly the relevant institutions do appear to have gone out of their way to provide a welcome to the Japanese and to have collaborated in ensuring Japanese needs are met. Power broker collaboration, and by implication the emergence of a civic-business elite, would, like cooperative union-management relations, represent a departure from typical 'arms length' relationships in post-war Britain, though there were a few exceptions to this rule before the Japanese became significant investors in the U. K. (Harvey, Smith and Wilkinson 1984).

The extension of corporate influence to external constituents, to the extent that it is significant, may be welcomed by many, due to its implications of cooperation and common purpose. Critics such as Bonis view this situation less favourably:

A kind of disguised Imperialism results when the organization seeks to control the external elements: customers, suppliers, subcontractors, members of other organizations, politicians and political organizations, the press, public opinion, pressure groups [...] (Bonis 1980: 163).

A final point of importance regarding Japanese direct manufacturing investment in the U. K. is the apparently long-term perspectives which the Japanese have brought with them. This is reflected in their aggressive marketing strategies, in their slow and careful decision making over location and in the commitment they are making to internal training and policies of long-term employment. This long-term perspective relates, of course, to the guidance of MITI and the Ministry of Finance in Japan and to the long-term, low interest loans available to Japanese manufacturers from financial institutions. The practices brought by the Japanese to the U. K. rely heavily, then, on the ability to take a long-term perspective. This contrasts with the situation of the typical British company which is heavily reliant on the stock market and ploughed-back profit as sources of investment, which means relatively short-term horizons and a *modus operandi* of short-term profit rather than long-term growth (Ackroyd et al. 1988). This implies that British *economic* culture is not currently in tune with the changes being attempted by the major manufacturing companies.

Complimentary to Japanese 'long-termism' is the emphasis placed by Japanese companies on strategic marketing. Japanese strategic marketing places a strong emphasis on market share (Wong, Saunders and Doyle 1987). Market dominance typically allows one higher margins (by increasing the barriers to entry of that market), which gives a company the elbow room to pay premium salaries, provide staff benefits and high job security for core workers and so on. Once in this position a company may be in a self-sustaining cycle. Comments such as "the Japanese have 'market share' tatooed across their hearts" (made to one of the authors by a director of an inward investment agency) make sense in this context.

To summarize the cultural consequences of direct Japanese manufacturing investment in the U. K., there is a very different experience of work which is more intense and disciplined, but at the same time implies wider skills and responsibilities for shopfloor workers, a dispersal of specialists and a delegation of authority to the level of the work team; employment and personnel practices are more paternalistic in an attempt to create loyalty and commitment; trade unionism takes on a different form, with representation at company rather than occupational level and with leaders acting not as adversaries but as partners in 'mutually beneficial' collaboration; and there is the possibility (though there is less evidence in this regard) that collaboration with external agencies becomes more extensive.

The critics see Japanese practice as illiberal — as a set of insidious control devices. The advocates see the strengthening of company-constituent relations as morally desirable. As Peter Wickens, Nissan U. K.'s personnel director, put it:

It is the concept of loyalty to the company which so wrankles left wing opponents of these new initiatives. Failing to realize that the intention is that all shall benefit, they attack what they believe are companies' attempts to usurp the traditional loyalty of workers to union [...]. Companies *do* seek employee loyalty and they *do* want to develop an environment where industrial action is inconceivable! (Wickens 1987).

What is clear is that to the extent that Japanese companies are successful in creating the close and collaborative relations with their constituents which they clearly desire, independent power bases in British society will be eroded.

Japanese companies, however, together employ less people than, say, Ford alone. So is Japanese influence on British industrial culture really of great import? The answer, according to survey and other findings on British and other Western companies in the U. K. attempting to emulate Japanese practices, is clearly yes.

Emulation of Japanese Practice

The establishment of manufacturing facilities in the North East of England by Nissan has laid bare the differences in productivity, performance and competitiveness between Japanese corporations and those British and foreign ones already operating in the U. K. The labour content of a Nissan car is claimed to be US $ 550 compared with US $ 890 from Ford at Halewood (*Independent* 11 February 1988), and Vauxhall Motors chairman John Bagshaw has suggested a cost advantage by the new Nissan plant over Vauxhall's British operations of between G. B. Stirling 250 and G. B. Stirling 500 per car (*Guardian* 16 December 1986). Such direct competition appears to have focused the minds of British managements and the response is very clearly to ape Japanese-style production and working practices. 'Adapt or die' has become the slogan of Britain's manufacturers, and this ultimatum is being presented to workforces and unions across the U. K.

Our survey of manufacturers appearing in the 1986 *Times 1,000* list (reported in Oliver and Wilkinson 1988) indicated a wave of attempts across all sectors to implement Japanese-style manufacturing and working practices over the last few years. Over 60% of the companies surveyed either used or were planning the introduction of Japanese-style practices such as JIT production, JIT supplies and total quality control techniques and, even more had recently implemented, or were planning, Japanese-style working practices such as group working and flexible labour deployment. These results are consistent with those of a similar survey reported by Voss and Robinson (1987).

What most emulating companies appear not to have done, yet, however, is to have introduced the 'cultural supports' necessary to encourage the working practices and shopfloor behaviour achieved by Japanese companies. These can be difficult to achieve on established production sites with established traditions and vested interests. The problems faced by emulating companies on this count were demonstrated clearly in a strike by Ford's blue-collar workers at the beginning of 1988. The strike was widely reported as being as much to do with the imposition of Japanese-style working practices as it was about pay, a typical picket line slogan being 'We're Brits not Nips'. At the time of writing, blue-collar workers had resumed work after management had conceded to negotiate and consult over changing work practices, but supervisors and other white-collar staffs were expressing their own concerns that the new working practices implied a dilution of authority and responsibility. Ironically, the strike had a pervasive and immediate impact on Ford across Europe because they had already implemented Japanese-style single sourcing policies, tightly integrating their European operations (*Independent* 17 February 1988). Clearly, Ford has not yet generated the cultural supports necessary for such a system of production. Difficulties in creating work cultures supportive of Japanese levels of quality and productivity are also documented by Turnbull (1986) regarding Lucas Electrical (automotive components) and by Smith (1988) in his study of the Rover Car group. Rover have introduced an extensive induction programme to encourage involvement in the company. Smith recounts

[...] that during the induction course (at Rover) a number of references to Japan [...] recalled the last war and, implicitly, the British way of life being defended. It was generally acknowledged that the home came before the company; that you worked for money and not out of slavish devotion; and that when holiday time came round you took your full entitlement. One participant remarked to murmurs of assent that his mortgage was with the Halifax, not the Rover group.

The intention to change the cultural base of British manufacturing is there, at least at the level of the firm, though most apparent successes documented so far appear to have occurred under threat of closure or investment strike. At GM's Bedford van plant for instance, acceptance of a company advisory board independent of the trade unions, a breakdown of demarcations, the establishment of managerial prerogatives over flexible labour deployment and management's right to use temporary workers and subcontractors when considered appropriate, was gained under threat of an investment strike by the Japanese partner in the joint venture, Isuzu (*Financial Times* 6 June 1987). Similarly, luxury coach manufacturer Plaxtons insisted on a no-strike flexibility package with its four unions before giving the go-ahead for a G. B. Stirling 1.25 million investment programme (*Financial Times* 26 October 1987). A squeeze on profits and intense international competition led AB electronics to embark on a strategy of spinning off business units to greenfield sites, with single status facilities and only one union for each site. The managing director concluded that:

We will never willingly start up another venture with a multiplicity of unions and I would make the recommendation to any inward investor that he should always seek to reach agreement on representation with one union (Merrette 1987).

Perhaps the biggest problem facing emulating companies in their adoption of Japanese-style methods, however, comes from their typically short-term horizons. Long-term, low interest financing would be useful for the appropriate marketing strategy, for the training and development required and for the long-term relationships among the organization and its constituents which is implied. Interestingly, a recent report by the Manpower Services Commission (1987) contrasted 'technology-driven' Japanese companies with their 'finance-driven' British counterparts. This raises questions of government support to industry, and relations between manufacturing and finance capital.

The state has been pro-active in attracting foreign investors to the U. K. – including Nissan. But the government implies that British businesses must raise their rates of return to investors if they are to attract capital – it's up to them. Profits for manufacturing industry have significantly increased during the 1980s, which can only help in giving firms the opportunity to look to the longer term, and the welfare state has been deliberately eroded, which theoretically could heighten the salience of company paternalism as a strategy for generating employee dependence and loyalty. However, a recent report by the National Institute (reported in *Financial Times* 28 May 1987) states that Britain's 'moderately favourable' productivity performance in the 1980s still leaves a 'formidable' gap with its rivals. That of Japan and West Germany, for instance, is around 80 per cent higher. In contrast, the same report showed Britain a clear second bottom (after Ireland in a league table of 12 industrial nations) in terms of unit hourly labour costs. America's were 61% higher and Japan's 29%. The report concluded the Britain's advantage of very cheap labour was 'more than offset' by very low productivity. The productivity improvements which come with Japanese-style practice are unlikely to be attained in companies unwilling or unable to give long-term commitments. These are essential if training and development programmes are not to be seen as mere 'costs', and probably equally important in gaining loyalty and dedication from employees and other company constituents. Hence the refusal of the present government to intervene in industry (apart from labour legislation) could provide the single biggest obstacle to British companies' attempts to emulate Japanese-style practice.

A recent House of Lords Select Committee advocated a package of measures which, it seems to the authors, would 'fit' the attempts of British companies to implement the changes to their organizational cultures which they seek. The package includes a new 'attitude' to manufacturing, to be gained through youth 'inculcation' and persuading 'all in industry' that they 'share a common interest in improving the productivity of British industry'; MITI-style guidance and 'common assumption' creation; subsidized loans to manufacturing industry; special government support to earmarked industries and projects; infrastructure improvements; measures to improve manufacturing management; and a shift from the 'tyranny' of quarterly financial reporting. The government was dismissive of the report (Coates and Hillard 1987). It is something of an irony then, that a government which welcomed the arrival of Nissan and pointed to the company as providing model work practices appears not to be more actively supporting firms − beyond labour legislation − in their efforts to introduce such practices.

Similar measures have been advocated by the past leader of the Social Democratic Party, David Owen, and by the 1988 Labour Party leadership. Were these parties to get into power, it is not clear whether the route pursued would best be described as 'authoritarian' or 'social democratic' (see Clegg et al., this volume).

Conclusions

British industrial culture is presently undergoing radical change due to the widespread introduction of new production, personnel and industrial relations practices. Led by Japanese companies investing in the U.K. which provide both the competitive spur and the model to be emulated, manu-facturing organizations are changing their approach to asset (including human asset) management and transforming the way in which they run their businesses. The new production and working practices entail a shift towards flexibility and teamwork within semi-autonomous groups and the transfer of specialist and supervisory responsibilities to this level; increasing asset utilization also means an intensification of work with bell-to-bell discipline. The personnel practices which provide the 'cultural supports' to such work practices are also peculiar to recent British industrial culture. Rigorous selection and appraisals, which take account of personality and biographical factors, company-organized induction and socialization, pol-icies of long-term employment and internal training and promotion, are all aimed at contributing towards a homogeneity of goals and an identi-fication with the company rather than the trade union or professional association. Trade unions themselves become incorporated, if not margin-alized, and single unions represent all employees in the company rather than the craft or occupational group. Comparisons with enterprise unions in Japan are not far-fetched. Further research is necessary to uncover the extent to which 'power broker collaboration' is increasing, but this is implied by the new management practices.

How far the erosion of independence of individuals and institutions (es-pecially unions) in the U. K. may go is unclear. Not surprisingly there is some cynicism among British workers towards company paternalism, and the Ford strike alone makes it clear that unions' loss of membership and power in the 1980s has not yet led to their complete emasculation. Equally, and perhaps ironically, the government's laissez-faire economic policies do not appear to be helping British-owned companies in their attempts to emulate the Japanese. On the other hand, companies' 'adapt or die' imperative is a powerful ideological counter to the slogan 'We're Brits not Nips', and the determination to force through change at the level of the firm is unequivocal.

References

ACAS/WINvest (1986): *Successful industrial relations: the experience of overseas companies in Wales*, Cardiff: ACAS Wales.

Ackroyd, Stephen, Gibson Burrell, Michael Hughes and Alan Whitaker (1988): The Japanization of British industry? *Industrial Relations Journal* 19, 1: 11 – 23.

Anglo-Japan Economic Institute (1987): *News and views from Japan 268*, London: Anglo-Japan Economic Institute.

Bassett, Philip (1986): *Strike-free: The new industrial relations in Britain*, London: Macmillan.

BBC [British Broadcasting Service] (1987): *Chopsticks, bulldozers and Newcastle brown*, London: British Broadcasting Corporation.

Beaumont, Philip (1987): *The decline of trade union organization*, London: Croom Helm.

Bevan, Wyn (1987): Creating a no-strike environment: the trade union view, Text of a speech given to the CBI Conference on Strike-free Deals, London, 24 June 1987.

Bonis, John (1980): Organization and environment, in: M. Lockett and R. Spear (eds.), *Organizations as systems*, 163, Milton Keynes: Open University Press.

Coates, David and John Hillard (1987): *The economic revival of modern Britain*, Aldershot: Edward Elgar.

Crowther, Stuart and Philip Garrahan (1988): Invitation to Sunderland: corporate power and the local economy, *Industrial Relations Journal* 19, 1: 51 – 59.

Dunning, John (1986): *Japanese participation in British industry*, London: Croom Helm.

Gleave, Simon (1987): How Japanese are Japanese factories in Britain? A study of Japanese personnel management in Japan and Britain, MBA dissertation, Cardiff Business School.

Gregory, Martin (1986): The no-strike deal in action, *Personnel Management* 18, December, 30 – 34.

Harvey, Brian, Stephen Smith and Barry Wilkinson (1984): *Managers and corporate social policy*, London: Macmillan.

Kelly, John (1987): *Labour and the union*, London: Verso.

Komatsu U. K. Ltd. (1987): *Komatsu employee handbook*, Birtley, England: Komatsu U. K. Ltd.

Linn, Ian (1986): *Single union deals: a case study of the Norsk Hydro Plant at Immingham, Humberside,* Barnsley: Northern College in Association with TGWU Region 10.

Manpower Services Commission (1987): *Management development and technological innovation in Japan*, London: Manpower Services Commission.

Marchington, Michael and Roger Armstrong (1986): The nature of the new joint consultation, *Industrial Relations Journal* 17, 2: 158 – 170.

McFadden, Ian and David Towler (1987): Nissan – the challenge to the trade union movement, Report to the Northern Regional TUC, April.

Merrette, Edwin (1987): Industrial change: a practical experience, Paper presented to the ACAS Wales Conference on Industrial Change, Swansea, Wales, 11 November.

Morris, Jon (1988 a): The who, why and where of Japanese manufacturing investment in the U. K., *Industrial Relations Journal* 19, 1: 31 – 40.

Morris, Jon (1989): *Japan into Europe! The impact of Japanese manufacturing in the EEC*, London: Wheatsheaf.

Oliver, Nick and Barry Wilkinson (1988): Manufacturing and personnel strategy in Western and Japanese-owned companies in Britain, Cardiff, Cardiff Business School Occasional Paper.

Pang, Ken Khi (1987): Japanese management practices in overseas subsidiaries: A case approach, MBA dissertation, Cardiff Business School.

Pang, Ken Khi and Nick Oliver (1988): Personnel strategy in eleven Japanese manufacturing companies in the U. K., *Personnel Review* 17, 3: 16–21.

Reitsperger, Wolf (1986): Japanese management: coping with British industrial relations, *Journal of Management Studies* 23, 1: 72–88.

Schonberger, Richard (1982): *Japanese manufacturing techniques*, New York: The Free Press.

Smith, Dennis (1988): The Japanese example in South West Birmingham, *Industrial Relations Journal* 19, 1: 41–50.

Takamiya, Makoto (1981): Japanese multinationals in Europe: international operations and their public policy implications, *Columbia Journal of World Business* Summer: 5–17.

TGWU [Transport and General Workers Union and Northern College Research Unit] (1987): *Change at work*, London: TGWU.

Turnbull, Peter (1988): The limits to Japanization − just-in-time, labour relations and the U. K. automotive industry, *New Technology, Work and Employment* 3/1: 7–20.

Voss, Christopher and Stephen Robinson (1987): The application of just-in-time techniques, *International Journal of Operations and Production Management* 7, 4: 46–52.

White, Michael and Malcolm Trevor (1983): *Under Japanese management*, London: Heinemann.

Wickens, Peter (1985): Nissan: The Thinking Behind the Union Agreement, *Personnel Management* August: 18–21.

Wickens, Peter (1987): *The road to Nissan*, London: Macmillan.

WINvest (1986): *The Japanese experience in Wales*, Publisher: WINvest, Cardiff. (Report prepared by: Arthur D. Little Ltd.)

Wong, Veronica, John Saunders and Peter Doyle (1987): Japanese marketing strategies in the United Kingdom, *Long Range Planning* 20, 6: 54–63.

The Dwarves of Capitalism:
The Structure of Production
and the Economic Culture
of the Small Manufacturing Firm

Jane Marceau

Introduction

Once thought to be destined to extinction, the small firm sector has made a comeback in OECD countries. In the rhetoric of researchers and politicians alike the dwarves of capitalism have taken on some of the giants' cast-off clothing. The fuddy-duddy image of the corner store and the black oil of the welding workshop have been replaced in the public mind by the spark and energy emanating from the high-technology whizz kids, who create not only new products but also new urban spaces such as Silicon Valley in the USA, the M4 corridor in England and 'Silicon Glen' in Scotland. The literature now abounds with research and reports arguing the importance of the small manufacturing firm's place in industrial capitalism and advocating greater attention to the small entrepreneur in the economic and social policies of governments of many hues. Questions asked by observers cover many issues: are small firms the product leaders of the future? the saviours of depressed regions? the source of the constant innovation which means that in future central industries will not 'mature' and their workforces and regions decline? the source of the employment we need to rescue the public coffers from the 'crisis' of the welfare state? (see, for example, Fothergill and Gudgin 1982, Keeble and Wever 1986, Oakey 1984, Rothwell and Zegveld 1982, Storey 1982 and 1985). In the debate economists, geographers and sociologists have all had their say, though they have often come to differing conclusions.

This chapter looks more closely at the place of the small firm in the manufacturing sectors of advanced industrial societies and more particularly at the economic culture of the small firms concerned. It suggests that much which seems 'typical' of this culture can only be understood in relation to the technologies, employment practices and other operating strategies of larger firms in the central areas of the manufacturing field.

The purpose of the chapter is twofold. First, it is to suggest the need for a reinterpretation of the apparent revival of the small firm and to support a rather different approach to understanding small firm growth and decline in the manufacturing sector. Second, the chapter uses that approach to suggest a different interpretation of existing data on the economic culture of the small firm. The chapter suggests that, far from being generated by 'smallness' as such, by inherent characteristics, by the constraints on opportunities arising from lack of management skill or from inadequate access to finance, the economic culture of the small firm needs to be interpreted as determined by the technologies employed in the large enterprises which have long dominated manufacturing in advanced industrial societies. The argument suggests that the level of technology, including both physical plant and managerial strategies, used in large companies will generate a particular kind of economic culture in small ones. This is because in manufacturing small firms are essentially 'created' by large ones: indeed the founders of small firms very frequently come from large ones. As they go, they take with them the level of education and technical skills, the social characteristics and managerial capacity level typical of employees at their hierarchical levels in the firms they were employed in. This approach suggests that as the large 'seedbed' firms change, so the population of small entrepreneurs and the economic culture of the enterprise they create will also change. (We are talking here of 'new' entrepreneurs, of course, rather than the 'heirs' of small concerns who inherit their businesses, although the argument can be extended to them, too.) The implication of this approach is that the characteristics of the entrepreneurial population as a whole in manufacturing will often be dependent on the technological strategies of large, bureaucratic, concerns. Public policies in relation to large firms, notably in the social security and labour relations areas, combine with other aspects of competitive strategy and internal organization in large enterprises to play a significant part in the generation of small firms even where they do not target such firms directly. Clearly there will always be some, more peripheral, manufacturing activities where the relationship is not so direct, but even there indirect influences can probably be found.

Using the perspective of the significance of these relationships, the chapter suggests an important dynamic of *change* in the population of small firms over time and the change in their associated economic culture. From this perspective, the explosion of small firms at the leading edge of technology should not be seen as the forerunner of a new industrial system, driven largely by individual science-oriented entrepreneurship, but rather as the latest act in a drama of continuing change in the productive structure.

The chapter suggests that in a period of rapidly changing technology the links between large and small firms will become clearer. While the small firm sector as a whole may 'revive' in the very early days of fundamental technological change, much of this 'revival' will prove over time to be ephemeral. As a tool of analysis simply counting the numbers of apparently free-standing enterprises is not enough: it indicates little about the nature of the population concerned and its changing fortunes.

For long, few data at all were available on the small entrepreneurial population. More recently, more sociological studies have greatly improved on the undifferentiated picture of the 'entrepreneur' painted by psychologists (McClelland 1953) or of the 'small firm' painted by economists and policy advisers such as Bolton. They have, for example, pointed to the difference between the 'Craftsman' and the 'Opportunistic' entrepreneur (Marceau 1983, Smith 1967), in social origins, education, labour experience and 'culture'. They have shown the distinctions which need to be made even within the world of micro-businesses (Scase and Goffee 1982). Differences can now also be seen as between retailing (Bechhofer and Elliott 1980), construction (Scase and Goffee 1982) and baking (Bertaux and Bertaux-Wiame 1981). All these studies have been valuable in exploring a sociologically much neglected stratum and in indicating some of the factors likely to influence 'success'.

None of these studies, however, have looked at *change* among the dwarves of capitalism. With some exceptions their methodology has led them to focus on small firms and their owner-operators as though they were in practice as independent as their formal, legal, free-standing status would suggest. While independence may be the effective norm in the service sector — and even there inroads are being made by franchising arrangements, affecting perhaps 80,000 businesses (Beesley and Wilson 1984: 131–132) — it has never been the general case in much of manufacturing. In manufacturing, notably in the key metal trades industries, much production has been carried out through subcontracting arrangements which subordinate the operating decisions of the smaller 'partner' to those of the large one.

This dependency means that as large firms alter their technologies, employment practices and other operating strategies, so the characteristics and the economic culture of their smaller suppliers may be expected to change. The studies referred to above were carried out in the mid-to-late 1970s: their timing meant that they were investigating a situation at the end of a very long period of technological stability and maturity where firms competed on price rather than on product. Focusing on the characteristics of entrepreneurs regarded as 'small independent businessmen', they neglected to ask questions about the origin and development of the population or even to see the major changes which even then were beginning to take place. Seeing the operation and success of the business as largely 'independent' and due to the characteristics of the entrepreneur, they failed to investigate the structural factors behind the growth, stability or failure of the enterprise.

Increasingly, however, it is clear that the 'shape' of the productive structure is determined by the decisions made by large and giant enterprises: it is their decisions about product, production technology and market which provide the niches occupied by their small *confrères*. The end of the period of technological maturity and the growth of radically new technologies, managerial and physical, indicate more clearly the dynamics behind the 'small firm revival' and the direction of the sociological changes to be found in the productive culture of small manufacturing firms.

The Small Firm Revival

First, some background data on the position of small firms in advanced industrial economies. Far from disappearing as predicted by Marx in the nineteenth century and others in the twentieth, the small firm sector has shown a remarkable capacity both to survive and, at times, to grow. The extent of their success, however, depends on the criteria defining the population concerned, and definitions of small firms vary greatly. 'Small' may mean numbers of people employed, market share, turnover or, more subtly, degree of decision making or operating dependency. Even as measured by one criterion, such as numbers of people employed, the companies described as small vary enormously in size. The OECD uses 200 employees as the cut-off point. Most countries use 100. Many researchers use 50. Others, such as Birch (1979), use 20.

Clearly, the definitions have enormous impact both on the 'size' of the small firm sector and on its significance in the economy. Using 100 employees as the cut-off point in most OECD countries means that 'small firms' employ between 20% and 60% of the labour force, with the average perhaps around 40%. Thus, for example, in Australia, Enterprise Australia calculated in 1981 that there were approximately 750,000 enterprises (other estimates, such as that of Johns et al. 1983, have a somewhat lower figure). Of these, nearly 93% were small. More than 700,000 employed fewer than 10 people, and 600,000 fewer than five, with 50,000 employing between 10 and 100. For each one of the top 500 giants there were 1,000 tiny enterprises of fewer than 100 workers, many employing fewer than 5 people. In the late 1970s in Australia these enterprises of fewer than 100 workers together employed 41% of all people working in the private sector and were responsible for nearly a third of the value added by that sector (Johns et al. 1978: 11). For the economy as a whole, their operations were highly significant.

Since the early 1980s, the position in the total economy of small firms, in Australia as in other OECD countries, seems to have been strengthening. Data from the Survey of Employment and Earnings and the Labour Force survey have been used by the Bureau of Industry Economics (BIE) in Canberra to show that in the 1980s small firms 'continued to contribute significantly to employment, accounting for nearly 52% of the total private sector workforce' in 1986 (BIE 1987: 3). Small firms, defined by the BIE as those employing fewer than 100 in manufacturing and fewer than 20 in most other sectors, were thus accounting for a growing proportion of the labour force. They were concentrated in construction, 'other services', transport, storage and the wholesale and retail trade but were nonetheless also important in manufacturing. Between 1984 and 1986 employment in small firms in all sectors grew: in manufacturing *all* the growth was in small firms (BIE 1987: 23).

A similar picture can be built up elsewhere. Thus, in Britain in the 1980s researchers such as Keeble (1985) have shown a significant resurgence in the numbers of small firms in both services and manufacturing, both absolutely and relative to large corporations, and in 1984 Gudgin showed a substantial increase in the rate of new independent business formation. The total number of U. K. new firm births in production industries, mostly manufacturing, rose each year between 1980 and 1983, a rise over the period of 31% (Ganguly 1984, quoted Keeble and Kelly 1986: 75).

In other parts of Europe, too, a similar resurgence has been documented. Thus, Baroin and Fracheboud and Aydalot in 1984 and Greffe also in 1984 showed that both in France and elsewhere in Europe new small firms were creating new jobs. In 1986 Korte was able to conclude that:

SMEs [small and medium enterprises] gained considerably in importance virtually throughout Europe in terms of their employment shares in the seventies and early eighties [...] in some cases [...] very greatly [...]. This seems to have been particularly true for establishments with 10 – 49 employees, either because large establishments have shrunk or because smaller ones have increased their employment share. By the early 1980s, 42% of EEC regions had at least one fifth of their manufacturing employment in firms of this size (Korte, in Keeble and Weever 1986: 42).

Much of this growth has been in firms in the service sector but it has also been important in manufacturing, and the rest of this paper will look more particularly at the manufacturing sector. It will use Australian data to illustrate more general processes.

Principal among the explanations offered for the growth in numbers of small firms are theories based on one of three factors: recession-push; growth in real incomes; and the impact of technological change, notably, of course, that of micro-electronics and the associated information technology. There is some evidence for each of the theories, but each also has important limitations. The 'recession-push' theory suggests that many new firm creations can be shown to be the result of unemployment which is said to push especially the long-term unemployed to attempt to create their own posts by founding an enterprise (Bamford 1984). Indeed, like Australia, many European countries, notably France, have encouraged this trend with special provisions for the unemployed to capitalize welfare benefits, to obtain cheap loans or gain access to specially built new premises. Some gains in numbers of small and especially very small firms have undoubtedly been made through this channel. The gain may, however, be only temporary since there is some evidence that the market niches occupied by these new companies appear on the down section of a Kondratiev long wave. The niches were once occupied by large firms, who reappropriate them on the upturn when they can once more exercise dominance over the market (Shutt and Whittington 1987, Storey 1982).

The theory based on the positive impact of growth in real income suggests that in times of real income growth, consumers develop new demands for less standardized products, leaving market niches for the craft or artisan producer to provide handmade, custombuilt or small batch items. Indeed, an increase in 'specialty' items available at higher prices is noticeable worldwide, not only in the yuppie sections of New York and London. The argument depends, however, to some degree at least, on the assumption that large firms are only able to produce economically in large batches. New technology, encouraging the transfer from economies of scale to economies of scope, may bring back large firm competition into this market.

The impact of technological change is, of course, central to most discussion about the 'revival' of the small firm sector. The nature of the micro-electronics 'revolution' is such that it radically transforms both *products* and *process*, and does so because of both the speed and nature of the changes involved. It is argued by many that the technology lends itself particularly well to use by small, flexible manufacturing firms. It is further argued that the central importance of the input of scientific research and engineering skills, coupled with the lessened need for complex production organizations, encourages 'inventors' concerned to break away from large enterprises and create their own companies, exploiting both their scientific knowledge and the rarity of their skills. However, these scientists depend very heavily on the research of others, located in large 'intellectual' organizations, notably universities, which themselves are also a source of new entrepreneurs and on the large firms which commission them to design and manufacture new products or components. Much is written about these firms as though they were free-standing, independent enterprises, which, of course, in some senses they are. In other senses, however, they are tied into a much more complex industrial fabric. In part, this is because the technology involves changes in both *product* and *process*. In looking at small, high-technology firms, the focus has too often been on the product rather than the process. Much depends, moreover, on whether the observer takes a national, regional or local perspective.

While all three theories help understand some of the apparent revival of small firms, they all have their limitations. In particular, they suggest little about the dynamics of the productive structure as a whole in which the small firms concerned are embedded. More promising, because addressing this dynamic, are theories relating small firm sector growth to the changing operating strategies of the large firms which continue to dominate all OECD economies (Shutt and Whittington 1987).

The Context of the Revival:
The Shape of the Industrial Structure

The 'shape' of the industrial structure of modern western societies has now for several decades been dominated by large and frequently multinational corporations, many of which are as powerful as and have a budget similar to that of some national governments (see, for example, Vernon 1974 and the work of Wheelwright (1978) and his colleagues at the University of Sydney, for instance Crough et al 1980). While it may now be true that the dominant force in the world economy is financial rather than industrial capitalism, it is by no means the case that inside national economies large firms have forfeited their power. While they may not be growing at the pace of earlier decades, and in some cases they may be shedding labour, there is no evidence at present, it seems, which suggests that they are not the dominant actors in national economies. Their actions, their investments, their production decisions seem, on the contrary, still to be at the heart of economic performance, a place recognized by much public industrial policy. In Australia, for instance, in the private sector at the start of the 1980s large enterprises dominated employment: constituting less than half of 1% of the total number of enterprises, they nonetheless employed more than half the working population. The top 500 enterprises represented only a tiny fraction of the one half of 1%, but they employed a third of all the people at work (Enterprise Australia 1980: 34 – 35). Manufacturing was especially concentrated: firms of more than 100 people employed 68% of the workforce in the sector. Multinational enterprises at the same time produced 66% of all manufactured goods. The proportions have changed only a little over the last few years (BIE 1987), not enough to signal the start of a radically new trend.

As stated above, this paper argues that the overall position and decline or increase in numbers of small *manufacturing* firms are to be understood principally, in Australia and elsewhere, as a function of decisions made by the large firms dominating central areas of manufacturing in the economy as a whole.

The paper takes the situation in the core metals industry as exemplifying the argument. Since the productive structure of an advanced industrial society is extremely complex, the processes described will be less evident in some sectors. In many senses, however, the engineering industries can be seen as the backbone of the system since, although pharmaceuticals, chemicals etc. are different in composition, production in all fields relies on equipment produced in the metals sector while some major consumer products are fabricated principally in metals. In some important senses, therefore, the metals industry can be seen as the 'basic' industry. The relationships generated within the metals trades broadly construed can be seen as the model for that of other industries where some fabrication is required and where micro-electronic technologies are transforming the productive process.

Several aspects of the organization of engineering enterprises are important here. First, historically the *central* enterprises involved have tended to be large, to be internally hierarchical and to employ many workers. A core of these workers is composed of skilled tradesmen, supplemented on the one hand by supervisors and on the other by trades assistants or process workers. In these firms production controllers have always relied on technology which maximizes control of the work process at the same time as they have had to recognize the importance of skilled tasks, particularly in the workshop. The work environment of these enterprises has therefore always included significant tension between the control demands by management, tending towards loss of initiative by workers, and the demands of the workshop technology which left skilled workers in relatively great control of such areas as the speed of work, and, a field where the skill of the operator mattered greatly, of the quality of the finished component or consumer good (Shaiken 1985). This tension has created an important motivation for entrepreneurship in the past (Smith 1967).

Second, organization of the work environment in major engineering enterprises, whether making cars, white goods, major components for vehicles or machine tools, for many decades dependend increasingly on the standardization of products made in the factory so as to realize maximum economies of scale. The importance of economies of scale meant that in complex products, especially in the age of mechanical rather than electronic technology, there were many components of the product and phases of the process which could not profitably be fabricated or undertaken inside the companies themselves. Thus, for such things as the production of prototypes or the non-metal components of the finished product or for specialist small batches, the large firms relied on small enterprises. These small enterprises were often in some senses also the firms' own 'products' since they were created by their own ex-workers who saw the opportunities and wanted to work for themselves (Marceau 1983).

Where ex-workers have been the source of the small companies producing the specialist components and small batches needed by their ex-employer (and other similar companies), one may expect that the economic culture of these firms will reflect the social background, education and work experience of the entrepreneurs concerned.

Similarly by extension, when large firms alter their technologies and operating strategies, new needs and niches will become apparent. In each case, one may hypothesize that a different kind of entrepreneur will be 'spun off'. These entrepreneurs, generated by different sections of the organization from their counterparts at an earlier period of technology and productive organization, will have differing socio-economic characteristics and their firms a different economic culture.

The Craftsman-Entrepreneur

Empirical studies of small manufacturing firms in the USA, in Europe and in Australia have shown the existence of a similar type of small manufacturing businessman. His (and such businessmen are usually male) characteristics are summarized in the label 'Craftsman-Entrepreneur' applied by Smith (1967), or the 'life-style' entrepreneur used by others such as Scase and Goffee (1982) or, more simply, the working-class entrepreneur (Marceau in Hunt, Jackson and Marceau 1981, Marceau 1983). It is this Craftsman-Entrepreneur (C-E) who typifies the characteristics and values which many have thought of as quintessentially those of the small businessman.

The image built up through the work of Smith, Marceau, Scase and Goffee and other observers is of the craft worker who acquired a specialized and, as formally recognized, relatively low level of skill first at school and then at work; who, before becoming an entrepreneur, was employed in the workshops of a company, probably large but possibly medium or small, which made products in the same or a similar field. In practice, as for example, Hunt, Jackson and Marceau found in Europe, he may well set up his business as a formal or informal subcontractor to his old company, producing a component which the company needs but finds unprofitable to produce itself. Beyond that he may diversify to other, but also related, products and sell to other, but mainly local, customers but he usually has few or no long-term plans for product development and invests little time and few resources in marketing efforts. Empirical evidence suggests that while the companies so formed may persist for very long periods of time they will not grow much, or grow only very slowly (Hunt, Jackson and Marceau 1981, Marceau 1983, Storey 1982). Such entrepreneurs, therefore, while they may grow richer than their non-independent peers will share many of their attitudes and values and remain not very far from the skilled working class. Even more important, they will share many of the unfavourable aspects of the opportunity structure with their worker peers: hence their difficulties in obtaining adequate access to capital.

The closeness of this kind of entrepreneur to the working class can be seen in a number of ways as exemplified in my study of 200 small manufacturers mostly in the metal trades in Sydney and Melbourne in 1982. First, they were frequently drawn from families whose head was either a manual worker (21%) or in the manual 'entrepreneurial working class' typified by plumbers, carpenters, automotive repairers or small manufacturing based on a craft skill (49%). Together these two categories covered 70% of the whole sample and nearly 90% of the companies in the metal trades.

Second, their education approximated that of the skilled working class. In my study the biggest single group had a principally technical education, including 26% who had completed an apprenticeship and 21.5% who had a post-secondary technical diploma. The last figure included a quarter who had also completed basic apprenticeship and gone on to specialize further. More than half, including those who had completed the apprenticeship, had ceased their education at the rough equivalent of upper secondary level or below.

Third, their work experience had been gained at a low hierarchical level in their employing organizations. Before creating their businesses, a third had worked only in trades or lower-level technical positions; while a further third had some supervisory or managerial positions, these included the heirs to their fathers' businesses, many of whom were tradesmen by training. It also seems that the majority of supervisory positions held were at foreman level. The employment experience was almost always in a firm in the same or a similar sector as each entrepreneur's own business.

Finally, the socio-economic position of many of the entrepreneurs meant that each must rely on savings for capital, thus starting and often continuing in a small way. Some had managed to build up a small network of businesses and had owned or still owned other enterprises — most of which were also in the same or similar sectors, producing closely related products and the associated services — but few had accumulated large capital sums. In most cases the entrepreneur had to rely initially on his family for clerical and managerial labour, being unable to afford specialist assistance. Family labour was particularly crucial in the early stages of the business, and most of the enterprises studied could not have survived without the 'free' services of the owner's wife (a situation also found in France among bakers by Bertaux and Bertaux-Wiame [1981] in the 1970s).

The small firm owners' motivations for entrepreneurship relate essentially to their past experiences and reflect their frustration at the weight of the constraints on their activities when employed by others, a frustration frequently reported by skilled factory workers (see, for instance, Shaiken 1985). Smith reported that among his respondents, the principal motivation for entrepreneurship was effectively to escape close supervision and a situation where many felt marginal at work, identifying neither with fellow workers nor with managers (Smith 1967). They wanted to set up their own firms to produce a 'good product for a fair price'. The entrepreneurs studied in Paris, in Sydney and in Melbourne were remarkably similar. All mentioned only one central motivation for entrepreneurship — independence, the chance to take one's own decisions and be one's own boss — to which some added a closely related set of motivations, expressed as 'job satisfaction', 'self-satisfaction' or 'flexibility' by some and by others as challenge, achievement, opportunity and security for the family or financial reward.

The economic culture of these firms reflects these motivations. Many such owners are risk-averse and conservative and do not encourage innovation or a market orientation. They see the business as a means to combine independence with a reasonable and reasonably secure income and, as many studies have shown, often do not wish the business to grow beyond the limits of their personal control. The operation of each business reflects the owner's experience and motivations. Thus, in personnel policy, for instance, the search is for 'reliable' and stable personnel, motivated by the same concept of a 'fair day's work for a fair day's pay' as the entrepreneur himself. Since he possesses trade skills similar to those of his workers, the entrepreneur tends to work alongside his employees. The scale of operation and level of profitability mean that few or no staff are available for specific tasks of control: the operation has to depend on the 'family atmosphere' and the loyalty and reliability of the workers retained often through non-price aspects of the workplace, such as conditions of work, job flexibility and interest and so on. Both the values at the heart of the enterprise and the ordering of the productive system are thus typical of the craft trades-man. As the organizational and productive technologies of core firms change, such entrepreneurs will become increasingly rare: they belong to a passing entrepreneurial population.

The Opportunistic-Entrepreneur

The opposite of the Craftsman-Entrepreneur in Smith's characterizations is the Opportunistic-Entrepreneur (O-E), the prototype from a few decades ago of the whizz kids who create and manage today's high-technology companies. In contrast to the C-E, the O-E is characterized, says Smith, by lengthy education, containing both technical and non-technical com-ponents, probably at degree level (see also Keeble and Kelly 1986: 99). His work experience before setting up his own enterprise includes both technical and managerial elements and his reference group is management. He tends to be from higher social origins (Hunt, Jackson and Marceau 1981). Unlike his C-E counterpart, he is effective in many forms of communication and shows confidence and flexibility in dealing with the social and economic environment. He delegates authority or responsibility in order to build a larger organization, hires on a universalistic basis and is sophisticated in his use of both marketing and other competitive strategies. He is aware of and oriented to the future and makes plans for company growth. He is the prototype of the niche marketer, deciding to set up a company to fill a gap in the market which comes from an original idea (usually scientific) or from one generated through experience of his employing company's product. He may or may not have his old company as his major or sole client. In comparison with the Craftsman-Entrepreneur he is likely to build a flexible firm which has considerable growth potential and to plan for future development. In short, he is the epitome of the middle-class owner – manager, likely to be from an entrepreneurial or professional family and to be interested in enterprise for profit rather than life style. His capital comes from loans rather than savings, and few or no family members are involved in the enterprise.

Exemplars of the Opportunistic-Entrepreneur were also both found in my 1982 study in Sydney and Melbourne and in the earlier one in Paris. In both Melbourne and Paris, for instance, they flourished in the printing and plastics extrusion fields. More obvious exemplars are, of course, the high technology firms at the forefront of the creation of new products, especially in computing, notably in software but also in hardware. These are the fast-growing firms of Silicon Valley, of the Cambridgeshire countryside and the Scottish glens. It is they who typify the new wave of entrepreneurs and who are currently changing the composition of the pool of small businessmen.

Changes in the Large Firm — Small Firm Nexus

Evidence is now becoming available from many countries which suggests that the radical nature of new technologies, understood as both the physical equipment and the ways in which it is utilized in the productive process, frequently provoke change in the internal organization of the companies which adopt it. They also cause the boundaries of production by a firm to be rethought and in many circumstances to change. Experience with some elements of the organization of the productive process which originated in Japan and which are now being introduced into North America, Europe and, increasingly, Australia suggests that the new technology will have two consequences important to the discussion in this paper. The first is that it will lead to a major readjustment in the market between large and small enterprises. The second is that this readjustment will itself further stimulate the generation of small enterprises through a reorganization of the division of manufacturing production which was established at an earlier stage of technological, organizational and social development. This new division of production will lead to a new population of entrepreneurs.

Changes in the division of production will be generated by adoption of the new core technologies for a number of reasons. First, the *products* (including machine tools) of the new technology are extremely complex. They require constant R & D, complex design and sophisticated machines for production. They lend themselves in the same way as the earlier products of the metals industries to subdivision and subcontracting. The main difference is that the skills needed by the subcontracting organization are at a higher scientific and professional level, requiring of the subcontractors a better education labour force and more up-to-date machinery. The products once translated into *process* technologies also tend to encourage a changed enterprise organization in both engineering and non-engineering industries and an altered division of labour. (This is already happening in the food industry, for example in the U.K. — see Child 1987.)

The trends can be seen in data gathered from different countries. In the face of a variety of changes in their competitive situation, firms of many kinds have been altering their organizational structures. John Child, for example, in a paper presented to an EGOS Conference in July 1987, describes the growing trend to deconstruct companies and to develop a variety of new contractual forms. Some of these changes are due to and some facilitated by new technologies: the challenges which spark the reorganizations may stem from sources at least once removed from technological change per se. Analysis of the reorganization sheds a rather different light on the small firm 'revival'. Far from being the traditional entrepreneurial free-standing enterprises, many new firms are in fact both creations and outposts of core enterprises in the sectors concerned. Shutt and Whittington (1987), for example, noted that in the U. K. from the mid-1970s onwards, large firms, while stabilizing their output, decreased employment per establishment but increased the number of establishments in a manner which paralleled the perceived revival of small firms. These two developments, they say, are not simply parallel but inter-related and '[...] the rise of small firms and small plants can at least partly be attributed to the changing strategies of large firms' (1987: 15). We return to this below.

These changing strategies, suggest Shutt and Whittington, are responses by large firms to three novel strategic challenges, all of which push them to use or to create smaller units of production. The first of these challenges is the need to reassert control over the labour process. At a time when the profitability of capital has been dropping in Europe, capital has felt the need to restructure its links with labour and create a new 'social structure of accumulation' (Gorden, Gowards and Reich, quoted in Shutt and Whittington 1987: 16). Creating new and smaller units to escape 'excessive' labour problems is not a new strategy — Bamford (1984) shows how this has happened over many years in Italy, for example — but seems to be increasingly common (van Tulder and Junne 1987).

The second challenge is to overcome the innovation risk which is associated with an accelerating rate of technological change. Responding to this risk has led major enterprises to experiment with radically new product and process innovations and to restructure their organizations accordingly (van Tulder and Junne 1987).

The third challenge lies in the intensification of demand risk, exemplified for many companies in the turndown of demand during the 1980—82 recession. Their analysis of enterprise activities leads Shutt and Whittington to argue that

large firms are currently responding to increased innovation risk, prolonged demand risk and the crisis of control over the labour process by various strategies of fragmentation. Large firms are fragmenting production both into smaller plants within their ownership and into small firms which are independently owned but economically dependent (1987: 17).

The firms' strategic responses to altered competitive conditions can be seen in the decentralization of production whereby large plants are broken up, creating both smaller plants and new subsidiaries; in increasing 'development' where large firms cease to own units but retain revenue links with them, as exemplified in franchising or licensing; and in a strategy leading to the disintegration of production and innovation. In the last case, firms cease to own units but retain control through market power (especially in vertical disintegration) through minority shareholding and through their underlying power to repurchase the units. In this way, ownership is shifted, often through worker or management buy-outs, but control is retained.

Similarly, Child also notes that firms in mature economies are responding to new challenges by changing the organization of transactions. Companies are, he says, tending to slim down and simplify their constituent units, sometimes by uncoupling these into separate activity areas and sometimes by sourcing more goods and services externally rather than encompassing the whole productive process within their boundaries, with a consequent shift from hierarchically coordinated transactions towards market-based ones (1987: 3–4). This can be seen not only in electronics sourcing but also in disparate industries such as food, construction, retailing and clothing.

Building on the work of Shutt and Whittington, and examining the results of the changes underway, Child outlines a range of organizational modes which are used to coordinate and control these 'spun-off' or 'fragmented' units and all of which are in use today. The modes are: integrated hierarchy, semi-hierarchy, co-contracting, coordinated contracting, coordinated revenue links and the spot network. The four in the middle are the ones which concern us here because they are the ones which show both the greatest difference from the present situation and give the most important clues about future trends.

The 'semi-hierarchical' firm is familiar on the landscape of much of Europe and is increasingly visible in Australia. This is seen in the multi-divisional firm or the parent-subsidiary where the parent is a holding company. The holding companies are in charge of a diverse range of firms and have financial control of subsidiaries. This firm, at least until 1981, was perhaps particularly well developed in the French 'group' systems of hierarchical control through participations sufficient to ensure common strategy (Allard et al. 1978, Bauer and Cohen 1981) but not outright ownership. Child quotes Buhner (1987) as arguing that the more loosely coupled holding mode may be well suited to take advantage of entrepreneurial opportunities in areas of new technology, which suggests that the arrangements are likely to become more widespread in the future.

It is, however, subcontracting which is of especial importance here. Subcontracting was, of course, frequent among the Craftsmen-Entrepreneurs described above in this paper but, it is clear that subcontracting, far from being associated only with an earlier form of technology and competitive conditions, is especially well suited to the organization of production using the new technologies. In some cases, subcontracting has now become what Child calls co-contracting, as in the example of European aerospace where a 'mutual organization', composed of a set of independent co-contractors engaging in a recurring relationship, has been set up. In other cases, subcontracting has become 'coordinated contracting' or the 'quasi firm' (1987: 15). In this the prime contractor or producer operates with a set of subcontractors as agents who form a recurring relationship which may persist over many years. This is the Japanese automotive-industry model.

New technologies facilitate these new arrangements and may lead to the situation where at one end of the continuum there exists, in Lambooy's words (1986), the 'hollow corporation' which is solely concerned with the design and marketing functions of the production process, with the remaining functions farmed out to subcontractors in one of the modes described by Child.

Many transformations of organizational structures are coming about because of the introduction of some new physical technology, notably that associated with CAD−CAM (Computer Aided Design−Computer Aided Manufacturing), which is believed to be most productive and hence profitable if introduced in conjunction with other organizational ideas borrowed from Japan. Thus, big companies in Australia as elsewhere are introducing not only new machines but also a completely new shopfloor organization and materials supply policy. The Just-In-Time (JIT) system of inventory control, allied to the *kanban* method of materials supply to machinery and delegation to workers of responsibility for quality control, means fundamental restructuring inside large enterprises in Australia as elsewhere.

The impact of the transformations, however, does not stop at the walls of the factory. The implications of this change for suppliers and hence for the productive structure as a whole are enormous. Thus, for example, JIT pushes responsibility for stockholding outside the walls of the enterprises concerned. More important, it means that the supplier companies themselves, many of which are relatively small, must in turn invest both in new machinery and in an altered organization of the labour process so that they can fulfil the new bargains made with clients and produce the required components at very short notice and at a very high level of quality. Faced with the new demands, many small suppliers take both fright and umbrage. In Australia, their reaction was recently typified by one supplier in New South Wales who responded to a client's demand for extra speed by shouting 'What do you think this is, a bloody pizza parlour?'.

The dependence of the reorganized core company on the reliability of the suppliers selected causes the more powerful enterprise to extend to its suppliers the emphasis on control previously reserved for its own workers. The suppliers chosen in effect become an external labour force with whom new and binding contracts must be negotiated. In order to rationalize their own internal operations the car companies, for example, who worldwide are some of the firms furthest advanced in this field, decided in the early 1980s in America and Europe, and are now deciding in Australia, that they must improve the production methods of their suppliers, many of whom were the typical Craftsmen-Entrepreneurs described above. Thus, for example, as van Tulder and Junne reported in 1987, in 1983 General Motors demanded that its electronics and machine tool equipment suppliers adopt its Manufacturing Automation Protocol (MAP) which laid down stringent standards of quality and designated approved methods of production. Firms not willing or able to apply this protocol within a given period of time were told that they would be removed from the list of the company's preferred suppliers. Other core enterprises, notably in France but also in other European countries, are following a similar line (van Tulder and Junne 1987). This reorganization and reaching out by core companies in an attempt to control suppliers has far-reaching effects on the productive structure which are beginning to be clearly discernible in Europe, although as yet scarcely talked about in Australia.

A first effect is that many medium and small companies will go out of business. In Europe and America it is clear, especially in the automotive industry, that the core companies are beginning to enforce concentration in the number and size of their major contractors. While many firms who are contractors to car firms are medium and large, their own subcontracting arrangements involve many small enterprises. Small firms, notably those generated by the earlier technology and retaining the economic culture of the Craftsman-Entrepreneur, are often not able to cope with the high quality standards demanded. Many go out of business, as happened in Italy a few years after Fiat decided that it would only produce the suspension system and technologically important parts of the car in-house, the rest being subcontracted out. The result was a decline of two thirds in the number of suppliers (van Tulder and Junne 1987). While in Australia the ability of the core firms to coerce their suppliers will be limited by the geographical dispersion of suppliers and the present need to import significant quantities of components, the net effect will be similar.

A second effect of the decisions of the large companies on their suppliers will be the virtual integration of many suppliers into the core firm. Thus, for example, as van Tulder and Junne say, advances in information technology provide companies with the opportunity not only to transfer responsibility for part of their activity onto independent suppliers but also to control the 'independents' by integrating the latter's planning into the core enterprise's own computerized information system, thus rendering much independence in decision making by suppliers illusory.

A third effect is the pushing of productive risk further and further out from the core companies concerned. As the immediate suppliers become 'integrated', so they in turn have to introduce new productive technology and internal organization. This means that they too will subcontract out a great deal of their business, increasing the number of 'tied' companies over a wide range of sectors and geographical locations, and it is these who will both hold the stocks and take the risks associated with fluctuations in demand.

Many of these companies will thus in effect be ultimately dependent on the core companies. While the ties will be most direct with the final component suppliers, the others will also become increasingly tied in. This is because the concentration on higher value-added investments and on research-intensive activities has, as van Tulder and Junne (1987) suggest, increased the attention which most core firms pay to the structuring of the subcontractor system. There seem, they say, to be two alternative strategies: the US – European model where all subcontractors do business not only with the large core firm but also each other, and the Japanese model where there is a more or less formalized hierarchical structure in which subsubcontractors are able only to service their 'superiors' rather than do business elsewhere, since servicing other clients increases the firm's freedom from the control of the large firm. While the 'European' model is less stringent, in part at least because of the dispersion of central production units, the 'Japanization' of the core firm – supplier relationship seems to be increasing everywhere. In Europe current variants are many. One example of the new relationships can be seen in the 'co-maker' scheme in Holland in which Philips provides capital and knowhow to smaller firms which in effect become an advanced base for Philips' own production system (Child 1987; van Tulder and Junne 1987). Co-maker-like arrangements are becoming increasingly common, Child says, as major firms seek to find new ways of 'economizing' in their productive relationships.

For these reasons, it is clear in many manufacturing sectors that the networks of production are increasingly tightly meshed, and both the number and type of small firms in the producer population will experience growing dependence on their large clients. Forced to innovate radically, many will be unable to respond. Those least able because they are the products of an earlier system of production and lack the education and professional experience as well, very often, as the capital to respond adequately to the new challenges will go out of business. A new breed of entrepreneur, neither the 'Craftsman' nor the classic 'Opportunistic' but rather the 'Managerial-Entrepreneur', seems likely to appear.

Small Firms at the Leading Edge

In apparent contrast to the sectors in which large companies increasingly seek to control and regulate the activities of their smaller counterparts stand the high technology sectors in which most new and fast-growing companies are burgeoning and producing the products which later become the components and processes used in the core companies just discussed.

As many studies, such as those by Oakey (1984) and Keeble and Kelly (1986), show, the new firms these entrepreneurs create grow faster than the national average, create new products frequently, invest heavily in R & D, provide (probably) higher income returns to the founders and hire only or principally highly skilled labour. As we saw above, they are flexible and market oriented and rely on staff professionalism to maintain quality and output. Their economic culture is in many ways, then, the opposite of that of the Craftsman-Entrepreneur. At present, they seem to be more truly free-standing.

Will these firms, then, be the forerunners in a productive system in which they will maintain their current place and in which, in high technology areas at least, small firms will remain at the leading edge? This paper suggests that this is probably unlikely. It seems more likely that they will conform to the same patterns of linkages between companies as their longer established counter-parts since they will be subject to similar forces in the marketplace and will recreate a similar productive structure.

There are several reasons which make this conformity likely. The new firms are not static. Despite the restrictions of the niches into which many such companies are forced (Oakey 1984: 16), some will become quite large firms. In the Cambridgeshire — Hertfordshire complex of small firms studied by Keeble and Kelly in 1985 some firms founded only a few years previously had already reached more than 100 employees, with more between 50 and 100. These are already on the borderline of changing status to medium rather than small enterprises. It is precisely those growing fastest which risk being taken over by larger competitors who are watching their progress. By 1985, 8.5% of the Keeble and Kelly sample had already been taken over, and van Tulder and Junne have described how many firms have been bought out by large competitors anxious to have, for instance, in-house chip design capacity. Many large firms watch and wait, allowing the small to take development risks and pouncing when the moment is right (van Tulder and Junne 1987). More will be absorbed as the field diversifies.

Second, there will be more diversity in the currently rather homogeneous sector, bringing the hi-tech firms more into line with patterns established by the older manufacturing sectors. Some may spawn new small firms. In contrast, some may contract as their products can be produced with less labour, as already seems to be happening in Silicon Valley (personal communication 1983). In some significant ways the operations of the hi-tech companies already resemble those of firms in other fields. Many have established similar production strategies in their larger counterparts and already subcontract much of the manufacture and distribution of their products to firms located elsewhere (Keeble and Kelly 1986, Rothwell and Zegveld 1982). Already, as the most successful ones grow, they are beginning to participate in the whole gamut of new contractual relationships with larger firms which is described by John Child in the paper mentioned above.

Third, although the small firms in question here are making high-technology *products*, many of their market niches are based on the manufacture of specialist sub-components. This may make them vulnerable to larger competitors. As Oakey suggests,

... if large production runs become feasible at some later date, it is likely that larger firms will move into these small firm production niches to take over either the firm itself or much of the small firm's emerging market (1984: 16).

Fourth, the seedbeds of new hi-tech companies are themselves reorganizing. While some large companies continue to dominate the high-technology sectors, notably in the production of hardware, the internal organizational patterns of many of these companies have in the past made it hard for them to provide the environment appropriate to develop many of the new ideas emerging from universities and the companies' own R & D departments. It is for this reason that in the past (and at present) new firms have spun off and been spun off (through individual action or management or labour buy-outs) to fill new market niches, notably in the ever-changing software and design areas where capital barriers to entry are low. Universities, too, similarly large and inflexible organizations, have also been sources of new high-technology entrepreneurs (Keeble 1986). From the small firms thus created further small firms have later spun off. However, the inflexibilities in large organizations which encouraged the spin off of new small firms are being modified. Many firms are developing 'intrapreneurship' schemes in a bid to keep their best inventors. Others are creating small units for the same purpose (Child 1987). Universities in countries such as the U.K. and Australia are being reformed to make them more flexible, and joint ventures with industrial concerns are becoming increasingly common.

Thus, for these reasons, while small high-technology firms may seem to hold very different positions in the structure of production from their lower technology *confrères*, these positions may prove to be unstable and their differences a function rather of conditions in the early days of development of a fast-moving field than of some intrinsic capacity.

Conclusion

It therefore seems that, while in the manufacturing arena the number of small firms is growing fast and that such growth is indeed primarily a function of the pace and type of technological change, there are powerful countervailing forces in the manufacturing sector as a whole. The presence of these forces means that many existing small firms will go out of business while others will be drawn into a complex mesh of contractual relations with other companies which, while in many cases leaving the smaller partner apparently independent, in reality will mean many constraints. The products of new technologies are too important for large firms to leave their manufacture to chance, and large firms are too powerful and too acquisitive to leave lucrative markets untapped. Finally, large firms, using the very technology created in part by the small ones are now in a position to invent new productive structures and to create more flexible organizational forms while still retaining control. The long reach of the financial and manufacturing 'group' typified by the experience of France seems unlikely to neglect the highly productive small advanced technology firms commonly considered by many observers to lie outside their span of control. Rather, it seems that while at first glance the shape of the productive structure over the coming decades will seem more complex, with the development of a greater variety of new organizational forms in the different spheres of activity, the structure as a whole will continue to be driven by the large and powerful in the arena who will readapt their strategies appropriately. While at any given time many small companies will be freestanding, their numbers will be determined by the large.

Given this conclusion, it seems to follow that the 'economic culture' of small manufacturing firms will continue in most cases to be dominated by that of the large. The only difference will be in the kind of entrepreneurs and productive forms generated. The Craftsman-Entrepreneurs will disappear. While at any point of time there will probably be at the leading edge of technology a sector of small independent manufacturing companies founded and managed by Opportunistic-Entrepreneurs, as the technology becomes routinized and the products absorbed into both the processes and products of the larger entities, existing firms will gradually be absorbed or find their activities more or less directly restructured by the large. The coming age will be that of the Managerial-Entrepreneur.

In conclusion then, this chapter suggests that it is important to look at the level of technology and the organizational structures generated in order to understand the 'shape' of the productive structure in the industrial sectors of modern western societies and, in particular, the economic cultures and relative shares of small enterprises. Level of technology and production organization need to be investigated not only as they exist *inside* the major companies but also as part of the linkages generated with 'outsiders' such as suppliers to see how the kinds of relationships generated inside the firm are reproduced outside in those developed between core and periphery. Immediately the same attempts at control and the same division of labour will become apparent. Through discussion of these relationships, this paper attempts to point to a possible approach to the analysis of the productive structure and its changes and of the economic culture of the component firms. At any one time it is clear that there is a mix of entrepreneurial types, corresponding to the mix of levels of skill and education in both the population at large and, more importantly, the set of tasks available in and needed by large or core enterprises. The operations of small manufacturing firms, it is argued here, are essentially residual: much of what they do, their nature and their economic culture, is determined for them by their large competitors and *patrons*. In recent years the 'leading edge' technologies have been drained out of large enterprises by new entrepreneurs. The organizational reactions of large firms have frequently been oriented rather more to past than to future conditions and their monolithic structures, generated in an earlier technological age, for some time proved slow to adapt to new conditions. Coupled with recession, this left room for new entrants skilled in new technologies whose numbers will ultimately alter the population of small manufacturing enterprises considerably, as their older counterparts will either close down or stagnate. However, the argument of this paper is that large firms seem once again poised to lead the way in technological innovation and that it is they who will continue to determine the shape and conditions of the productive structure in western industrial countries and most particularly in Australia. Leaving some highly innovative firms to take the risks which they find unacceptably high, large firms will move in when conditions are right and re-enmesh most of their smaller brethren in a productive net which allows some freedom to small firms to manoeuvre but which ultimately will determine who succeeds and who fails in an increasingly subtly controlled productive environment and market place. This is another of the lessons to be learned from Japan.

References

Allard, P., M. Beaud, B. Bellon, A. M. Levy and S. Lienart (1978): *Dictionnaire des groupes industriels et financiers en France*, Paris: Le Seuil.

Armington, C. and M. Odle (1982): Small business — how many jobs? *The Brookings Review* Winter: 14–17.

Aydalot, P. (1986): The location of new firm creation: the French case, in: D. Keeble and E. Wever (eds.), *New firms and regional development in Europe*, 105–123, London: Croom Helm.

Bamford, J. (1984): Small business in Italy — the submerged economy, in: C. Levicki (ed.), *Small business: theory and policy*, 97–110, London: Croom Helm.

Baroin, D. and P. Fracheboud (1983): *La contribution des PME à l'emploi en Europe*, Notes et Etudes Documentaires Nos. 4715–6, Paris: Documentation Française.

Bauer, M. and E. Cohen (1981): *Qui gouverne les groupes industriels?* Paris: Le Seuil.

Bechhofer, F. and B. Elliott (1980): *The petite bourgeoisie*, London: Macmillan.

Beesley, M. and P. Wilson (1984): Public policy and small firms in Britain, in: C. Levicki (ed.), *Small business: theory and policy*, 111–126, London: Croom Helm.

Bertaux, D. and I. Bertaux-Wiame (1981): Artisanal bakery in France: how it lives and why it survives, in: F. Bechhofer and B. Elliott (eds.), *The petite bourgeoisie: comparative studies of the uneasy stratum*, 155–181, London: Macmillan.

BIE [Bureau of Industry Economics], Small Business Research Unit (1987): *Small business review*, Canberra: Australian Government Publishing Service.

Birch, D. (1979): The job generation process, Working paper, MIT Program on Neighborhood and Regional Change, Cambridge, Mass.: MIT.

Blois, K. (1984): Large customers and their suppliers, *European Journal of Marketing* 11/4: 281–290.

Boreel, M. and L. van de Bunt (1987): Change in technology and organisational response, Paper presented to the Eighth EGOS Colloquium, Antwerp, 22–24 July on 'Technology as the two-edged sword of organizational change'.

Buhner, R. (1987): Management-Holding, *Die Betriebswirtschaft* 47: 40–49.

Campbell, I. and K. Strahan (1984): *The northern suburbs industry project*, 3 volumes, Melbourne: Department of Employment and Training.

Child, J. (1987): Information technology, organisation and the response to strategic challenges, Paper presented to the Eighth EGOS Colloquium, Antwerp, 22 – 24 July on 'Technology as the two-edged sword of organizational change'.

Collins, O. and D. Moore (1964): *The enterprising man*, East Lansing, MI: Michigan State University, Business Studies.

Cross, M. (1981): *New firms and regional economic development*, Farnborough: Gower Publishing Co.

Crough, G., T. Wheelwright and T. Wilshire (1980): *Australia and world capitalism*, Melbourne: Penguin.

Deeks, J. (1976): *The small firm owner-manager: entrepreneurial behavior and management practice*, New York and London: Praeger.

Dohse, K., U. Jurgens and T. Malsch (1985): From 'Fordism' to 'Toyotism'? The social organization of the labour process in the Japanese motor industry, *Politics and Society* 14 – 2: 115 – 146.

Ebers, M., U. Berger and M. Lieb (1987): The two worlds of computer aided manufacturing, Paper presented to the Eighth EGOS Colloquium, Antwerp, 22 – 24 July on 'Technology as the two-edged sword of organizational change'.

Enterprise Australia (1980): *The enterprises of Australia*, Sydney: Enterprise Australia.

Fothergill, S. and G. Gudgin (1982): *Unequal growth: urban and regional employment changes in the U.K.*, London: Heinemann Educational Books.

Ganguly, A. (1984): Business starts and stops: U.K. county analysis 1980 – 83, *British Business* 18 – 24 January: 106 – 110.

Greffe, X. (1984): *Les PME créent-elles des emplois?* Paris: Economica.

Gudgin, G. (1984): *Employment creation by small and medium sized firms in the U.K.*, Cambridge: Department of Applied Economics.

Hunt, D., J. Jackson and J. Marceau (1981): *The ownership, operations and employment potential of small manufacturing enterprises*, Bruxelles: Commission of the European Communities.

Johns, B., W. Dunlop and W. Sheehan (1978): *Small business in Australia*, Sydney: Allen and Unwin.

Johns, B., W. Dunlop and W. Sheehan (1983): (Revised edition) *Small business in Australia: problems and prospects*, Sydney: Allen and Unwin.

Keeble, D. (1985): Industrial change in the United Kingdom, in: W. Lever (ed.), *Industrial change in the United Kingdom*, Chapter One, Harlow: Longman.

Keeble, D. and T. Kelly (1986): New firms and high technology industry in the United Kingdom: the case of computer electronics, in: D. Keeble and E. Wever (eds.), *New firms and regional development in Europe*, 75 – 104, London: Croom Helm.

Keeble, D. and E. Wever (eds.) (1986): *New firms and regional development in Europe*, 42, London: Croom Helm.

Lambooy, J. (1986): Information and internationalisation: dynamics of the relations of small and medium sized enterprises in a network environment, Paper presented to a Table Ronde 'Les PME innovatrices et leur environment local et économique'. Aix-en-Provence, 4 – 5 July.

Marceau, J. (1983): *Small manufacturing enterprises in Australia*, Melbourne: Department of Employment and Training.

Massey, D. and R. Meegan (1979): The geography of industrial organization, *Progress in Planning* 10: 159 – 237.

McClelland, D. (1953): *The achievement motive*, New York: Appleton-Century-Crofts.

Oakey, R. (1984): *High technology small firms*, London: Frances Pinter.

O. E. C. D. (1986): *The role of large firms in local job creation*, Paris: Organization for Economic Co-operation and Development.

Rothwell, R. and W. Zegveld (1981): *Industrial innovation and public policy*, London: Frances Pinter.

Rothwell, R. and W. Zegveld (1982): *Innovation and the small and medium sized firm*, London: Frances Pinter.

Scase, R. and R. Goffee (1982): *The entrepreneurial middle class*, London: Croom Helm.

Shaiken, H. (1985): *Work transformed: automation and labour in the computer age*, New York: Holt, Rinehart and Winston.

Shutt, J. and R. Whittington (1987): Fragmentation strategies and the rise of small units: cases from the North West, *Regional Studies* 21, 1: 13 – 23.

Smith, N. (1967): *The entrepreneur and his firm: the relationship between man and type of company*, East Lansing, MI: Bureau of Business and Economic Research, Michigan State University.

Storey, D. (1982): *Entrepreneurship and the new firm*, London: Croom Helm.

Storey, D. (ed.) (1985): *Small firms and regional economic development: Britain, Ireland and the United States*, Cambridge: Cambridge University Press.

van Tulder, R. (1987): Technology and the changing structure of European multinationals, Paper presented to the Eighth EGOS Colloquium, Antwerp, 22 – 24 July on 'Technology as the two-edged sword of organizational change'.

van Tulder, R. and G. Junne (1987): *European multinationals in core technologies*, Chichester: Wiley.

Vernon, R. (ed.) (1974): *Big business and the state*, London: Macmillan.

Victorian Chamber of Manufactures (1981 a): *Manufacturing industry in Australia*, Green Paper No. 6, Melbourne: VCM.

Victorian Chamber of Manufactures (1981 b): *Manufacturing industry in Victoria*, Green Paper No. 7, Melbourne: VCM.

Wheelwright, E. (1978): *Capitalism, socialism or barbarism? The Australian predicament*, Brookvale: ANZ Book Co.

Wilson, P. and P. Gorb (1983): How large and small firms can grow together, *Long Range Planning*, 16, 2: 19 – 27.

Part IV
Culture's Consequences: Values in Action

The Cash Value of Confucian Values

Michael Harris Bond and Geert Hofstede

> Do not repeat the tactics which have gained you one victory, but let your methods be regulated by the infinite variety of circumstances.
>
> Sun Tzu, *The art of war*

This is a short chapter intended to summarize a line of research that we have been pursuing separately and together for the last two decades. Given the scope of the project, we propose only to adumbrate the issues and findings, pointing the interested reader to the appropriate references.

The Psychological Study of Values

Psychologists have long been interested in values, especially as they link with expectancies to predict behaviour (Feather 1979). Cross-cultural psychologists were ready converts to this interest because differences in typical behaviours from culture to culture seemed so easily explained by reference to putative differences in values (Zavalloni 1980). Two steps were needed, however, to give direction and coherence to this use of values. First, a comprehensive mapping of the value domain was required so that some simplification of the constructs could be achieved (Schwartz and Bilsky 1987). Secondly, the world's cultures would have to be located on this taxonomy, so that explanations of cultural differences involving values became less *post hoc* and opportunistic (see, e. g., Bond et al. 1985).

One of the best-known studies on the effects of different cultural values on behaviour was that of McClelland (1961). He tried to show that there was an empirical link between a country's level of achievement themes in school storybooks and its economic growth. The sceptics were not far behind, of course. McClelland's measures of economic growth have been disputed (e. g., Franke 1987) and so have the meanings of his measures of achievement themes in schoolbooks (e. g., Hofstede 1980: 171). To others, values could be construed as mere epiphenomena, Marxian reflections of the conditions of production. As countries modernized, conditions of life would converge out of the diversity imposed by cultural beginnings, homogenizing values in their wake (see Yang, in press, for arguments and data on the 'convergence' hypothesis).

Be that as it may, psychologists would still be keen to discover *which* values were linked to economic performance at both individual and cultural levels (see Leung and Bond, 1989, for a discussion of the level issue). Such knowledge could then be used to direct attention towards socialization practices regarding values and towards theory building about the linkages among values, the conditions of production and economic performance (see, e. g., Redding 1988, Triandis 1984).

The Values of Nations and Their Economic Performance

At this point, one must confront the issue of procedure. If this exploration is to be scientific, then some act of inter-subjective measurement must be undertaken. The rich insights of a Weber or a Parsons must be translated into measurement operations. Regrettably, we must therefore now part company with those who deny the validity of such a possibility either for aesthetic or epistemological reasons. As Thomas Aquinas aptly put the matter, 'No one believes anything he does not first believe to be believable'. And there is no point arguing over irreconcilable irreducibles.

If, however, one is seeking to link values and economic performance scientifically, it seems evident that one must sample from as wide a selection of economic units as possible. Broad selections iron out peculiarities in the data arising from temporary economic realignments produced by developments such as resource discovery, for example. Hofstede's (1980) study of work-related values in 40 countries is the largest such study, easily eclipsing any previous attempt. He factor analyzed the country averages of responses to his work-value survey, extracting four factors. Each country was then given a score on each of these four dimensions, providing a value map which could be used to anchor cross-cultural research on values and behaviour.

In an effort to validate his factors Hofstede correlated his country scores for a given factor with other country-level data, like automobile speed limits, civil unrest, proportion of GNP devoted to foreign aid and so forth. One empirical result of that Olympian undertaking was the discovery of a .82 correlation between a country's GNP in 1970 and its score on the factor labelled 'individualism'. Was this .82 correlation accidental and hence a red herring? Given that the correlation was (a) based on a sample of 40 countries and (b) replicated in both Hofstede's samples of 1967 and 1972, this conclusion seems unlikely. So, the values constituting the 'individualism' factor appear worth the detailed consideration Hofstede gave them in Chapter 5 of his 1980 book as components of a country's economic performance.

The Missing Link

None of Hofstede's four factors correlated with economic growth, a measure of economic performance unrelated to GNP. The rich countries do not necessarily get richer, nor poorer for that matter. So, the data show that a country cannot ride the bow-wave of convergence towards individualism, presuming that the inexorable tide of modernization will eventually sweep it into the land of milk and honey. So, the hunt was still very much on for that mix of values that related to economic advance. For, it must be acknowledged, the secret hope has always been that the critical values, once identified, could be inculcated at a societal level, thereby pushing eager contenders towards the promised land. Indeed, one consequence of McClelland's earlier theory was the development of traning programmes to enhance achievement motivation in developing countries.

The Whisper from the East

Economic analysts were quick to note the extraordinary growth levels among the Five Dragons of East Asia over the last two decades. They were less able to identify the economic mechanisms responsible (Hicks and Redding 1983 a). This is hardly surprising given the daunting array of factors; legal, political and economic, which characterizes the present realities of Japan, Taiwan, Hong Kong, Singapore and South Korea (Redding 1988).

Herman Kahn (1979) was one of the first to suggest that the common cultural heritage of Confucianism might be the Rosetta Stone for translating the Dragons' successes. The sprawling Rorschach of Confucianism quickly became everybody's explanatory starting point. The fact that Confucianism had once been used to explain China's economic torpor was quickly forgotten. No matter, however, because Confucianism was an elephant of many parts, as the Sufi story reminds us, and creative thinkers selected those anatomical features that fitted their reasoning (see, e. g., Hwang 1986).

Table 1   Values Loading > .55 on the Factor Analysis of Standardized CVS Country Means

CVS I *(Integration)*	CVS II *(Confucian work dynamism)*
Tolerance of others (.86)	Ordering relationships (.64)
Harmony with others (.86)	Thrift (.63)
Solidarity with others (.61)	Persistence (.76)
Non-competitiveness (.85)	Having a sense of shame (.61)
Trustworthiness (.69)	Reciprocation (−.58)
Contentedness (.65)	Personal steadiness (−.76)
Being conservative (.56)	Protecting your 'face' (−.72)
A close, intimate friend (.75)	Respect for tradition (−.62)
Filial piety (−.74)	
Patriotism (−.62)	
Chastity in women (−.70)	
CVS III *(Human-heartedness)*	CVS IV *(Moral discipline)*
Kindness (.72)	Moderation (.65)
Patience (.88)	Keeping oneself disinterested and pure (.56)
Courtesy (.76)	Having few desires (.67)
Sense of righteousness (−.57)	Adaptability (−.71)
Patriotism (−.62)	Prudence (−.58)

The Chinese Value Survey

For reasons of his own, Bond was developing an instrument to measure Chinese values, many of them of course Confucian in their nature. One of his concerns was to ensure that Oriental frameworks were represented in any theorizing about values. Social science is Western in origin and value surveys, such as Hofstede's, are the products of Western minds. The dimensions of value discovered by Hofstede could also be found in other Western instruments (Hofstede and Bond 1984), but could they be found in one culled from an Oriental tradition?

The answer, it turned out, was that three of Hofstede's four culture-level dimensions of values overlapped with three of the four in the Chinese Value Survey (CVS).

Indeed, the first CVS factor, 'integration', located countries in ways that correlated .68 with their 1984 GNP's just as Hofstede's individualism had done in an earlier era. Not surprisingly, the Eastern values of integration measured in 1983 located countries in ways that correlated .65 with the Western values of individualism measured in 1972. The economic elephant of wealth was thus locatable across time by value measures derived from dramatically different cultural traditions. The link between values and wealth was robust!

The second CVS factor did not produce correlations with any of the Hofstede factors. It appeared to be a uniquely Oriental factor with a number of Confucian themes, such as ordering relationships by status and observing that order. Perhaps, then, the use of the CVS had suggested an additional dimension of values necessary to make the value taxonomy more comprehensive. This potential seemed vindicated when it was discovered that this second factor, and none of the others, located countries in ways that correlated (.70) with their rate of economic growth across a twenty-year period from 1965 – 1984. This value complex was tendentiously labelled 'Confucian work dynamism'. The missing link had been forged!

Confucian Work Dynamism and Economic Growth

Hofstede and Bond (1988) have speculated about how the particular values constituting Confucian work dynamism may be implicated in recent economic growth. So, for example, the relative indifference to 'protecting one's face' (surprise!) in the high-growth countries may be related to focusing on the task at hand and ignoring concerns about the social ramifications of interpersonal events. It should be borne in mind, however, that whatever the reasoning, these key values must be orchestrated within a complex latticework of varying economic, legal, political and demographic factors to make sense of recent growth in East Asia (Hicks and Redding 1983 b, Redding 1988). Of course, this very complexity of factors suggests that the values have some independent explanatory use and are not mere epiphenomena.

It should be made clear that the measurements in question were taken from university students who are hardly representative of their cultures as a whole. Instead, they probably represent that group of the population which will constitute the bedrock of middle and upper management in a given country. This is an important consideration in light of Redding's (1988) analysis of the entrepreneurial role in the growth of the Five Dragons. Briefly, he argued that structural supports propose and entrepreneurial behaviours dispose. Both are needed to achieve growth. Entrepreneurial behaviours include initiating and co-ordinating activities, but do not need to be performed by the same person or persons.

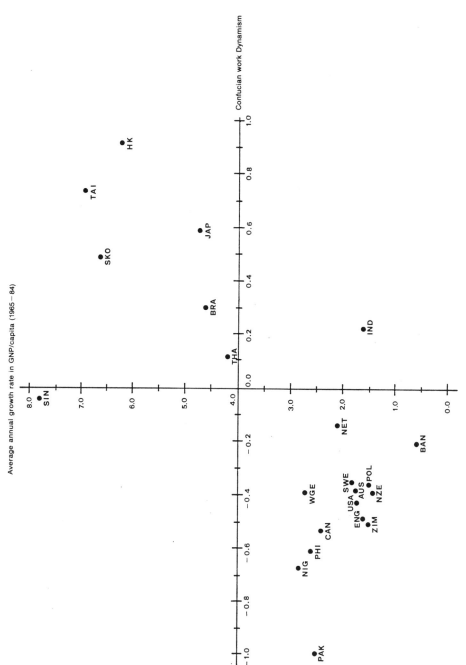

Figure 1   Average annual growth rate in GNP/capita (1965 – 84) as a function of Confucian work dynamism

Could it be that the CVS has identified a critical complex of values necessary to the worldview of those actors in the drama who perform the co-ordinating activities? Without such personnel as back-up, the initiating activities of entrepreneurs founder for want of effective follow-through. Of course, such values do not ensure that growth will occur, as we see in Fig. 1 for the case of India and Bangladesh, where the lack of structural supports depresses the initiating activities of the enterpreneurial role. No amount of co-ordinating skills in future middle management can sustain a fire with neither sparks nor fuel. Should these factors be brought into play, however, the potential for growth appears to be present in the values of this key group.

In passing, it is worth noting that different values may be important in rank and file workers for countries experiencing high levels of sustained growth. In those sectors of the population a different aspect of the Confucian heritage may be relevant. Further survey research could address this possibility.

As argued elsewhere (Bond 1988), the values that relate to growth in one historical period are unlikely to do so in another. Shifting world conditions create opportunities which can be more effectively exploited by the actors in certain types of political environment than others. Our eventual theories will therefore be time-bound.

Conclusion

For the time being attention is focused on East Asia. The use of the CVS has enabled us to validate the earlier intuitions that something Oriental in cultural tradition was critical in bringing the growth here to a boil. Further, the instrument has permitted a sharpening of the rampant speculation by showing empirically just which values, Confucian and otherwise, are *and are not*, related to this economic upsurge. As William James reminded us, the usefulness of scientific constructs lies in their capacity to provide empirical linkages. This is their 'cash value', as he put it, and Confucian values have proven their worth in predicting economic growth. A new method has yielded a new explanatory linkage.

References

Bond, Michael Harris (1988): Invitation to a wedding: Chinese values and global economic growth, in: D. Sinha and H. S. R. Kao (eds.), *Social values and development: the Asian perspective*, 197–209, New Delhi: Sage.

Bond, Michael Harris, Kwok-Choi Wan, Kwok Leung, and Robert Giacalone (1985): How are responses to verbal insult related to cultural collectivism and power distance? *Journal of Cross-Cultural Psychology* 16: 111 – 127.

Feather, Norman T. (1979): Values, expectancy, and action, *Australian Psychologist* 14: 243 – 260.

Franke, Richard H. (1987): *Achievement motivation and national economic performance*, Proceedings of the 25th Annual Meeting, The Southern Management Association, New Orleans.

Hicks, George and S. Gordon Redding (1983 a): The story of the East Asian economic miracle: I. Economic theory be damned, *Euro-Asia Business Review* 2: 24 – 32.

Hicks, George and S. Gordon Redding (1983 b): The story of the East Asian economic miracle: II. The culture connection, *Euro-Asia Business Review* 2: 18 – 22.

Hofstede, Geert (1980): *Culture's consequences: international differences in work-related values*, Beverly Hills, Cal.: Sage.

Hofstede, Geert and Michael Harris Bond (1984): Hofstede's culture dimensions: an independent validation using Rokeach's value survey, *Journal of Cross-Cultural Psychology* 15: 417 – 433.

Hofstede, Geert and Michael Harris Bond (1988): The Confucius connection: from cultural roots to economic growth, *Organizational Dynamics* 16: 4 – 21.

Hwang, Kwang-Kuo (1986): *Dao* and the transformative power of Confucianism: a theory of East Asian modernization, Unpublished manuscript, National Taiwan Unversity.

Kahn, Herman (1979): *World economic development: 1979 and beyond*, London: Croom Helm.

Leung, Kwok and Michael Harris Bond (1989): On the empirical identification of dimensions for cross-cultural comparisons, *Journal of Cross-Cultural Psychology* 20, 133 – 155.

McClelland, David C. (1961): *The achieving society*, Princeton, N. J.: Van Nostrand Reinhold.

Redding, S. Gordon (1988): The role of the entrepreneur in the new Asian capitalism, in: P. L. Berger and H. H. M. Hsiao (eds.), *In search of an East Asian development model*, New Brunswick: Transaction Books.

Schwartz, Shalom H. and Wolfgang Bilsky (1987 a): Toward a universal psychological structure of human values, *Journal of Personality and Social Psychology* 53: 550 – 562.

Schwartz, Shalom H. and Wolfgang Bilsky (1987 b): Chinese values and the search for culture-free dimensions of culture, *Journal of Cross-Cultural Psychology* 18: 143 – 157.

Triandis, Harry C. (1984): Toward a psychological theory of economic growth, *International Journal of Psychology* 19: 79 – 95.

Zavalloni, M. (1980): Values, in: H. C. Triandis and R. W. Brislin (eds.), *Handbook of cross-cultural psychology: social psychology* 5: 73 – 122, Boston: Allyn and Bacon.

Ethnicity and Religion in the Development of Family Capitalism: Seui-Seung-Yahn Immigrants from Hong Kong to Scotland

How can greedy human beings trust each other enough to go into business together? The conventional answer is that greed is somehow culturally restrained. In the jargon of the economists, 'economic man' stands for an abstracted entity as 'culture-free' as that other great artefact of early twentieth-century European rationality, the 'intelligence test'. For social scientists this has meant that 'the economy' and 'culture' have been seen as two great independent variables or value-systems (or whatever), which have to some extent conflicted with each other or, at the very least, had an independent causal effect upon each other and upon individual and social actions. Which of the two has a more fundamental effect has been a touchstone to differentiate between Marxism and its opponents, between different Marxist schools and (in a less overt way) between different functionalist or structuralist schools.

When we write of an 'economic culture', we are implicitly drawing upon a century of European debates in which tradition, language, morality and religion have been seen to discipline, or to modify, or to be a mere super-structure of or even to be 'over-determined in the last instance by' the operation of need, greed and the material base. These academic debates correspond to popular European conceptions of problems of deciding right and wrong (tough and tender, consumption vs. production, economic vs. 'social') and, therefore, can actually influence and shape policy debates. It is much harder, however, to make the imagery of 'culture' and 'economy', as independent variables in dialectical interaction, work in the analysis of cultures where the economy itself may be seen as a moral process. None-theless, if we are to answer crudely cultural-determinist models of the development of East Asian firms, we must develop alternative accounts of the general processes of the construction of economic morality. When we do this, we may be able to shed some light on the question of how trust is established between individuals to allow the employment of capital on a large scale and the growth of firms.

A traditional location of this debate has concerned the relationship between protestant Christianity and capitalism (Tawney 1926, Weber 1930). Very crudely, the possible positions in this debate were that protestantism created the conditions for the rise of capitalism, or, contrariwise, that capitalism created the conditions for the birth of protestantism or, in the muddled middle, that the whole process had something of the chicken and the egg about it. The historical debate has spawned a contemporary organizational and social-psychological debate (Furnham 1984) over the importance of a concept taken from this debate, the 'protestant ethic', presented as a reified ideal-type of individualistic striving. Common to all sides of these debates is the ascription of at least analytical autonomy to religion and forms of the organization of production.

In this paper I propose to look at the relationship between protestant Christianity, often thought of as a specifically Western religion, and the economic life of a group of Hong Kong Chinese fishermen and its emigré communities. To avoid identifying them too closely, I will refer to them in this paper as the 'Duck Islanders'. I shall speculate as to whether that relation between their religious and economic life can be thought of as one of cause and effect. Does their religion promote capitalist organization among them because it promotes individualistic striving? – or, paradoxically, because it promotes solidarity and trust which facilitate the accumulation and cooperative employment of capital? A second important theoretical question will be whether it is helpful in any sense to see this relationship as existing in the context of a specific ethnicity, nationality or 'area' (i.e. region of the world in the sense of 'area' studies). Do the Chinese, for example, take an 'ethnic culture' with them, or do they only become capitalists outside of China? Or is the real question the one that Wong (1979 a) has posed in his path-breaking study of Shanghainese in Hong Kong, as to what use do capitalists make of the ethnic networks of their own cultural community?

Questions of the mutual effects of the mode of production and culture are usually posed with large national collectivities taken as examples. Following Max Weber, ideal-types are constructed of the behaviour of the industrialists, technological innovators and workforces and (although Weber partly at least saw the value of ideal-types in the empirical study of divergence from them) the construction of logical connections among these ideal-types has become the most common method of the analysis of social trends. An extremist such as Outhwaite (1975) can even state that ideal-types *are* the method of the social sciences. In such an atmosphere it is perhaps unsurprising that grand theory of capitalism is allowed to substitute for the kind of empirical study of the behaviour of actual capitalists that Wong (1979 a) has cautiously attempted.

A devastating critique of ideal-typical method can be found in Jennifer Platt's (1971) re-working of the Bethnal Green Community studies. She shows, for example, that Willmott and Young's concern to present an overall picture of women's life-histories lead them to obscure important differences between women which are indicative of trends and changes they miss. At the risk of sounding positivist, this paper seeks to reaffirm her assertion that exceptions to rules are important to a scientific approach. This is so even if those exceptions are found amongst small, despised or obscure groups of people. Of course, 'social facts' in the Durkheimian sense are usually statistical trends; but social *theory* should account both for the trend and the exception to the trend, otherwise the exception does falsify the rule. *Verstehen* cannot be exempted from logic or refutation. A sociological career, spent in the study and service of pariah groups, such as Gypsies and South Chinese boat-dwellers, has left me with the conviction that models of cause and effect based on ideal-typification of large-scale trends in national histories allow considerable space for ethnocentric self-deception.

The problem that sociologists of really small minorities always face, however, in comparison with the sociologists of large collectivities, is that their audience is rarely familiar with the background of the minority; the corresponding advantage is that the scholar's version of that historical background is less open to challenge. What follows must inevitably be taken as rather tentative.

The Duck Islanders are exceptional in every way. They preserve a Seui-Seung-Yahn (water-dweller) identity when others abandon it and preserve a sense of community between the well-off and the poor, where most poor Seui-Seung-Yahn have simply ceased to be part of the community. They have embraced Christianity, which most other Seui-Seung-Yahn reject but, unlike most Chinese Christians outside China, they have joined a church that remains fiercely Chinese and un-Europeanized in culture; yet within that sectarian and inward-looking church the Duck Islanders are notably outward-looking.

The Duck Island community was created during the Second World War when a section of the Hong Kong Seui-Seung-Yahn (fisherfolk) community converted to the Jan-Jesu-Gaau-Wui (True Jesus Church). Across the world there are today perhaps 1,500 Duck Islanders. An understanding of the nature of this community requires an understanding both of the special position of fisherfolk in Hong Kong society, and of the distinctive doctrines and social attitudes of the True Jesus Church.

Hong Kong fisherfolk belong to a socio-economic stratum which has been perceived as distinct in Cantonese-speaking areas of South China for perhaps 1,500 years (Acton and Acton 1982, Anderson 1970). The community in fact includes two slightly different strata: (a) river and canal transporters of goods and (b) coastal and river fishermen. Both of these are referred to by ordinary Cantonese as 'Tanka', a highly pejorative word for which a number of improbable folk-etymologies are current; members of the community resent the term 'Tanka' and refer to themselves as 'Seui-Seung-Yahn', water-dwelling people.

Before 1950 the Seui-Seung-Yahn were seen both by Chinese scholarship from imperial times down to the U. S.-trained sociologists at Lignan (now Zhongshan) University in the 1930s (Wu 1936, 1937) and by Hong Kong-based European scholarship (Balfour 1970) as an *ethnic* group. They were treated as a pariah group, ineligible for marriage with peasants, and in places not even allowed to step foot on land, supposedly by imperial decree (although in fact all the imperial decrees that have been found actually do the opposite and restore privileges to the 'Tanka' people supposedly lost in the past). Prejudice against this pariah group took a distinctly racist ideological form, stigmatizing the 'Tanka' as supposedly aboriginal descendents of 'Tan' people who lived in Guangdung before the migration south of Han Chinese. They were said to be darker in colour, to have a distinct dialect, a greater incidence of green eyes, six-toed children and so forth (Ho 1965).

After 1945, policy to improve the situation of the Seui-Seung-Yahn at first reflected this ethnic perception of their situation. Both in China and in Hong Kong separate educational provision was launched for them (Acton 1981). But in the post-war world the taken-for-grantedness of ethnicity of pre-war racial thought no longer existed. In China national minorities policy required a bureaucratic processing of candidates for national minority status (Wong 1979 b). The report on the investigation into the Tanka in the People's Republic started in 1956 has not been published, but a reading of Fei's (1980) discussion of the process easily enables us to understand why they never have been listed as a national minority. In Hong Kong social anthropology reached the New Territories, and a series of papers by Ward (1955, 1966, 1967), based on repeated ethnographic visits to the island of Kau Sai, reached the conclusion that with minor exceptions the Seui-Seung-Yahn were ethnically indistinguishable from the Cantonese, with similar models of the world, marriage and death practices and religious beliefs similar to those of other Han Chinese. Other scholars endorsed this (Anderson 1978, Kani 1967) and even their language, apart from its specialized fishing vocabulary, is said to be virtually the same as ordinary Cantonese (Anderson 1972, McCoy 1965).

I have argued (Acton 1985) that this reassessment of the ethnic status of the Seui-Seung-Yahn is misguided in its cut and dried approach to whether groups are or are not ethnic. Distinct kinship organization, history and (contrary to McCoy) language, do, actually, give the Seui-Seung-Yahn many of the characteristics conventionally ascribed by sociologists as constituting ethnic identity. I argued that the de-ethnicization of perceptions of the Seui-Seung-Yahn was a consequence of the change in their position in the economy. (I argued this partly by comparison with the reverse process of ethnicization of Gypsies in academic and policy perceptions going on at the same time in Europe, where the disappearance of traditional trades delegitimated the perception of them as an occupational stratum.)

In the South China of the late twentieth century sea-fishing is no longer a suspect pariah trade, but a vital part of the modern economy. In both Hong Kong and Guangdung, despite the difference of regime, there has been a massive public investment to modernize marine and riverboat technology and marketing, through the encouragement of cooperatives both in transportation and in fishing, and even, in Hong Kong, in housing. The numbers of people still within the fishing and water-transport industries, however, fell dramatically, from around 50,000 to 35,000 in Hong Kong in the 1970s alone. The living standards of those within a more capital intensive industry rose, while those who left it, so the conventional wisdom goes, were assimilated into the general Cantonese population. Both in Guangzhou and Hong Kong non-Seui-Seung-Yahn children sought entrance to the special schools; the last such school in Guangzhou was integrated into the general school system in 1978, while in Hong Kong the numbers of schools declined from the peak of 14 primary schools and one secondary school in 1980 to 10 primary schools and one secondary school in 1987. The total number of pupils, however, has grown slightly, because although the schools on remote islands have shrunk, the numbers of pupils in schools in urban areas, now almost indistinguishable in character from other urban schools, have risen. The voluntary charitable and religious schools for boat-dwellers have now all disappeared.

Although there are some organizations which maintain links with and promote the welfare of Seui-Seung-Yahn who no longer fish (Acton 1981), the membership of these is obviously only a fraction of those who have left the fishing industry. Whereas in the post-war years there were official estimates of the numbers of the 'Tanka' community, no one would now venture such an estimate because the community has ceased to be well defined. The wealthiest of those who remain fishermen have diversified their investment into the stock exchange and into manufacturing industry like any other capitalists; although they may contribute to charities for fisherfolk along with the other charitable contributions which mark a

Hong Kong capitalist's social standing, their acknowledgment of Seui-Seung-Yahn identity — or, should we say, in this context, origins — remains private, because, although government policy is favourable and living conditions improved, much popular prejudice remains.

The True Jesus Church

I am not aware of any formal academic history of the True Jesus Church, still less of its presence in Hong Kong. According to its own literature (True Jesus Church 1976), it was founded in Peking in 1917. The practice of 'speaking in tongues', seen as a sign of 'baptism in the Holy Ghost' mark it as one of the many Pentecostal denominations founded around the world in the first two decades of this century (Hollenweger 1972). Among Pentecostals, it is distinctive in possessing 'Seventh Day' principles; i. e. it celebrates the *Sabbath* on Saturday, not on Sunday. It is difficult to know whether their thinking on this is derived from Seventh Day Adventist or Baptist thought or whether independently arrived at, since the church sees itself as having by inspiration revived the practice of the early church as revealed and justified in its reading of the Bible and discounts, therefore, any notion that it has borrowed any of its practices from earlier or European churches. Some of its formulations as to its independence might be seen, however, to reflect the ideas of pre-1949 phases of the Three-Self Movement (cf. Soo 1980: ch. 8). Contemptuous of most Sunday-worshipping churches, it has occasionally sought links with other, usually tiny, Seventh-day Pentecostal sects around the world, but usually finds them unsound on Baptism, which it holds to be inefficacious unless carried out by someone themselves correctly baptised, in the name of Jesus, by total immersion in 'living water', face downwards upon immersion, face upwards on coming out of the water, followed by washing of the feet. It describes itself as 'a revived apostolic church, [preaching] [...] a full gospel of salvation based on the truth in the Bible, accompanied by signs and miracles and the gifts of the Holy Spirit' (True Jesus Church 1976).

After 1949 its international headquarters were moved to Taiwan and only recently has personal communication with its adherents still in the People's Republic of China been eased. Until recently its influence was mainly limited to areas of substantial Chinese presence, such as Malaysia and Singapore and, to a lesser extent, two other East Asian countries, Korea and Japan. As, however, the children of its converts have entered white-collar occupations and become part of the student and professional Chinese diaspora, presences have been established in India, Thailand, the Philippines, Europe and North America, while missions have also been established in Africa. In the countries of their more recent expansion there are now growing numbers of non-Chinese converts. Within Taiwan it was described by the late head of the Elim Pentecostal missionary work there as being seen by other Christians as highly sectarian and isolationist (J. K. MacGillivray, personal communication 1982); he expressed great surprise at the relatively open and outward-looking attitudes in Hong Kong and the U. K. In 1987, at a meeting of their London church, I put it to a Malaysian Chinese student that the True Jesus Church was increasingly prepared to be open to fellowship with Christians from other churches, but more so outside Taiwan. After thinking a moment, he replied that yes, the church in Taiwan might be a bit more conservative, but — *'like China itself'* — it might be opening up.

Although the message of the True Jesus Church is addressed to all humanity, outside of Asia membership is clearly a token of Chinese ethnicity for many of its members. They pay little attention to the European festivals of Christmas and Easter, seen as pagan events which have been incorporated into Christianity. (In any case, these are busy times in the restaurant trade.) They do, however, celebrate the Chinese New Year (although as a secular, not a religious, event) and some congregations, in a spirit of missionary concession to European culture, will mark January 1st by a special service. In the U. K. maintaining Chinese culture is clearly important. In the early years of immigration to the U. K. parents used to send their children home from Scotland to Duck Island in Hong Kong to receive a Chinese education at the Fish Marketing Organization school on the island. In 1980 there were still 40 children there, in two classes.

In the last decade, however, the True Jesus Church in Scotland, dominated by Duck Island emigrants, has set up its own educational institutions. With the aid and materials that the Hong Kong High Commission supplies for Chinese classes they run a number of Chinese classes on Sundays and weekdays. They run these on a scrupulously secular basis 'as a service to the Chinese community in general', drawing in numbers of non-church-members. By 1987, there were only three children in the F. M. O. school on Duck Island.

Although, however, in the U. K. the True Jesus Church serves as a marker and sustainer of Chinese ethnicity in general, in Hong Kong it is more frequently a marker of specifically Seui-Seung-Yahn identity, a fact which must be borne carefully in mind when considering the economic culture of the Scottish-based group.

The Hong Kong church dates back to the period of Japanese occupation during World War II. A Malaysian Chinese lady fish merchant began to preach and pray for healing among the fishermen from whom she bought prawns and other items. Many of the oldest Duck Islanders, including the village head, have vivid memories of her preaching. After a number of healing miracles a congregation was established, drawing Seui-Seung-Yahn from the North-Eastern part of the New Territories of Hong Kong. The post-war years, however, brought a double challenge to these converts. First, they were no longer visited by the lady who had first preached to them and their contact with the parent True Jesus Church became largely postal for some years. Secondly, after 1949, the original site of their church fell on the Communist side of the border with Hong Kong and was expropriated. Faced with this the congregation took a decision with far-reaching effects. Following the biblical injunction, 'Come out from among them and be ye separate', they decided to build a new church and establish a completely new village on the then uninhabited Duck Island.

At first, like most Seui-Seung-Yahn, they were poor, stigmatized and lived mostly on boats; but as the years passed, the school was established and a housing cooperative (with some overseas assistance) built houses. To the effects of the economic assistance given to the fishing cooperatives by the Hong Kong Government were added the effects of the industry and sobriety which, as John Wesley pointed out, attend any religious revival, promoting thrift and consequently the habit of saving for a rainy day. When the community was forced to face up to the manpower shake-out consequent upon the mechanization of the fishing industry, a number of strategies were possible. Some could continue fishing more efficiently. Some individuals contributed to family income by seeking factory jobs in Kowloon; many of these later returned to family businesses, but some have remained permanently as employees of other enterprises. More importantly, in the 1970s economic activities were diversified within Hong Kong, particularly into sea-fish farming on Duck Island, and substantial chain migration took place from the 1960s onwards following the original lead of one man following a friend who was not a Duck Islander.

Clearly, although the Duck Islanders do not perceive themselves as having been in any sense wealthy in the 1960s (and certainly not by comparison with today), their thrifty saving habits had generated a sufficient economic surplus both to finance emigration and to diversify economic activities in Hong Kong.

Of these two, economically emigration is vastly more important. Community members estimate that between 80 – 90% of the 1,500 people who would call themselves Duck Islanders now live outside Hong Kong (some 1,000 in the U. K.), leaving only 2 – 300 people in Hong Kong, many of them elderly, mostly living on Duck Island itself, although a few, whose jobs or business lead them to the urban areas, live there, returning to Duck Island for the Sabbath. On the Island itself, in 1987 there were only ten active fishing boats and these were line-fishing sampans, very much smaller than the substantial net-fishing junks of former years. The fishing boats were still said, however, to be a larger source of income than the declining seafish-farming business which had been started in the 1970s. Remittances from abroad are also important. Some Duck Islanders living in Scotland keep up houses on the Island; many of the houses built during the 1960s now stand empty, however, even though recently the government finally brought mains water and electricity to the island.

Although there are now small numbers of Duck Islanders in a number of countries, the main receivers of emigration have been Scotland and England. In Scotland perhaps 300 live in Edinburgh, while a smaller group lives in three small towns in the North-East of Scotland (which I will refer to as the Three Towns Community). In England there is a largish community in Newcastle-on-Tyne and two smaller communities in southern coastal towns. These communities were established by chain migration. A few members of the community came over first and followed the same economic strategy as other Hong Kong New Territories immigrants to the U.K.; they first worked as waiters and cooks in existing Chinese restaurants, then established their own, then brought over their kinsmen, who in turn established more restaurants. These establishments vary in size from small 'carry-out' (Scots for 'take-away') and 'chop-suey' houses, to restaurants where more distinguished Cantonese cuisine is on offer. Although only in this generation have the Duck Islanders become food professionals, like all Cantonese communities they have a reverential — almost sacramental — approach to cooking and eating.

The question we must now ask is how the economic culture of these Scottish Duck Islanders differs (a) from that of other Seui-Seung-Yahn, (b) from the Duck Island economy as it was established in Hong Kong after the war, (c) from that of other Chinese in the U.K. and (d) from that of non-Seui-Seung-Yahn True Jesus Church members.

Economy and Economic Culture of the Duck Islanders

Both in Duck Island today and in the U.K. the label that best fits the economic organization of the Duck Islanders is 'family capitalism'. There is a distinct watershed between 'family capitalism' and 'formal capitalism' (see Acton 1984 which, again drawing on Wong 1979 a, contrasts different models of ethnic mobilization between capitalists of Gypsy ethnicity who have or have not passed this watershed). Family capitalists seek to employ kin and acquaintances, whereas formal capitalists advertise posts and have to maintain an image of scrupulous fairness by not showing favouritism to family members. Family capitalists will openly capitalize upon their ethnic networks, making a virtue of their support of them. Formal capitalists may in fact make use of ethnic networks, or even cater to specific ethnic markets, but they have risen above crude and public ethnic symbolism — they identify with a class, 'responsible business leaders no matter what their background' rather than an ethnicity, 'our own kind of people'. Where family capitalists use all their money to consolidate or expand their own business, formal capitalists will both seek finance in the market and hedge their bets by investing their own money elsewhere. Formal capitalists appeal to the legal structures of the state to create trust, whether between directors and shareholders or between managers and employees; family capitalists locate trustworthiness via ethnic and kin networks, which tends to limit the growth of their firms.

The transition from being 'the boss' or 'the governor' to being 'the managing director' is one that needs to be studied. No Duck Islanders I met had made it, however, and indeed this marked a clear distinction between them and other Seui-Seung-Yahn in Hong Kong. The need to shake-out labour from the fishing industry has inevitably led the wealthier Seui-Seung-Yahn to take a more ruthless attitude towards more distant kin and ethnic connections. The new respectability of the Seui-Seung-Yahn community at large in Hong Kong has partly been achieved by a divorce between its poorer and richer sections. In the 1970s, while many of the poorer Seui-Seung-Yahn moved into resettlement estates or other land-based dwellings, some from choice or necessity remained on their boats; richer Seui-Seung-Yahn and government officials would, largely erroneously, refer to the inhabitants of the floating villages in the typhoon shelters as not being real 'Tanka', but only 'boat squatters' (SoCo. 1978). This is very similar to the way rich Gypsies in the U. K. will claim (and sometimes really believe) that poor Gypsies living in caravans by the side of the road are not really Gypsies at all. As we have noted above, the wealthier fishermen have entered the world of the stock market and formal capitalism; they have to distance themselves from a rough image.

This is not true at all of the Duck Islanders. The community which formed in the 1940s has not divorced into rich and poor. The admonitions of Zechariah (7.10) about the widow, the fatherless, the sojourner and the poor, are taken rather seriously among them; it is a caring community. Wealth is seen as in some sense held in trust. The 'Three Towns' community was described to me in 1981 as 'five restaurants in three towns which keep sixty people alive'.

One consequence of this is that the Duck Islanders have preserved an ethnic concept of Seui-Seung-Yahn identity. Although the ten boats still working on Duck Island, and its declining fish farm are the only remaining connection with the sea, their fishing background remains culturally important to the Duck Islanders. They emphasize that they have changed: one of the first ways in which they will test a new acquaintance is by turning over a fish during a meal to reject Seui-Seung-Yahn (and wider Cantonese) superstition; but the sea remains an enduring part of their collective consciousness. The passages dealing with Jesus' disciples' fishing activities are favourite parts of the bible and fishing imagery can play a large part in sermons. In one sermon in Scotland the preacher even referred to himself and the congregation as 'Ngodeih Danka...'. The context was the persecution of the Jews in the Old Testament; the message was that 'we fisherfolk' know all about that; the use of the word 'Danka' in that context had all the force that a Black American preacher would have if he started a sentence in a sermon 'We Niggers ...' — an embracing of that which the oppressor considers stigmatizing. The same sermon contained passages in 'Seui-Seung-wa', fishermen's dialect, which baffled not only myself but the Malaysian Cantonese speaker sitting next to me; perhaps the Duck Islanders do not realize that the scholars have declared there is no such thing as Seui-Seung-wa.

One might ask whether this ethnically based 'family capitalism' is properly described as capitalist at all. I would argue that it is. What Ward (1967) describes as a 'post-peasant economy' is radically different from the community of independent primary producers who needed little more than their skills to compete and catch fish. The cooperatives which assisted the modernization of the fishing industry and the start of the fish-farming were financial cooperatives — mutual credit associations rather than true producer cooperatives as in the People's Republic. The Duck Islanders help one another — but the businesses definitely belong to individuals, however much those individuals may see ownership as a religious trust. The fish farming is declining as the individual owners of particular cages retire or give up, and those cages then remain disused; it is not managed as a collective enterprise. Equally in Scotland there is a clear awareness of the importance of capital accumulation by individuals in successful business — how could it be otherwise?

Might we nonetheless suggest that the Duck Islanders' protestant Christianity has, so far from facilitating and encouraging their turn to capitalism, moderated and restrained it? Superficially this hypothesis might seem to have some supporting evidence, for example, in the economic specialization of the community. It has turned from one trade, fishing, to another, restauranteering. By contrast, in the London True Jesus church, dominated by Malaysian Chinese, among the professions represented there are — as in the English Chinese community at large — a fair proportion of accountants and student accountants. The Duck Islanders in Scotland, on the other hand, have virtually no accountants among them and have been forced to rely on Scottish accountants — not always wisely chosen at first — to handle their tax affairs. A number of the family businesses in Edinburgh use the services of two Malaysian Chinese accountants who are not, however, church members.

One restaurant-owner and lay-preacher employed an accountant who compounded neglect of his tax returns by dying in the middle of an appeal procedure a few years ago. The restaurant-owner had gone to London to prepare for an evangelistic mission in another country when a relative in Scotland opened his mail to find that the Commissioners of the Inland Revenue had set up a hearing for the very next day. He flew back to find that they were asking for more money than he had, or than he thought he could possibly owe. He told them so, and that they could take everything he had if they wished, but that he had to leave to go about the Lord's work at 4.00 p. m. sharp. Eventually a compromise was reached on a figure which he could pay by selling two buildings. When I met him in 1987, he was 'working for the Lord full time'. He had decided that business was hard and 'everybody thinks' people in business are dishonest. He wondered whether the Commissioners of the Inland Revenue might not have been prejudiced against Chinese persons. But, he said, all the Duck Islanders now took great trouble to get their accounts done properly.

In this respect, perhaps, the Duck Islanders are more like formal than family capitalists. Family capitalists in the U. K. are often rather proud of their ability to evade tax, a moral position which we may even find creeping into official discourse with right-wing economists' celebration of the so-called 'black economy'. The Duck Islanders deeply resent any implication that as small businessmen they are bound to be on the fiddle somewhere; honesty is a critical value for them.

For example, in 1981 I heard a sermon in which part of the theme was the need for truthfulness and honesty. Into this the preacher dropped a single sentence — that for example — 'we in the restaurant trade', because of the large amounts of cash handled, might be tempted not to declare it all for tax.

In the course of my life I have heard many sermons on sin from many different kinds of pulpit; never have I ever heard one that had such an effect as this. A collective intake of breath was followed by a silence of agonized introspection that was almost palpable. The afternoon after that sermon it had been planned for me to make various visits with the preacher; instead I spent most of the afternoon waiting outside various houses while the preacher was engaged in urgent pastoral visits at the request of church members; I remember thinking it had been a brave sermon to preach.

Not the least attractive characteristic of the Duck Islanders is the candour of this moral introspection. For example, the principle of non-violence which they espouse is also difficult to uphold. The same man who preached the sermon referred to above told me of an occasion when he had been serving in the family 'carry-out' restaurant. Late one night just as he and a cousin were closing the kitchen down after locking the front door, three young men knocked on the door and begged to be served, pleading that they had been working late and had no other chance to get a meal. So the Duck Islanders yielded to persuasion, relit the gas and served the young men — who promptly tried to run out without paying. 'I was so angry' the preacher recalled, "we jumped over the counter, we run after them, we tell them 'You pay for your meal!' ", and as he told me he clenched his fists at the memory. What worried him was the thought that if they hadn't paid, his anger might have led him so far as to hit them.

A Malaysian Chinese family head visiting Edinburgh from the London church told me that they had let a room in their house to two students, one Nigerian and one English. After a while relations had deteriorated and as the students refused to leave the house, and things got so bad, the family moved out to stay with relatives. The father of this family asked, 'Do you think they realize that because we are Christians, we will not go to court against them? What do you think we should do?' One cannot help wondering whether serving Chinese take-away meals to the crowds that turn out of Scottish pubs of an evening would be quite so safe or lucrative if some of the customers realized the scruples of these gentle restauranteurs. I learnt later that eventually and with great reluctance, the family went to court.

The concern with economic morality perhaps marks a difference between preaching of the Duck Islanders and other True Jesus Church teaching that I heard or read. By and large True Jesus Church teaching is preoc-cupied with theological correctness. The Church is marked out in most of the world as a minority sect which has to define its boundaries by pro-claiming correct doctrine, even within families where one is a church member and one not. The Duck Islanders, however, are mostly preaching to each other and do not have the same need to scarify the heretic; not unnaturally this means that, although they follow the theological method of the True Jesus Church, with long rhetorical arguments full of Scripture quotes often taken out of context, their sermons also are full of practical advice and reflection on the problems of daily living which, mostly being in the same business, they tend to share. In short, the Duck Islander sermons still reflect what Durkheim called 'mechanical solidarity'. Even those few Duck Islanders who have given up the practice of religion are still part of the community, still treated with affectionate tolerance; indeed I and my family were lodged with one such person on a visit to Scotland — underlying this perhaps was the thought that if this person saw that I was interested in the church, that might re-kindle his interest. It is also worth noting that this non-religious Duck Islander was as hospitable as all his relatives; when one Duck Islander asks a favour of another, it is granted almost without reflection. This is possible, of course, because everyone knows what is right and proper to ask as a favour.

More important, perhaps, than preaching in shaping this integration of religious morality into domestic and economic life was their practice of family Bible study. This brings together in private homes family and friends who live nearby: always a much smaller group than would be at a church service. This Bible study is fitted around the working day; back on Duck Island it was held before the fishing boats set sail and then, again, when the fishermen had returned and eaten. In Scotland it is held, like the main Saturday service, in the afternoon between the lunch-time and early evening sessions in the restaurants and then, again, at around one o'clock in the middle of the night after the restaurants have finally closed. Everybody present reads verses from one or two specific chapters of the Bible and then someone leads a meditation. Unlike a sermon, where a fusillade of disparate texts is dragooned into support of a prepared message, the meditation may draw disparate messages from contextualized texts. It seems likely to me that the self-searching economic morality of the Duck Islanders is underpinned far more by this fairly intimate practice of bible study, than by the exhortations of the sermons. The sermons express the ideology, but the bible studies create, recreate and adapt it.

Is it, then, simply the case that the Duck Islanders' religion has simply restrained and moderated their adaptation to capitalism? Certainly, religion has constrained their economic behaviour; but I think it would be a mistake to see it as simply having done this. In some ways the Duck Islanders are poised to move from family capitalism to formal capitalism without paying the price of loss of community and loss of identity that other Seui-Seung-Yahn in Hong Kong (and other Chinese immigrants abroad) have suffered. They have built up an accommodation between the trust based on ethnic and kin networks and that based on universal legal structures, because of the implicit universalism of their religion, which values scrupulous honesty towards all people and not only their own. In some ways the whole community acts like a single firm, say a moderate-sized restaurant chain.

The community has built up its family businesses. It has found and spent the money to provide beautiful church buildings: it is reaching the point where it has a further surplus to invest and where the stock market might provide an outlet. On a visit to Duck Island late in 1987 I heard a sermon which moved by easy stages from the blessedness of Sabbath rest to the need to cast worldly care aside because the love of God gives much greater pleasure. For instance, the preacher said, looking round, all the congregation knew that one of them had lent a large sum of money to someone who had bought stocks and shares just before the catastrophic slide in the stock market in October 1987. But that did not matter, he said, it was unimportant compared with the blessedness of rest in Christ. It was a very gentle rebuke, and what was being rebuked was undue concern over a loss rather than the investment.

It is a sobering thought that someone for whom profit is not the main motivating force may actually be more willing to take an economic risk, if they think it right, than someone for whom profits (and the fear of loss) is the be-all and end-all of business.

It is also a paradox that, although the True Jesus Church in Scotland preserves a strong distinctive identity for its members and, although it is somewhat of a 'total institution', providing religious, social, educational and sporting activities which can take every moment of a member's time; it is also a means of social integration into the Scottish community, simply because it provides a social status for its members to which other people in Scotland can relate. For example in the Three Towns Community, the leader of the church, who is also the leading restaurant-owner, is self-evidently to other businessmen-cum-church elder/deacons in the town the same kind of animal as themselves. One Pentecostal minister told me, confidingly, that though they might seem a little strange, they were 'real, borned-again Christians' — even if they did baptize babies. They visit the services of other churches and are visited in turn. The church leader belongs to the chamber of commerce; he played a big part in opposing the starting up of a disco (which, it was widely felt in Three Towns might be the occasion of sin). In short, the distinctive identity of the True Jesus Church has meant that the Duck Islanders can achieve a corporate integration, rather than an individual assimilation into Scottish society.

There are of course many isolated ordinary Chinese restaurant families in Scotland who have achieved neither. The True Jesus Church has begun to see its educational programme as in some way a service to such families, without necessarily imposing conversion on them. In fact, one leading church member has actually taken a formal job in Edinburgh with the Lothian Community Relations Council. The Duck Islanders then, are a community who have already adopted formal and legal structures of business within their family capitalism, and who possess an economic surplus which they are going to want to invest rather than to consume, and who have already begun to adopt a role of social leadership and liaison vis-à-vis sections of the wider Chinese community in Scotland. It certainly does not seem impossible to me that they might come to have the kind of economic impact that, say, the great Quaker families: Rowntrees, Cadbury and Fry, had on the confectionery industry. The difference between the Duck Islanders' adaptation to capitalism, and that of other Seui-Seung-Yahn is, perhaps, not so much that the Duck Islanders have been more restrained, but that they have had the communal strength to ensure that the adoption of capitalist economic methods serves their purposes and community, rather than allowing themselves to be subordinated to the 'imperatives' of the market and the break-up of their community.

The story of the Duck Islanders is, then, one that has only really just begun. I am conscious that my limited experience is an extremely slender base upon which to build speculation about their future contribution to the overseas Chinese economy. If they were themselves asked what they would wish outsiders to learn from them, many would probably reply in terms of a correct understanding of baptism; but the world itself − and this is my plea both to other scholars and to the Duck Islanders themselves − may have broader economic lessons to learn from their development about how to have enterprise without individual competitiveness and aggression, and how to gain profits without abandoning morality. This may sound rather off-puttingly pious; but it would be misleading to conclude without emphasizing something of the sheer charm of the Duck Islanders.

My first visit to Duck Island in 1980 was in the company of two Fish Market Organization Education Officials; until I saw the church building on the Island I was unaware of the existence of the True Jesus Church; to find an island entirely populated by seventh-day pentecostals was certainly a surprise. One of the two officials with whom I visited the island was a young lady of strikingly fashionable appearance, whose main interests were swimming, dancing, American detective fiction and the possibility of graduate study in Canada − the very opposite in style to the Duck Islanders. I asked her whether the Fish Marketing Organization schoolteachers on the island might not feel somewhat isolated when everyone else on the island belonged to this strange religious sect. 'Oh no', she replied, 'they are not like that, everyone likes them, they are always helpful and cooperative, they don't cause any trouble, they are always peaceful and quiet, they just practise their religion, they do no harm, everybody likes them'. It is not only their trust of each other which is an economic asset to them, but also the trust they inspire in others.

Only time can tell whether economic success will dilute and dissipate this unique community, or whether it can continue to transcend the temptations of wealth to contribute its integrity to the economic culture of Scotland.

Acknowledgements

I owe many debts of gratitude especially to the Fish Marketing Organization and other officials for information and interviews and to the British Academy for grant-aid both for my initial fieldwork in 1980 and for travel to Hong Kong to give this paper in 1988. But the largest debt of all, of course, is to the Duck Islanders themselves, for their never-failing welcome, hospitality and tolerance.

References

Acton, T. (1981): Education as a by-product of fish marketing, *Journal of the Hong Kong Branch of the Royal Asiatic Society* 21: 120 – 143. (Actually, although dated 1981, this was published in 1983.)

Acton, T. (1984): The rich have no country, the poor have no class, Paper given to the British Sociological Association Conference.

Acton, T. (1985): The social construction of the ethnic identity of commercial nomadic groups, in: J. Grumet (ed.), *Papers from the fourth and fifth annual meetings*, 4 – 23, New York: Gypsy Lore Society, North American Chapter.

Acton, T. and B. Acton (1982): Boat dwellers of South China, *China Now* 102: 26 – 29.

Anderson, E. (1970): The boat people of South China, *Anthropos* 65: 248 – 256.

Anderson, E. (1972): *Essays on South China's boat people*, Taipei: Orient Cultural Service.

Anderson, E. (1978): *The floating world of Castle Peak Bay*, Ann Arbor, MI: Michigan University Microfilms International.

Balfour, S. (1970): Hong Kong before the British, *Journal of the Hong Kong Branch of the Royal Asiatic Society* 10: 134 [reprinted from *Tien Hsia Monthly* (Shanghai) Vols. 11 & 12].

Fei, H. T. (1980): Ethnic identification in China, *Social Sciences in China* 1: 94 – 107.

Furnham, A. 81984): The protestant work ethic: a review of the psychological literature, *European Journal of Psychology* 14: 87 – 104.

Ho, K. E. (1965): A study of the boat people, *Journal of Oriental Studies of Hong Kong University* 10: 1 – 41.

Hollenweger, W. J. (1972): *The pentecostals*, London: SCM Press.

Kani, H. (1967): *A general survey of the boat people in Hong Kong*, Hong Kong: Chinese University of Hong Kong New Asia Research Institute Monograph No. 5.

McCoy, J. (1965): The dialects of the Hong Kong boat people: Kau Sai, *Journal of the Hong Kong Branch of the Royal Asiatic Society* 5: 46−64.

Outhwaite, W. (1975): *Understanding social life: The method called verstehen*, London: Allen & Unwin.

Platt, J. (1971): *Social research in Bethnal Green: an evaluation of the work of the Institute of Community Studies*, London: Macmillan.

SoCo (Society for Community Organization) (1978): A Survey of Boat People in Hong Kong (in Chinese), Hong Kong: SoCO.

Soo, M. W. (1980): Christianity in a colonial and Chinese context − the internal organisation and external relations of the Swatow Baptist Church in Hong Kong, London University Ph. D. Thesis.

Tawney, R. H. (1926): *Religion and the rise of capitalism: an historical study*, (The 1922 Holland Memorial Lectures), London: John Murray.

True Jesus Church (1976): *Words of life I*, Singapore: English Literature Evangelical Centre of the International Assembly of the True Jesus Church.

Ward, B. E. (1955): A Hong Kong fishing village, *Journal of Oriental Studies of Hong Kong University* 1: 195−214.

Ward, B. E. (1966): Sociological self-awareness: some uses of the conscious model, *MAN* 1: 201.

Ward, B. E. (1967): Chinese fishermen in Hong Kong: their post-peasant economy, in: M. Freedman (ed.), *Social Organisation: Essays presented to Raymond Firth*, 271−288, London: Cass.

Weber, M. (1930): *The Protestant Ethic and the Spirit of Capitalism* (tr. T. Parson, with an introduction by R. H. Tawney), London: Allen and Unwin.

Willmott, P. and M. Young (1957): *Family and kinship in East London*, London: Routledge and Kegan Paul.

Willmott, P. and M. Young (1960): *Family and class in a London suburb*, London: Routledge and Kegan Paul.

Willmott, P. and M. Young (1973): *The symmetrical family*, London: Routledge and Kegan Paul.

Wong, S. L. (1979 a): Industrial entrepreneurship and ethnicity: a study of the Shanghainese cotton spinners in Hong Kong, Oxford University D. Phil. Thesis.

Wong, S. L. (1979 b): *Sociology and socialism in contemporary China*, London: Routledge and Kegan Paul.

Wu, Y. L. (1936): The boat people of Shanam, *Nankai Social and Economic Quarterly* 9, 3: 613−665.

Wu, Y. L. (1937): Life and culture of the Shanam boat people, *Nankai Social and Economic Quarterly* 9, 4: 807−854.

Charismatic Capitalism: Direct Selling Organizations in the USA and Asia

Nicole Woolsey Biggart

Direct selling organizations (DSOs) such as Amway, Tupperware, Shaklee and Mary Kay Cosmetics are a distinctively American form of enterprise. DSOs first developed in the United States in the 19th century as a response to changes in the national commodity distribution system and assumed their modern form in the 1930s in reaction to New Deal employment regulations in the United States. They grew rapidly in the 1960s and 1970s with changes in America's labour force composition, in particular the recruitment of women to paid labour. In addition, direct selling organizations utilize nationalistic American symbols and Western individualist ideologies to appeal to recruits. The reasons for the development, growth and persistence of DSOs in the United States are several and fairly straightforward responses to American economic, political and social conditions.

Nonetheless, despite direct selling's emergence from and adaptation to United States society, DSOs are beginning to explode as a form of enterprise in Asia. Shaklee, Amway and Avon have rapidly growing presences in several Asian economies. Indeed, Japan has outstripped the United States in per capita participation in direct selling and in sales per direct selling distributor (the name for a DSO salesperson). In 1985 American and Japanese distributors each sold about $ 8 billion in goods. In 1987 the Japanese sold more than twice as much — $ 17.5 billion — while sales in the United States remained flat at $ 8 billion. In June 1988 rapidly multiplying Korean direct sellers formed a trade association. A consultant to the industry in Asia said DSO growth in Taiwan is 'the most explosive in the world', and 'Korea is not far behind'. The reasons for the current diffusion of DSOs throughout Asia, it is clear, however, cannot be the same as the reasons direct selling developed and grew in the United States: the institutional history and settings are simply too different.

The purpose of this chapter is threefold. It is, first, a brief review of the factors that gave rise to direct selling organization in the United States. Second, it is as an introduction to direct selling, a widespread but understudied economic phenomenon. I present in ideal-typical form the distinctive structural characteristics of DSOs, particularly as they deviate from bureaucratically-organized firm enterprise. Finally, based on scholarship about Asian society and enterprise, I offer tentative suggestions as to why direct selling appears to be finding a fertile environment in Asian nations while they are faltering in Europe. I hypothesize that social structural arrangements in Asia, while different from those in the United States, nonetheless make the region fertile for the development of this form of enterprise. The data and ideas in this paper draw from a larger study of the history and dynamics of the direct selling industry in the United States. See (Biggart 1989) for further information about data sources, data collection and analytic methods.

The Origins of Direct Selling Organizations in the USA

Direct selling, as an activity, is thousands of years old. Independent itinerant peddlers have sold goods from backpacks and carts for thousands of years. In the United States 'Yankee Peddlers' were an important means for distributing commodities throughout the colonial economy. Their importance declined by the 1840s, however, with the rise of a nation-spanning transportation network and the establishment of retail stores. Ironically, direct sellers made a comeback after the Civil War as a response to the success of mass merchandisers: manufacturers, displeased with having their goods sold next to a variety of other commodities in department stores, solicited salespeople to sell only their products. These travelling distributors became the first organized direct salesforces.

Organized independent distributors were a modest but stable presence through the 1920s in the United States. A wide variety of goods were sold by door-to-door salesmen: vacuum cleaners, pots and pans, shoes, books, brushes and home medicinals. A number of DSOs including Avon, Wearever, Encyclopaedia Britannica and Fuller Brush trace their origins to the period between the Civil War and World War I. At least 200,000 Americans were direct selling distributors in the 1920s.

Although enjoying a stable existence in the 1920s, direct selling was directly threatened by New Deal employment reforms of the 1930s. Then, as now, direct selling was an inefficient way to distribute goods. Selling tends to be a secondary income opportunity for most distributors and competes with family, hobbies and a primary job for the time of the worker. Salespeople are highly dispersed, poorly (if at all) trained and unmanaged.

The logic of direct selling, however, allows even unskilled, less-than-committed salespeople to profit a company as long as the overhead is kept sufficiently low. Even if the average distributor contributes only $ 10 a month profit to a DSO, enough distributors added to a salesforce without the costs of supervision and a work site can result in a very profitable business. The minimum wage law and payroll taxes proposed by New Deal reforms of the Roosevelt administration would have imposed unbearable overheads on the direct selling industry. The anticipated New Deal burdens on employers were predicated on the bureaucratic organization of work where the employer had the undivided, supervised and presumably productive time of employees. Direct selling had none of these conditions.

Direct selling resolved this employment regulation challenge by declaring distributors 'independent contractors'. The industry relinquished the employment relation and the right to use authoritative management controls in exchange for freedom from employment taxes and regulations and minimum wages.

While direct selling companies escaped the threat of expensive state regulations, they were faced with another challenge: the new need to control a dispersed salesforce without the use of managerial controls. DSOs pursued a number of strategies, but by the 1950s the most important were the development of self-controls and peer controls; distributors were urged to control themselves and each other. These non-managerial control strategies worked because of the character of the organizational structure of DSOs as they developed after World War II, particularly in the 'network DSO' variant, the form of direct selling that grew the most and grew the fastest in the 1960s and 1970s. In addition, the increased recruitment of women to direct selling probably contributed to the success of this form of enterprise. Women find the peer controls as they are expressed in DSOs to be friendly, even nurturing, and more acceptable than the authoritative relations associated with bureaucratic workplaces.

The Structure of Direct Selling Organizations

DSOs organize independent salespeople, often called distributors or consultants, who sell products and services directly to consumers through personal demonstrations, primarily in private homes. Demonstrations are either 'one-on-one' or, frequently, in 'parties' such as the ones made famous by Tupperware and Stanley Home Products. Distributors profit by selling products at retail prices which they purchase at wholesale cost from the DSO or from another distributor. As independent contractors, they purchase as individuals the products they sell and pay the cost of promotional

materials such as samples and advertising literature. Further, they control
the level of their work activity. Members[1] of network DSOs also recruit
and train ('sponsor') new organizational members who are likewise independent contractors. Members usually receive financial incentives, typically
a percentage of a recruit's sales, for sponsoring new distributors. Network[2]
DSOs are distinctive for this recruitment strategy which gives its organization a pyramid-like social network structure[3]: a distributor sponsors
others, each of whom is encouraged to sponsor others in turn. Each level
of sponsorship accrues to the financial benefit of the original sponsor and
any intermediate sponsor in the 'line'. Distributors therefore, have a financial interest not only in their own selling and recruiting success but in
the success of distributors below or 'downline' from them. Intense social
relations typically emerge from these financial relations as sponsors become
obsessed with the success of their recruits.

According to the Direct Selling Association, an industry trade association,
in 1983 the direct selling industry generated more than $ 8 billion in sales
and engaged 5 million workers in full-time (25%) or part-time work (75%).
Direct sales workers do not usually rely on selling as a primary source of
income, however. According to a 1977 survey conducted by Louis Harris
and Associates for the industry, direct sales income represents a median
of 9% of total annual household income of all DSO members, and 27%
of household income for members who work 20 or more hours per week
(1977: 15). 80% are women. Direct sales has vocational but also clearly
avocational adherents. DSOs, whose only true employees are in relatively
small administrative centers, would seem to represent loosely organized
market relationships between members of a line who encourage each others'

---

[1] Direct sales people are not 'members' in the sense of being employees or dues-paying
supporters; they are legally independent businesspersons. However, they are members in
the social sense of having associational relations and a common orientation.
[2] The direct selling industry recognizes a subset of DSOs that are called multilevel marketing
organizations. Multilevel marketing organizations have two essential features, the sponsorship structure I describe, and the wholesale sale of products by distributors to others
they have sponsored (downline distributors). A number of DSOs, including Mary Kay
Cosmetics, have the sponsorship structure without the marketing feature (Mary Kay
consultants purchase all products directly from the company). In this paper, I am concerned
with all DSOs that have the social relationsships created by levels of sponsorship. This
represents the majority of DSOs and in recent years has represented the fastest growing
sector of the industry in the United States. Direct selling of all types, including network
DSOs, are growing in Asia.
[3] In true pyramids sponsors may be rewarded simply for recruiting persons into the company,
rewards which are unrelated to the sale of goods. These are illegal in the United States.
DSO sponsors only receive rewards if the recruit sells products. Therefore, DSOs have
been found by courts to be legal.

Table 1   Models of Organization Structure

	Bureaucratic Organization[1]	Direct Selling Organization
Authority	Rests in universal rules; individuals empowered by office; office held by virtue of experience or expertise	Rests in substantive philosophy joined to belief in value of entrepreneurialism; individuals empowered by philosophical commitment
Normative system/social controls	Impersonal controls such as rules and supervision; segmental distribution of authority, financial rewards, status	Self-control (discipline) and personalistic peer controls; totalistic relations
Stratification	Hierarchical, differential distribution of authority, financial rewards, status	Undifferentiated authority structure joined to a status hierarchy; administration may be hierarchical
Differentiation	Horizontal differentiation of functions; vertical differentiation of authority and expertise	Differentiated between administrative staff and sales force; saleswork minimally differentiated
Compensation and incentives	Financial rewards, especially salary, primary	Combination of material, purposive, and solidary incentives
Recruitment and advancement	Universalist appointment based on training and expertise; tenure constitutes a career	Particularist recruitment for commitment potential; limited notion of career; tenure constitutes a way of life

[1] Adapted from Weber 1978: 217–226.

sales success out of pecuniary self-interest. In fact, DSOs are highly structured, and more closely resemble a moral community than a market.[4]

The following describes in ideal-typical form the important social structural features that modern DSOs share in some degree (Table 1). Not all DSOs, and not all members, embrace these features equally; my study of American DSOs posits the features of organizations that approach a pure type or what McKelvey and Aldrich (1983) call an 'organizational form'. In this comparative analysis I contrast six DSO structural dimensions with another ideal-type to provide a widely understood point of reference: the bureaucratic firm as described by Weber (1978). From an economic perspective

---

[4] Sociologists are beginning to explore the socially structured character of market relationships and challenge the view of markets as composed of autonomous individuals. See, for example, Abolafia (1984).

DSOs and firms are not directly comparable: economists would describe the DSO as a firm with a market of independent buyers (distributors) who sell to consumers. This conceptualization, however, does not capture the social reality of direct selling organizations: distributors do not operate like a market — they are socially and financially interdependent and often morally proscribed from competitive relations. Moreover, from the points of views of the actors involved, DSOs and firms are directly comparable. Each represents a social and economic alternative, a distinctive way of life in the economy.

Authority

Bureaucratic authority rests in universal rules to which the membership submits as individuals. DSOs, which have few rules, base their authority on a belief in entrepreneurialism, usually combined with belief in a substantive philosophy. Moreover, this entrepreneurial — substantive philosophy is frequently attributed to a charismatic leader, usually a founder. The leader's vision is expressed in the products and services offered for sale and in entrepreneurial association with the organization, which takes on value beyond its remunerative properties. DSOs tend to vary by their mix of these two bases of commitment, entrepreneurialism and a companion philosophy, although both are typically present. Shaklee, for example, stresses its vision of an ecologically harmonious world where people do not upset the natural balance through the indiscriminate use of non-biodegradable products. In addition, they claim the importance to health and happiness of using natural food products, rather than those developed for commercial convenience. Shaklee's products are an expression of belief in environmentalism, and members' shared use and promotion of products is a demonstration of commitment to a way of life as much as a means of profit. Amway, in contrast, stresses the value of entrepreneurial association which provides members with the opportunity to establish financially successful independent businesses; money, however, is both a means by which the member secures status, self-appreciation, social contacts, and security, as well as a valued end. Mary Kay Cosmetics asserts the importance of such traditional feminine values as attractiveness and family life, while promoting the self-actualizing potential of maintaining a business.

Although bureaucratic enterprises occasionally have 'charismatic' leaders insofar as these leaders possess personal magnetism and a persuasive business philosophy, among modern secular organizations it is usually social movement organizations (e. g., Trice and Beyer 1983), not routine economic enterprises, that embrace charismatic elements. DSOs, however, are extraordinary in the extent to which they rely on a leader's vision as a justification and guide to economic activity. Recently organized DSOs such as Shaklee, Mary Kay Cosmetics and Amway utilize their founders to sustain commitment: the writings of Dr. Forrest Shaklee, as well as living founders Mary Kay Ash, Rich DeVos and Jay Van Andel, are sources of intense interest and inspiration to members.[5] Each of these founders has been celebrated in a biography or autobiography that is widely read by the membership. Visits by leaders are the occasion for devotion and expressive behavior.

DSOs, like many religious groups, combine charismatic elements with value-rational organization (Peven 1968, Satow 1975). Orientation toward a leader's vision; the egalitarian, familial and emotional character of membership; and the stress on selling as a way of life rather than as instrumental activity have analogues in religious groups. In addition, the membership of a DSO may assume the character of a discipleship. This is especially apparent in proselytizing (recruiting) activities and in frequent group rallies that celebrate organizational beliefs. DSOs, like some political organizations, appropriate much of the social structural form of religious organization (O'Toole 1976), but supply a unique philosophical content, although a belief in the substantive value of entrepreneurialism is common to DSOs.

A number of informants compared DSO membership with church affiliation. For example, an Amway distributor said, 'I found a family that I had never had. There was a tremendous amount of love and acceptance, understanding and support in growing. I am a strongly religiously oriented person and there is a similar feeling in my church'. According to the Harris survey, active salespeople are more likely than the general public to be religious (and politically conservative), suggesting the familiarity and acceptability to DSO members of churchlike structural arrangements (Louis Harris: 14).

Legal-rational and traditional organization, not charisma or value-rationality, are most commonly associated with economic enterprise. But according to Weber, 'charisma is by no means alien to the economy' (1978: 1118), although Weber saw charismatic economic activity primarily linked

---

[5] While DSOs date from the 1800s, the use of such personalized forms of control as charismatic leadership, the multilevel marketing structure, and expressive practices appear to date from the 1930s and 1940s. DSOs founded prior to that time, even those operating today, have a less personalized character and more closely resemble the sales units of firms (cf. Kogan 1958).

to impermanent enterprise such as adventure or booty capitalism (e. g., piracy). Moreover, Weber's own study of the Protestant ethic as expressed by Calvinism shows the affinity of value-rationality to economic activity, in that instance, an entrepreneurialism oriented 'solely toward a transcendental end, salvation' (1958: 118).

It appears that charismatically led DSOs may suffer a problem typical of such organizations, the problem of succession on the death or retirement of the leader (although the recency of many of these organizations makes such a conclusion tentative). The retirement of Shaklee's founder in favour of a professional manager created a brief crisis. The new president's attempts to develop Shaklee's product line were perceived by long-term members as opposed to the founder's vision, according to one member. Protests by distributors modified what were instrumentally based business decisions. Another Shaklee informant spoke of an instance where the new president and other professional managers were photographed with a group of top distributors. The distributors arranged for the managers to stand at the ends of the group picture so they could be cut out of the photograph later if they failed to subordinate themselves successfully to founder Dr. Forrest Shaklee's philosophy.

The administrative staff of DSOs, which may be bureaucratically organized, derive their authority from their ability to interpret the organization's philosophy. Distributors accept the staff's decisions based on their presumed ability to further the interests of the organization's purpose, not for reasons of superior bureaucratic authority.

Normative System and Social Controls

Bureaucratic organization controls action largely through impersonal means such as rules and the routinization of work processes. Even apparently personal forms of managerial control such as supervision and discipline are in fact impersonal; supervisors do not act as individuals, but as agents of the organization (Scott 1981: 277–279). Personalized relations are subordinated to the impersonal in the modern firm; the personal finds expression in informal networks. Bureaucratic controls are justified through a managerial ideology that asserts the right of owners to control their property, and supervisors to manage workers as owners' agents because of superior knowledge and ability (Bendix 1956, Hill 1981: 39–40).

DSO members are geographically dispersed and work independently; there is no office to which they report. Bureaucratic controls of most forms are unsuited to this arrangement. Instead, DSOs rely on variants of two strategies used by autonomous professional organizations such as universities and law firms: self-control and peer control (in addition to incentives, which are discussed separately). Self-control emerges from internalizing the organization's philosophy, often by use and commitment to the products, and by discipline to the sales plan of activity. Recent recruits, for example, are usually encouraged to make a suggested number of sales contacts within a given period. Members are encouraged to compete with themselves in achieving sales goals and are taught that they will achieve whatever level of success they choose.

Individualism and self-determination are strong underlying ideologies. DSO members are supplied self-help books and motivational tape recordings. (Several independent firms have emerged to sell such materials to the growing market of DSO distributors.) Success in DSOs is portrayed as more than instrumental financial achievement. Rather, it is a sign of personal growth, something to be valued for itself; it is a measure of a person's discipline and, implicitly, of his or her worth. Failure, likewise, is more than a business upset. According to one Amway informant, 'I don't think of people who leave as bad people. I think of them as people who, for whatever reason, chose not to be successful'.

The other source of control is face-to-face peer relations, especially with members of one's line. The sponsorship structure, which profits those who recruit new members, resembles the internal subcontract system used in British and American factories prior to 1900. Under this arrangement, management subcontracted work to employees who could in turn recruit workers and control production at a profit (Hill 1981: 18, Nelson 1975: 39). Unlike those bureaucratically organized factories where work could be directly supervised, however, DSOs must rely on the commitment of dispersed workers. Sponsors, in this situation, act as motivators and supports for their downline members, encouraging their sales efforts. Discipline and negative sanctions have little utility in such an arrangement and would contradict the independent status of distributors. Criticism, for example, is explicitly forbidden in Mary Kay and discouraged in Shaklee.

Praise, in contrast, is freely given, especially in public meetings. Meetings are frequent, usually at least once a week and sometimes more often. They are occasions to inspire commitment, to celebrate the organizational philosophy and to recognize successful distributors, often through elaborate ceremonies, rituals and singing. These expressive practices have no regular counterpart in bureaucracies where a wider array of control strategies is possible.

Peer control in DSOs is highly personalized, in contrast to peer controls in professional organizations which typically have an administrative component (Scott 1981: 223). Sponsors conduct meetings for members of a line to share information and experience. In contrast to bureaucratic organizations, which may also rely on face-to-face meetings to convey norms as well as information, DSO relations are notably personal, even familial. Recruits are called 'offspring' in the Mary Kay 'sisterhood'. A Shaklee distributor whose line becomes inactive is 'orphaned' and may be 'adopted' by another line. The totalistic, familial orientation is more than metaphor; committed members frequently become involved in each others' non-work lives.

Family-like peer controls and the system of positive reinforcement would be threatened by competition within the organization, especially within a line. Unlike most capitalist enterprises, DSOs build in mechanisms for avoiding competition.[6] Mary Kay consultants are instructed to ask customers if they have ever bought the company's products; if so, they are referred to the customer's original consultant for subsequent purchases. Mary Kay has an award for the most selfless (non-competitive) consultant, the 'Miss Go-Give' award. One large Shaklee line sponsored a subsidiary association whose members promise to service recruits who move away without adopting them (profiting from their sales). A Shaklee distributor choosing to change lines must remain inactive for six months, a policy designed to discourage 'raiding' of distributors between lines. These organizational arrangements help to manage the inevitable tension inherent in an organization which simultaneously promotes aggressive individualism and non-competitive loyalty to line.

Bureaucratic impersonality extends to viewing workers segmentally, that is, only as workers. Firms often attempt to exclude ties that compete with loyalty to the organization, maintaining a clear separation of spheres. Theorists, however, have described organizations that 'try to incorporate and thus co-opt the family into serving the organization's ends' (Kanter 1977: 10, see also Coser 1975). DSOs adopt this latter strategy. Amway and Shaklee encourage the development of husband-wife businesses and the sponsorship of family members. Shaklee invites and entertains distributors' children at conventions. Husbands of Mary Kay consultants may attend spousal support sessions at annual meetings; those not attending are sent telegrams thanking them for the support of their wives' businesses. DSO membership is described by members as valuable even for non-participating family members. According to an Amway salesperson, 'There are things that we do for my daughter that I know I wouldn't have done

---

[6] Of course, in its ideal form, bureaucracy does not generate internal competition.

without this business. I am teaching her the principles of free enterprise. There is not a greater gift that I can offer her.'

Extending social controls beyond the bounds of work relations gives meaning to the organization's philosophy as a way of life and organizational peer relations as familial.

Stratification

In bureaucracies authority is stratified; 'each lower office is under the control and supervision of a higher one' (Weber 1978: 218). Rewards such as privilege, prestige and financial remuneration are likewise distributed unequally by rank. The inequality of bureaucratic organization is justified by the greater expertise and responsibility of superior officials.

The pyramid-like structure of DSOs might suggest that it is also unequally ordered. In fact, DSOs have an undifferentiated authority structure joined to a status hierachy. All distributors have equal authority to sell products under a contractual arrangement with the DSO administration and no distributor may control, dismiss or discipline another. (Even the DSO headquarters may not unilaterally dismiss a distributor; it may only terminate its sales agreement if the distributor fails to meet contractual obligations.)

A line does not constitute a hierarchy of authority. Distributions receive new titles and financial rewards by achieving established sales and recruiting goals. This 'advancement' does not, however, grant the distributor greater authority over downline members, although it usually results in greater personal influence. It is possible and not unusual for a downline member to achieve a greater level of financial success and a superior title than his or her sponsor.

Status, however, is clearly attached to higher levels of sales and recruiting (and, therefore, financial) success. Privileges, such as invitations to expense-paid meetings, accrue to higher level distributors who form a cadre of virtuosi, a status elite. Sales bonuses, such as cars and luxury goods, are desired symbols of status. Shaklee, for example, awards cars of greater or lesser value based on sustained sales of different amounts. The cars are leased by the company for the distributors' use for two years. At one regional Shaklee meeting distributors who had received cars were asked to stand and introduce themselves in order of the number of cars they had received. The person having earned the most cars, six, was the last introduced and most honored.

Differentiation

Firms differentiate work, not only by level, but by function. Differentiation allows officials to develop expertise in specialized areas, contributing to bureaucracy's efficient, rationalized character. Differentiation, however, requires that firms, especially large ones, develop co-ordinating mechanisms for bridging the work processes and understandings of unlike workers. Direct supervision, liaison roles and mutual task dependence are examples of bureaucratic co-ordinating strategies (Lawrence and Lorsch 1967, Mintzberg 1979, Walton and Dutton 1969).

DSOs are minimally differentiated; the primary division of labour is between the administrative staff and the salesforce. Saleswork is largely undifferentiated; while some members choose to spend more time recruiting or selling, most distributors do both. The highest level distributors spend more time 'managing' (training and motivating) their downline members than they do other activities, but most members perform some combination of the same tasks. Co-ordination, therefore, is accomplished almost entirely through the standardization of work skills and processes, allowing even very large DSOs to have a relatively small number of administrators. For example, Shaklee Corporation has an administrative staff of 1,500 and 1.5 million distributors. The undifferentiated nature of work contributes to the mechanical type of solidarity described by Durkheim (1949).

The sameness of distributors' work experiences, dilemmas and aspirations underlies one of the distinctive motivational strategies employed almost universally by DSOs: the use of exemplars and testimonials. Because everyone performs the same work under similar conditions and can aspire to the same higher ranks (there is no theoretical limit to the number of higher level titles), the experience and advice of successful distributors assumes great importance. Some successful distributors travel regularly to speak at meetings. Favorite testimonials are widely circulated as tape recordings.

Compensation and Incentives

Workers in firms work primarily for money in the form of salaries (Weber 1978: 222). DSOs rely on a combination of remunerative, value-fulfilment and solidary incentives.

Financial and purposive or value incentives are fused in DSOs; distributors achieve profit through the promotion of products and the establishment of businesses that have ideological importance. Informants stressed continually the difference between working for money in a bureaucratic enterprise, and working in DSOs to promote something in which they believed for which they could also earn money. One Shaklee distributor's comment was typical '[This organization places] a possibility at my fingertips for tremendous financial *and* personal satisfaction — growth in every direction possible.' Active salespeople are concerned with earnings, but far less than inactive salespeople. Active members, according to the Harris survey, find that 'their satisfactions in other areas sustain their involvement' (Louis Harris 1977: 12); for committed members material interests are subordinate to solidary incentives such as friendship and peer recognition. In fact, as in many professional organizations, the capitalist nature of the enterprise is often obscured or made to seem secondary. Shaklee consultants do not speak of selling products, they 'share' products. Mary Kay consultants emphasize their role as teachers rather than as salespersons.

DSOs are notable for the extent to which they employ symbolic awards. Inexpensive items such as pins, ribbons, jewelry and certificates are awarded for even small amounts of sales and are presented publicly at meetings. Persons achieving higher levels of sales and recruiting success are awarded items of value such as jewelry, fur coats, cars and expensive vacations, sometimes personally by the founder. Mary Kay salespeople wear items of clothing that indicate to members their recruiting and sales success. Mary Kay also awards numerous pieces of gem-studded jewelry, many of which have symbolic meaning. Very successful consultants, like military personnel, may be decorated with a dozen items of jewelry on status-ranked clothes.

The presentation of awards is an occasion for celebration of an individual's success by his or her peers. One Amway distributor said, 'When you get to [a middle achievement] level you get your first standing ovation, probably ever in your life. Performers tell me that is the most exhilarating experience and one of the reasons they keep going back to perform.' Symbolic awards and expressive peer acclamation are rare in firms, and typically occur only on an extraordinary achievement or at retirement; many workers never receive such recognition. DSOs routinely give praise and bestow awards which are signs of personal accomplishment and furtherance of the organization's philosophy. They have the character of 'honorific gifts' that allow members 'to share in the social, political or religious esteem and honor' in which the leader is held (Weber 1978: 1119).

The presence of ideal, symbolic and honorary incentives does not negate the importance of purely material rewards. Many distributors are attracted to the organization because of the opportunity to earn money in a flexible setting and because of the tax benefits that accrue to self-employed workers in the United States. Long-term members, however, largely embrace the ideational premises of the organization which both supplants and gives greater meaning to their material pursuits.

Recruitment and Advancement

Bureaucratic officials are selected according to universalistic criteria; candidates' qualifications are measured against impersonal standards and credentials may be used as evidence of expertise. DSOs, in contrast, rely on particularist selection criteria: the potential for a recruit's commitment to the organization. Recruits are usually persons with affective ties to members, such as family members and friends, or are satisfied customers of DSO products. Recruits sign contracts with the organization agreeing to conduct their activities in approved ways. Absolute standards of competence and credentials are not criteria for membership.

DSO membership may constitute a career, but not in the usual bureaucratic sense of hierarchical achievement or seniority. Success measures are explicit (e. g., monthly sales volumes, number of recruits), and advancement does not depend on the approval of superiors. Committed salespeople often use the term 'career' to speak of their activities (especially in DSOs like Amway that emphasize entrepreneurialism), but career in this usage often includes a notion of sales as a way of life, not merely a pursuit of livelihood.

Institutional Foundations of Economic Organization

Economic organizations, if they are to prosper, must fit into a conducive social and political environment. Direct selling has worked well in the United States because it has adapted to regulatory and market conditions, but also because of its ideological compatibility with American individualistic and meritocratic culture. Self-controls are based on a belief in the ability of individuals to control their fate. Certainly, the network DSOs succeed in part because of the relatively open character of social ties between individuals in the United States which permit the successful use of peer controls by unrelated persons.

While objective economic conditions suggested to some American direct selling executives that Europe was likewise a fertile market for their products and recruiting efforts, they have found this not to be uniformly the case. Northern Europeans did not greet direct selling with the enthusiasm of Americans. Laws there restrict market entry and access to homes far more than in the United States. The ideological climate is hostile, too, according to one industry executive:

In Europe the [DSOs] are in bad shape because Europe is much more socialistic, and the free enterprise spirit [...] it's not there. It's definitely a matter of spirit in this business and that's lacking. Plus they have a retailer antipathy [against tradespeople] which we have overcome here for the most part. It [remains] very strong there. I would say sales are flat to poor there.

A historical legacy of distaste for commerce, generous employment benefits in social democratic countries, and perhaps in some nations a more participative bureaucratic firm, pose obstacles to direct selling organizations.

This same executive noted, however, that Italy and Spain were good arenas for direct selling. These are countries with fewer worker protections and social welfare benefits. They are also countries with growing informal sectors where petty businesses flourish, suggesting that the 'entrepreneurial spirit' is alive in southern Europe.

If the outlook for much of Europe is bleak, the nations of the western Pacific rim are absorbing DSOs at a rapid rate. The diffusion of this type of organization is only beginning but success is promising, according to several executives. Between 1985 and 1987 the number of direct sellers in Japan tripled from an estimated 1 to 3 million, according to an industry executive. The Japanese government is exerting pressure on DSOs to recruit only adults over 21 years because large numbers of students have been quitting school to pursue direct selling.

Japanese distributors sold $ 17.5 billion worth of goods in 1987, but if automobile sales are included, the number jumps substantially: 75% of new cars are sold by door-to-door salespeople in Japan, more than $ 25 billion worth in recent years (Englade 1985). Between 1985 and 1987 direct selling grew an estimated 200% in Malaysia, 150% in Singapore, and 30% in Hong Kong (World Federation of Direct Selling Associations 1986).[7] The prospects are so good in Asia that Amway has shifted its international focus from Europe to the Pacific basin, which now represents 75% of its international revenues. An industry executive estimated that Amway will do $ 700 million in Japan in 1988 — the same as its American sales —

---

[7] The World Federation of Direct Selling Associations reported that in 1985 Hong Kong had 20,000 distributors and $ 15 million in retail sales; Malaysia had 95,000 distributors and $ 135 million in sales and Singapore had 15,000 distributors and $ 23 million in sales. Officials say that, at best, the figures are rough estimates (World Federation of Direct Selling Associations). Figures for 1987 are from a 1988 unpublished internal document.

after only 5 years of doing business in Japan.[8] Japan is Avon's largest foreign market (Hayes 1987).

Why is direct selling growing rapidly in Asia? Only tentative answers are possible: the newness of this enterprise form in the East and the lack of systematic information collected by either researchers or the industry demand hypotheses rather than conclusions. But the work of scholars interested in Japanese and Chinese society and enterprise, and my interviews with several industry executives, combine to suggest ways in which DSOs are ideally suited to social conditions in Asian nations.

In an important article in the *American Journal of Sociology* Mark Granovetter (1985) argued, in opposition to neoclassical economics, that economic activity can only be properly understood in the context of social institutions and relations: economic activity is *embedded* in society. It is culturally informed and channelled by the character and network of interpersonal relations.

Granovetter's 'embeddedness' argument was unintendedly invoked by Asian direct selling executives as reasons for the success of DSOs in the East. Three social factors, especially, were suggested as reasons direct selling organizations are suited to the Asian environment: cultural values, the structure of social relations and the importance of family ties. Each reason suggests why the DSO form — developed in and suited to America — also 'embeds' readily in Asia. Moreover, these executives' conjectures are given support by scholars of Asian enterprise and society.

Direct selling organizations incorporate two social values, individualism and community. Success is attributed to individual entrepreneurs who are recognized for their personal achievements with financial and social rewards. But individual distributors are part of a community — sponsorship lines of fellow distributors 'related' to them in the enterprise. Individuals are expected to heed the advice of upline sponsors and usually to support the selling and recruiting activities of members of their line.

Although the values of individualism and community are both inherent to direct selling organization, economic individualism clearly dominates in American DSOs. Scholarship would predict, and my interviews confirm, that communitarianism is stronger in Asian direct selling, especially in Japan where social scientists describe the group as the primary social unit and where 'individual autonomy is minimized' (Nakane 1970: 10). Japanese communitarianism is associated with common membership in an institutional setting, whether a patrilocal household, a place of work or a school

---

[8] Amway is privately held and does not publish financial data.

class. The primacy of group interests and the subordination of individual interests can spur on enterprise. Indeed, it has been described as a critical factor in Japan's industrial success (Vogel 1979).

A communitarian ethic is present in Chinese society, too, but is less all-encompassing and anchored primarily in the patrilineal family. Unlike Japan, however, individualism in the pursuit of interests and mobility are also important to the Chinese. The simultaneous presence of the values of familism and individualism create tensions in Chinese institutions, including enterprise. 'Both the Chinese and Japanese cultural traditions extol, as social ideals, "complementarity of relations" and "harmonious human relations in an organization". [...] [But unlike the Japanese there is] the pervasive ambition for [Chinese] individuals to strike out on their own' (Wong 1986: 312).

Americans, the Japanese and the Chinese embrace different values regarding the individual and the group. As Edwin Winkler (1987: 173) put it:

Americans' primary values are individualistic and underneath, most of their secondary values are individualistic as well. The primary values of Japanese are communitarian and, underneath, so are most of their secondary values. However, the primary values of Chinese are communitarian but, underneath, most of their secondary values are highly individualistic.

DSOs, with their foundation on both communitarian and individualistic values, can be moulded to these various settings. One would expect, however, that Japanese DSOs will take shape differently from those in the United States and in Taiwan, with the Japanese stressing relations in the line and team-based awards rather than success for individuals, and the Taiwanese emphasizing the familial aspects of direct selling. One Asian direct selling executive noted, too, that direct selling provides an outlet for frustrated individualism in Japan.

In addition, the structure of relations in Japanese and Chinese society parallels those in DSOs. As one Amway executive put it 'these are very structured societies' referring to the widespread presence of status hierarchies in Asian nations. Hierarchical relations in Japan, as in Chinese societies, are based on the Confucian doctrine of obeisance to superiors − whether a parent, an elder brother or the state. Social hierarchy has deep roots in Asia extending back to a feudal heritage in Japan, and to the stratified estates of imperial China. Status ranking systems (*shikaku seido*) are present today in Japanese enterprise and grant esteem and small perquisites to a select few among formally equal workers (Cole 1971: 109−113). In contrast, according to Ruth Benedict, Americans 'uphold the virtue of equality even when we violate it and we fight hierarchy with a righteous indignation', but the Japanese 'confidence in hierarchy' is basic in her whole notion of 'man's relation to his fellow man' (1944: 43, 45).

In DSOs, all distributors are legal equals — independent entrepreneurs. In the absence of an employment relation no person has authority over the other, and no distributor is required to obey another. DSOs, however, have clearly defined status hierarchies and sponsorship lineages. In the absence of authority relations the 'suggestions' of upline sponsors and status superiors carry a moral imperative that in fact substitutes for bureaucratic controls. In the Unites States, where entrepreneurial autonomy is prized, tensions may form around the directives of status superiors (Butterfield 1985: 79). The tensions are less apparent in Asian direct selling: executives attribute Asians' familiarity with and ready acquiescence to status superiors as a reason for DSOs' organized and disciplined character in the East.

In addition to a status hierarchy, DSOs are distinctive for their familylike lines — genealogies of fictive parents and siblings who recruit and encourage each other in economic pursuits. In the United States actual relatives are often recruited into direct selling, thereby utilizing affective bonds to sustain financial activity. In America, though, this combination of family and business is exceptional, not a common cultural pattern. Chinese economies, though, are notable for the extent to which they are comprised of family firms and utilize family labour. Japanese firms often employ a form of familism to create bonds between unrelated workers and management (Abegglen 1958, Clark 1974: 38–41). Moreover, in both Japanese and Chinese societies actual family bonds, through both marriage and consanguinity, are especially strong, and extended family units more likely to remain intact than in the United States.[9] Direct selling organization, with its personalized recruiting and familial organizational relations, is especially suited to situations where family networks are large and form the basis of economic activity.

Other factors surely promote direct selling in Asia, for example, a propensity for self-discipline (Benedict 1944: 228–252), and limited income and advancement opportunities for women workers.[10] In addition, Asians unlike many Europeans, have a generally high regard for enterprise.

---

[9] Family units, while generally strong in Asia, are composed differently in different Asian societies, however.

[10] Industry officials noted that direct selling succeeds in some countries, including Asian ones, where women have few or poor ways of entering the labor force. This is an important reason for the success of direct selling in Mexico, for example.

The conditions that are contributing to direct selling's explosive growth in Asia are certainly not the conditions that gave rise to it in America. Their histories, social institutions and cultural values are too different. In both instances, though, this flexible form of enterprise takes root because of the character of the political and social, as well as economic, structures of society.[11]

References

Abegglen, James C. (1958): *The Japanese factory: aspects of its social organization*, Glencoe, IL: Free Press.

Abolafia, Mitchel (1984): Structured anarchy: formal organization in the commodity futures industry, in: P. Adler and P. Adler (eds.), *The social dynamics of financial markets*, 129–150, Greenwich, Conn.: JAI Press.

Bendix, Reinhard (1956): *Work and authority in industry*, New York: Wiley.

Benedict, Ruth (1946): *The chrysanthemum and the sword*, New York: New American Library.

Biggart, Nicole Woolsey (1989): *Charismatic capitalism: direct selling organizations in America*, Chicago: University of Chicago Press.

Butterfield, Stephen (1985): *Amway: the cult of free enterprise*, Boston: South End.

Clark, James (1974): *The Japanese company*, New Haven, Conn.: Yale University Press.

Cole, Robert E. (1971): *Japanese blue collar*, Berkeley, Cal.: University of California Press.

Coser, Lewis (1975): *Greedy institutions*, New York: Free Press.

Durkheim, Emile (1949): *Division of labor in society*, George Simpson (tr. 1983), Glencoe, IL: Free Press.

Englade, Kenneth (1985): Door to door car salesmen in Japan reap billions, *Toronto Globe and Mail* July 23.

Granovetter, Mark (1985): Economic action and social structure: the problem of embeddedness, *American Journal of Sociology* 3: 481–510.

Hamilton, Gary G. and Nicole Woolsey Biggart (1988): Market, culture, and authority: a comparative analysis of management and organization in Japan, Taiwan, and South and Korea, *American Journal of Sociology* 94: 52–94.

Hayes, Thomas C. (1987): Puzzling out foreign profits, *New York Times* Nov. 9, D1: 7.

Hill, Stephen (1981): *Competition and control at work: the new industrial sociology*, Cambridge, MA: M.I.T. Press.

Kanter, Rosabeth Moss (1977): *Work and family in the United States: a critical review and agenda for research and policy*, New York: Russell Sage Foundation.

Kogan, Herman (1958): *The great EB: the story of the Encyclopaedia Brittanica*, Chicago: University of Chicago Press.

---

[11] Gary Hamilton and I (1988) make this same argument.

Lawrence, Paul R. and Jay W. Lorsch (1967): *Organization and environment: managing differentiation and integration*, Homewood, IL: Irwin.

Louis Harris and Associates, Inc. (1977): *Highlights of a comprehensive survey of the direct selling industry*, Washington, D. C.: Direct Selling Association.

McKelvey, Bill and Howard Aldrich (1983): Populations, natural selection, and applied organizational science, *Administrative Science Quarterly* 28: 101 – 128.

Mintzberg, Henry (1979): *The structuring of organizations*, Englewood Cliffs, N. J.: Prentice-Hall.

Nakane, Chie (1970): *Japanese Society*, Berkeley, CA: University of California Press.

Nelson, Daniel (1975): *Managers and workers: origins of the new factory system in the United States 1880 – 1920*, Madison, Wisc.: The University of Wisconsin Press.

O'Toole, Roger (1976): 'Underground' traditions in the Study of Sectarianism: non-religious uses of the concept 'sect', *Journal for the Scientific Study of Religion* 15: 145 – 156.

Peven, Dorothy E. (1968): The use of religious revival techniques to indoctrinate personnel: the home party sales organization, *Sociological Quarterly* 9: 97 – 106.

Satow, Roberta Lynn (1975): Value-rational authority and professional organizations: Weber's missing type, *Administrative Science Quarterly* 20: 526 – 531.

Scott, W. Richard (1981): *Organizations: rational, natural and open systems*, Englewood Cliffs, NJ: Prentice-Hall.

Trice, Harrison and Janice M. Beyer (1983): The routinization of charisma in two social movement organizations, Paper presented at the Academy of Management Meetings, August, 1983.

Vogel, Ezra (1979): *Japan as number one*, Cambridge, Mass.: Harvard University Press.

Walton, Richard E. and John M. Dutton (1969): The management of interdepartmental conflict: A model and review, *Administrative Science Quarterly* 14: 73 – 84.

Weber, Max (1958): *The protestant ethic and the spirit of capitalism*, Talcott Parsons (tr.), New York: Scribner's.

Weber, Max (1978): *Economy and society*, Guenther Roth and Claus Wittich (eds.), Berkeley: University of California Press.

Winkler, Edwin (1987): Statism and familism in Taiwan, in: George C. Lodge and Ezra Vogel (eds.), *Ideology and National Competitiveness: an analysis of nine countries*, 173 – 206, Boston, Massachusetts: Harvard Business School Press.

Wong, Siu-Lun (1986): Modernization and Chinese culture in Hong Kong, *China Quarterly* 406: 306 – 325.

World Federation of Direct Selling Associations (1986): *Direct selling: a world of business*, Washington, D. C.: World Federation of Direct Selling Associations.

Notes on Contributors

Stewart Clegg was Professor and Head of the Department of Sociology at the University of New England, Armidale, Australia and in 1990 moves to a Chair of Management at the University of St. Andrews, Scotland. The author and editor of many books, his interests include the kind of comparative work this volume suggests, the sociology of power and organizations and empirical studies of class structure in a comparative context and organization analysis. He is a past editor of the *Australian and New Zealand Journal of Sociology*, a current editor of *Organization Studies* and a consulting editor for *Work, Employment and Society* and *International Sociology*. He is a Fellow of the Australian Academy of Social Sciences.

Gordon Redding is Professor of Management Studies and head of department at the University of Hong Kong. After a first degree at Cambridge, he spent ten years in the U.K. department store industry in general management before undertaking a doctorate at the Manchester Business School. In Hong Kong since 1973, his primary research interests are in cross-cultural management and organizational comparisons. He has specialized particularly in the Overseas Chinese and has published extensively in this area.

Monica Cartner is Research Co-ordinator in the Graduate School of Business and Government Management, Victoria University of Wellington, New Zealand. Formerly a social worker, she has worked in social sciences research for several years, particular interests being organizational theory and cultural aspects of managerial behaviour. Current major projects include bibliographic work for the East-West Centre in Hawaii and a long-term study of overseas Chinese managers and businesses.

Winton Higgins is an Associate Professor in Politics at Macquarie University, Sydney. Originally trained as a lawyer, he has studied at the Universities of London, Sydney and Stockholm and has published extensively on Sweden and Social Democracy. The present contribution is one of a number of collaborations between him and Stewart Clegg in organization analysis, and he is currently working on a major study of Ernst Wigforss.

Tony Spybey is a Senior Lecturer in Sociology at Plymouth Polytechnic. He worked and travelled extensively in Africa, Central America, the Caribbean and South and Southeast Asia, before taking up an academic career. He studied initially at Southampton and gained his Ph.D. at the University of Bradford. He has worked at the University of Twente in The Netherlands and has been a visiting Professor at the Copenhagen School of Economics and at the University of Uppsala, Sweden.

Richard Whitley is Reader in Sociology at the Manchester Business School and was the first Visiting Professor for the Citicorp Doctoral Programme at the Department of Management Studies, University of Hong Kong, in 1988. He has published widely in the field of the sociology of the sciences, business elites and organizations and is currently the Managing Editor of the *Sociology of the Sciences Yearbook* and President of the International Sociological Associations's Research Committee on the Sociology of Science.

Gary Hamilton is Professor and Chair of Sociology at the University of California, Davis. He has written widely on topics relating to the historical, comparative analysis of China and is currently involved in a major research programme on the institutional foundations of East Asian economies, funded in part by the National Science Foundation.

William Zeile is a doctoral candidate in economics at the University of California, Davis, and he is writing his dissertation on international trade and industrial organization in the Far East. He is involved with Prof. Hamilton and others in the National Science Foundation project.

Wan-Jin Kim is an Assistant Professor in economics at Seoul National University and recently completed his Ph. D. in economics at the University of California, Berkeley. He is involved with Prof. Hamilton in the National Science Foundation project.

Stephen Wilks is Senior Lecturer in the Institute of Public Adminstration and Management at the University of Liverpool. He qualified as a Chartered Accountant before taking up an academic career as a political scientist. He has written widely in the field of comparative political economy and since 1983 has been Research Co-ordinator for the major Economic and Social Research Council's twelve project programme of research on Comparative Government – Industry Relations.

Simon Tam is a lecturer in the Department of Management Studies at the University of Hong Kong. His managerial and business career started in 1968, which led him very soon to directorate and ownership levels. In recent years he decided to spoil himself by suspending his business engagements in order to follow his curiosity. He is now registered with the London School of Economics for a Ph. D., his topic being Hong Kong Chinese business behaviour.

Bob Tricker is Professor of Accounting and Finance in the Department of Management Studies at the University of Hong Kong. After study at

Oxford and Harvard, in 1967 he became the first Professor of Information Systems in Britain at Warwick University. He subsequently directed the Oxford Management Centre (now Templeton College) and founded the Corporate Policy Group at Nuffield College, Oxford to study board level direction of companies. His research interests are in the fields of corporate strategy and governance and the nature of information in the organization context.

Peter Standish is Visiting Professor of Accounting at INSEAD (Institut Européen d'Administration des Affaires), Fontainbleau, France, having previously held the chairs of Business Administration and of Accounting and Financial Reporting at Harvard Business School and London Business School respectively. He has published widely on aspects of finanical reporting, inflation accounting and processes for setting accounting standards. His principal research interests are in the concept of national accounting codes, the principal example of such a code, the French 'Plan comptable général' and in the institutional frameworks appropriate for the development of such codes.

Malcolm Lewis is a Senior Lecturer in Management at Otago University, New Zealand. He has an M. A. from Wellington, New Zealand, an M. Phil. from Liverpool and his Ph. D. from Cape Town. He is also an Incorporated Engineer and continues an interest in electronics. His major research activities are in technology development and its implications for organization theory and business policy, but he also has a strong interest in the philosophy of the social sciences and in social power. Much of his teaching has been on MBA programmes where he has encouraged students to study alternative world views.

Alan MacGregor is a Senior Lecturer in the Department of Accounting and Finance at the University of Otago, New Zealand. He has an MBA and Ph. D. in Accounting Theory from Cranfield Institute of Technology and is professionally qualified in the U. K., Australia and New Zealand. His research interests include the 'Weltanschauung' of accounting theorists, the role of accounting as a control in the culture of which it is part and the relationship between accounting risk measures and arbitrage pricing theory. He is currently joint editor of the *Pacific Accounting Review,* a research journal sponsored by the New Zealand Society of Accountants.

Max Boisot was, until recently, Director and Dean of the China-EEC Management Programme (CEMP) in Beijing. He has an M. Sc. and a Master of City Planning from M. I. T. and his Ph. D. from Imperial College, London University. He originally studied architecture at Cambridge and ran a practice in London. He is based in Paris and is presently on leave of absence from the École Supérieure de Commerce de Paris, where he teaches business policy.

John Child is Dean of the Faculty of Management and Modern Languages and Professor of Organizational Behaviour at Aston University, England. In 1985 he was Professor in the China-EEC Management Programme (CEMP) in Beijing and is a member of the Euro-China Association for Management and has also worked with the Chinese Academy of Medical Sciences and the People's University of China. His main research interests are enterprise organization, information technology and comparative management, including China, and he has published extensively on these and related topics.

Hiroshi Mannari is Professor of Sociology at Kwansei Gakuin University, Japan. His research interests include social stratification, mobility and cross-national studies of industrial and other complex organizations, and he has published extensively in these topics. His current major project is a comparative study of Japanese and French firms facing flexible technology.

Robert Marsh is Professor in Sociology at Brown University, Providence, and has previously taught at the Universities of Michigan, Ann Arbor, Cornell and Duke. He was a Visiting Research Fellow at the Centre for East Asian Studies at Stanford in 1983 and held the Manpower, Research and Training Research Chair at the U.S. Naval Academy, Annapolis in 1987 – 88. He has conducted extensive research in East Asia on problems of complex organizations, developing nations and sociological theory and has published widely in these fields.

Barry Wilkinson and *Nick Oliver* are both lecturers in Organizational Behaviour and Personnel Management at the Cardiff Business School, University of Wales College of Cardiff. Their wide-ranging interests in the sociology and psychology of organizations were brought together from 1986 in a major study of the Japanization of British industry. Currently, they are jointly pursuing research on the development and impact of computer-aided production management systems in 'total quality' organizations and on the spread of Japanese manufacturing systems across the world.

Jane Marceau is Professor of Public Policy and Head of the Public Policy Programme of the Australian National University. Before taking up her current appointment at the ANU, she was the Eleanor Rathbone Professor of Sociology at the University of Liverpool and has published extensively in the fields of business elites, policy research and the sociology of education.

Michael Bond is Senior Lecturer in Psychology at the Chinese University of Hong Kong and also acts as a cross-cultural management trainer for multi-national corporations in Hong Kong, where he has lived since 1974. His research and publications are devoted mainly to a comparison of the psychological and social functioning of the Chinese people with people from Western countries.

Geert Hofstede is Professor of Organizational Anthropology and International Management at the Department of Economics and Business Administration of the University of Limburg, The Netherlands. Originally trained as a mechanical engineer, he worked in staff and line management jobs for ten years in Dutch companies. His doctoral thesis *The game of budget control* gained wide acclaim. He was the Manager of Personnel Research with IBM in Europe before beginning his academic career, which has included research and teaching at IMEDE in Lausanne, INSEAD in Fontainebleau, the European Institute for Advanced Studies in Management in Brussels and IIASA in Laxenburg, Austria. He is the Director of the Institute for Research on Intercultural Cooperation (IIRC), which is presently heavily concerned with the study of corporate cultures. Prof. Hofstede is widely published academically and has acted in a consultant role to public and private organizations in addition to his academic work.

Thomas Acton is a Reader in Romany studies at the Thames Polytechnic, where he has worked since 1974. He obtained his Ph. D. from Oxford for a study of the British Gypsies. Although his major interest and publications relate to the Romany society, he has also conducted research among the South Chinese fisherfolk and has a general interest in ethnic minority economic development.

Nicole Biggart is Associate Professor of Management and Sociology at the University of California, Davis. Her current interests include Asian business and the relationship of economic structure to social structure. She received her Ph. D. in Sociology from the University of California, Berkeley and has published in these and other areas.

Index

Abegglen, J. 82, 88 – 90, 96
AB Electronics 350
Abercrombie, N. 42
Abernathy, W. 54, 55, 59
Abrahamson, B. 63
Accountants 219 – 221, 223 – 226,
    242 – 244
Accounting 19, 56, 60, 61, 215 – 245
Acton, T. A. 4, 25, 381 – 408
AEU 341
Albrow, M. 255
Aldrich, H. 322, 326
Alford, R. 25
America, see USA
American Law Institute 190
Amway 409 – 427
Anderson, P. 31, 136
Anthony, P. 146
Aoki, M. 82, 88, 92
Apple, N. 64, 70
Aris, S. 190
Armstrong, J. 137, 138, 147
Armstrong, P. 219
ASEAN 92
Asian Wall Street Journal 106
Aston School 12, 322
Attewell, P. 259
Australia 6, 9, 18, 19, 21, 33, 58, 59,
    72, 73, 191, 227, 228, 358, 359,
    361, 369, 371, 375
Authority 16, 95
Automation 318, 321

Baker, H. 207
Balogh, T. 133
Bamford, J. 360
Bangladesh 389
Bank management 20, 249 – 275
Barnett, C. 132
Bass, D. 254
Bauer, M. 80, 83, 93
Bauman, Z. 31

Baxter, W. 220
Beechey, V. 253
Belgium 34, 231
Bell, P. 222
Benston, G. 223, 239
Berger, P. 1, 24, 31 – 33, 42, 49, 51,
    131, 146, 149
Berle, A. 190, 199
Biggart, N. 3, 25, 43, 49, 56, 57, 82,
    92, 97, 107, 120, 409 – 428
Birrell, R. 260
Blau, P. 256, 322 – 325
Boisot, M. 8, 23, 26, 281 – 313
Bond, M. 4, 25, 383 – 390
Boreham, P. 34, 35, 45, 51, 66, 73
Boulding, K. 222
Bowles, M. 260, 261, 272
Boyd, R. 149
Braverman, H. 10, 14, 251, 253, 256,
    265
Brazil 109
Britan, see also UK, 6, 7, 18, 19, 54,
    58, 59, 72, 135 – 139, 194, 227,
    228, 238, 282, 359
  culture 18, 144 – 146, 148
  economic culture 347
  industrial culture 333
  industrial relations 8, 10
British Civil Service 133 – 137, 144,
    146
Brocklesby, S. 257 – 259, 262 – 264,
    272
Brostroem, A. 63
Bruno, M. 73
Buchanan, D. 252
Bullock, Lord 190, 192
Burawoy, M. 252, 253
Bureaucracy 137 – 143, 413, 416, 419
  beyond 79 – 104
Burnham, J. 190
Burrell, G. 255, 256